VISIONS OF DANTE IN ENGLISH POETRY

COSTERUS   NEW SERIES
VOL 72

Edited by

C.C. Barfoot, Hans Bertens, Theo D'haen
and Erik Kooper

AMSTERDAM 1989

VISIONS OF DANTE IN ENGLISH POETRY

translations of the *Commedia*
from Jonathan Richardson to William Blake

V. Tinkler-Villani

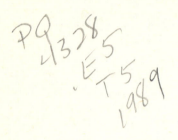

CIP-GEGEVENS KONINKLIJKE BIBLIOTHEEK, DEN HAAG

Tinkler-Villani, Valeria

Visions of Dante in English poetry : translations of the
Commedia from Jonathan Richardson to William Blake /
Valeria Tinkler-Villani. — Amsterdam : Rodopi. — Ill. —
(Costerus, ISSN 0165-9618 ; New Series, vol. 72)
Met bibliogr..
ISBN 90-5183-078-5
SISO enge 852.7 UDC 820
Trefw.: Dante Alighieri "La divina commedia" ; Engelse
letterkunde.
©Editions Rodopi B.V., Amsterdam 1989
Printed in The Netherlands

for Trevor

Contents

List of illustrations

All illustrations are to found between pp. 262 and 263

Note

The edition used for quotations from Dante is *La Divina Commedia*, edited by Natalino Sapegno. For my translations of the original I am heavily indebted to the translations of the *Divina Commedia* by John D. Sinclair, Charles Singleton and C.H. Sisson. In the chapter on William Blake I have referred to Henry Francis Cary's translation of the *Divina Commedia*, this being the version most probably used by Blake.

Translations of quotations from the *Divina Commedia* are provided in the footnotes. Translations of the original and of critics's remarks in my text are provided to facilitate the reading of my argument.

If two successive references are the same, the second is footnoted.

I refer to the Italian or the English versions of the titles of Dante's works according to the translator's own use. Thus, Cary's version of *Inferno* is *Hell*, whereas Boyd's is *Inferno*.

Acknowledgements

In accordance with tradition at Leyden University, many of the debts I owe must remain implicit. These are the debts to the many present and past colleagues at Leyden University who have assisted me in various ways during the writing and final preparation of this work.

I may, however, express my gratitude to the late Seymour Betsky, whose confidence in me was always greater than my own. Similarly inspirational was my father, to whom I am more grateful than I can say. His readings of Dante are still clear in my memory, and to these I owe much of my love and understanding of the *Commedia*.

Sincere thanks are due to John Fitzgerald and Alan Crowe, without whose expertise the technical preparation of these pages would have been even more laborious than it has been. I must also express my thanks to the British Museum and to Cambridge University Library for their remarkable and kindly assistance with rare materials.

My greatest debts are personal ones. I thank my sons, Conrad and Paul, for their understanding and their interest in what I do, as well as for the many beneficial interruptions. Conrad's help with the printing out of early drafts has not been forgotten. I also thank my mother for her interest in my career and her loving care since childhood. But my greatest debt of gratitude goes to my husband Trevor for being my most rigorous critic. His enthusiasm and assistance has supported me at every step on the way, for he has been 'my master, my authority; the one alone from whom I have learned the exact style which does me honour now'.

1

Introduction

Dante's *Divina Commedia*, which was finished by the time of the author's death in 1321, was translated into English in its entirety only five centuries later, in 1802. Yet within a mere two decades of the appearance of this first complete translation the *Commedia* had become a central text in English poetry.[1] What happened in English poetry in the eighteenth century and the first years of the nineteenth that made poets and translators turn to Dante and his *Commedia*? This is the general question which is central to the present study.[2]

The sudden flourishing of Dante translations and interest in Dante in England coincides with the aesthetic revolution which took place in the late eighteenth century, and therefore a study of the one may be expected to shed some light on the other. The approach adopted in this study was indicated by specific questions posed by the course of Dante's reputation in England. How did translators read and interpret Dante? What features of their contemporary literature did they see as analogous to features of Dante's poem? What models, what techniques, what diction were available to them? Viewed from this angle, an analysis of the presence of Dante in English poetry can provide an insight into the English literary climate of the time; and this is my objective in this study, to read early translations of Dante in order to explore the temper of a period, thus offering indications of some characteristics and limitations of eighteenth-century poetry.

In *A Defense of Poetry* (1821) Shelley stated that 'The *Divina Commedia* and *Paradise Lost* have conferred upon modern mythology a systematic form'.[3] The present study will offer indications of the truth of this remark, by shedding some light on the process by which Dante provided English poetry with a mythology, and on the ways in which this mythology became intertwined with the Miltonic tradition in English poetry. Translations of Dante's *Commedia* contributed to strengthening and modifying the Miltonic tradition in English poetry, so that some aspects of Milton's poetry were carried over into nineteenth-century poetics.

The present work will concentrate mainly on the period between 1719 and 1820 – that is to say, from the first translation of an episode from the *Commedia* to the work of Henry Francis Cary and William Blake. It will include William Blake's last work (his translation of Dante into his illustrations to the *Commedia*, finished in 1824) but will exclude the use of Dante by other Romantics such as we find in Shelley's *Prometheus Unbound*, published in 1820.[4]

A number of issues form the historical context and the methodological framework of this study of the translation of Dante into English. It is these issues that the rest of this introductory chapter will deal with.

Dante in England

Translations of Dante into English steadily increase in number and range during the course of the eighteenth century. Initially, translators focus on one episode – the drama of Ugolino in *Inferno*. Jonathan Richardson the elder is the first, producing a blank verse version of the Ugolino episode in 1719. Gray and the Earl of Carlisle are the authors of verse translations of the same episode (1742 and 1772 respectively). Joseph Warton follows with a prose rendering of Ugolino included in the first volume of *An Essay on the Genius and Writings of Pope* (vol 1 1756, vol 2 1782), and Thomas Warton's prose translation of Ugolino forms a digression in the third volume of his *History of English Poetry* (1781).

From one episode, translators move on to tackling a few cantos, a whole *cantica*, and eventually the whole work. So a further step in the course of Dante translations into English is William Hayley's version of the first three cantos of *Inferno* in 1782. Then, in the same year, Charles Rogers published his version of the whole of the *Inferno*. Henry Boyd added his version of the first *cantica* in 1785, and published his translation of the whole *Commedia* in 1802.

Rogers and Boyd's versions have been branded as 'bad' translations or paraphrases, and so the first English version of Dante accepted as a proper translation in the current Dante canon is Henry Francis Cary's *The Vision of Dante* (*Inferno* 1805-6, *The Vision, or Hell, Purgatory, and Paradise of Dante Alighieri*, 1814). In the wake of Cary's Dante, many attempted a version of one or more *cantiche* of the *Commedia*. There were 38 versions in the nineteenth century, but the authors were not the major scholars or poets of the century, being mostly lawyers, men of the Church, doctors, ladies of leisure.[5] In our century, on the contrary, translations have been equally numerous, but are usually the work of either scholars or writers of stature, such as Laurence Binyon (1943), John D. Sinclair (1946), Dorothy L. Sayers (1954) and Geoffrey L. Bickersteth (1955).[6]

In the United States, three twentieth-century translations stand out for their specific contribution to the Dante canon. John Ciardi broke new ground by adopting a colloquial style, reproducing Dante's immediacy and manipulation of the vernacular. Charles Singleton's monumental work on the three *cantiche*, with both text and commentary, followed the author's publication of three seminal critical volumes on Dante, and was expected to provide the standard English edition of Dante's work. Even so, another translation followed: Mark Musa's *The Divine Comedy* (1971) is now replacing Sayers' version in the Penguin edition of the *Commedia*.

According to Dudley Fitts, quoted on the book-jacket of the John Ciardi translation, this was the 'version definitive for our time'. But even in the eighties translations continue to be produced, in both Britain and the United States. In 1980 Charles Sisson published his *Divine Comedy* – a revolutionary gesture in Dante translations, since the text is not interrupted by footnotes, summary of the argument, or even line numbers. The poem appears not as a translation addressed to scholars, but an English text for readers of poetry. Sisson was followed, in 1983, by Allen Mandelbaum's beautifully printed 'California Dante'. Also in 1983 Tom Phillips, a painter, produced in his illustrations the most brilliant translation of Dante, and then proceeded to add, by way of commentary, a rendering of the verse. Even in our own decade, therefore, translations of the *Commedia* into English continue to appear. A 'final' translation, it seems, is not to be achieved.

As for the popularity of Dante among English poets and critics, this suddenly flared up at the end of the eighteenth century. So, whereas the major scholars and critics of the eighteenth century, such as Edmund Burke and Samuel Johnson, hardly knew Dante, by the middle of the nineteenth century a complete reversal had taken place.[7] In 1840 Thomas Carlyle stated that the Olympus of letters is shared by two poets only, Dante and Shakespeare – 'the Saints of poetry'.[8] Ruskin went even further when, in the *Stones of Venice*, he claimed that Dante was 'the central man in all the world, as representing in perfect balance the imaginative, moral and intellectual faculties, all at their highest'.[9] Since then, studies on Dante have done nothing but increase in number as well as profundity and seriousness.

In our century it was probably Ezra Pound who gave special impetus to the critical discourse on Dante, but it is T.S. Eliot who defines the significance of Dante in English poetry.[10] Eliot firmly states the irrelevance of whatever could be an obstacle to the modern reader of the *Commedia*. There is no need to understand Dante, believe what he believed, or even to know any facts about the *Commedia*, its author and his time.[11] The fundamental difference between the *Commedia* and modern poems in what reception theorists call the repertoire – the 'extratextual' reality of the poem, made up of social, historical and cultural norms – is therefore of no importance.[12] In addition, Eliot takes Dante's allegory and establishes its equivalence with the analogous feature of contemporary poetry, the image: 'allegory means clear visual images', he says. And Eliot underlines the universality of Dante's poetry when he states that 'there is no poet, in any tongue

... who stands so firmly as a model for all poets' (*Dante*, p. 268). From Eliot's views on Dante there follows an inescapable conclusion: '... the last canto of *Paradiso* ... is to my thinking the highest point that poetry has ever reached or ever can reach' (*Dante*, p. 251). In Eliot's words on Dante the past is integrated with the present; but in the last quoted statement the validity of Dante's poetry as the standard for poets is extended even into the future.

In fact, the course of Dante's reputation among poets is even more striking than his reputation among critics. Some eighteenth-century poets were aware of the existence of Dante, but it would be pure speculation to claim more than this.[13] It is only with William Blake that Dante became a significant and influential voice in English literature. But we are by then well into the nineteenth century, and by that time Blake was only one name out of many who were influenced by Dante. Lord Byron saw Dante as another example of that figure we have come to call the 'Byronic' hero, a figure fundamental to Byron's vision of man and of the protagonist of poems. The influence of Dante on Byron is more direct in Byron's translations of the Francesca episode in *terza rima*, and in his own *Prophecy of Dante* (1821). In this poem, Byron creates a figure of Dante approaching death, 'now overwrought/ With the world's war, and years, and banishment', who becomes the defender of civic liberties, the poet of his race, and the prophet of the future of his people.[14] Shelley, too, translated Dante (two sonnets and a *canzone*, besides some passages from the *Commedia*), and imitated Dante in his own poems such as *The Triumph of Life* (1822), and *Prometheus Unbound* (1820).[15]

As the century progresses, the interest among poets in Dante continues. Tennyson, Browning, and Rossetti all wrote poems directly inspired from passages from the *Commedia*, or from Dante's life.[16] And in our century the 'divine poet' becomes one of the Muses of English poetry. W.B. Yeats sees Dante as the final mask:

> And yet,
> The chief imagination of Christendom,
> Dante Alighieri, so utterly found himself
> That he had made that hollow face of his
> More plain to the mind's eye than any face
> But that of Christ.   ('Ego Dominus Tuus', 1918)[17]

In these lines Yeats connects the opening of *Inferno*, with its wood in which the poet/protagonist Dante had lost himself, to the final vision in *Paradiso*, where the poet/protagonist receives the vision of the mystery of the incarnation – the union of the divine and the human. Dante and Christ face each other in that vision, in an image of self-reflection and final salvation which Blake used in his illustrations, for it reflected the central myth of his own vision of man. Some of the early translators did produce a version of this moment in Dante's poem in terms of vision and salvation, but others did not.

The English Dante is the figure of a prophetic poet, who is an outsider banished for life – an exile, whose visionary powers show him life and man for what they are. In modern poetry he becomes the touchstone and the standard. As an example of the function Dante assumes in recent poetry one can take an exchange between Seamus Heaney and Donald Davie. In 'An Afterwards', Heaney creates an image of the poet as Ugolino, devouring other poets' brains in order to give body to his own creations. And as a poet he is himself an Ugolino, since first he translates the episode from *Inferno*, and then uses it to shape his own poem.[18] Donald Davie picks up and develops Heaney's idea. In 'Summer Lightning', which is dedicated to Heaney, (and in which a phrase from 'An Afterwards' is quoted) Davie calls poetry 'the one/ Game that we play here', and suggests that 'This calls for Comedy, never more demonic/ Then when Divine'.[19] Dante has become the linking thread running through the 'daisy-chain' of poets.

Dante as universal man and poet had already taken shape in Blake's illustrations to the *Commedia*, which show the influence of the preceding translations (such as those by Boyd and Cary), and of current views of Dante (such as that of William Hayley). To read and study the early responses to Dante, the early translations of the *Commedia*, some related texts, and the illustrations by Blake is to trace the process which resulted in the creation of this figure of Dante.

Dante is a living presence in twentieth-century English culture. From this vantage-point it becomes all the more remarkable that before the nineteenth century Dante is virtually absent from the English literary scene. The standard explanation for this relies on the nature of classical and neoclassical literature, which would accept the work of Petrarch, Ariosto and Tasso, but not the unsophisticated work of Dante.[20] This was true for the whole of Europe, and even in Italy Dante's fame was very low in the sixteenth and seventeenth centuries.[21]

As for the reasons which could explain the sudden vogue of Dante in the late eighteenth century, there are also standard explanations. To begin with, Dante was known in the seventeenth and eighteenth century, but was disliked. If views on his work were expressed at all, they were dismissive and disparaging, like Voltaire's remarks on Dante in his *Essai Sur La Poèsie Epique* (1728). However – the standard explanations continue – a number of historical changes contributed to bringing Dante to the foreground. Oscar Kuhns (1904) mentions in particular the arrival in England of Italian expatriates, who brought with them a revaluation of Dante as a patriot for Italian independence; Dante becomes 'the prophet of a united fatherland'. Friederich (1950) relies mainly on the claim that neoclassical ideals would have been closer to those of 'the Petrarchans and the Arcadians', and mentions Vico in particular as the thinker who introduced a historical approval of Dante. Doughty (1950) points to a few chance events which placed Dante in the foreground: Voltaire's remarks on Dante, which would greatly increase familiarity with his name; the Grand Tour, which would contribute to an interest in Dante; Sir Joshua Reynolds' picture of Ugolino exhibited at the Royal Academy in 1733. But as the main reason for the new vogue for Dante Doughty emphasizes the Gothic Revival. Brand (1957) repeats most of these explanations, concluding that the Romantics appropriated Dante, because his manner was very close to theirs.[22]

These explanations have become the commonplace surrounding the reception of Dante in English literature, and have hardly been questioned by later critics. Dorothy L. Sayers very specifically attributes the sudden rise in Dante's fame to the phenomenon of the craze for the gothic, 'horrid' novels.[23] William De Sua expands somewhat more on the topic, and says that the *Commedia* seemed 'to many critics, bizarre, Gothic, and barbarian'; but that the relaxation of the rules, the change in the standards of reason, decorum and taste meant that the neoclassical strictures were loosened sufficiently for Dante's *Commedia* to be granted some literary status.[24] In both cases, the writers accept these views as obvious tenets, and do not attempt to test their validity and explore the dynamics of the process of change.

The time has certainly come for a fresh assessment of these claims. All the explanations mentioned by the critics are valid up to a point, and in all probability the cumulative effect of them all contributed to the growing vogue for Dante. But in fact, when considered in isolation, many of them appear very narrow and often inaccurate. The presence of Italian patriots in England is noticeable particularly in the early nineteenth century, and it helps explain the specific quality of views on Dante at that time – such as those Byron expresses in his *Prophecy of Dante*.[25] Giambattista Vico's theories and views in justification of the autonomy of art were, indeed, discussed and expounded in the eighteenth century, in the three laborious editions of his *Principi di Scienza Nuova* (1725, 1730, 1744), in which Vico expresses his view that Dante was the typical poet of the modern world. But Vico's views were first introduced into England by Coleridge, and we are by then into the third decade of the nineteenth century.[26]

Doughty's arguments are not satisfactory either. Some of his explanations simply create a new question – why did Voltaire think of attacking Dante, why did the Grand Tour traveller bring back an interest in Dante and not in Arnaut Daniel or Boccaccio? Brand's remarks, also, are misleading, being to some extent a misrepresentation of the process which took place. The Romantics did not appropriate Dante because his manner was similar to theirs: their manner had been partly shaped by the images, structures, and visions of Dante as these had been translated into English poetry.

Even the case of Petrarch is not as dissimilar from that of Dante as it might at first appear.[27] The Elizabethans had discovered the usefulness of the sonnet and of the diction provided by Petrarchism in providing pattern and method for their own poetry, but their adaptations do not reveal a particularly deep understanding of Petrarch's own vision and achievement. Neither was Petrarch's work translated in its entirety, at that time. The *Canzoniere* had been translated into French, for example, by 1600, and by that date more than two hundred editions of the Italian text had been published all over Europe – with the exception of England. In fact, the complete *Canzoniere* was not translated into English until 1850. This does not suggest that Petrarch was ignored for an even longer time than Dante, but that the course of the fortunes of Dante and Petrarch in England follows a parallel track. As George Watson puts it, 'a second age of Petrarchan translations hardly begins before the 1760's' – and therefore Petrarch is rediscovered in the second half of the eighteenth century. Translations of individual poems from the *Canzoniere* increase at this time, and the names one comes across are familiar to the student of the reception of Dante in England. Horace Walpole, William Roscoe, and Charles Burney (author of the very first translation of Dante's *Commedia*, which is, however, now lost) are mentioned by Watson as instrumental in rediscovering Petrarch; and the third translation of the *Trionfi* into English is by Henry Boyd, author of the first extant translation of the *Commedia*.

However, rather than a contrast between the neoclassicists, with their affinity to the ideals of Petrarchism, and the Gothic Revivalists, who responded to the appeal of Dante's verse, we must see in the movements within the eighteenth century one articulated and complex whole. The Gothic Revival takes its place within the increasingly imaginative, descriptive and meditative poetry of the eighteenth century; and the taste for this kind of poetry can in fact explain the popularity of some parts of Petrarch's poetry, for 'Where the Elizabethans heavily preferred "In Vita", the taste of the last two-hundred years has moved towards the remorseful, tragic poems of "In Morte"'.[28]

The standard explanations of the course of Dante's fame are in fact based on a dismissive view of the eighteenth century. Doughty puts this very clearly when he says that 'The Augustan Age in England was, in taste and mental and emotional attitudes, remote from the medieval world of Dante. Its rationalistic spirit was too clear yet narrow, too unimaginative and anti-mystical, too realistic and sophisticated to respond to the deep conceptions and appeal of Dante's verse.'[29] The analysis of the texts which report and bear witness to the response of readers to Dante confirms a very different view.

Long before the Gothic Revival, the eighteenth-century mind had turned outward and borrowed from many sources to enrich its own varied field: it had turned to Longinus and Boileau, or the picaresque novel of Cervantes, testifying to its own intellectual mobility.[30] Interest in and borrowing from other cultures naturally involves translation – the interest in the epic resulting in translations of Homer, and the interest in the sublime in the translation of Boileau.[31] Moreover, it is in the eighteenth century that the classic translations of Ariosto and Tasso by Harington and Fairfax are felt to be insufficient, so that the need arises for a contemporary response to the text. Hence, in 1783 John Hoole issued his translation of the *Orlando Furioso*, with a second edition appearing two years later, in 1785 – the very year in which William Boyd published his *Inferno*, in a volume which also included translations of selected cantos of Ariosto's work. The same John Hoole also translated Tasso's *Jerusalem Delivered* in 1763, although he had already been preceded by Thomas Hooke in 1738 and by P. Doyle's *The Delivery of Jerusalem* in 1761.[32]

The renewed popularity of Petrarch, Ariosto and Tasso testifies also to the interest of the eighteenth century in different kinds of poetry, and in translation as such. Translation received a particular impulse in the eighteenth century, both in the sense that many translations were produced, and in the sense that many writers expressed views on the theory of translation – even if these views were at times tentative.[33]

Apart, therefore, from various specific routes by which Dante might have made his way into England, a more general but accurate explanation of Dante's growing popularity in England lies in the very nature of the eighteenth-century mind and its interests. The Grand Tour traveller brought back an interest in many foreign authors and their work, of which Dante is one. Such a general tendency, of course, creates a need for translations.

But maybe the case of Dante translations in particular should be connected to another strand of eighteenth-century English culture: the heritage of the social, political and religious upheavals which shook England throughout the seventeenth century, including the Glorious Revolution of 1688 – a heritage which is not only political but also cultural. Political activism connected with the theory of limited monarchy continued well into the eighteenth century. There were many societies, at the time, which kept alive the ideals of reform and even of republicanism, radicalism and revolution. Such were, besides many small groups, the Society for the Commemoration of the Revolution (of 1688), which met annually, the Society for Constitutional Reformation (SCI), and the London Corresponding Society (LCS), which met weekly, and one of the most active members of which was a very important Antiquary, Thomas Hollis (followed, after his death, by his cousins).[34]

These societies represent the organized sections of the committed public, but the feelings they had sprung from were widespread. The American Revolution, to begin with, though opposed by the king, the nobles loyal to him, and the higher clergy, was received quite differently by the artisan classes, the gentry, and the lower clergy, who often strongly sympathized with the colonists' struggle for independence. There was, in short, in England a strong radical movement which was, for all intents and purposes, the descendant of the forces which stirred England at the time of the Glorious Revolution of 1688. Among the most committed members of this movement (although not usually members of the societies) were many writers, artists and engravers. To give a few examples, the radical camp is represented, in painting, by Barry, West, Banks, Fuseli and Blake, in poetry by the young Wordsworth and Coleridge, Burns, and, again, Blake, in prose by novelists like Godwin, Wollstonecraft and Bage and Holcroft, by a philosopher like Godwin, an agriculturalist like Young, and by polemicists like Paine, Priestley, and Horne Tooke. The views of all these writers were supported and given currency by the radical publisher Joseph Johnson. The range and depth of radical sentiment varies greatly among these names, and many eventually changed camp. Nevertheless the intensive activity of all these writers, and the various strands of their commitment did help to give shape to an alternative tradition, and an alternative ideology. Both are characterized by a critique of the established system, a love of liberty and hate of corruption, and more nationalistic ways of writing. The production of radical pamphlets and the work of the societies reached its peak in the 1790's, and then diminished, but other, less politically orientated movements remained active.

Another society, of a different nature, which played a particularly important role in the culture of the time was the Society of Antiquaries, founded in 1718. The members of this society focused their studies, which were in various fields, on England's past. In history, this meant a close study of anything connected with the myth of gothic liberty – the system of civic liberty of the Saxon kings, lost to the Normans and then lost again to the Stuarts. In literature, it led to studies on Celtic poetry, nordic mythology, and a re-assessment of native English traditions in poetry. In architecture, Antiquaries supported the gothic style, and in particular the style of gothic ruins in gardens – a style which was native to England's soil, and which belonged to England's own past. Thus, rather than emblems of decay and mortality, gothic ruins were reminders of the defence of English liberties.[35]

The work of the Antiquaries in this area highlighted the connection between a sentimental appreciation of England's past and the aesthetic perception of art and nature. History and political ideals, therefore, became intertwined with the taste for ruins, and with landscape gardening. But landscape gardening has taught a further point: that, paradoxically, the love for England's past could be expressed by the use of the Italian garden as opposed to the French garden. The Italian garden reproduced a mixed form, both in structure and in the experience of the viewer, variety and irregularity being the standard of taste here, as they were becoming in literature. More importantly, the choice of an Italian garden corresponded to notions of the retreat from active political life, an interest in the country party, and generally an opposition to royal or aristocratic rule.[36] If the preference for Italy as a model for landscape gardening was partly due to an ideological choice, motivated by a political myth, the same motivation could apply to literature, and help explain the growing appreciation of Dante, whose life and poetry (unlike those of Petrarch and Tasso, for example) are filled with political themes and the love of civic liberties.

The cumulative evidence emerging from my analysis of the responses of early readers of Dante, of translations of Dante, and of the illustrations of the *Commedia* by Blake may shed some light on this issue. I will, therefore, return to it in the conclusion to the present work, while in the course of the analysis I will confine myself to pointing out relevant details.

The professional space of the present work

Some of the issues considered have hardly been dealt with in any depth. There have been a number of historical and bibliographical studies and a number of critical short studies of limited scope.[37] All the primary material – reviews, letters, extracts from long works – containing references to Dante, from the time of Chaucer down to the translation by Cary, has been collected and published by Paget Toynbee.[38] Charles Dédéyan built on Toynbee's collection by commenting on the progress of Dante in England, and highlighting the pattern of increasing popularity of Dante in English literature.[39] English translations of Dante have been studied by William De Sua in his *Dante into English* (1964). The significance of Dante for the creative work of poets 'from Shelley to T.S.Eliot' is examined by Steve Ellis in *Dante and English Poetry* (1983).

Ellis examines how the work of English poets has been moved by Dante's vision, images and structures, and he also describes the picture of Dante which these poets have presented to the reader: the 'Byronic Dante' and the 'Dante of the Vita Nuova' being just two of the faces Dante has assumed in the course of

English literary history. But Ellis virtually neglects the pre-Romantic reception of Dante; and in so doing he misses something of the nature and manner of the growth of the early views of Dante, such as the Byronic Dante, and in fact misunderstands and misreads the first translators' contributions to the growth of such views.

The neglect by both De Sua and Ellis of the eighteenth century leaves unprobed the most obscure but decisive moment for the reception of Dante in England. De Sua, however, does briefly survey the period, and his work addresses some of the questions examined here. A closer look at *Dante into English* will help define the professional space of the present study.

De Sua is the first critic who attempts to link Dante translations and English literature. His, therefore, is a pioneer study, and deserves recognition for this fact. De Sua produces a precise division of Dante translators into the early renovators, who paraphrase their model, the romantic reflectors, who write metaphrase, the Victorians, who write literal and often unpoetic versions, and the craftsmen and critics of the twentieth century. De Sua himself best summarizes his concerns and the originality of his approach. Comparing his work to the critical bibliography of Cunningham (see note 38), De Sua states that 'This study... devotes considerably more time than does Dr. Cunningham's to characterizing the methods and theories of translation of the neoclassicists, the Romantics, the Victorians, and the moderns... [De Sua's own work] is as much a history of translation theory as it is an examination of the practice of Dante translation'.[40] However, the contribution of the work to both the history of translation theory and the practice of Dante translation is weakened by a lack of clarity in the method and system of study the author follows, a lack of clarity which the actual analysis of translations does not dispel.

In the first pages of the 'Preface' we read that 'In addition to the practical criticism of Dante, the subject of literary theory also comes within the scope of this study'. To these various topics De Sua proceeds to add others: 'moreover, canons of poetic style, diction, and versification also enter' and 'an analysis of the specific problems posed by Dante's language and metre, ... will be undertaken together with the particular solutions offered by the various translators'. But when De Sua continues by saying 'these, then, are the motive and method of this study' the reader cannot take this seriously. There is no method in the list of subjects mentioned: the various facets of the work are only listed, and the connectives such as 'in addition' or 'moreover', as well as vague phrases such as 'also enter' or 'come within the scope', tell the reader little about the systematic procedure followed. We still do not know how the translations have been examined and selected, what reading of Dante the author considers to be adequate as a standard on which to base comparisons, what theoretical standpoint will be adopted to evaluate the practice of translation and the theories of literature and the theories of translation.

After reading the book, the reader remains in doubt about two further important aspects of the study: the objectivity and thoroughness of the actual reading of the texts, and the validity of the chronological framework produced. The first problem is well exemplified by the treatment of Boyd's translation. De Sua states that this version is characteristic of the 'paraphrasing' method of eighteenth-century translators, who had little respect for their original and wanted to recreate it, and he then proceeds to look closely at two passages. The first example, the concluding lines of the Ugolino episode, would illustrate 'Boyd's deafness to Dante's exquisite echoing of sense in sound – a classical principle he ignored.' After quoting three lines from Dante and the corresponding lines by Boyd, De Sua points out that Boyd misses 'the gnawing cacophonous effect of the plosives and quick vowels' (p. 14), and also that 'Dante's concise imagery (occhi torti, teschio, denti, osso) is dissipated, replaced with more general nouns ("repast", "look," "haste", "game").' Both of these contentions seem on the surface to be true; so far as the latter is concerned, however, De Sua neglects to point out the simultaneous addition of adjectives ('*dire* repast', '*malignant* look', '*furious* haste', '*savage* game', emphases added) and what this might tell the critic about Boyd's manner of rendering Dante and its possible effect on the reader. And far from failing to reproduce Dante's echoing of sense in sound, Boyd does this, even to excess, in *Inferno* and in *Paradiso* – only he does not do it in the same lines or in the same way as the original. Boyd uses the alliteration characteristic of Anglo Saxon poetry, or of Spenser, thereby reproducing Dante's echo of sense in sound in a traditionally English way. De Sua's analysis of the text, therefore, is not thorough, because he points out only those aspects of the original which support his contention, without looking objectively at what Boyd offers the reader in place of the original, and also because he does not sift the text systematically, for otherwise he would surely not have missed Boyd's use of alliteration.

De Sua's method is to see how stylistically similar some specific turns of phrase or expressions selected more or less at random actually are, and how the different prosodic choices – *terza rima* versus prose or blank verse – affect an individual line. There is no attempt to probe into how Dante's world has been distorted, and what has been presented to the reader in its place. Moreover, the use made of the texts is very limited. Boyd is dismissed after a reading of only three lines from the Ugolino episode (*Inferno*, Canto XXXIII), twelve lines from the Francesca episode (*Inferno*, Canto V), and a few of the translator's general remarks. Cary is treated similarly, with thirty-two lines of text being quoted. Of these, three are from *Purgatorio*, the rest from *Inferno*, with none at all from *Paradiso*. De Sua's textual analysis is clearly unsatisfactory in that from a text of more than 14,000 lines so few are quoted (and seem to have been consulted); and it is even more unsatisfactory in that while the poetry of Hell is observed very briefly, the very different poetry of Paradise receives no attention at all.

The second major problem with De Sua's work is the doubtful validity both of the strict chronological framework, and also, connected with this, of the means whereby 'the prevailing methods of the age' were discovered. In his conclusion, De Sua suggests that the examination of translations has led to the identification of 'a quartet of more or less distinct methods of translation corresponding roughly to the four literary periods in which Dante has been translated into English' (pp. 122-123). But we have already seen how weak the actual examination of the translation was. Furthermore, the author himself is compelled to admit that 'the methods migrate, undergo individual modifications, enjoy revivals, and continue to be practised in alien periods...'. But still this does not suggest to him the reductive nature of a strict chronological framework, which does not take into consideration that the same translator might attempt to solve the problems of the poetry of *Inferno* and *Paradiso* in distinctive ways, or even the problems of a 'purple passage' differently from those presented by a tense dialogue between two characters.

De Sua sees the irregularities in his pattern only as the survival of an earlier method into a later age – not as independent methods of translating. Nor does he consider that any one translator might perhaps have preferred to indulge his own views and translate in a 'modern' critical way, but that his publisher or a different purpose led him to adopt a different approach. To give but one example, De Sua, faithfully following his chronological framework, says that 'Shadwell is a Romantic translator in the Victorian age, Sinclair and Huse literalists among the moderns ...'. But there is an obvious reason why, to select one name, Sinclair is a 'literalist' (that is, a 'Victorian translator'). Sinclair wrote his translation 'to serve readers who have little or no knowledge of Italian and who wish to know the matter of Dante's poem'.[41] Moreover, Sinclair's translation was published with the Italian text opposite the English translation, and includes commentary essential for the student and presented in a way which is methodologically valid, making this edition very suitable for students of Dante still at an elementary level. But neither authorial intention, nor other aspects of a translation play any role in De Sua's approach. He therefore misses the chance of realizing that his chronology itself is at fault – for Boyd is partly a 'Romantic' translator – and of seeing how a chronological approach such as his is too inflexible to account for the varied ways in which translators render different aspects of an original.[42]

De Sua's *Dante into English* leaves the impression that when its author started his work he had already made certain assumptions about the method of translation of a particular period, and its general validity, and that his analysis of the translations and the examples chosen is a simple reflection of these assumptions. De Sua certainly seems to accept, for example, the traditional view that eighteenth-century translators, like Pope with his Homer, re-wrote the original in neoclassical terms. Hence, Boyd's translation, which belongs chronologically to the eighteenth century, is examined on the basis of how it does or does not reflect this traditional assumption. Later methods are not tested against the earlier text, and examples do not qualify, modify or enrich the basic view, but simply confirm it or point to occasional aberrations, as in the case of Boyd's blindness to the neoclassical poetic technique of echoing sense in sound. Moreover, the analysis of Boyd's translation does not produce its own values; De Sua accepts and adopts the view that paraphrase is bad translation. His discussion, therefore, is flawed by a lack of clarity and flexibility in authorial stance and methods of approach, and a lack of insight into poetry. His greatest flaw, however, is the uncertain approach to translation.

The present work and translation studies

'Traduttore traditore' the Italians say; and if to study a version of a great poem in a different language seems a vain effort, a study of translations of Dante seems even irreverent, for Dante himself warned that it is impossible to translate poetry 'senza rompere tutta sua dolcezza e armonia'.[43] However, the expectations concerning translations have changed in our century, so that although many scholars and artists, like Pirandello, would say that the translator is like an actor (or in fact almost any reader) in that he can never reproduce the author's original intention, they would also agree with Pirandello when he says that the problem resides in methodology – in a viable critical view of translation.[44] In recent years a group of researchers (including Susan Bassnett-McGuire, James Holmes, André Lefevere, Gideon Toury and others) have in fact developed a more descriptive and systematic approach to translation studies. Although the material for my exploration consists mainly of translations of Dante's *Commedia*, this study is not intended as a contribution to the field of translation studies. In a succinct definition of this field, James Holmes distinguishes three phases of the translation process:

...the first of the three phases described here the translator shares with every reader of literary text, the third with every writer; the second, however, that of developing a target text map from his source-text map by means of correspondence rules, is uniquely a translational (or at least a specific kind of metatextual) operation, and as such deserves our special attention.[45]

The focus of the present study is not on the second phase, but on the first and third. For the translator is seen, first of all, as a reader of Dante, who faces a text built upon a selection of social norms, literary allusions, and a philosophical framework which are often at variance with those which shape the literature of his own culture. He must, therefore, attempt to find analogous features in his own time, which enable him to recreate a total referential context for the text in front of him.[46] Secondly, the translator of Dante is a writer, who produces an English text shaped by the models current in English poetry at the time.[47] In finding equivalences, as a reader, and in his choice and combination of models, as a writer, the translator reveals the power, flexibility and significance of features of his own culture.

However, I do rely on the same basic view of translation as developed in translation description studies. This view is not normative and prescriptive, nor is it aimed at distinguishing a 'good' from a 'bad' rendering of a particular passage or text – it is not, that is, 'source-oriented'. Rather, a comparison is made between a passage from the original and a passage from a translation to highlight what particular solution has been chosen for a particular problem, and why. Accordingly, I analyse translations like Charles Rogers' *Inferno* (1782) and Boyd's *Commedia* (1802), which have been branded as 'bad' translations by many critics. In fact, the study of these translations will prove to be necessary in order to build up a larger picture of responses to and translations of Dante in the given period.

More specifically useful to my discussion is a work such as F.T. Steiner's collection of texts on the translation theory current between 1650 and 1800, and his comments on it. In particular, I have selected two of F.T. Steiner's views as central to this study. First, from his evidence Steiner concludes that translation played a very important role in eighteenth-century culture. 'Translation was not only an art and a cultural process, but a metaphor for salvation and an analogy to other arts of understanding', according to Steiner, and it is for this reason that he believes that his historical survey of English translation theory between 1650 and 1800 'will also be valuable to students of eighteenth-century literature'.[48]

A similar standpoint lies behind the present work. The reception of Dante in English literature, studied through the translations of the *Divina Commedia*, exemplifies in a striking manner the confrontation – which created the peculiar tension in the eighteenth century – between the poetry of reasoning and argument, and the poetry of sensibility. Moreover, the mapping of this confrontation can be seen as being of general significance, of more far reaching interest than its limitation to the eighteenth century suggests. Traditional criticism has seen the confrontation between reason and sensibility in the eighteenth century as the result of the dualistic nature of neoclassical taste – with on the one hand an attraction to reason, clarity and elegance, and on the other to pathos, sublimity and even horror. But one can take a broader and deeper view, and agree with other critics in seeing this duality as the basic duality within English poetry, between what Joseph A. Wittreich calls the 'line of wit' and 'the line of vision', active at all times, between which, in varying degrees, English poetry always oscillates, and which reached its sharpest tension in the eighteenth century.[49] Dante becomes a catalyst helping to carry certain features of the poetic views of Young and Blake into the nineteenth century.

The second view of Steiner's adopted here is his distinction between the translator as painter (that is, close imitator and commentator), and the translator as creator. For the historicist study of early translators of Dante highlights another point. From the very start there arises a distinction between two kinds of translation: translation as commentary, and translation as imaginative recreation. The translator may decide to tackle a particular author because he admires his work and feels that the reader should have access to it; usually, this translator feels that his sensibility and knowledge give him a particular claim on that poet's creation – he is in possession of the truth about it. On the other hand, a translator may decide to produce a version of another poet because the latter's images and structures enable him to give body to his own vision; he feels he has something to communicate, and translating that poet provides him with the means. In this case, he is creating almost *ab ovo*: he is conscious of producing not a copy, but an analogue, an equivalent in modern terms of whatever he sees as being of particular importance and validity in the original.

This is not essentially a diachronic matter: De Sua's contention that Boyd intended to re-write Dante, while Cary translated his work literally because he was the first to have a high regard for his original, that later again the Victorians were literal translators because of current ideas about translation, and that the twentieth century was more critical and scholarly can only be attained by an extreme simplification of the analysis. A more accurate examination of the texts and of how the translators rendered their original provides a different picture. Both Boyd and Cary were trying to make Dante accessible to readers, but wavered between this intention and the attempt to recreate his poetry. The only basic difference is that Cary is more of a scholar and steps into the shoes of a creative writer very seldom, while Boyd does it continuously. A combination of the two approaches is, in varying degrees, always present in translations from different translators and different ages. The same recreating impulse which Boyd manifests at times in his translation, and Blake in his illustrations, also emerges in Shelley's, Browning's and Heaney's poems, and in Sisson's translation.

It remains possible of course to trace some kind of diachronic pattern in the spread of these two kinds of translations. In the case of Dante, the line of commentary starts with the 1719 rendering of Ugolino, finds its climax in Cary's version, and then becomes submerged in the Romantic poets' intense personal response to Dante. It clearly reappears in the numerous scholarly translations of the late nineteenth and twentieth centuries – in particular those of Binyon, Bickersteth, Sayers, Sinclair, and Singleton, which have been considered as the standard versions of Dante in English. The recreative approach begins with the early translators of the Ugolino episode in the second half of the eighteenth century, whose imagination is fired by Dante's images. It continues, mixed with the alternative approach, in Boyd's work, and finds its climax in Blake. It then disappears temporarily from translation, but is carried on in the use poets make of Dante in their own poetry – first by the Romantics and later by Browning and Rossetti, Pound and Eliot. It reappears in translation only in the very recent renderings of Dante by the modern poets C.H. Sisson and Allen Mandelbaum, and by the painter Tom Phillips.

But essentially the spread of commentary and recreative translation is a synchronic issue: there are two approaches to translation, and they intermingle according to the individual translator's varying responses to his original. The central eighteenth-century translation, Pope's translation of Homer, is itself one of the most striking examples of a text where both intentions are evident. The second chapter of this study will, accordingly, briefly consider Pope's Homer in order to illustrate the nature and effects of the two approaches to translation. Cowper's translation of Homer at the end of the eighteenth century will also be glanced at, for Cowper's choices and his standpoint are very different from Pope's. These two versions of Homer can provide the historicist framework of reference for translations of Dante in the eighteenth century.

Before leaving the subject of translation, however, one further point must be dealt with. In the penultimate chapter of this study the focus will be on William Blake, and in particular on his illustrations of the *Commedia*. Although traditionally illustrations are reckoned to belong to the field of figurative art, they are regarded here as a kind of translation. Like a translator, in his work on Dante Blake reveals the ways in which he read the *Commedia* and the forms and images which were available to him, and which he selected to give shape to his vision of Dante. These forms and images are often shared by poetry and painting, and particularly so in the case of Blake. Such a view is not idiosyncratic, and I return for support to the essay by Pirandello referred to in the opening of this section, entitled 'Illustratori, Attori e Traduttori' (1908). Here Pirandello shows how an actor, like a translator, gives his own voice to the matter of the original text; and both the actor and the illustrator translate a living but immaterial artistic creation into visible, living reality (p. 235).

Translations of Dante can only offer particular visions of his work; and translations of Dante in the eighteenth and early nineteenth century were often given shape, as will be seen, in terms of English visionary poetry. In Blake the phrase 'visions of Dante' retains its metaphorical meaning, but also assumes literal meaning.

The present work: its connecting threads and its structure

The examination of the early translations of Dante into English does not present excessive methodological problems, since the focus is limited to just one episode, or a few cantos. With complete translations of the whole *Divina Commedia*, however, not only the amount of material but also the variety of poetic and philosophical issues are much greater. A few of these issues must be extracted from their contexts to serve as connecting threads in the examination of translations, and even though the present work does not presume to study the world of Dante or add anything to primary Dante scholarship, nevertheless the issues selected must be representative of important aspects of both the translations and the original. Fortunately, two issues of this kind presented themselves as inescapable.

It has been clear from the start that Dante has appealed to English translators and poets mainly for his power to create intensely visual poetry, and because he produced a vision of human life through the presentation of characters – particularly that of the autobiographical protagonist. It is therefore these two aspects – the visible world Dante creates, and the figure of the protagonist as different from that of the narrator – that this study will use as connecting threads.

That there are two figures in the *Divina Commedia* – Dante the narrator, and Dante the voyager – and that Dante the writer is not necessarily Dante the narrator, and is certainly not Dante the voyager is a realization which translators have partly had to discover for themselves, partly to accept from scholars in the course of the twentieth century. The pattern of change is perfectly illustrated in the movement from the identification of Dante the writer with Dante the voyager (as it appears in some early translators) to the recognition of the presence in the

Commedia of Dante the narrator as a figure quite separate from Dante the voyager (as for example in Allen Mandelbaum's recent translation).

But it is the visual element of Dante that has particularly attracted the interest of English translators and scholars. The fact that so many artists – Sir Joshua Reynolds, Flaxman, Fuseli, Blake – produced paintings and illustrations inspired by episodes from the *Commedia* is one expression of this interest; but in addition we also have the continuous assessments of the visual element in Dante by translators, poets and scholars, from the eighteenth century to the present day. Cary mentions that it was Dante's way 'to define all his images in such a manner as to bring them within the circle of our vision, and to subject them to the power of the pencil.'[50] Ruskin finds that the emotion inspired by natural landscape is not expressed, in the Middle Ages, by 'visible art', and concludes that 'we must ... take up written landscape instead, and examine this medieval sentiment as we find it embodied in the poem of Dante.'[51] T.S. Eliot recognizes the central function of the visual particularly in the translation of a great poem into a different culture, and says 'speech varies, but our eyes are all the same .... Dante's attempt is to make us see what he saw.'[52] C.H. Sisson uses very similar words in the introduction to his translation in 1980:

> The moment comes – sooner rather than later, later rather than sooner, according to the difficulty (for him) of the passage – when the translator sees through to the original matter – the actual objects – of the original. It is at this moment that his own words form, and he has to take what he is given, and to say what he sees (p. ix).

Within the continuity of this concern with Dante's visual manner there is what amounts to a reversal in the understanding of it. Cary and Coleridge saw it as 'too graphic', while Sisson is vividly aware of the indirectness of Dante's manner, which makes the reader create the images. The pattern seems to come full circle in the translation of *Inferno* by the painter Tom Phillips (1983), who wrote his version of the poetry as an explanation of, and comment on his illustrations of that *cantica*.

That Dante's visible world and his protagonist are important matters in the original, and therefore are fully justified as a focus of this exploration, needs to be briefly established. Just as in English literature, so on the Italian scene the many illustrators have shown us Dante's sense of the real and concrete. The presence of a definable iconography, the statuesque nature of many of Dante's characters, the variety and efficacy of his similes, the continuous reference to eyes and the importance of vision are all facets of this stress on Dante's creation of a concrete world, not just in *Inferno* but even in *Paradiso*, as C.F. Goffis says: 'Il senso del reale, che noi abbiamo ammirato nell'Inferno è nerbo dello spirito dantesco, che nel Paradiso gli consente di tradurre una realtà metafisica in forme nuove e concrete ...'.[53]

This solidity of the world of the *Commedia* is increased by the fact that there is a figure observing it and experiencing it. One of the first commentators of the *Commedia* pointed out the presence of a protagonist-like figure in the poem: 'Dante pone se in forma comune d'uomo ... inchinante alle sensualitadi'.[54] Many commentators have occasionally referred to this figure as a matter of course, but without developing its implications into a reading of the poem, and without using it systematically – until this century. It was following the work of Charles Singleton, Erich Auerbach and particularly A.C. Charity that Italian criticism recognized the centrality of the issue. Angelo Jacomuzzi's views are very similar to those of Charity, and are shared by a number of Italian critics, such as G. Contini, to whom Jacomuzzi refers:

> Ma l'indicazione continiana, quando la sottolineatura (Dante 'personaggio-*poeta*') si traduca nella distinzione *personaggio/poeta* ch'essa implica, oltre che esser un necessario criterio esegetico e un efficace scandaglio euristico, può svolgere la funzione d'un importante criterio metodologico ....[55]

The main consequence of this view is the resulting distinction between two levels of significance in the poem, corresponding to the two different angles of vision within it, and consequently between two levels of reading. The reader has to interact with the text, to follow the imperfect, developing vision of the protagonist, while interpreting it on the basis of the higher vision and guidance of the narrator. The issue of 'vision', in this context, therefore assumes a richer meaning. The vision of the protagonist, of the strange world around him, will turn into the beatific vision which unifies the experience of the two figures. The present work will be sympathetic to the prophetic reading of the *Commedia*, as developed by Singleton, Charity and Jacomuzzi, without agreeing with the excesses to which such a reading has led a critic like Mineo.

The present work is divided into three parts. Part one focuses on the eighteenth century: the example of the translation of Homer by Pope and by Cowper make up Chapter 2, references to Dante in magazines and letters Chapter 3, early translations of the Ugolino episode Chapter 4, Hayley's translations of the first three cantos of *Inferno* Chapter 5, and Rogers' translation of the whole of *Inferno* Chapter 6. Chapter 7 will offer a brief conclusion to part one. Part two analyses the first two complete translations of the *Commedia*, by Henry Boyd (Chapter 8), and by Henry Francis Cary (Chapter 9), and is also rounded off by a brief conclusion (Chapter 10). Part three will extend the discussion into the analysis of Blake's Dante (Chapter 11) and with a final conclusion (Chapter 12).

PART I

THE EIGHTEENTH CENTURY

2

Pope's and Cowper's translations of Homer: the context of Dante translations

Pope's translation of Homer

Pope was writing within a tradition of English translations of Homer,[1] but very consciously adopted a progressive and innovative stance in relation to his predecessors. In the footnote explaining the ritual sacrifice in Book I of the *Iliad*, he says

> If we consider this Passage, it is not made to shine in poetry. All that can be done is to give it Numbers, and endeavour to set the Particulars in a distinct View. But if we take it in another Light, and as a Piece of Learning, it is valuable for being the most exact Account of the ancient Sacrifices any where left to us ... [a detailed description of the ritual procedure in sacrifices follows].
>
> I am obliged to take notice how intirely Mr. *Dryden* has mistaken the Sense of this Passage, and the Custom of Antiquity; ... . Some of the mistakes ... he was led into by Chapman's Translation.[2]

Pope sees Homer at this point not as a poet, but as a chronicler of customs, manners and rites of the past. Moreover, he goes on to claim that both the seventeenth and the sixteenth centuries had misinterpreted Homer's historical world, and hence also his poems; and in the same breath he claims his own role in discovering it and making it available to the reader. This is the alternative pleasure poetry offers; the reading 'will double their [the readers'] Pleasure' if they reflect that they are 'growing acquainted with Nations and People that are now no more' (p. 14). Part of Pope's own task as a translator is to pass on this historical knowledge to his readers, hence the inclusion, in the published edition of Pope's *Iliad* and *Odyssey*, of Parnell's 'Life and Times of Homer', and hence the commentaries, footnotes, essays. That the scholarship he offers is now out of date is beside the point. The important fact is that Pope felt he had to include the best scholarship of the time, use it within his own translation to highlight certain moments of the story, and in fact carry out research and make discoveries, whenever possible, for himself.

The effect of this on his translation is a new closeness to the text, a kind of literalness, in this respect, and a greater seriousness of tone. An example can best illustrate how it all works. This is the passage describing the sacrifice in the quotation referred to:

Ὡς ἔφατ' εὐχόμενος, τοῦ δ' ἔκλυε Φοῖβος Ἀπόλλων.
αὐτὰρ ἐπεί ῥ' εὔξαντο καὶ οὐλοχύτας προβάλοντο,
αὐέρυσαν μὲν πρῶτα καὶ ἔσφαξαν καὶ ἔδειραν,
μηρούς τ' ἐξέταμον κατά τε κνίση ἐκάλυψαν   460
δίπτυχα ποιήσαντες, ἐπ' αὐτῶν δ' ὠμοθέτησαν.
καῖε δ' ἐπὶ σχίζῃς ὁ γέρων, ἐπὶ δ' αἴθοπα οἶνον
λεῖβε· νέοι δὲ παρ' αὐτὸν ἔχον πεμπώβολα χερσίν.
αὐτὰρ ἐπεὶ κατὰ μῆρ' ἐκάη καὶ σπλάγχν' ἐπάσαντο,
μίστυλλόν τ' ἄρα τᾶλλα καὶ ἀμφ' ὀβελοῖσιν ἔπειραν,   465
ὤπτησάν τε περιφραδέως, ἐρύσαντό τε πάντα.
αὐτὰρ ἐπεὶ παύσαντο πόνου τετύκοντό τε δαῖτα,
δαίνυντ', οὐδέ τι θυμὸς ἐδεύετο δαιτὸς ἐΐσης.[3]

So *Chryses* pray'd, *Apollo* heard his Pray'r:
And now the *Greeks* their Hecatomb prepare;
Between their Horns the salted Barley threw,
And with their Heads to Heav'n the Victims slew:
The Limbs they sever from th'inclosing Hide;
The Thighs, selected to the Gods, divide:
On these, in double Cawls involv'd with Art,
The choicest Morsels lay from ev'ry Part.
The Priest himself before his Altar stands,
And burns the Off'ring with his holy Hands,
Pours the black Wine, and sees the Flames aspire;
The Youth with Instruments surround the Fire:
The Thighs thus sacrific'd, and Entrails drest,
Th'Assistants part, transfix and roast the rest:
Then spread the Tables, the Repast prepare,
Each takes his Seat, and each receives his Share.
When now the Rage of Hunger was represt,
With pure Libations they conclude the Feast;   (Book I, ll. 598-615, pp. 116-17)

The same passage in the well-established Victorian translation of Andrew Lang, Walter Leaf and Ernest Myers is as follows:

So spake he in prayer, and Phoebus Apollo heard him. Now when they had prayed and sprinkled the barley meal, first they drew back the victims' heads and slaughtered and flayed them, and cut slices from the thighs and wrapped them in fat, making a double fold, and laid raw collops thereon, and the old man burnt them on cleft wood and made a libation over them of gleaming wine; and at his side the young men in their hands held five-pronged forks. Now when the thighs were burnt and they had tasted the vitals, then sliced they all the rest and pierced it through with spits, and roasted them carefully, and drew all off again.

So when they had rest from the task and had made ready the banquet, they feasted, nor was their heart aught stinted of the fair banquet.[4]

Pope's generalizing mind turns the five-pronged forks ('πεμπώβολα') into 'instruments'; he turns the old man ('ὁ γέρων') and the young men ('νέοι') into 'Priest' and 'Assistants'. Also, the fat is laid in a double fold, according to Leaf, and 'in double Cawls involv'd with Art' in Pope: a very eighteenth-century expression for a very eighteenth-century notion. De Sua would call this taking liberties with the text, and rewrite it according to contemporary canons and ideas. And yet Pope himself complains of Dryden's misunderstanding of the details of the text, so that in Dryden's version 'in effect there is no Sacrifice at all'. Thus Pope does take the original seriously within a historicist view which is flexible enough to make allowances for very different conventions. This goes beyond an attention to details, because it reflects the fact that 'the ancient Poets and in particular *Homer*, [have] written with a care and respect to Religion', while no modern poet, continues Pope, will leave behind a similarly accurate record of contemporary rites (note to line 600, p. 116).

Pope follows Dryden, therefore, in the elaborate, neoclassical diction and the use of the heroic couplet for his translation, but adopts an innovative attitude by assuming the role of the historian unveiling past facts. Two observations can be made here. First, the term 'literal' is a relative notion. Translation, in Pope's hands and in fact in Pope's day, has become more literal than it ever was before.[5] Accordingly, Boyd's paraphrase could be considered quite literal in a similar manner, even though perhaps its closeness to the original might be relative, and restricted to specific aspects of the original. The second observation is that Pope's new literalness concerning the facts of the past world results in an increased seriousness, causing him to use solemn language and tone, which leads in itself to a departure from the original. It is known that the *Iliad* begins with majestic, public postures and ends with more private, inner sentiments. This growth is lost in Pope's version. His seriousness of purpose, dominated by a desire to re-establish the majesty of Homer, and his indubitably greater skill in public rather than private poetry, lead him to extend the celebratory, ritualistic tone to the end of the epic.[6]

Thus, paradoxically, the desire to rediscover the original, literal meaning can lead to apparently non-literal renderings. In the same first book, not long after the passage quoted, Pope refuses to imitate his predecessors and produce, as a version of one of Homer's epithets, something like '*the venerable Ox-ey'd* Juno' (Dryden; 'βοῶπις πότνια Ἥρη'). Pope explains that he agrees with Madame Dacier in the view that 'βου' is 'only an augmentative Particle', and that, moreover, 'the Imagination that Oxen have larger Eyes than ordinary is ill grounded, and has no Foundation in Truth;...' hence, he will translate with a 'Paraphrase': 'Full on the Sire the Goddess of the Skies/ Roll'd the large Orbs of her majestic Eyes' (Book I, 712-713, and note 713, p. 121). It is easy for us to smile at what is probably a 'literal' reconstruction, but motivated by the Augustan dislike of a comparison between an ox and a goddess; and in fact, Pope's version here has little to do with Juno's beauty, but with her majesty. The point is, again, that Pope is mainly attempting to correct tradition, and re-establish truth. This reference to Juno follows the dispute between the goddess and Jupiter, which had been rendered, before Pope and certainly by Dryden, with some licence. In a note to the passage on Juno Pope says that 'Mr Dryden ... has translated all this with the utmost Severity upon the Ladies, and spirited the whole with satirical Additions of his own' (note 698, p. 121). He disagrees with Dryden's attitude, and again agrees with Madame Dacier who prefers to give 'the whole Passage a more important Turn, and incline us to think that *Homer* design'd to represent the Folly and Danger of Prying into the Secrets of Providence.' What we have seen, therefore, in this paragraph are examples of conscious, worked-out attempts by Pope at achieving some measure of true literalness in translation.

Less factual, but motivated by a similar compulsion to set the record straight about Homer, is Pope's intention to rescue Homer from the burlesque tradition of interpretation in which some predecessors had rendered his work. Homer was the father of western poetry, the author of the greatest heroic poems, combining Art and Nature, and he had to be rendered as such. The echoes of the Roman authors – Virgil and Ovid – as well as the English – especially Milton but even Spenser (in the pictorialism of some almost emblematic tableaux) – served to give to Pope's Homer the character of a universal poem, and insert it within English epic tradition.

But in addition to his historicist approach to the original, Pope also uses Homer's verse to give shape and voice to his own poetic views, and so, after observing the process and the results of Pope's attempt to unveil the truth about his writer, we must now turn to an analysis of the ways in which Pope used Homer to give utterance to his own beliefs. According to Maynard Mack, Pope's personal response to Homer must have been very great, since he 'had the urge to ... make him ... contemporaneous and exemplary to the age' (p. xlvi). The two terms Mack uses are indeed useful in distinguishing Pope's aims. To make Homer contemporaneous involves the deliberate attempt to build a bridge between past author and present reader, and includes the strategies discussed in the previous paragraphs (such as the attempt to be more literal, the extension of the celebratory tone, the connection made with Milton and other authors). To make him exemplary means to channel those views and beliefs that the translator sees as central to his own age, including those in Pope's own poetry, through Homer, and attempt to solve the poetic issues of the present by means of the past.

Pope can be seen making Homer exemplary when he uses him to prove a universal truth, and one which he felt was very central to his age. In his own *Essay on Criticism* he had argued that imagination is indivisible from judgement, and that both are necessary to the workings and products of the mind. Homer, who was considered the poet of Art and of Nature, would be the proof that the two powers of man must be allies. Hence Pope's particular stress, in his preface, on that aspect of Homer which had received little attention, that is, on 'Invention'. The traditional comparison with Virgil offers Pope suitable material with which to expand on this view; Virgil might share with Homer the claim to 'Judgement', but 'his [Homer's] Invention remains yet unrival'd'. Pope seems to move towards views of original genius and the power of the imagination of poets in the second half of the eighteenth century when he says that 'It is the Invention that in different degrees distinguishes all great Genius's ... . Whatever Praises might be given to works of Judgement, there is not even a single Beauty in them to which the Invention must not contribute.' This seems confirmed by the synonyms which specify the meaning of 'Invention': 'the Force of the Poet's Imagination, (p. 4), and 'the boundless walk for his Imagination' take us as far as 'the Warmth of his Rapture' and even into 'Poetical *Fire*'. It is the same fire, says Pope, that flashed in Statius and burned like a furnace in Shakespeare and Milton. As far as the translator is concerned, 'It is not to be doubted that the *Fire* of the poem is what a *Translator* should principally regard, as it is most likely to expire in his managing' (pp. 17-18).

The pre-romantic vocabulary must not blind the reader to the fact that Pope's boundlessness is very much within bounds. He might use the same words that Edward Young was to use in his *Conjectures on Original Compositions* (1759), but his meaning is different. Particularly Pope's use of the vocabulary of the sublime deserves a brief explanation. When Pope refers to 'the sublime', he uses a term which will gather together many varied strands of aesthetic ideas and poetic taste which had ɔeen rejected by the neoclassical poetics. But Pope's sublime is of that early kind which was perfectly at home within Augustan taste. It has no element of pain or terror, no notion characteristic of Burke and those who followed him. Even when, in some scenes of the *Iliad* as well as in his own poetry, Pope seems to create a night-piece, he is more often than not simply letting the reader derive a comforting feeling about his own time and state by comparing it with the impending doom of the Trojans, and the 'darksome' setting of Eloisa's speeches. Pope's 'genius', or 'boundless', or 'vast' are not those of the later sublime. His 'vast' is the vast of Addison, Akenside, or Lord Kames, who as late as 1762 still saw it as 'within proper bounds';[7] his nature leaves no place for the revelation of the supernatural, but is still the neoclassical order, the harmonious regularity of the divine. Pope's mention of Longinus indicates the allegiance to that early sublime, the sublime of man not nature, of Raphael not Michelangelo. If one insists on reading these signs as early forms of later developments, one can only see them as latent.

Up to this point we have considered two aspects of Pope's more recreative response to Homer: the fact that through a discussion of Homer he argues the relative merits of judgement and imagination, and his allegiance to early forms of the idea of the sublime. Before moving to the versification, two more aspects of Pope's translation of Homer must be mentioned, because they clarify two elements of eighteenth-century poetry which must be kept in mind as shaping the context of Dante translations. The first is the great importance of the 'sentiments' of authors, particularly past authors – their 'sententious statements', as the eighteenth century understood the word, communicating the authors' philosophy; and the second is the pictorial, descriptive aspect of the poetry of the age.

The present-day reader of Pope's 'Preface' to his translation might find it difficult to believe, but Pope was voicing the basic views of his age when he said that 'a particular care should be taken to express with all Plainness those Moral sentences and Proverbial Speeches which are so numerous in this Poet' (p. 19), or that 'What were alone sufficient to prove the Grandeur and Excellence of his Sentiments in general, is that they have so remarkable a parity with those of the Scripture' (p. 9). Pope is reading Homer in the only way he can – as an eighteenth-century reader, and his translation of Homer follows from that. The eighteenth century inherited an ethical approach to the ancients, and added to it its own need to move from the survey of particularity to the observation of universal needs and truths. The circumstances of the heroes' lives and actions were read to discover the moral sentiments voiced by their author. Accordingly, Pope's Homeric heroes face death and destiny with a self-consciousness which is certainly not Homeric, so that their own unique fate becomes a crucial example of general human destiny. In fact, generalization and abstraction of moral and religious values are the most obvious additions of Pope to his Homer.

'"Sentiment"', as R. Brower points out, 'is closely connected for Pope and his contemporaries with description, a point emphasized more than once in the notes'.[8] Often a scene in Pope turns from action to picture, and more importantly from an expression of 'moral Sentences and Instructions' into pictures. Brower concludes that 'After the belief in Homer's truth to General Nature, the most important governing idea of Pope's translation is the pictorial' (p. 130). Characteristic of Pope's pictorial additions are words like 'shining', 'bright', 'fire', which are words of the kind listed by Josephine Miles as especially favoured in the mid-eighteenth century.[9] Being both descriptive and suggestive of spiritual significance, these words underline the connection between the two governing ideas: pictures are 'universal Pictures', and show the moral value of the specific. Notable in this connection is Pope's mention of Spenser and Milton, and the occasional imitation of their pictorial techniques. But at this point one further element of the dynamics of translation begins to become clear: it is not always possible to distinguish between the two apparently contradictory aims. Is Pope using Milton to insert Homer 'historically' within the English tradition Homer belongs to, and is Pope therefore revealing to the reader a truth which has been hidden by time and its changes? Or is Pope in fact rewriting Homer by creating an equivalent of Homer's heroic world in terms of the English epic tradition, which, through the work of Spenser and Milton, had become more spiritual and passive? Truly it becomes difficult to distinguish between Pope's intention of making Homer 'contemporary' and of making him 'exemplary' to the eighteenth century.

But finally Pope's intention of making Homer 'exemplary' – his allegiance to translation as recreation – can only be identified as a definite aspect of his translation if Pope's own skills as a poet and sensitive craftsman succeed in shaping the borrowed world into a unified poem. Whatever he intends to voice, and whatever he gives voice to unawares, he must succeed in creating that unity which alone is poetry. This can only be done through the English language the ancient poet is made to speak, and the rhyme and rhythms the translator produces. Pope's *Iliad* is indeed a poem with a validity of its own, and therefore it is an eighteenth-century, rather than ancient, poem. In the matter of language and versification, the historicist approach recedes into the background. Pope is very well aware of the distinction between the world created in a poem and the language the poet speaks, and the different duties of the translator:

> It is the first grand Duty of an Interpreter to give his Author entire and unmaim'd; and for the rest, the *Diction* and *Versification* only are his proper Province; since these must be his own, but the others [the 'parts of the Poem' such as 'Fable', 'Manners' and 'Sentiments', and the particular 'Images, Descriptions and Similes'] he is to take as he finds them (p. 17).

The translator is, admittedly, an interpreter, but he must produce neither a too literal rendition of the sense, nor a 'rash Paraphrase'. As far as diction and versification go, he must indeed create an equivalent, a contemporary analogue of the original. He must turn one language and rhythm into another language and rhythm. Pope uses the neoclassical diction of Dryden and the heroic couplet of the eighteenth century. In some ways these features represent appropriate eighteenth-century versions of analogous features in Homer; in other respects they cannot but greatly distort Homer, and produce 'something parallel, tho' not the same.'[10]

There is nothing original in this. Pope here accepts and adopts the principles of translation characteristic of his age; in fact he practically restates what Dryden had said about translation in his 'Dedication' to the *Aeneis*, where Dryden had explained his method as the selection of the middle path 'betwixt the two Extremes of Paraphrase and literal Translation'. He had then proceeded to specify the translator's particular responsibility:

> I have endevour'd to make Virgil speak such English as he woul'd himself have spoken if he had been born in England and in this present age.[11]

These words can be taken to express Pope's standpoint; in fact, Pope's own words in the quotation above simply expand on Dryden's.[12]

The combination of an innovative approach and a traditional approach, of the historicist closeness to the text and personal transformation of the message, of the 'matter' of the poem and its diction and versification might seem to indicate a kind of absolute split in Pope's translation. But this is not what this discussion wants to suggest. First of all, it has been shown that opposites mingle and become confused in particular instances, and secondly that the attempt to be literal at times results in a departure from the original. But it is particularly important to realize that, if there is a split, it occurs, and becomes finally resolved, in the translator himself. In the case of Pope, his Preface makes it quite clear where the split occurs. On one side of the split, we continuously read about 'the parts of the poem', the 'Marvelous Fable' (p. 7), the knowledge of 'Nations and People', the 'Vision of Things nowhere else to be found' (p. 14), the 'true Mirror of that ancient World', and the creation of 'a new and boundless Walk for his Imagination' (p. 5) – in short, we read about the work itself as a product, the fact that 'Our Author's Work is a wild Paradise...' (p. 3). On the one hand, therefore, we have Pope's concern to reproduce correctly the world of the poem. On the other side of the split Pope becomes conscious of the presence of the writer's personality: 'the Reader is hurry'd out of himself by the Force of the Poet's Imagination, and turns in one place to a Hearer, in another to a Spectator'. Thus a distinction arises between the 'work', and the 'Author'. Aspects of the poem ('Exact Disposition, Just Thought') may be 'found in a thousand; but this Poetical *Fire*, this *Vivida vis animi*, in a very few' (p. 4). And the endeavour of 'any one who translates Homer, is above all things to keep alive that Spirit and Fire which makes his Chief Character'. This chief character cannot be discovered in the writer's learning or his fame, but in the poetic act itself; therefore Pope advises the translator 'to study his Author rather from his own Text than from any

Commentaries, how learned soever, or whatever Figure they may make in the Estimation of the World' (pp. 22-3).

The implication of these statements goes further than the obvious belief that the translator must be a poet of equal gifts and similar stature to the writer of the original. To translate Homer in these terms means to recognize the truth of his world, as well as the greatness of his soul, but also one's own ability to rise to the challenge of reproducing both of these. The translator moves into the world's past, bridging the interval with the language of the present. The process remains ambiguous in so far as there is a temporal journey which may be to the past, or from the past. But one thing is quite certain: if Pope claims to reproduce Homer's world closely, and to make Homer speak as if he had been born in eighteenth-century England, this is the same as saying that he sees Homer reincarnated in himself. He is one of the 'few' who have the poetic fire he referred to, and it is here that, in Steiner's words, 'translation was ... a metaphor for salvation' (see p. 15 above). Finally, therefore, the literal and the recreative approaches to translation seem reconciled, in the case of Pope, in the identification between the translator and the original writer.

Cowper's translation of Homer

Pope's Homer finds its counterpart in the last decade of the eighteenth century in Cowper's translation of the *Iliad* and the *Odyssey*. Cowper translated in Miltonic blank verse, disagreed with the use of couplets, and attacked the idea that the translator should imagine to himself how the original author would have written, had he lived in England in the times of the translator. His approach to his work, therefore, seems very different from Pope's, and offers an indication of the contexts within which Dante translations are placed. I return to Cowper's ideas later, when I discuss Rogers' translation of *Inferno* at the end of Chapter 8, but a brief excursion into Cowper's *Iliad* will therefore be useful at this point.

Cowper's 'Preface' to his *Iliad of Homer* (1791) is not long, but in it he expresses views on translation in general as well as ideas concerning the translation of Homer in particular (including the models to be chosen). He goes beyond translation, however, and in his preferences and choices he expresses views on the writing of poetry at the end of the century.

To begin with the first of these three aspects of Cowper's 'Preface' (his views on translation in general), he takes a strong position regarding fidelity to the original:

> ... the sense of the author is required, and we do not surrender it willingly even to the plea of necessity. Fidelity is indeed of the very essence of translation, and the term itself implies it.[13]

In fact, at this point Cowper gives voice to the view that if we do not respect fidelity 'we may call our work an *imitation*, if we please, or perhaps a *paraphrase*, but it is no longer the same author only in a different dress, and therefore it is not translation' (p. x).

In language and style, too, Cowper considers that the translator should attempt to find 'the exact medium' between free and servile translation; he seems to distrust the translator's reliance on imagination when he objects to 'an opinion commonly received' – 'that a translator should imagine to himself the style which his author would probably have used, had the language into which he is rendered been his own'. The problem with this approach is, according to Cowper, that each translator would 'fall on a manner quite different from all the rest', which implies that probably no-one would find 'the right' manner (p. xi).

However, 'fidelity' in the rendering of the sense of the original does not mean quite the same thing to Cowper – or, as we have already seen, to Pope – as it does to us. For example, Cowper admits to translating some epithets 'in one way or other', and to leaving some out, if they were repeated – the reason for this selection being so obvious that 'it need not be mentioned'. Cowper's stance of improving his original becomes evident also when he states which the most difficult passages to translate were: 'It is difficult to kill a sheep with dignity in a modern language, to flay and prepare it for the table, detailing every circumstance of the process' (p. xvi). This is the passage examined earlier (pp. 24-5 above) in the translations of Pope and of Lang, Leaf and Myers, and Cowper's consciousness of having to labour in order to translate his original with 'dignity' is clearly close to Pope's position:

> So Chryses prayed, whom Phoebus heard well-pleased;
> Then prayed the Grecians also, and with meal
> Sprinkled the victims, their retracted necks
> First pierced, then flay'd them; the disjointed thighs
> They, next, invested with the double caul,
> Which with crude slices thin they overspread.
> The priest burned incense, and libation poured
> Large on the hissing brands, while, him beside,
> Busy with spit and prong, stood many a youth
> Trained to the task. The thighs with fire consumed,
> They gave to each their portion of the maw,
> Then slashed the remnant, pierced it with the spits,
> And managing with culinary skill
> The roast, withdrew it from the spits again.

Their whole task thus accomplished, and the board
Set forth, they feasted, and were all sufficed.
When neither hunger more nor thirst remained
Unsatisfied, boys crown'd the beakers high
with wine delicious . . .   (Book I, ll. 562-580, pp. 15-16)

What was said of Pope's version of the *Iliad* in comparison with that of Lang, Leaf and Myers' can be said of Cowper's, too. He also turns the old man into a Priest, and though he does not change the 'young men' into 'Assistants', his long paraphrase fulfils the same purpose ('many a youth/ Trained for the task'). As for the preparation of the sacrifice, Cowper is less ceremonial than Pope, who presents a slow-moving, solemn ritual, but he still heightens the dignity of the task by compressing descriptions ('the retracted necks', 'the disjointed thighs') and choosing phrases with connotations of solemnity ('invested', 'overspread', 'burned incense', 'hissing brands'). Similarly, the epithet for Juno, which Pope had paraphrased in order to avoid the comparison of a goddess with an ox, is also paraphrased by Cowper, who, rather than 'ox-eyed Juno', has a shortened version of Pope's 'large Orbs of her majestic eyes': 'the Goddess ample-eyed' (Book I, l. 677).

Fidelity is, therefore, a relative term to describe Cowper's stance, both in respect to the matter and to the manner of the translation. Cowper himself states that his language is 'not verbose', and his diction is 'often plain and unelevated' because Homer himself is grand and lofty only in the right places, and therefore his translator must vary his own diction. Yet it is difficult to reconcile his use of words like 'plain' and 'not verbose' with a statement such as this: 'I have also everywhere used an unabbreviated fullness of phrase as most suited to the nature of the work ...' (p. xv). It seems, at this point, that what is mainly important is 'the nature of the work', not the sense and style of the particular passage.

In fact, Cowper's recreative stance in relation to his original, which already makes a brief appearance in these statements, emerges most obviously in what I have listed as the second aspect of Cowper's preface (his remarks on a contemporary version of Homer). He chooses Milton as the model for Homer because he considers that Milton's style is the English analogue of Homer's.[14] The 'similitude' is mainly a question of manner, and 'no person familiar with both [Homer and Milton] can read either without being reminded of the other.' But it is particularly English blank verse that seems to be the contemporary analogue of Homer's lines, and 'A translator of Homer ... seems directed by Homer himself to the use of blank verse, as to that alone in which he can be rendered with any tolerable representation of his manner in this particular' (p. xiii). The Miltonic style and in particular blank verse are the most suitable for rendering the basic aspects of Homer's poetry, which Cowper identifies as Homer's 'energy' and 'harmony' – energy being communicated by Miltonic diction, and harmony by blank verse. 'Energy' is the main characteristic of Milton's diction, and 'so long as Milton's works, whether his prose or his verse, shall exist, so long there will be abundant proof that no subject, however important, however sublime, can demand greater force of expression that is within the compass of the English language' (p. xii). As for 'harmony', it is to be found in blank verse, particularly in that of Milton, who had a perfect ear for judging variety of effect, with which, in fact, 'harmony' seems to be considered by Cowper as synonymous.

It is at this point that Cowper leaves for a moment the direct concern with translation, and turns to the third aspect of his preface – poetry in general, contrasting the use of rhyme with the use of blank verse. He accepts the view that 'the author is certainly best entitled to applause who succeeds against the greatest difficulty, and in verse that calls for the most artificial management in its construction' (p. xiii). Rhyme, he states, is easy to write: it is regular and smooth, and the poet's labour needs to be exercised only within the limited range of the rhyme scheme itself ('rhyme' being used by Cowper, seemingly, as synonymous with 'couplets', p. xiv). But the writer of blank verse has a much harder task: he must 'exhibit all the variations, as he proceeds, of which ten syllables are susceptible; between the first syllable and the last there is no place at which he must not occasionally pause, and the place of the pause must be perpetually shifted' (p. xiv). Moreover, the harmony of the whole depends not only on the variety of effect within the line, but also on the variety of effect of a number of lines in combination – each line having to be different in the distribution of pauses from the line preceding it and the one which follows it. Only in this way can the poem be 'musical'. And in fact, variety in itself seems to be more important than musicality, for 'a line, rough in itself, has yet its recommendations; it saves the ear the pain of an irksome monotony, and seems even to add greater smoothness to others' (p. xiii). Milton's *Paradise Lost* well exemplifies this practice. In addition to the difficulty of creating variety in the distribution of pauses, blank verse also requires 'a style in general more elaborate than rhyme requires, farther removed from the vernacular idiom both in the language itself and in the arrangement of it...' (p. xiv). There is, therefore, no doubt in Cowper's mind that this is the more difficult medium for writing poetry, and should earn its composer the most applause.

In his stress on fidelity, not only in matter, but also in manner, and the need to create an analogue of the original, Cowper seems to give voice to what De Sua calls a 'new vision' of translation developed by the Romantic translator (Cary being one example), who tries to 'produce a translation that will have an aesthetic effect similar to that the model has in the source language'. In this respect Cowper differs considerably from the eighteenth-century translator who tries to create a new original, 'regardless of how it reflected the qualities of the model' (De Sua, p. 28). This is, of course, true in so far as the very notion of an aesthetic effect would have been foreign to writers and artists before the eighteenth century. But the comparison between Cowper and Pope's stance indicates the existence of other notions.

Both Pope and Cowper produce a version which has 'dignity'. Cowper is more restrained in this respect, probably not only out of personal preference, but also because he did not need to redirect tradition. Pope had attempted to rescue Homer from the burlesque translations which had preceded his, and he had therefore placed great emphasis on dignity and ritual. Cowper could simply rely on Pope's achievement. Therefore, the position of a translation – at a particular moment in the course of translations of that author – is also an important feature of a translation, partly determining a translator's attitude. This notion must be kept in mind in reading the translations of Dante.

A second notion is revealed by the fact that, in practice, Cowper distances himself from Pope's attitude in his 'Preface', but translates in a relatively similar manner in practice. This is not so much a question of a gap between theory and practice, as of understanding the words used in their historical context. Cowper's fidelity is still much closer to Pope's than to our notion of the word, so that the critic who attempts to assess the shifts in taste and attitudes of a particular age must not just rely on the views expressed by writers and translators, but also be guided by a careful reading of the text.

Thirdly, Cowper's words on poetry in general highlight the change in the current views on the sublime style. This highest poetic style derived its elaborate diction from Pope's Homer, and continued to do so throughout the eighteenth century. But the eighteenth century took sublimity into different regions. First, poets and translators escaped from the fetters of the couplets into the freedom of blank verse. Moreover, they extended sublimity from pictorialism and use of visual images to musical effect. In addition, it is remarkable that Cowper extends a discussion of translating Homer into a discussion of English poetry. The value of a translation resides in English poetry: Milton is the epitome of the poet of sublimity, not just for his use of space, but also for his use of a harmony which includes roughness and irregularity, and for his use of energy, and these latter two are the aesthetic qualities valued at the end of the eighteenth century. This connection between translation and the contemporary taste in native poetry is a belief that Mack claims for Pope:

> For Pope, Homer was a poet with certain supreme qualities, and to render these qualities
> as he perceived them, in his own poetic medium, was his first criterion of truth to his
> author. In other words, the 'truth' of the rendering lay in the English poetry (p. lxxxix).

Pope's 'first criterion' must surely be the final criterion of any translation, since
no reader can possibly fully respond to a version of an earlier poem which only
reproduces the more literal, historical truth this expresses. The diction and
versification must make the poem speak a language the reader can interact with.
The historical world, on the one hand, and the diction and versification, on the
other, must be fused in a synthesis by the poetic vision the translator has
recognized (and already used in the shaping of the diction and versification).

Beyond the changes traceable between Pope and Cowper, or between
translators of Dante such as Hayley, Rogers, Boyd or Cary, a basic similarity
remains. Certainly many a twentieth-century translator regards his task in exactly
the same way as Pope regarded his. C.H. Sisson seems to echo Pope's words
when he says that the translator 'must see through his original to the matter – the
actual objects – of the original. It is at that point that his own words form, and
he has to take what he is given and to say what he sees.' Sisson distinguishes
between the 'matter' and the 'words', the one given, the other his own, just as
Pope distinguished between the 'Author', on the one hand, and the 'Diction' and
'Versification', on the other. The similarity between the translator's approach in
the eighteenth century and today is underlined when Sisson quotes Dryden to
express his view of the translator's task. He must speak

> in his own voice as modified by the presence of that august original – for it must still be
> his own voice, even though his success is to be measured by the degree to which it
> resembles that imaginary English in which his author 'wou'd himself have spoken'.[15]

The attempt to form a bridge to the past, and the creative re-enactment of a voice
uttering universal poetic truth in different mediums are both encapsulated in this
one sentence. The translator will speak in 'his own voice', like Pirandello's actor,
but the truth of what he says will be warranted by the 'august original'. Also in
this sense translation can be 'salvation', and the choice of a text can be an
ideological gesture, indicating the choices and beliefs of the translator. I will refer
to this issue again in the final conclusion of this study, on the basis of the analysis
of the translations of Dante.

3

The 'real reader' of Dante:

a survey of early references to Dante

In a brief survey of early translations of Dante, Dorothy Sayers, herself the author of one of the best known versions of the *Divina Commedia* of this century, summarizes the commonplace concerning the reception of Dante in the eighteenth century:

> The credit of his [Dante's] re-discovery in this country belongs to the eighteenth century. This might seem odd; but in fact it was not so much the Age of Reason that discovered the *Divine Comedy* as the Gothic Revival that discovered the *Inferno*. This was the First Gothic Revival – not the moral and ecclesiastical Gothic of Ruskin and Pugin, but the picturesque and Hell-fire Gothic of 'Monk' Lewis and the 'horrid' novels.[1]

This commonplace, like all others, is true up to a certain point, in this case to the extent that it accommodates the 'horror', 'wildness', and 'terror' so many readers of the times noticed in Dante. But it is in fact a great simplification of a complex phenomenon which deserves to be examined more critically. For in order to produce a neat definition Sayers is forced to rely on a number of sweeping generalizations, which have since been proved very inaccurate. Unfortunately, the process of criticism does not move in steps which are automatically synchronized with each other, and so, even when it became clearer and clearer that the term 'Age of Reason' required continuous qualification, and, also, that the Gothic Revival was not the sudden and revolutionary movement it had at first seemed, the established view concerning the reception of Dante in England still remained that which Sayers had enunciated. A study of eighteenth-century translations of Dante's *Divina Commedia* should, therefore, attempt to correct this view and clarify the true nature of the climate of response to Dante and his poetry. Testing Sayers' words against those of the readers of the time offers a way of building a more accurate and better articulated picture of the shifts in taste and response of the age. This is what I intend to do in this third chapter.

This exploration will show how Sayers' summary is inaccurate in at least three major ways. First, the readers of the time, faced with Dante's poem, did indeed try to include another story of victims and punishers, the Middle Ages, and the dark recesses below the surface of the earth within their horizon of expectation

– in this case, the gothic novel; but Dante's poem disappointed their expectations, and only left them confused. They did not recognize the *Inferno* as a gothic story, and turned elsewhere for a frame of reference. Sublime thoughts, pathetic tragedy, and historical satire all seemed to offer better forms of access to the *Divina Commedia*. Secondly, Sayers stresses the importance of the 'horrid' novels, implying that it would be the sensational, and even pornographic, taste satisfied by 'Monk' Lewis that discovered Dante rather than the taste of those readers with moral and religious concerns. This chapter will show that this was not true of the early readers, and following chapters will show that this implication of Sayers was not true of the first published translations of the *Divina Commedia*, and that it was only partly true of some translations of the Ugolino episode. Thirdly, and more importantly, it could be said that it was the arguments around the sublime that gave access to Dante's poem, particularly because they justified the idea of translation. It was translation itself that discovered Dante.

The basic problem with a statement such as that of Sayers' is that it uses the generalization a later age can make in order to *systematize* a complex issue, rather than *explore* what was taking place at the time. The latter is the method followed here. Readers' references to Dante's poem in terms of the gothic and sublime will be considered first; these in fact enable one to observe from a fresh point of view the changes in the eighteenth-century sublime which were examined, for example, by Samuel Monk and Marjorie Hope Nicolson. This examination will lead on to readers' use of other labels to integrate Dante's poem, particularly the historical satire; and finally references to the Ugolino episode will complete the picture which serves as the context of the translations.[2]

The 'gothic', the 'sublime', the 'pathetic'

We are all familiar with the use of 'Gothick' in the early eighteenth century as a term to indicate architecture which was so different from the classical styles of Greece and Rome, chiefly for being 'fantastical and ... not founded neither in nature nor reason'.[3] Barbarians, invading the Empire and destroying its treasures, had replaced these styles with a manner of building characterized by lack of symmetry and of right proportions – by walls that were too thick, arches that were too steeply pointed, and towers that were too high. In his proposal for the repairs of St Paul's, Christopher Wren specifies that 'the Gothick rudeness of the old design' of the Tower was so irregular that 'the Tower from Top to Bottom, and the next adjacent Parts, are ... a heap of Deformities'.[4] The effect of such structures on the human mind was confusion.[5] This is exactly the way readers of Dante reacted to his attempt to connect his age and his work with classical, biblical and mythological worlds. In the presence of St Lucy, Charon and Virgil in the same book readers only saw confusion and a lack of discrimination and taste. So Dante's poem was labelled as both a barbaric muddle and an example of ugly gothic architecture. Martin Sherlock expands on the former view, and expresses himself very bluntly:

> The enlightened Italians will own, allowing all the merit of Dante, that his poem is the worst that there is in any language: ... when we read his poem at present, it must be considered as a mass of various kinds of knowledge gothickly heaped together without order and without design (Martin Sherlock, *Letters from an English Traveller*, 1780, *DEL* p. 376).

As late as 1780, therefore, this reader still sees Dante's work as the construction, by a Swiftian modern spider, of a gothic fortress, which does not offer a vision of order. But Sherlock's apparently total rejection of Dante's poem on the basis of its gothicism is not his final word on it, and later we will need to return to Sherlock. Roscoe makes use of an architectural comparison:

> Compared to the *Aeneid*, it [*Inferno*] is a piece of grand Gothic architecture at the side of a beautiful Roman temple (William Roscoe, *The Life of Lorenzo de Medici*, 1795, *DEL* p. 527).

Roscoe uses the vocabulary of the discussion of the sublime and beautiful. He clearly distinguishes between the 'grand' of Dante's work and the 'beautiful' of Virgil's; the former might be closer to the sublime in Burke's terms, but it is not in the tradition of order, is not therefore beautiful and consequently, he implies, it is not good. That only order offers a clarifying, even redeeming vision is implied in the opposition Roscoe makes between the general, morally blank 'architecture' and the specific and meaningful 'temple'.

Order in nature and society and the vision of order in literature are basic issues of eighteenth-century philosophy, and on them are based the identity of the self as well as civic and moral systems. Dante's *Inferno* is seen as an example of the loss of these values. This is implied in the preceding quotation and made very clear in the words of Hester Lynch Piozzi:

> Loss of ORDER in the ARRANGEMENTS of civil society would produce, nay does produce, the most fatal of consequences; while reward for industry and excitement to honourable actions are no more; the very words Loss and Gain, Virtue and Vice, must be erased from our new vocabulary, and Dante's Inscription on the Gates of Hell set in their place; for where all are equal within, these words do well without:
> Lasciate ogni speranza voi ch'entrate.
> Leave Hope Behind, all you who enter here.[6]

What is suggested is a possible didactic function of Dante's *Inferno*, illustrating the results of lack of social stability and moral integrity. But readers go no further than pointing out the great difference between classical art, which reveals the plan of nature, and Dante's irregularities.

The recognition of the gothic origin of Dante's poem leads to a strong rejection of it in the case of Sherlock and a milder reduction of its literary status by Roscoe. In fact, what these critics see as gothicism is not the horror of the gothic novels, which by Roscoe's time were already popular, but the outward framework, the 'mass of ... knowledge' of the poem. Nevertheless, even after rejecting the gothicism of the *Commedia* in such extreme terms, Sherlock still finds a saving grace in the form of Dante's sublimity: Longinus, he says, would have condemned the *Divina Commedia*, but 'on perusing the Canto of Count Ugolino, the sentimental soul of Longinus would have exclaimed "Homer has nothing so sublime!"' (*Original Letters on Several Subjects*, 1781, *DEL* p. 378). The timeless sublime, recognized by any sentimental soul, re-establishes, therefore, the balance which had been tipped against Dante by the historical gothic framework of the *Divina Commedia*.

The rejection of Dante's gothicism is confirmed by the comments of such writers of gothic novels as Horace Walpole, and such lovers of gothic novels as Anna Seward. The gothic taste characteristic of the last decades of the eighteenth century did not really accept even the *cantica* of *Inferno*. Horace Walpole, the Whig author of the first gothic novel, *The Castle of Otranto* (1764), says 'Dante was extravagant, absurd, disgusting, in short, a methodist parson in Bedlam' (*DEL* p. 339). The modern reader might remark that Walpole's devices in his own fiction are extravagant and absurd – such as the giant shape of an ancestor appearing piece by piece, his gigantic helmet falling directly on top of the prince on his way to his wedding and smashing him to death – and the prude might find the obvious references to incestuous tendencies disgusting. But the fact remains that Walpole in no way responds to Dante's *Inferno*. Here we have the writer of a 'horrid' novel who objects to a kind of preaching moralism he sees in Dante.

Anna Seward, the Swan of Lichfield, had an undoubted love for the gothic. Her correspondence records her fondness for Ossian, for 'her darling' *Vathek* (*DEL* p. 398) and for *The Mysteries of Udolpho*. She also openly displayed her taste for the terrible sublime. In her letters, for example, she repeatedly pictures herself as a heroine of Radcliffe's gothic novels; and on one occasion she recounts how she, alone of her company, dared approach the sea during a storm:

> I resolved to taste, amidst the incumbent gloom of a very lowering night, a scene congenial to my taste for the terrible graces. Requesting the stout arm of Mr Dewes' servant, I begun with him my sombre expedition. As I passed along the sands, the tide twice left its white surf upon my feet; and the vast curve of those fierce waves, that burst down with deafening roar, scarce three yards from me, sufficiently gratified my rage for the terrific.[7]

Her correspondence, a fascinating record of the exchanges between the cultured readers of the time, registers, as far as translations of Dante are concerned, her reactions to the translations by Hayley, Boyd and Cary, and records the latter's replies to her. That she clearly connected the name of Dante with the gothic taste is illustrated by a visit she made to the romantic 'ladies of Llangollen'. In describing this visit she refers to the famed library, 'fitted in the gothic style', but, most revealingly, of all the authors represented in it Seward mentions only the name of Dante, recording also the warm admiration of the ladies for this writer.

In spite of her love of the gothic, her own taste for the terrible sublime, the intense correspondence with translators, and her awareness of Dante's connection with the gothic, Anna Seward had a strong dislike for Dante. The extreme personal response to the gothic and the sublime contrasts with the absolute lack of such a response in the case of Dante's poem. At first, Dante is only a fashionable name someone like her ought to know; her letter of June 13, 1805 shows, in its muddled reference to the first canto of *Inferno*, that she could not have read even the opening of the poem with attention.[8] Being an articulate and profuse writer she makes it quite clear what it is that the lover of the gothic and sublime objects to in Dante: there is 'nothing for the heart, or even for the curiosity as to story, in this poem'; and further, 'The poet, being his own hero, involves by necessity, an unpleasant quantity of egotism' (*DEL* p. 401). The gothic taste might enable readers not to condemn outright the presence in a poem of ghosts and spectres, but the reader of gothic novels misses the exciting plot full of fantastic and surprising incidents, the sentimental hero and heroine, and, what is equally damning, the absence, practically, of natural scenery.

This last issue must have been of particular importance in confusing readers' reactions in their attempt to understand the world of Dante. The 'new philosophy' and the later sublime both rely on a new and more sharply focused view of nature. The gothic sections of Ann Radcliffe's novels, which carry the protagonists into the dark depths of the self, are usually embedded in sections where the sublime of nature takes the soul of the hero and the heroine on a flight towards the infinite and the divine. But in Dante's Hell there is very little nature, and what there is is not uplifting: there is too much terror, as Seward remarked. The sublime feelings that Addison, Gray and Walpole had discovered in themselves as, in a state of terror, they viewed the Alps were not to be felt in the reading of Dante. In other words, just as the basic features of the gothic novels are missing in Dante, so is the natural sublime, which included the gothic as a particular development of its vision, or as its other Janus face. Still it is the word 'sublime' which is used repeatedly with reference to Dante's poem particularly in the 1780's and 1790's, in a repetition which loses all significance except as a general indication of approval. It is to the use of this term that a study of readers' reaction to Dante must turn.

The word 'sublime' underwent so many adaptations, not only during the course of the century, but even in its use by different contemporary writers on aesthetics, that it has become a very slippery term. But what is relevant to the present study is its general growth, as sketched by such twentieth-century scholars as Samuel Monk and Marjorie Hope Nicolson.[9] To briefly summarize Monk's arguments, one can say that the sublime was not a new idea in the eighteenth century; it is simply the name the late seventeenth century gave to the high or grand style. The sublime of excellent thoughts and simple language, the sublime of Longinus, is the rhetorical sublime. But the rhetorical sublime included as a particular application the possibility of an appeal to the emotions – through the use of a style and diction appropriate to this aim, and this was sometimes called the 'pathetic'.

The idea of the 'pathetic' is a central issue in the notion of the sublime in England. The word existed as a critical term even earlier than 'sublime', and it indicated that aspect of the grand style which included the emotive involvement of the reader. The sublime as a critical term consisted of a rhetorical sublime and a pathetic sublime, the latter being the ideal medium for tragedy. The history of the sublime in England is more or less the history of the growing distinction between the two ideas, so that the sublime of passion, particularly the stronger passion of terror and the irrational, came to be regarded as the true sublime, while the rhetorical sublime fell into disrepute. The difference between the two is fundamental: the rhetorical sublime, which included the early pathetic, involved *persuading* the reader by stirring his emotions, and was therefore a means to an end, and controlled by judgement; while the later pathetic or terrible sublime implied the aesthetic *enjoyment* of certain feelings and sights, and is therefore connected purely with pleasure. For the various writers on the topic, the pathetic becomes a point of contention. Since the sublime astonishes and ravishes, it naturally includes the pathetic, many thought. But other writers, such as John Baillie, accepted as sublime only those emotions which instilled serenity in the mind.[10] It was to be, as Monk sees it, the task of English critics to join the idea of the 'pathetic' with that of the 'sublime', and this is what happens in the case of views on Dante.

In a letter to George Walpole (the third Earl of Orford and a nephew of Horace Walpole), an Italian teacher in London, Vincenzio Martinelli, discusses the *Commedia* of Dante in answer to Voltaire's attack on Dante. With reference to the sublime, Martinelli says

Le sue similitudini in grandissima parte sono bellissime e sforzo unicamente del suo ingegno, le sue descrizioni vivaci all'ultimo segno e sommamente originali, e il suo sublime resulta dall'altezza e insieme profonda verità di pensieri spiegati con parole le piú comuni, ed è questo quel sublime, che Longino sopra ogni altro commenda. La critica ordinaria, che i superficiali della Letteratura Italiana fanno dello stile di Dante, è di duro e d'oscuro. Oscurità piú o meno si trova in tutti gli Autori antichi, che non si possono intendere, se prima il lettore non si erudisce de i fatti che essi trattano....[11]

That Martinelli's words had resonance at the time is proved by the fact that this and another letter of his were included in the French edition of the *Commedia* in Paris in 1768, and also occasioned a reply by Voltaire.[12] Martinelli's words are of particular significance in the present context in that they enable us to establish that by 1758 some definite view about Dante's sublime had been voiced. In this case it is the early sublime which is found in Dante: high thoughts and simple language. The appeal to Longinus had of course become a way of trying to secure recognition for those works which seemed to fall outside the neoclassical canon. Martinelli's claims for Dante's poem could have been simply another weak and vague appeal to 'the sublime', were it not for the fact that he anticipates Sherlock in distinguishing between the gothic and the sublime in Dante: he points out that the obscurity of the poem resides only in the historical reality of Dante's world, while the sublimity is in the thoughts expressed by the poetry. Readers were remarkably consistent in suggesting this distinction, even though it seems only a half-realized insight.[13]

Perhaps the most eclectic critics of the eighteenth century were Joseph and Thomas Warton. Great classical scholars, their writings reveal a sensitivity and response to most of the movements and shifts of taste and sensibility in the second half of the eighteenth century. This lends to their criticism a measure of the tentative and some tension; thereby their criticism becomes an indicative reflection of the age, and yet it is also often in advance of its time. Already in 1756 Joseph Warton retells the story of Ugolino, and adds that

Perhaps the Inferno of Dante, is the next composition to the Iliad, in point of originality and sublimity. And with regard to the Pathetic, let this tale stand a testimony of his abilities: for my own part, I truly believe it was never carried to a greater height.[14]

Warton clearly moves away from the Longinian sublime into the later views on the sublime.

There are a number of observations to be made on the passage quoted. Warton changes the traditional comparison between Virgil and Homer which Pope, for one, used and extends it into one between Homer and Dante, or, in other instances, between Virgil, Homer and Dante, in a kind of gradual scale between the extremes of judgement and imagination. This is, in itself, a sign of the changing balance in the taste of the age.

Another such is the constellation of words used to describe Dante. Pope used words like 'genius' and 'sublime', but the combination of terms in the above quotation lends to them quite a different meaning: Dante was a 'genius' to Warton and some other readers of the time, but in combination with 'pathetic' and 'sublime' in the quotation above the word 'originality' moves closer to Edward Young's views as expressed in *Conjectures on Original Compositions*, published three years later, in 1759. The way in which the constellation of existing terms was used with a continual shift in significance indicates the manner in which new works and new feelings were being included and absorbed in the critical language of the times. Warton does not use the word 'gothic' at all in this case; the praise of Dante's poetry is, as with other readers, all in terms of its sublimity.

The term 'sublime' has expanded so as to include other developments in eighteenth-century taste. Whereas Monk sees the term as developing from the Longinian sublime to the sublime of terror and the vast, Marjorie Hope Nicolson sees its growth as originating in the feelings for the great and grand in God, and then being transferred to nature – first into space and subsequently onto the earth. Fed by observations of nature, developments in science and theology, and continental travel, astonishment at, and fear of nature turn into pleasure in its grandest phenomena. And while some artists only moved to an intellectual justification of the uses of this transformed concept of the sublime, others went further and clearly pledged their allegiance to the belief that the true sublime resides in emotional enjoyment, and the effect of sublimity is on the soul of man. Nicolson summarizes the mid-century sublime in these terms:

> In 1744, five years after Gray's grand tour, Thomson published the revised *Seasons*, Young the complete *Night Thoughts*, Akenside *The Pleasures of the Imagination*. In various ways, they brought together the strands of the rhetorical and natural Sublime, which had been developing in parallel, and made them into a pattern which the youthful Burke employed when in mid-century he wrote his *Philosophical Inquiry into the Origins of Our Ideas of the Sublime and Beautiful*.[15]

Nicolson's views differ from those of Monk, but complement, rather than contradict them. In fact, just as Monk's framework could help us trace the ways in which Dante began to be integrated by the critical views of the age, so the aspects of the sublime that Nicolson stresses can be seen to play an important role in familiarizing readers with Dante. It is easy to trace Monk's arguments in the early references to Dante, because he based his theory on the popularity of the Longinian sublime and the shift in significance of 'the pathetic', which are ideas and terms of current use in the eighteenth century. It is more difficult to do the same for Nicolson's arguments, because she attempts to discover the deeper movements in taste which educated persons in the eighteenth century were not themselves conscious of, and can therefore hardly be expected to have formulated in words. It will be the examination of the translations of Dante that will support the validity of Nicolson's ideas. There we shall see that the 'cosmic journey' poem, which had reversed its upwards thrust and turned downwards into the terrestrial excursion poem, plays a considerable role as a model for the translator of Dante.

But there is at least one reader who reacts to Dante exactly in Nicolson's terms, with a stress on the combination of the rhetorical and natural sublime, on the emotional effect of such sublime, and on spatial and temporal infinity:

> We are carried on from torment to torment: – and children who have been taught to find amusement in seeing a fly spin round upon a needle, might find, perhaps, in the Inferno of Dante, a recreation for their riper years. It is singular, that in the continued contemplation of such a subject, as the place of eternal punishment for so great a part of the human race, he should not once be elevated into grandeur of description or sublimity of sentiment ... (Anonymous, the *Monthly Magazine*, April 30 1799, *DEL* p. 574).

G.T., the anonymous writer of the essay, has read Dante according to the framework of ideas that Nicolson traces in the eighteenth-century mind, and the result is a rejection of Dante. The vital fact that must be underlined in assessing the significance of this rejection is that G.T. had attempted to read Dante in the original (and it is unfortunate that information as to which edition he read is lacking). Compared to the visions of the English poets, Dante's world treats time and place very poorly. Neither the idea of eternity nor the size of the place where such great crowds must be gathered had moved Dante into the visions of the new vastness discovered by the natural sublime, nor into the grand diction of the rhetorical sublime that one had come to expect of English poets. And these are precisely the elements that some translators will superimpose on the world and words of Dante, to satisfy both the expectations of readers and the current literary canon.

It is only a later reader who can see and accept with equanimity the different character of Dante's world with respect to nature:

> No person can have attended to the Divine Comedy without observing how little impression the forms of the external world appear to have made on the mind of Dante. His temper and his situation had led him to fix his observation almost exclusively on human nature. The exquisite opening of the eighth canto of Purgatorio affords a strong instance of this. He leaves to others the earth, the ocean, and the sky. His business is with man. (Macaulay, 'Criticism on the Principal Italian Writers', 1824)[16]

One cannot quite agree with Macaulay: the forms of nature play an important role in the *Commedia*, and occasion passages just as 'exquisite' as the one mentioned by the critic. But it is true that Dante's concern was with man's place in the world, and in any case it is significant that the critic's realization of this does not stop him from appreciating the poetry. G.T., on the contrary, simply cannot accommodate the newness of Dante's poem, because it is too different from the verbal grandiosity of the imaginings and visions of English poets such as those mentioned by Nicolson.

Also a late insight is the distinction between the gothic and sublime which was merely implied in the words of eighteenth-century readers – that the former leads to a rejection of the poem, the latter to approval of it. Isaac D'Israeli makes explicit the opposition between the gothic as the historical aspect of the *Divina Commedia* and its sublime poetry as the central issue of Dante's poem. In his *Curiosities of Literature* (1823) D'Israeli mentions a number of medieval works which could have been sources of the *Commedia*, and adds:

> In these extraordinary productions of a Gothic age we may assuredly discover Dante; but what are they more than the framework of his unimitated picture! It is only this mechanical part of his sublime conceptions that we can pretend to have discovered; other poets might have adopted these 'Visions;' but we should have had no *Divina Commedia* (*Curiosities of Literature*, vol. IV, *DEL* p. 508).

The distinction between the historical framework of Dante's poem and the poetic life of Dante's world is established here in terms of gothic and sublime respectively. The former is only a literal vision, the simple dream mode of medieval literature, which creates the structure of a poem; the latter is a true Vision, creating a metamorphic world according to the poet's conceptions. When D'Israeli adds some words he attributes to Dante, and has him say 'I found the *original* of my *hell* in the *world* which we inhabit', he is stressing the universality of the experience dramatized, as well as the relationship between reality and poetry. These insights are the achievement of a reader later than those who 'discovered' Dante, but are the fruit of the struggles, including the terms of rejection, of those earlier readers. When one re-evaluates the earlier readers' vague references to the sublime and pathetic as terms of approval, and their vague references to the gothic as the 'facts', 'knowledge', historical reality of Dante's poem, one realizes that D'Israeli is making explicit what they had only begun to see.

But for many readers, who required clear signposts in order to classify and therefore come to accept the texts they met, a vague insight and a vaguer term were not enough. And since no clearer word than 'sublime' was to be found in the available critical vocabulary, they chose the easy way out. Largely, therefore, the struggle to accept Dante's world took the other route, faced the other aspect of the work – its historical reality – and attempted to find a generic description that would classify it in those terms.

Epic, satire and the protagonist

Obviously the *Divina Commedia* was neither a celebration of the political and religious systems of its age, nor a masterpiece in the neoclassical tradition, and so as a generic description the term epic was not appropriate on either account. It is in the context of a discussion of the epic that Walpole rejected Dante. And Seward, similarly, had rejected 'an epic poem consisting wholly of dialogue and everlasting egoism'. Joseph Warton is also dissatisfied with the term epic. He can describe particular parts of Dante's poem in various ways, but finds it difficult to find a term which can be used for the poem in its totality. Eventually, however, he finds a way out. *Inferno* is sublime and Ugolino is pathetic. As for the *Divina Commedia* as a whole, it is perhaps not quite an epic, but it has similarities with another well respected and established genre, and Warton turns to that: 'Dante wrote his sublime and original poem, which is a kind of satirical epic, ...about the year 1310'.[17]

'Satire' appeared to accommodate Dante's *Divina Commedia* better than any other genre. From 1750 onwards Dante's poem is called 'gothic' a few times, 'sublime' very often, and 'pathetic' particularly with reference to Ugolino and a handful of other episodes – but it is also called a satire. Nugent, for example, says that in the intention of its author the *Commedia* was 'a downright satire on the government and its principal members, and a caricatura of the manners of his compatriots of both sexes' and Dante 'carefully concealed' this intention 'under a multitude of theological and mystical questions' (1769, *DEL* pp. 250, 251); he therefore inverts the two terms of the duality (the gothic/sublime/pathetic/mystical, and the satire of government and politics), and places the historical as the true subject of the poem. James Beattie, also, in 1783 says that in the three *cantiche* Dante 'intermixed satire with his poetical descriptions and allegories' (*DEL* p. 358). Roscoe, too, distinguishes between Dante's *Commedia*, Petrarch's sonnets and Boccaccio's *Decamerone* as 'three little books written for the purposes of satire, of gallantry, and of feminine amusement'. He uses the term satire again for parts of the *Commedia*. Another writer, Penrose, uses it in connection with Dante's conversation. To the above list can be added the name of Thomas Warton.

Thomas Warton is the epitome of the typical reader of Dante at that time – sensitive but puzzled, and can be taken as a test case; his writings are a mixture of all the elements already mentioned. He makes the familiar comparison between Dante and Virgil, but modifies this by making a comparison also between Dante and Spenser and Milton, a comparison which will become more common in the second half of the century. Shakespeare and even the Book of Job are also mentioned. The confusion of styles is still remarked upon: 'the groundwork of his [Dante's] hell is classical, yet with many Gothic and extravagant innovations' (in *The History of English Poetry*, 1781).[18] There is, also, again mention of the gothic elements of the poem, the writer being surprised that 'some of the Gothic painters' have not been inspired by the picture of the Terrestrial Paradise in Dante's *Purgatorio*.

Besides being in places gothic, Dante's poem is, according to Warton, an expression of the terrible sublime. But on some occasions the poem falls into bathos: in Dante 'the rest of Virgil's, or rather Homer's, infernal apparitions are dilated with new touches of the terrible, and sometimes made ridiculous...' (p. 64). On other occasions Warton perceives the opposite movement – from the ridiculous to the sublime: 'the grossest improprieties of this poem discover an originality of invention, and its absurdities often border on sublimity' (p. 65).

Warton clearly is at a loss: his response to Dante is mixed, and so he turns this way and that to find features of the existing literary canon which will accommodate this strange poem, features ranging from the 'tragical history' of Francesca to the 'true poetry' of Ugolino and to the 'horror' of some punishments. To make matters even more confusing, parts of Dante are perceived as gross, and Warton appears very uncertain of what to do with the least delicate passages in *Inferno*. It is touching to hear him almost refuse to translate them into English:

> In another department, Dante represents some of his criminals rolling themselves in human ordure. If his subject led him to such a description, he might have at least used decent expressions. But his diction is not here less sordid than his imagery. I am almost afraid to transcribe this gross passage, even in the disguise of the old Tuscan phraseology.
>
> > Quindi gíu nel fosso
> > Vidi gente attuffata in uno sterco
> > Che dagli uman privati parea mosso;
> > Et mentre che laggiú con l'occhio cerco;
> > Vidi un, co'l capo sí da merda lordo
> > Che non *parea s'era laico, o cherco*.[19]

Presumably, he cannot stop himself from including the passage because it represents something that must be dealt with. Eventually he feels compelled to clarify his entire mixed response to Dante, and at last cuts the Gordian knot by choosing the easiest way out: 'The truth is, Dante's poem is a satirical history of his own times' (p. 76). After all, ordure is not unknown even to Pope so long as it appears in satire, and in fact Warton's reaction is similar to the reaction of the 'Friend' in Pope's 'Epilogue to the Satires':

As hog to hog in huts of Westphaly:
If one, through Nature's bounty or his Lord's,
Has what the frugal, dirty soil affords,
From him the next receives it, thick or thin,
As pure a mess almost as it came in;
The blessed benefit, not there confined,
Drops to the third, who nuzzles close behind:
From tail to mouth, they feed and they carouse:
The last full fairly gives it to the House.
 F. This filthy simile, this beastly line,
Quite turns my stomach – *P.* So does flattery mine.
And all your courtly civet-cats can vent,
Perfume to you, to me is excrement.[20]

This is by no means the only case in which Pope makes use of ordure in his satires. Swift, too, used excrement – to indicate, for example, the all-too-human nature of his Yahoos, and the degenerate taste of Gulliver, who cannot stand the smell of a human being, and appreciates better that of horse manure.[21]

We seem to be at the opposite extreme from the gothic of the 'horrid' novels; the self-indulging escape into the sensational horror and even pornography of 'Monk' Lewis is the very opposite, in aesthetic terms, of the posture, concerns and intention of the moral satirist. Satire has at its core the act of moral choice, or the description of an (im)moral stance; and its focus is therefore on the working of the mind. In the words of Martin Price, satire was supposedly the dominion of the traditional 'order of the mind', but it can span the dialectic between the two extreme orders, the order of the flesh, and the order of charity.[22] This means first of all that it could, therefore, include the varied world of Dante's poem, which in structure seems to move through the three orders successively, from the flesh to the mind to charity or universal love. But more importantly it means that satire is open to forms of experience which are closed to most other traditional genres of the age. It is the mock form of satire and of comic poems, such as the *Dunciad* and the earlier *Hudibras*, that can accommodate some features of Dante's poem, such as its 'comedy', the lapses into bathos, and the concern with the contemporary political and social scene. The history of Florence and Dante's part in it certainly formed a first channel of ingress for Dante's work into England; for the first recorded mentions of Dante are in letters of travellers, and are informative and of a historical nature.[23]

But both epic and satire require a particular kind of hero. The heroic attitude of the protagonist of classical epic is an open acceptance of death, so long as it brings fame and honour; connected to this is the hero's valour, his dedication to action and not calculation – and hence Ulysses, for example, is not the epitome of the classical hero. The English epic hero had become more passive, his responsibility towards humanity more spiritual. But a certain heroic stature and integrity still had to be there. In satire the persona of the protagonist or speaker is also very important, since it provides the moral perspective on the basis of which the reader can determine the ethical model which is being presented. In most of Pope's satires the speaker himself provides the basic moral attitude, as, for example, in the above quotation from the 'Epilogue to the Satires', where the Friend's corruption is set off by the other speaker who is Pope himself – the autobiographical mode being used to add immediacy and significance.

Dante's hero, on the contrary, offered no perspective to the eighteenth-century reader. Unheroic, unenterprising, seemingly egoistic, unsympathetic, he exploded the epic mode. Furthermore, his behaviour seemed to be not merely irrelevant to the main action but inconsistent with it, so that even as a satiric tool he was useless, since he could not provide a point of reference which the reader could use. Indeed, he became a major stumbling block to readers' understanding of Dante's poem. Wolfgang Iser's description of the reading process helps explain why:

> ... if the reader is at present concerned with the conduct of the hero – which is therefore the theme of the moment – his attitude will be conditioned by the horizon of past attitudes towards the hero, from the point of view of the narrator, of the other characters, the plot, the hero himself, etc. This is how the structure of theme and horizon organizes the attitudes of the reader and at the same time builds up the perspective system of the text.[24]

In the case of Dante's poem, this process was seriously disturbed by the nature of its hero. The early reader of Dante had the greatest difficulty in placing Dante's protagonist within a total perspective of the text in front of him, since the text appeared to require an epic hero or one of the various forms of the central character of satires. G.T., the anonymous contributor to the *Monthly Magazine* we have already come across, in his long and very revealing essay in the issue of April 30, 1799, says:

> The author is 'the little hero of his tale:' and the hero's only adventure is that of being the traveller and spectator, without ever forming a part of what passes, or serving at all to connect the parts that do pass under his observation, except as being the endless relator of them: and they are as distinct from each other as he from them (*DEL* p. 573).

The reader of eighteenth-century English literature expected a 'hero' to be closely involved in all that passes, and to function in at least three ways: he had to hold the framework of the narrative together, provide a centre of active interest, and serve as a tool to communicate significance. All these features seem missing in Dante, whose protagonist is only a witness of the stories being told.

It is truly remarkable that G.T. should have noticed the presence of two different roles in which the figure of Dante is present in the poem – the first as 'traveller and spectator' and the second as 'relator' – without being able to connect these roles to an overall picture of Dante's purpose and technique. Because the hero plays no part in the action of the story, and because he does not even play an important role in unifying all the episodes, this reader is prevented from moving to a better understanding of the function of the protagonist's stance. Yet he had registered other features of the text which could have helped him to see that Dante was creating a considerable distance between reader and protagonist – through the presence of the narrator. For in discussing *Paradiso*, which he finds extremely boring, he says

> Cantos 15, 16 and 17 are almost exclusively occupied by a very reverend personage called Cocciguida [sic for Cacciaguida]: – and, as we see his name announced in the argument of three successive cantos, we begin to hope for some permanent interest, to which we have hitherto been total strangers. We listen with tolerable patience to the whole detail of his family in all its generations; and waiting to hear what celebrated sage or hero of history he will prove, he concludes, by declaring himself no less than the great great grandfather of Dante! – 'tritavo' – and like the shade of Anchises is seized, too, with prophetic spirit; and foretells the foundation of an empire! – No, – The banishment of Dante from Florence (*DEL* p. 575).

G.T. notices the important structural climax formed by the Cacciaguida episode, and the prophetic role which Dante – and his work – assume, but neither perception leads him to the insight that the *Divina Commedia* is a prophecy meant for the reader, not an epic in celebration of the writer. It is the autobiographical stance that puts G.T. off; he is looking for an epic hero, and only finds Dante himself. The epic model only highlights, by way of contrast, what seems to be the grotesque distortion of Dante's purpose.

Accustomed to the sentimental hero, the tragic hero or the gothic villain and so on, the reader of Dante simply could not combine the features before him into any meaningful picture. But what many readers of *Inferno* objected to particularly strongly was a specific feature of the protagonist – his ambiguous moral stance, as exemplified in the cruel and dishonest reaction to Alberigo in Cocytus, just after the meeting with Ugolino. In this particular instance, in spite of promising Fra Alberigo that he will clear his lids from the ice that encrusts them if he reveals his story, Dante afterwards refuses to do so,

> ... E io non lil'apersi,
> e cortesia fu lui esser villano.   (*Inferno*, XXXIII, 150-1)[25]

The present-day reader, having followed the protagonist and narrator through the harrowing experiences of Hell and having felt, therefore, its oppressive and inescapable grip, then realizes that the experience of Hell has corrupted the protagonist, turning him into a traitor like Ugolino. But the eighteenth-century reader, following the traditional way of reading the utterances of heroes of classical epic, namely with a view to discovering the opinions of their authors, reacted strongly to what he saw as the cruelty of Dante. Thus to the painter Fuseli it seemed that Dante 'betrayed a failure in moral feeling. *...the poet* refuses to render him [Alberigo] the service he promised. That is bad, you know; faith should be kept, even with a poor devil in Antenora' (*DEL* p. 430; emphasis added).[26]

To sum up, disappointed in their expectations of a genre they knew – gothic story or epic – as well as in their requirement of an ethically valid model, eighteenth-century readers turned to satirical history to accommodate the contrasting facets they saw in the *Commedia*. But this did not take them very far; for none of the readers mentioned in this context found in satire a way into the poem. On the contrary, as in the case of Thomas Warton, it became a retreat from the struggle of responding to the *Commedia*. Some of the dynamics of the general process in the eighteenth century are now easy to trace: for the first main issue is that, in addition to the gothic, many other features of the literature of the time – genres as well as aesthetic ideas – became channels through which familiarization could take place, and these must have had a cumulative effect. The second main issue is that this process involves a continued attack on the expectations of the reader, which will, in all probability, eventually succeed in modifying them. In this sense, the 'gothic' Sayers refers to was in fact instrumental in promoting an understanding of Dante because the fact that the attempt to read the poem as a gothic novel was unsuccessful is basically immaterial. The sustained struggle to harmonize the new poem with the existing ideas on poetry as well as fiction could itself, theoretically, result in communication. And, in the case of Dante, it did – but not for the whole of the *Commedia*. The poem as a whole was too varied for the reader to be able to comprehend it in its totality. Even the *cantica* of *Inferno* was too 'new' to stimulate responses which could enable the reader to recreate one complete aesthetic object. But a more limited segment of Dante's poem was, indeed, successful in stimulating the necessary responses.

Ugolino

The discovery of Dante comes when readers find some aspect of his poetry they can fully experience, in the sense that they can recognize in it something they know, find contemporary analogies, and insert it in the existing canon. They found all they wanted in the episode of Count Ugolino, since the sentimental, the gothic, and pathetic tragedy all provide ways of approaching this episode from *Inferno*. Sherlock had said that 'the sentimental soul' of Longinus would have recognized the sublimity of this episode, and indeed Ugolino is the hero of as sentimental a story as one could imagine. The popularity of this episode has been ascribed to the fact that it is characteristically 'romantic', stressing 'men' rather than structure, theology, or poetics; but in fact the features which made the tale popular are those of an eighteenth-century sentimental story. The reader follows the increasing torments of a father, who must look upon and endure the sufferings of his innocent children; and ethical values are apparently communicated through the exposure of terrible suffering the reader cannot but sympathize with. In fact the spot where Ugolino's story took place became a destination for the sentimental journey, although, like Tristram Shandy at the tomb of the lovers, the traveller, here John Durrant Breval, could be sorely disappointed:

> At Pisa I was desirous to see the *Torre di Fame*, remarkable for the disastrous End of Count Ugolin and his four or five Sons, pathetically described by the great Dante, but found the entrance walled up ... (*DEL* p. 204).

He adds that 'History scarce affords a severer Instance of Prelatical Revenge, than a whole Family immur'd in a Dungeon, and the Keys of it thrown into the River, to cut off all Possibility of Relief'. Thus by 1726, which is the latest date when this letter could have been written, the Ugolino episode was at least known to the continental traveller, who had some knowledge, even if inaccurate, of its history, and also of Dante's 'pathetic' rendition of it. In addition to serving as a shrine for sentimental travellers, Ugolino answers the expectations of the readers in being a historical figure, who steps out of the poem in which he appears and speaks – like one of the heroes of Dryden's historical plays; and like an extract from such a play, his story is presented as the dramatic monologue of a hero of tragedy telling a tale full of pathos.

More than any of these things, though, the episode of Count Ugolino is a gothic story. Eighteenth-century readers would have been able to read Dante's Ugolino episode as a barbaric tale from times past, as exploited by the Gothic Revival, or as a sensational fiction, as exploited by 'Monk' Lewis. Eighteenth-century readers would also have been able to read this episode as a psychological study, a form of the gothic which lent itself to a propagandist novel such as *Caleb Williams*. And it is significant in this context that, while the author of a 'horrid' novel, Walpole, was harshly critical of Dante, William Godwin, the author of *Caleb Williams*, expressed high esteem of the Italian poet and his work.[27] In fact Dante's Ugolino has all the features of the gothic as we have come to know it, with the hindsight of those who can follow the developments and growth of the sensational and horrid genre into the mode appropriate for tracing the inner movements of the mind. This is the aspect of the early gothic which merged imperceptibly into the no-exit existential situation of the heroes of dark romanticism, and later into the temporary use made of this mode to dramatize narratively the confrontation with the evil aspect of the self, surviving to the present day in novels such as many of Iris Murdoch's.

Therefore in the Ugolino episode, if not in the whole of *Inferno*, the eighteenth-century reader would have found a true gothic story. The Tower of Famine with its chink and its locked door, the tender agonizing presence of the children, and the vindictiveness of the priests are the setting and circumstances of a good gothic story. The dream and the hunt are the obsessions of the mind imprisoned, and make of Ugolino both a sentimental and a gothic hero. G.R. Thompson establishes as the main feature of the purely gothic vision the fact that it 'ends in despair, pain and annihilation. The gothic hero is ultimately torn apart by demons.' Dante's hero was too passive, unenterprising, and unsympathetic, but Ugolino can easily assume the role of the protagonist of Dante's *Inferno*. Together with other victims in despair, such as Paolo and Francesca, and Ulysses, he assumes this role not only because of the horror of his predicament, but also because he can turn imperceptibly from being the hero of the more outward gothic plot into the central figure characteristic of the dark romanticism of the nineteenth century. Thompson goes on to specify the difference between the gothic hero and the dark romantic hero:

> The Dark Romantic hero, by working in and through evil and darkness, by withholding final investment of belief in either good or evil, by enduring the treachery of his own mind, and by accepting his crucifixion by whatever demonic forces may exist, perhaps attains some Sysiphean or Promethean semblance of victory.[28]

Ugolino, a traitor punished on earth and in Hell, torn by the horrors of his story, in turn torments his own betrayer and murderer, Bishop Ruggieri, and therefore unifies the roles of gothic hero, dark romantic hero, and devil. He is, in fact, a type of Dante's Satan, and the active figure of the greatest tempter, whom Dante pictures as a monumental shape of icy immobility, eternally chewing three sinners.[29] Ugolino's grasp on the mind of the eighteenth-century reader lies in the fact that this sentimental father is also an icon of fallen man, and an anthropomorphic form of evil; and the fact that he is a traitor, a Cain with an unspecified guilt marking him, turns Ugolino into a romantic figure who, even in the pit of Hell, continues with his vain destructive struggle.

The ambivalence of the two views – the sensational gothic, and the dark romantic (which includes the psychologically-orientated gothic) – is clearly distinguishable in Richard Warton's translation of the Ugolino episode, which, in terms of its descriptive detail, seems to deserve the appellation of gothic. Published in 1804, it is therefore a relatively late translation, since by that time at least nine versions of the same episode had appeared, including two within translations of the whole of *Inferno*, and one within the whole *Commedia*. Since the present survey stops considering translations of episodes from the time versions of whole cantos begin appearing, this is perhaps an interesting context within which to look at this particular version of Ugolino.

The various translations that had appeared in the meantime owe some of their colouring to the gothic, but, as will be seen, this will be a minor feature of the translations. Warton's, on the contrary, is coloured specifically by the gothic and dark romantic. First of all, additions create the setting of a gothic novel; the Bishop is called a 'priest' more often than in the original (with the addition, in one instance, of the adjective 'Perfidious'), the word 'horror' is inserted whenever possible, and the addition of blood and charnel-house imagery works to turn Ugolino into a malignant monster. Thus, in the opening of the episode, Ugolino '...with unhallow'd fangs, like common food/ Grinded the naked scalp and suck'd the blood', the words here being far more specific and descriptive than in the original, as they are in the closing lines, of which the last four are a complete addition:

> The Spectre ceas'd: and kindling with disdain
> Snatched the torn scalp with eager fangs again.
> Still as he gnaws, the flesh, the vessels grow;
> Still as he quaffs the purple currents flow:
> Still o'er th' eternal wound the fibres spread:
> Such is their mutual doom: and such th' atonement paid.   (*DEL* p. 661)

This is the only reference to Ugolino as a 'spectre' I have seen, and the word confirms the translator's use of sensational gothic images, such as the abundant blood. Ugolino's 'eager fangs' in the closing lines round off his first appearance as a blood-sucking monster – clearly the forefather of the vampire. Yet, together with these horrid descriptions, the translator includes an inner struggle between love and guilt, which does not belong to the gothic villain. To begin with, at Ugolino's first appearance Warton adds a footnote in which he makes Ugolino, who was a traitor, more or less innocent by saying that he had 'by the wiles of the Bishop Ruggieri been led into a plot against his country' (*DEL* p. 658). He therefore justifies him to the reader, and presents his character as that of a basically good man, more sinned against than sinning. But to present Ugolino as an ambivalent figure (basically similar to the later Byronic hero) means that he must have on his brow the mark of Cain, and therefore the translator tries to have his cake and eat it. So he proceeds to underline the hero's consciousness of guilt, by making him recognize in the faces of his four children 'the likes of their sinful sire', where the adjective 'sinful' is an addition.

Ugolino must be recognized as one of the obsessive and recurring figures which make up the iconography of the English gothic, understood with the overtones discussed in the previous pages. But features of the more sensational gothic narratives were superimposed on Ugolino only in the first years of the nineteenth century, in a second stage of the reception of Dante in England – probably to satisfy, as it were, the taste of some readers. It is a fact that in the period surveyed the episode of Ugolino was never called 'gothic', but was usually referred to with terms connected to the 'pathetic' sublime. One other current term which was used for Ugolino – if only twice – was 'picturesque', and this is a reminder that, besides being a verbal icon, Ugolino also became a recurrent topic of figurative arts. An anonymous contributor to the *Quarterly Review* of January 1823 stated that 'Dante was brought into fashion in England by Sir Joshua Reynolds' Ugolino' (*DEL* p. 369).

Reynolds' contribution to the Royal Academy exhibition of 1773 is in fact an important landmark in the fortune of Dante in England, not only for the event in itself, but also because of the discussions it originated. References to Reynolds' Ugolino are frequent and even someone as unresponsive to Dante as Horace Walpole was moved to exclaim 'In what age were parental despair and the horrors of death pronounced with more expressive accents than in his picture of Count Ugolino?' (*DEL* p. 339). But if some admired, others criticized, and others again were moved to improve on the attempt. Fuseli criticizes the composition of the painting as well as some of its details – such as the muscularity of the presumably starving sons. Fuseli's own version of Ugolino was exhibited at the Royal Academy in 1806, and critics began to take sides: *Bell's Weekly Messenger* carried in its edition of May 25 of that year a sharp criticism of Fuseli's work. According to the anonymous reviewer, Fuseli 'entirely lost the passion he must have intended to enforce; he has substituted horror for pathos, and depictured ferocity instead of sympathy' (*DEL* II p. 31). William Blake, Fuseli's friend, was then moved to reply to this, and in a letter to the editor of the *Monthly Magazine* (July 1806) he disagrees strongly with the article in the *Messenger*, and concludes that in Fuseli's painting 'the effect of the whole is truly sublime' (*DEL* p. 456).

Blake himself had already used the group of Ugolino for the illustration of one of his own poems, to provide an icon for a particular moment in his own vision.[30] Flaxman, the friend of Blake and Fuseli, had published in Rome in 1793 his own illustrations to the *Divina Commedia*, which were subsequently used in so many editions of the *Commedia* in England, Italy, Germany and France, that Besso, having collected the evidence, was led to affirm that 'Per la divulgazione iconografica della Divina Commedia, il Flaxman ha avuto nella metà del secolo scorso quell'influenza che ebbe nell'epoca successiva l'opera del Doré'.[31]

Reynolds, Fuseli, Flaxman, and Blake initiate a long line of painters and illustrators, which runs parallel to the line of translators of Dante's text. As far as the eighteenth century is concerned, the connection between painters/illustrators and translators is very close and will have to be kept in mind. As is the case with the reactions of readers and translators of Dante, the reactions of the painter are phrased in terms of 'pathos', of 'horror', and particularly of the sublime. But, like poetry, painting confirms that the more sensational gothicism is exploited, in the case of Ugolino, only later, a good example being provided by the list of thirty-eight subjects for paintings proposed by Benjamin Robert Haydon in 1804 – the very same year of Richard Warton's 'gothic' translation. Besides one group of sacred and one group of Shakespearean topics, there is also a group which Haydon calls miscellaneous but which clearly has a common theme, the sensational gothic:

No. 2. Milton playing on his Organ – blind.
No. 8. A Woman contemplating the Body of a Man she has just murdered.
No. 9. Scene in a mad-house.
No.10. Ugolino.   (*Correspondence and Table Talk of R.B.Haydon*, DEL p. 666)

To sum up, in the minds of eighteenth-century readers of Dante, the *Commedia* moves from being read as a satirical historical poem to being read as a sublime poem of the inner vision – moves, that is, from the views of Thomas Warton to those of D'Israeli. The shift from satire to sublime poem corresponds, in fact, to the shift from one kind of reader to another. The majority of the early readers – the Wartons, Roscoe, Neville – read the original, and attempted to find analogous features in their own time to familiarize Dante's world, while many of the later readers, like Seward, read the *Commedia* in translation, and read the poem as if it were a version of their own literature. The sublime assumes an important role in this movement within the reception of Dante's poem, because a little-noticed result of the importance of the sublime is that it justifies the struggle to produce translations.

The historical, factual and anecdotal material brought back from Italy in the first half of the century led to an emphasis being placed on the historical reading of Dante, which in turn led to a rejection of Dante: 'Dante is now no longer read in Europe, because his work is continuously alluding to facts utterly unknown' (Anonymous, 1762, DEL p. 327). What this implies is that it was impossible to 'translate' into a meaningful contemporary context a historical past so different and specific. But the much greater importance gradually assumed by the sublime, particularly when the role of practical emotions was superseded by that of aesthetic emotions, and phenomena as perceived by sense gave way to phenomena as expressed in art, meant that translation was gradually perceived to be less and less of a hindrance. Already in 1725 a critic recognized the difference that the views on the sublime make to translation. Anthony Blackwell, describing the sublimity of the Bible, underlined this particular contribution of the sublime, saying that since it strikes like lightning and transports the soul into ecstasy, it is beyond criticism, beyond style and ornaments of language, and therefore 'translation cannot mar it'.[32]

The reception of Dante in the eighteenth century is characterized by the tentative efforts to find analogous features and corresponding ideas within contemporary aesthetics, but the movement is threefold. Critics for their criticism, and readers to rationalize what they read, search the existing critical vocabulary to find appropriate terms to accommodate the 'foreign' world or the response of their sensibility, while translators attempt to find the diction and the forms to render both Dante's world and the response to it as poetry.

4

The early translators

Jonathan Richardson, Thomas Gray and the Earl of Carlisle

Jonathan Richardson (1665-1745) was a painter, and also a writer of essays on painting and aesthetics. It is in one of his *Two Discourses* published in 1719 that he translated Dante's Count Ugolino episode into blank verse. That he should feel he had to introduce Dante before he moved to the translation is not surprising, since he himself would probably never have heard of the Italian poet if he had not been confronted with the reproduction of a bas-relief – then attributed to Michelangelo – representing Count Ugolino in prison. Thus through Michelangelo and through figurative art Dante's fame in England began.[1]

The aesthetic arguments around the early sublime – of grand, serene and excellent thoughts – and the late sublime – of the irrational and of irregular nature – that animated eighteenth-century poetics were also current in the figurative arts, and here they found their correspondence in the comparison between Raphael and Michelangelo. Raphael is the ideal sublime painter of correct judgement and purity of taste, who idealizes nature in an impersonal art copied from the Ancients and which the modern student must copy from him in turn. But Michelangelo becomes the original genius, whose art embodies energy. He imitates no one, and cannot, and indeed must not, himself be imitated. His is the sublime of art not as ideal form but as intensity of feeling, the product of an artist who has his own vision, and is true to it. And what more proof of the visionary and prophetic nature of Michelangelo's art could there be than the Sistine Chapel? By the beginning of the nineteenth century it was clearly Michelangelo rather than Raphael who was the example of greatness and sublimity. But during much of the eighteenth century the balanced struggle between the two views of art was very obvious; for it even animates the writings of Sir Joshua Reynolds, President of the Royal Academy between the years 1769-1790.

Monk notices that the 'President's taste was not quite at one with his theory'. In a letter to a young painter in 1769 Reynolds advises him to observe and study the Sistine Chapel when in Rome, but in his official role, in his theoretical writings, 'he thinks that he should give the advantage to Raphael'.[2] A similar pull between the same two forces can be glimpsed at times in Pope. His attempts to harmonize judgement and imagination in his writings seem to be grounded in neoclassical rules and taste; but his somewhat less public compositions in the grotto and the gardens at Twickenham reveal a more affective and personal response to his material. Jonathan Richardson, a friend of Pope's, was also a true neoclassical scholar, and consequently he recognized the greatness and sublimity of Raphael, but already in the first years of the century he, too, admitted the different sublimity of Michelangelo: 'his Style is his Own, not Antique, but he had a sort of Greatness in his utmost Degree.'[3] It is for his study of the idea of the sublime that Richardson is particularly known; he studied the sublime of Longinus and Boileau and applied these ideas to painting. He was original in some of his views; as Monk points out, in his preferences for 'Rembrandt and Zuccari as exemplars of the sublime in painting, he spoke only for himself, and not for his age'. Although he did not follow his insights into a strikingly original system of thought, still 'he was worthy of notice chiefly as an innovator'.[4] He was certainly an innovator in terms of his influence on the course of Dante's fame in England, since his own fame and the importance of his writings must have greatly contributed to the movement that introduced Dante into England.

In the choice and the limits of the episode from Dante which he translated, and in the mixed purpose of translating it, Jonathan Richardson establishes a pattern. Like those who followed him, his purpose was partly to make an obscure but interesting poem known to the reading public. This is what makes his version of importance for this study – it is the first significant translation of Dante's poetry, which was then considered 'very curious and very little known'.[5] But Dante's Count Ugolino also provided Richardson with a suitable example he could use to illustrate a basic idea in his essay – that there was a scale of arts which led from history to poetry, and then moved higher to sculpture and painting. This ulterior motive strongly affects the picture he leaves of Dante and his verse.

Richardson compares history with poetry, sculpture, and painting, in order to prove the gradual superiority of the second term of comparison over the first, and the third over the second, with the highest place belonging to painting. The part of the essay devoted to this argument is organized in such a way as to guide the reader by various means towards seeing the validity of this view. One of the ways in which Richardson manipulates the reader is by the very order in which the material is presented. He juxtaposes history (Giovanni Villani's chronicle of the strife between Pisa and Florence, in which Count Ugolino and Bishop Ruggieri were involved), poetry (Dante's lines from Canto XXXIII of *Inferno*), sculpture (the bas-relief attributed to Michelangelo), and a hypothetical painting, but does not compare them objectively in order to deduce a general statement by way of observation. Rather, the comparison itself is presented as an illustration of the statement of Richardson's convictions, which is placed first:

> As the business of painting is to raise and improve nature, it answers to poetry; (though upon occasion it can also be strictly historical) and as it serves to the other more noble end, this hieroglyphic language completes what words or writing began, and sculpture carried on, and thus perfects all that human nature is capable of in the communication of ideas ... (p. 256).

Not only Richardson's organization of the material, but also his appraisal of it is distorted so as to prove his contention. His support of the long-standing conviction of the superiority of painting and the relatively low position of history in 'the communication of ideas' guides Richardson in the summary of Villani's pages. Richardson provides what amounts to a quite literal translation of the original. However, he cuts out any reference to 'Fortune' and to 'the wrath of God', which in Villani function as reflections of mind and spirit on men and events.[6] Villani's pages are seen by Richardson, or represented by him here, as factual history only; and the same attitude is reflected, if not in the translation of Dante's poem, certainly in the presentation of the poet.

After the translation of Villani's relevant pages, Richardson continues by saying, 'the poet carried this story further than the historian could, by relating what passed in the prison' (p. 258), thereby limiting the contribution of poetry to the 'story' and to 'what passed', information not available to the chronicler. Moreover, Richardson does not mention Dante's fame in Italy or skill as a poet, but introduces him as a man and a political figure: 'This is Dante, who ... was ruined by the commotion of the times.' Instead of describing his writings, Richardson tells of the events that led to Dante's banishment – not because he was of 'the contrary party, but for being neuter, and a friend to his country'. It is the moral and political integrity of the man that Richardson reports to his readers. The identification of the poetry with factual events and of the poet with the protagonist of the poem is demonstrated beyond any doubt by the manner in which Richardson achieves the transition between the history of Dante and the Ugolino episode: 'This great man (in the 33rd canto of the 1st part of his Comedia) in his passage through hell introduces count Ugolino gnawing on the head of his treacherous and cruel enemy the archbishop, and telling his own sad story, at the appearance of Dante' (p. 259).

Richardson then moves to the actual translation of the episode from Dante's *Inferno*. It is in blank verse, visibly divided into paragraphs according to the sense and tone of the narrative.

La bocca sollevò dal fiero pasto
  quel peccator, forbendola a' capelli
  del capo ch'elli avea di retro guasto.   3
Poi cominciò: "Tu vuo' ch'io rinnovelli
  disperato dolor che 'l cor mi preme
  già pur pensando, pria ch'io ne fali.   6
Ma se le mie parole esser dien seme
  che frutti infamia al traditor ch'i rodo,
  parlare e lacrimar vedrai inseme.   9
Io non so chi tu se' né per che modo
  venuto se' qua giú; ma fiorentino
  mi sembri veramente quand'io t'odo.   12
Tu dei saper ch'i' fui conte Ugolino,
  e questi è l'archivescovo Ruggieri:
  or ti dirò perché i son tal vicino.   15
Che per l'effetto de' suoi mai pensieri,
  fidandomi di lui, io fossi preso
  e poscia morto, dir non è mestieri;   18
però quel che non puoi avere inteso,
  ciò è come la morte mia fu cruda,
  udirai, e saprai s'e' m'ha offeso."   (XXXIII 1-21)[7]

He from the horrid food his mouth withdrew,   1
And wiping with the clotted offal hair
His shudd'ring lips, raising his head thus spake.

  You will compel me to renew my grief
Which e'er I speak oppresses my sad heart;   5
But if I infamy accumulate
On him whose head I gnaw, I'll not forbear
To speak, tho' tears flow faster than words.

  I know not who you are, not by what power,
Whether of saints or devils, you hither came,   10
But by your speech you seem a Florentine;
Know then that I count Ugolino am,
Archbishop Ruggieri this; which known,
That I by him betray'd was put to death,
Is needless to relate, you sure have heard;   15
But what must be unknown to mortal men,
The cruel circumstances of my death,
These I will tell; which dreadful secret known,
You will conceive how just is my revenge.

At the very beginning, the original implants in the reader a vivid impression of a man's consciousness, through the means of that man's own powerful speech, which was intended as an emotional appeal to the protagonist's sympathy. The overall effect of Richardson's version is a toning down of the pathos Ugolino invokes, and an increased emphasis on factual events. A brief analysis of the words used and the changes made will illustrate how this is effected. In the first lines 'disperato dolore' ('desperate grief') becomes 'grief', and the feeling communicated by these lines, which in Dante show an Ugolino profoundly moved, is here weakened and softened into a 'sad heart'. The stress placed by Ugolino, in the following lines of the original, on the cruelty of his death, in order to make the listener realize how seriously he had been wronged, is changed by Richardson into a stress on 'the cruel circumstances' of his death, to which he adds that it is a 'dreadful secret'. Continuing with his focus on fact and act rather than ideas and feelings, Richardson cuts out line 16, with its stress on the evil thoughts of Ruggieri, and then proceeds to change Ugolino's trust in the bishop (line 17) into Ruggieri's actual betrayal of the politician – replacing a feeling with an act. Moreover, in the last line quoted, Dante's Ugolino says his words will show to what degree his 'neighbour' had wronged him – the stress being again on depth of guilt, underlined by the ironic use of the word 'neighbour'. This is quite different from Richardson's Ugolino, who will tell such a story of what happened that his present revenge will appear justified. There is, therefore, in the translation a continuous stress on the past fact and its consequences, rather than on the present suffering and the state of the man's soul.

In two passages that follow some phrases are very inaccurately translated and distort the poetic effect of the original. In the first passage Richardson's Ugolino sees through the cracks in the prison the 'approach of morn' ('lume'), while Dante's Ugolino had seen the passing of many months ('lune'). This underlined in the original one of the elements of the tragedy – the length of the imprisonment. In the second passage Ugolino recounts his dream (which presages his death and that of his family) of a hunt pursuing 'il lupo e' lupicini' (l. 29, 'the wolf and wolf cubs'), and tearing them to pieces. Richardson's hunt pursues 'the wolf and her whelps', and substituting the mother for the father already diminishes the similarity in the two situations, and therefore the effect of the forewarning. But that similarity and its consequent effect are even further diminished at the point when the dogs reach the wolves and rend the sides of 'lo padre e' figli' (l. 35, 'the father and the sons'). The change of words to translate 'lo padre e' figli' is dramatically very important, since at Ugolino's waking the reader is told that his children are also imprisoned. Richardson, however, renders this whole phrase with the one word 'prey', which is quite inadequate.

The distortions described in the previous paragraph, however, are relatively minor, being, in the first passage, possibly due to early editions of the *Commedia*, and, in the second passage, a matter of poetic sensibility.[8] Still, their combined effect is a reduction of the tension and pathos of the original. This is probably similar in spirit to Richardson's neglect of the idea of 'the pathetic' in his study of the sublime – he was simply not interested in that aspect of the sublime, but only in the sublime of nature. As it happens, the avoidance of this characteristic feature of the eighteenth-century climate does not distort the original as much as an emphatic stress on it does. In some of those passages which are potentially most 'pathetic', Richardson's version follows the original in the control and lack of excessive sentiment which is central to the effect of Dante's lines, as we see in the passage following the dream, in the final preparation for the resolution of the tragedy with its five successive deaths:

"Come un poco di raggio si fu messo
  nel doloroso carcere, e io scorsi
    per quattro visi il mio aspetto stesso,   57
ambo le man per lo dolor mi morsi;
  ed ei, pensando ch'i' 'l fessi per voglia
    di manicar, di subito levorsi   60
e disser: 'Padre, assai ci fia men doglia
  se tu mangi di noi: tu ne vestisti
    queste misere carni, e tu le spoglia'.   63
Queta'mi allor per non farli piú tristi;
  lo dí e l'altro stemmo tutti muti;
    ahi dura terra, perché non t'apristi?"   (XXXIII 55-66)[9]

  But when the light of the succeeding morn   50
Faintly appear'd, and I beheld my own
In the four faces of my wretched sons,
I, in my clenched fists, fasten'd my teeth;
They judging 'twas for hunger rose at once,
You, sir, have giv'n us being, you have cloath'd   55
Us with this miserable flesh, 'tis yours,
Sustain yourself with it, the grief to us
Is less to dye, than thus to see your woes.
Thus spake my boys; I like a statue then
Was silent, still, and not to add to theirs,   60
Doubled the weight of my own miseries:

The narrative in the original moves in units connected by simple logic; the fourth line does, it is true, follow on from the previous tercet with a rhetorical heightening of tone, but the story is based on the chronology of how things happened and the logic of the successions of thoughts in Ugolino's mind. Richardson's version moves in the same manner.

    The closeness of Richardson's version to the original is particularly evident if we look at other eighteenth-century versions of this same passage – such as Gray's, for instance:

"Till a new Sun arose with weakly gleam
And wan, such as mought entrance find within   60
That house of Woe: but oh! when I beheld
My sons & in four faces saw my own

Despair reflected, either hand I gnawed
For Angeuish, which they construed Hunger; straight
Ariseing all they cried, 'far less shall be   65
Our suffering, Sir, if you resume your gift;
These miserable limbs with flesh you clothed;
Take back what once was yours.' I swallowd down
My struggling Sorrow, not to heighten theirs.
That day & yet another, mute we sate   70
And motionless: Oh! Earth! couldst thou not gape
Quick to devour me? ... "[10]

In Gray's version, which, like Richardson's, is in blank verse, the recurrent enjambments create a rhythm and a pace quite different from the original's feeling of enclosure and oppression. There is a progression in the poetry, which heightens both the narrative movement and the dramatic story told by the speaking voice of Ugolino. For example, 'straight/ Ariseing' adds physical movement to the action of this drama. Also, other additions increase tension; so, 'straight/ Ariseing' is balanced by 'mute we sate/ And motionless' (where the second phrase is an addition), and Ugolino's biting of his hands is balanced by the added images of 'I *swallowd down/* My struggling Sorrow' and of the earth *devouring* Ugolino (emphases added). These balanced effects, together with the impulsive movement and speech of the children, create an interplay of feelings and passions which is dramatic, in the sense that it is a moving and dynamic story. There is a large element of the 'pathetic' here; and one could pick out any phrase to show how the effect created is at variance with the brief but powerful directness of Dante's storytelling. In the very first lines, 'weakly gleam/ And wan' takes the place of 'a little ray', 'house of Woe' is an abstraction from 'painful prison', and 'father' has become 'Sir'.

Gray wrote this translation as an exercise when he was learning Italian; and it seems also an exercise in preparation for Gray's most idiosyncratic poems, based on his interest in northern mythology and poetry. I am not referring to 'The Bard' as much as to 'The Fatal Sisters' and 'The Descent of Odin' (1757, 1760 and 1761 respectively). These two paraphrases of passages from Icelandic sagas were written some twenty years after the version of Ugolino, but they are later, finished pieces, while the latter was an early exercise the author did not think worthy of publication; they can therefore all be seen as emerging from Gray's life-long taste for primitivist poetry. This is confirmed by the texts of the two Scandinavian poems. In 'The Descent of Odin', the journey to the dwelling of Hela, goddess of the dead, is turned obviously into a journey into Hell, and even the iconography is specifically altered. So, the 'Whelp' which Odin met 'on the road' becomes Cerberus ('He the Dog of Darkness spied') and while in the original Odin '...came to the deep/ Dwelling of Hela', in Gray's story '... full before his fearless eyes/ The

portals nine of hell arise.'[11] Similarly, in 'The Fatal Sisters' (which is the vision
of a character in *Njals Saga*) Gray adds a parenthetical clause in the second line,
introducing the idea of Hell which is not in the original ('Haste, the loom of hell
prepare').[12] In each, the original had an abundance of gore, which Gray further
emphasizes.

Gray's imitations of Nordic poetry, therefore, seem motivated by interests
similar to his translation of Dante, and they all belong within the same context.
This context has nothing in common with the later sensational gothic, but with the
scholarly interest in northern mythology. Therefore Gray's poetry, together with
his antiquarian studies, contribute to the course of Dante's fame in England by
associating Dante's poetry with northern primitivist poetry and its nationalistic
focus on England's past.[13]

The Earl of Carlisle's version of Ugolino (1772) shows how far from the
controlled tone of the original a translation could move:

> Now in the gloomy cell a ray of light
> New horrors added by dispelling night.
> When looking on my boys, in frantic fit
> Of maddening grief, my senseless hands I bit.
> Alas! for hunger they mistake my rage,   65
> 'Let us,' they cried, 'our Father's pains assuage:
> 'Twas he, our Sire, who call'd us into day,
> Clad with this painful flesh our mortal clay,
> That flesh he gave he sure may take away.' –
>   But why should I prolong the horrid tale?   70
> Dismay and silent woe again prevail.
> No more that day we spoke. – Why in thy womb
> Then, cruel Earth, did we not meet our doom?[14]

While Gray had highlighted the movement and position of the characters within
the setting, Carlisle eliminates any references to these aspects of the situation.
The children do not stand up, but they only speak; 'stemmo tutti muti' ('we all sat
dumb', as Bickersteth and others translated it, or 'we stayed all silent', as
Singleton and others translate it) becomes 'Dismay and silent woe again prevail',
thus changing a tense posture into an inert visual allegory. All physical movement
has been eliminated, leaving only a 'horrid tale'. But even the tale itself is reduced
to a basic situation, because the small details which in Dante only serve to
contribute to the human drama acquire a life of their own and move into the
foreground. For example, Dante's brief mention of the first light of dawn ('un
poco di raggio si fu messo', 'a small ray of sunlight made its way') becomes a
major element in creating a picture of terror; also, Ugolino biting his own hands
is described with an abundance of adjectives which lengthen and magnify the
significance of this action; and, to give another example, the children's very grand

and formal speech would sound utterly out of place were it not for the effect it has of underlining the lack of control in Ugolino himself. It is these various details which stand out and overwhelm the reader with a picture in which only the sensational and extreme have a place. And it is a picture in which everything contributes to the presentation of Ugolino himself. At one point, for instance, the narrative flow is interrupted by another of Ugolino's gestures, in this case a rhetorical question, which again places him in the centre of the picture: 'But why should I prolong the horrid tale?', asks Carlisle's Ugolino, who then proceeds to curse the earth and then carry on with the tale. The consequence is that the tale itself loses its narrative interest, while the human drama is buried under operatic gestures.

Drama and opera are key words in the understanding of both Carlisle's view of Ugolino and also the models he used to give voice to this view. Carlisle does indeed turn to the eighteenth-century stage to find his models, and one must attempt to narrow down and qualify what this implies, and in what ways his translation is, and is not, dramatic. Since all physical movement has been excluded from it, Carlisle's 'Ugolino' cannot be called dramatic, if the term is taken in its primary, general meaning of suitable for acting on the stage, unless one is thinking of the more static acting of eighteenth-century opera. Nor does the human drama in Carlisle turn inwards and centre upon the tragedy of Ugolino, since there is no interplay of characters, passions or forces, either inside or outside the main character. The struggle of Ugolino in the original poem is not dissimilar to classical tragedy: Ugolino seems to be unable to overcome the inner clash between his will and his impotence. What impresses the reader in Carlisle's version, however, is not the tragic doom of this powerful man trapped within his fate, but only his wild state of paroxysm. For what Carlisle is interested in is the basic situation of the character, which he can manipulate by pushing it to the extremes of passion – a technique characteristic of opera. Like the characters in Dryden's *Aureng-Zebe*, Carlisle's Ugolino leaves the limits of reality and reason and enters the regions of madness. But unlike in Dryden's play, here there are no other characters or scenes to reintroduce sanity and a solution. The horrors, the 'frantic fit' and 'maddening grief', which are not in the least denied in Dante's poetry, in fact reduce the horrific effect of the indirectness of the original, with its picture of the powerlessness of love and the turning inwards of Ugolino's grief. The formal address of the children's plea further destroys the *pathos* of the scene, creating in its place the rhetorical pathetic of formal eighteenth-century heroic tragedy.

It is precisely the excessive and extravagant diction which is referred to in the previous paragraph, and which Carlisle borrows from Dryden, that particularly distorts the original. In Dante, the reader responds to the restraint in the poetry by filling in the gaps with his own responsive imagination, which is given more than sufficient stimuli. The reader of Carlisle is overwhelmed to such an extent as to be reduced to passivity by the picture of wild passions and the language of excess. Logic itself is forgotten in favour of a telling word, such as the 'senseless' the translator adds (l. 64 of the passage quoted above); this might conceivably suggest the madness of Ugolino, but, since it refers to Ugolino's own hands which he bites, it would literally mean that he does not feel the biting at all. The 'Alas!' that follows also seems out of place; for it is an exclamation which expresses passion, and yet here it introduces a sentence in which Ugolino simply reports, word for word, the children's response to the biting of his hands. Rational control has broken down in the poetry as well as in the character.

Richardson's version is much more subdued, and his additions or changes are of limited import. Richardson ignores the words 'doloroso' and 'dolor' in lines 56 and 58, but maintains the outward statement of Ugolino's grief by adding line 67, where Ugolino is made to say '[I] ... doubled the weight of my own miseries'. These words are not fully appropriate to the tension the original builds up, since they indicate that Ugolino is concerned, however indirectly, with his own state, while Dante's lines attempt to affect the reader with the sufferings of the innocent children, with Ugolino, at this point, presenting himself purely as a father. Richardson's other addition, his comparison of Ugolino to a statue, seems to provide a suitable image for Ugolino's increasing withdrawal, his immobility and silence, following on from line 49, 'Io non piangea, si dentro impetrai' ('I did not weep, I so turned to stone within'), and seems to anticipate some of the best known criticism of Dante. It was Francesco de Sanctis who saw Ugolino as 'una colossale statua di odio' ('a colossal statue of hatred'),[15] and his words on the whole episode are a cornerstone in Dante criticism. Some of De Sanctis' critical pronouncements are still considered valid; others have been contested. Mario Marcazzan rejects the view of Ugolino as a statue. In his reading of Canto XXXIII, he points out how comparing Ugolino to a statue betrays the dynamism of the character – by which he must mean the dynamism in presentation, and of inner rather than outward movement – and also betrays Dante's intention of picturing a man robbed of dignity and pride, a man left with 'la bestialità di quell'odio' ('the bestiality of that hate').[16] Marcazzan's words are proved true in Richardson's version; the latter's introduction of the image of Ugolino as a statue corresponds to the nature of his whole episode, which is much more static than the original. He does not overwhelm the reader in the same way as Carlisle, but instead he offers what is mostly a measured and factual story, rather than a complex tissue of tensions.

However, by extracting the episode from its context all three translators do distort the original in a fundamental manner, but in varying degrees according to the length of the passage they extract. The protagonist's experience in his meeting with Ugolino, as told by the narrator, consists of three distinct moments: the very first meeting between the protagonist and Ugolino in the last lines of Canto XXXII; what one might call the episode of Ugolino proper in Canto XXXIII (beginning with the raising of his head from the skull, continuing with the tale he tells, and closing with the lowering of the head onto the skull again); and the protagonist's reaction, in the form of a curse on the city of Pisa for what it had done to Ugolino and his children. All three moments play a very important part in revealing the function the total episode has within the *Commedia*. However, all three translators begin with the first line of Canto XXXIII, thereby cutting out completely the first moment of the meeting. And they all introduce Ugolino in a similar manner, as a comparison of the first tercet indicates:

> He from the horrid food his mouth withdrew,
> And wiping with the clotted offal hair
> His shudd'ring lips, raising his head thus spake   (Richardson)

> From his dire food the greisly Fellon raised
> His gore-dyed lips, which on the clotter'd locks
> Of th' half devoured Head he wiped, & thus
> Began;   (Gray)

> Now from the fell repast and horrid food,
> The Sinner rose, but first (the clotted blood
> With hair depending from the mangled head)
> His jaws he wiped, and thus he wildly said: (Carlisle)

The reader who approaches the original after the translations will perhaps read into the text all it suggests and see the images the translators spell out:

> La bocca sollevò dal fiero pasto
> quel peccator, forbendola a' capelli
> del capo ch'elli avea di retro guasto.   3
> Poi cominciò: ...   (Dante; trans. in note 7)

The original does not deny that Ugolino had 'gore-dyed lips' as Gray says, and the reader can certainly be justified in visualizing lips dripping with red blood. But Dante avoids specific details or colours, and uses words with no horrific connotations: the word 'fiero' does mean 'as a savage beast', but still has connotations of pride; even the suggestive word 'guasto' is fairly colourless. There is certainly nothing in the original to warrant Richardson's 'shuddering lips'.

Maybe the English authors found that the original lacked graphic detail; maybe they were, in a way, interpolating from the previous canto, where Dante is slightly more detailed. The very first description of the sight Dante as traveller is faced with as he meets Ugolino and Ruggieri is one of movement, the act of biting:

> e come 'l pan per fame si manduca,   127
>   così 'l sovran li denti all'altro pose
>   là 've il cervel s'aggiugne con la nuca:[17]

But it is this hungry bite that is horrific, more than the mention of 'il cervello' ('the brain'); and even in this first description Dante is suggestive but restrained, as in the expression 'il teschio e *l'altre cose*' ('the skull and *the other things*', emphasis added). What all three translators attempt to do is to interpret the text and to make apparent what it is they see: here, the horrid gore, which seems to have been far from unusual in English writings of the age. Gore was common on the English stage and in Primitivist poetry, and even Pope had added it to his Homer. To label this as gothic, however, is to simplify matters to excess; Richard Warton's 'unhallow'd fangs' were gothic, but the colouring these translators add to the original comes from various aspects of the poetry of the time, and consists, quite simply, of the current ways of reading a poetry made up of such signs as the far away past, battles, death, and guilt.

Had the translators attempted to interpret Ugolino in the light of the rest of the *Commedia*, the results might have been different, but since they tackled Ugolino on its own, their response is limited accordingly, as one would expect. For Dante's technique in the Ugolino episode is particularly complex, his achievement particularly pregnant with meaning, and both technique and significance depend on the position and the function the passage has within the total poem. Dante must have found it hard to balance the opposing functions of his Ugolino. For Ugolino must horrify the reader, not with the outward show of gore but with the bestiality of the action, the 'sí bestial segno' (XXXII, 133; 'such a bestial mark'), yet at the same time the reader has to be brought to see the sinner as a man, even as a tender father. The paradox of the Ugolino episode, the power it has over the reader, lies in this tension between the sinner deep down in Cocytus and the story he tells. One of the ways in which Dante achieves this double vision is by creating a break between Canto XXXII, where Ugolino appears engaged in his beastly occupation, and Canto XXXIII, where he leaves off biting into the skull and assumes a new role. The language highlights this break.

The beginning of Canto XXXIII is practically unique in the *Divina Commedia*. As de Sanctis said, we know immediately that we are approaching something different.[18] Here the language used by the narrator is suddenly more elevated: Marcazzan calls it 'lo stacco dall'uno all'altro canto, l'esordio epico e solenne' ('the sudden shift from the one canto to the other, the epic and solemn opening').[19] Also in the tale told by Ugolino in the same canto it is the language

Ugolino uses that suggests the human being beneath the sinner (as previously in the case of Farinata degli Uberti, for example). But in both cases the language is solemn because it is stern and direct, rather than grand because elaborate and sensational. Therefore, extracting the episode from its context means the loss of this tool (the different language used in Cantos XXXII and XXXIII) in creating meaning. Even within the episode, moreover, each translator, unlike Dante, follows a particular model and adopts a uniform tone and diction. Naturally, however, the translator could only really move to a flexible and varied use of language within the episode if he had first understood the whole of the poem, including the function of the episode within it.

Extracting the episode from its context means the loss of the contrast and link not only with the poetry preceding it, but also with the poetry following it, both of which, in the case of Ugolino, are equally vital in determining the significance of the episode. All three translators begin their versions with the first lines of Canto XXXIII, and all three stop before the curse on Pisa. Gray stops with the end of the tale, which is the moment appropriate to his chosen emphasis on the tragic story of the family. Richardson, followed by Carlisle, stops only slightly later, with the description of Ugolino setting his teeth into the skull again. Admittedly, Ugolino's final lowering of the head into the skull in another horrific bite does seem the natural conclusion of the episode which started with the raising of that head. However, as was the case with Gray, so Richardson's choice of the concluding moment is of a piece with the rest of his approach; for just as Richardson had cut out references beyond the factual in Villani, so he now concludes the episode with the end of the action.

But the Ugolino episode is not just a purple passage in Dante's poem – it is a high point of the whole *Commedia*, well integrated within it, which gathers various threads to a climactic point. Neither is it only a moment in the journey of the protagonist; it is also a revelation of the state of his consciousness. Hence it is the protagonist's curse which follows Ugolino's tale that completes the meaning of the episode. When the reader is faced with the picture of this terrifying sinner gnawing a skull but then hears his words of grief and tenderness, he is forced to reflect not only on Dante's idea of divine justice in *Inferno*, but also on the rhetorical purpose of Ugolino's speech; when he hears the protagonist explode with a curse on Pisa which is as cruel as Ruggieri's betrayal, the reader is confronted with the effect of the experience of travelling through Hell. The sudden shift between Ugolino's final withdrawal into silence (at the end of his tale) and the protagonist's curse creates a break in the text – the second break within the Ugolino episode considered in its totality, which should force the reader to collate ideas of cruelty, trust, innocence and justice, and lead him to realize that the protagonist has been emotionally and rhetorically moved into abandoning his moral stance and has, in fact, lost his values. The reader who has recognized and coped with this sudden break in the story would then be equipped to understand why the protagonist goes back on his promise to Alberigo, something which appears incomprehensible after a reading of the translations .considered so far.

The total effect Richardson creates is appropriate to his purpose. The reader of Richardson is impressed by the outward effect of the scene and the story told, rather than the pathos of the man. Had Richardson stressed the idea of fatherhood, the innocence of the children, the powerlessness of affections, he would have rendered poetry which does not simply tell a story no chronicler could have witnessed with his own eyes, but poetry which communicates ideas of justice or the 'dialettica dell'odio e della pietà' ('the tense interrelation of hate and pity'), so central to the *Divina Commedia*.[20] But this would not have served his argument, which is that figurative arts, here the bas-relief and the hypothetical painting, go beyond the telling of a story, since 'There are certain Ideas which cannot be communicated by Words, but by Sculpture and Painting only' (p. 262), for 'Sculpture carries us yet further than Poetry, and gives us Ideas that no Words can: Such Forms of things, such Airs of Heads, such Expressions of Passions cannot be described by Language' (p. 255).

One feels particularly disappointed, because Richardson, one would have thought, was uniquely equipped to cope with the juxtaposition, in Dante's Ugolino, of the visual and the verbal. Dante's Ugolino is both an impressive figure of a man, and a manipulator of words. Ugolino appears at first as a figure of Dante's Lucifer, a mechanical man-eating machine, man depraved to the lowest level of cannibalism, and deprived of all but automatic movement. When, at the call of the poet's voice, he raises his head, he is, for the moment, raised again into humanity, and slowly the features of that sinner become more and more human; but then the process is reversed in front of our very eyes, and Ugolino returns to being a beast. The protagonist follows him, and his own degradation universalizes that seemingly extraordinary state. But in addition to the metamorphic shape of Ugolino there are the words that he utters. Very interesting in this context is Mario Marcazzan's comment. He sees the dynamism of the episode as the shift from the horror of the physical detail of Ugolino visualized in Hell – which is what most of the translators give us – to the suggestive words which tell the inner truth of the character:

> Il testo non da torto a quegli interpreti che illustrano nell'esordio del canto la repugnanza dei particolari ...; ma il movimento dalla prima alla seconda terzina, dai resti dell'atroce imbandiglione ai gesti silenziosi e resoluti, *alla parola che riscatta quell'abisso di miseria e*

annulla quell'orrore,ha un respiro poetico e umano d'incomparabile potenza (emphasis added).[21]

Marcazzan points out in this episode 'l'esaltazione, nella parola, della natura umana' ('the ennobling of human nature through language'), but the language of eighteenth-century poetry does not seem to have the right words. Richardson, it seems, was right after all – at least as far as the eighteenth century is concerned: he certainly proves even to us that in that age sculpture offered a better 'language' with which to reproduce Dante's text than the poetic language used by, say, Gray. Richardson's description of the bas-relief representing Ugolino proves that this is a translation of the original which is richer in significance than any of the versions in poetry that we have discussed, including Richardson's own.

It is really only speculation to say that Richardson selected the limits of the episode in order to suit his purpose. But the fact remains that what he gave to the eighteenth-century reader is one perspective on Ugolino. The conclusion of Canto XXXII, the main story, and the curse which follows the final bite create three levels of significance. Richardson only picks out one of the three, and in this way he is able to prove that sculpture can, indeed, communicate ideas better than poetry. The bas-relief, Richardson says, 'shows us the Count sitting with his four Sons, one dead, over their Heads Famine, underneath, Arno' (pp. 262); and so the central picture of Ugolino's desperate grief for his children is linked on the one hand to the power of animal appetites over human feelings, translating Dante's 'piú che 'l dolor, poté 'l digiuno' ('fasting was stronger than grief'), and on the other hand to the presence of Arno, which suggests both the geographical and the historical dimension of the tragedy and translates the speaker's curse, that makes the river rise to punish Pisa's crime against nature itself. In other words the bas-relief, being composed, as it is, of three elements, renders the full complexity of Dante's Ugolino.

Whether Richardson was consciously manipulating the material at his disposal or not, he certainly bequeathed to those who followed him a picture of Ugolino with little depth and potential. From this moment on translators of the Ugolino episode will be obsessed by the impressive figure of Ugolino in Hell, with its horror and disgust, and will not penetrate either to the more general truth the episode serves to communicate or to the episode's function within the *Divina Commedia*. Had Richardson been moved by a completely different motive – say, to prove that sculpture and poetry were equally effective in communicating ideas, or that one ought to read literature as one looks at a bas-relief – he might have discovered the basic issues at work in the last cantos of *Inferno*, and he would

then have given to readers and translators access to a very different view of
Dante's poetry.

The lost translations of Charles Burney and William Huggins

Between the early translations of Richardson (1719) and Gray (1737-40, though
published only in 1884) and the later translation of Carlisle (1772), other
translations of Dante were produced, which were, however, left unpublished and
eventually lost: Charles Burney translated the whole of *Inferno* in 1761, and
William Huggins the whole of the *Divina Commedia* in 1760. Burney and Huggins
embody in their approaches the mixed response to a text. Burney translated the
Inferno, his daughter reports (*DEL* p. 323), to console himself for the loss of his
wife, and this must indicate a personal, if curious, rapport with the original.
Huggins seems to have had a less intimate reason for producing the translation:
he had travelled in Italy and, according to Toynbee (*DEL* p. 307), came back with
a desire to spread an acquaintance with the literature of that country. So, after
Ariosto, he translated Dante. At his death he had left a manuscript ready for
publication, with instructions for it to be published, but this was never done – and
thus Huggins loses the claim he could have had to have been the first recognized
translator of the *Divina Commedia*, or even of *Inferno*.

Only one extract of Huggins' translation appeared in print. *The British Magazine*
published in 1760 Dante's version of the Lord's Prayer (which forms the first
seven tercets of *Purgatorio* XI) followed by Huggins' translation:

> *Sicut meus mos*
> As literally as possible.
> Our Father blest, who art in Heav'n above
> Not circumscrib'd: but thro' consummate love,
> Which to those primal essences you bear,
> Thy name be hallowed; thy power rare,
> By ev'ry creature: as it is but meet,
> All thanks be render'd to thy affluence sweet:
> Advance to us the peace of thy wish'd reign
> As, of ourselves, to that we can't attain,
> If it comes not, with all our skill humane.
> As, in the heav'ns, thy angels of their will
> Make sacrifice, and sign Hosanna still,
> So, may, on earth, mankind thy law fulfill.
> Our daily manna give to us this day,
> Without it, thro' this wild and thorny way,
> Who strives to travel, will more backward stray.
> And, like as are those wrongs, which we receive,
> In others pardon, so thy pardon give
> Benignant: nor survey out merit small,

And feeble virtue, so propense to fall,
Suffer not our old enemy to tempt;
But, from his punctures keep us still exempt.
                    Amen.[22]

The prosodic mode Gray had chosen for his version of Dante's poetry had been blank verse, which, with its unrhymed movement divided into paragraph units and made varied by enjambments, underlined the narrative flow of the story told, and was the perfect medium for a speaking voice telling a tale of pathos. Carlisle, on the other hand, had preferred the heroic couplet of dramatic poetry, which sustains the formal and mannered style of the utterance, has the ring of thought in movement, and provides an alternation between stasis and progression. Huggins takes a middle course between these two. He uses the rhyming pattern of the heroic couplet, but avoids the packed closeness of the couplet unit and varies his punctuation considerably, adding to the aa bb rhyme the syntactic complexity of the verse paragraph.

Dorothy Sayers, who, in her short article which surveys Dante translations, does not pause on either Boyd or Rogers, does quote Huggins, pointing out, in her one sentence on his version, how 'the pull of the terzine' forces Huggins into turning his couplet into tercets. This is possibly the case, although Sayers' notion could be affected by her view that, to the translator of Dante, the choice is '*terza rima* or nothing'.[23] A close examination of Huggins' work, however, makes it appear more likely that he was striving for variety within bounds. There is a juxtaposition of the staccato movement of the couplet rhyme and the varied blank verse paragraph; two units of six lines enclose three tercets. In this Huggins is, as he says, following the original 'as literally as possible'. Dante's first six lines form one syntactic movement. The three tercets which follow stand each on their own, as the thoughts are organized into units of three lines. This second unit of three tercets forms the core of the prayer, and the translator remains faithful to this pattern of the original. Like Dante, Huggins then balances the whole into one total, well-proportioned composition by concluding with a second syntactically independent movement of six lines. The translator is building up a very carefully constructed total unit, consisting of three couplet-rhymes (one syntactic unit), plus three tercets (three syntactic units), plus three couplet-rhymes (one syntactic unit). The addition of 'Amen', which is not in the original, stresses the homiletic nature of the poem, as well as the unified nature of its form. Had this translator already noticed the importance, in thought and in rhythm, of the three-in-one pattern of the tercet, as reflecting the image of the Trinity? The obvious care taken in the making of this translation makes one very much regret that this version of Dante has been lost. The solutions Huggins found for his translation were probably very different from those of other contemporary translators of Dante, and a more extended analysis of his lines might have confirmed what is merely suggested in the short extract available: that Huggins was striving towards a movement and rhythm which left behind the enclosure of Pope's couplets and opened the poetry out into more extended and varied units, characteristic of the blank verse paragraph later preferred by Cowper.

5

William Hayley

The translations considered so far, even taken together, only provide us with a very fragmentary picture of Dante. From the point of view of the models used, Richardson, Gray, Carlisle, and Huggins looked in different directions; from the point of view of the reason for translating, each was moved by a different motive; from the point of view of availability, it is doubtful whether Gray or Huggins' work was known even to a small circle of acquaintances, while Carlisle's was printed and therefore certainly available, and Richardson's *Two Discourses* was one of the major works on aesthetics of the age. In their differences these translators are the vanguard in the discovery of Dante as well as in the attempt to adapt English models to the original text, and they opened the way to a more deliberate and planned experiment. This step was taken by William Hayley (1745-1820), author, critic, and patron, mainly in his translation of the first three cantos of *Inferno* in 1782.

Histories of English literature hardly mention Hayley's work, except in connection with the support he gave to poets like Blake and Cowper. Yet for two or three decades after 1780 Hayley was an important figure in the world of letters, and a very popular poet. Hazlitt, Hunt, Coleridge, Lamb, Southey, Crabb Robinson and Byron all read Hayley's work and testify, in their references, to his status at the time. Byron refers to him satirically in *Don Juan* and in *English Bards and Scotch Reviewers*. In the latter, a recent production of Hayley is referred to as 'in vain attempting something new', while a few lines further one of Hayley's best known works is mentioned: 'Triumphant first see *Temper's Triumphs* shine!/ At least I'm sure they triumphed over mine'.[1] This dismissal of *The Triumphs of Temper* is, if anything, further proof of its popularity, which is sufficiently illustrated by the details of its publication – twenty-four times between 1781 and 1817, including American editions, as well as a translation into German in 1788.

But Hayley's popularity did not survive long into the nineteenth century. Already in 1815 Leigh Hunt stated, in a long note in *The Feast of Poets* to which I will refer again, that 'It would appear from some specimen in his notes, that Mr. Hayley would have cut a more advantageous figure as a translator than as an original poet...'.[2] These words suggest the beginning of the decline of Hayley's fame, especially as a poet, leading to a practically complete neglect of the man and his work by present-day scholars. But, interestingly for this study, the 'specimen' referred to by Hunt will almost certainly have been Hayley's translation of the first cantos of Dante's *Inferno*, included in the notes to Hayley's *Essay on Epic Poetry*.

In Donald Reiman's view, Hayley's fame died with the neoclassical canon: 'Hayley's poetry represented the values of traditional correctness and decorum in an age gradually beginning to value originality and sincerity'; consequently soon 'Hayley's writings became generally irrelevant to the Romantic context'.[3] But an objective look at the evidence, together with a reading of Hayley's major poem, will indicate a very different view; for Hayley's work is filled not only with neoclassical values, but also with the tension between the poles of 'neoclassicism' and 'romanticism', in which Dante plays an important role.

I intend to look at Leigh Hunt's comments on Hayley, side by side with Hayley's own words on ideas of decorum and originality – in particular, his preface to his poem the *Triumphs of Temper*; subsequently, a reading of this poem will test what Hayley actually does in his poetry. The analysis of the poem might seem to take us, at times, away from the main thrust of the present study; but the reason for the sustained analysis of this poem is that in the *Triumphs* Hayley is heavily indebted to Dante. Therefore a study of the models used in conjunction with Dante will tell us something of the manner in which the latter was introduced to the reading public. This will all constitute the first section of my analysis of William Hayley's contribution to the presence of Dante in England. In a second section, I will consider Hayley's translation of the first three cantos of *Inferno*.

Hayley's *Triumphs of Temper*

As far as contemporary comments on Hayley go, Leigh Hunt's words may be typical. He objects to the *Triumphs of Temper* because of 'that smooth-tongued and overwrought complimentary style', and this is probably the kind of remark Reiman would have based his argument on; but Hunt also says 'There is something not inelegant or unfancyful in the conduct of Mr. Hayley's Triumphs of Temper' (p. vii). This remark provides us with two separate insights: first of all, it admits, however begrudgingly, that both decorum and originality exist side by side in the poem; and, secondly, it suggests that these were the standards by which works were judged at the time. Hunt evaluates Hayley's poem on the basis of two requirements, and finds them both present, at least in some measure.

That Hayley's work represents the traditional value of decorum needs no demonstration. Heroic couplets which move at a regular pace (even using padding where needed), an overt didactic pose, lengthy informative notes, and an extensive use of metaphors and classical references justify Reiman's evaluation. But running parallel to these features is a continuous straining for novelty and for the imaginative.

A search for novelty is present in many of Hayley's works. Hayley declares that the reason he wrote his *Plays of Three Acts* in rhyme was to add novelty.[4] The same wish to freshen up traditional forms is evident in the *Essay on Epic Poetry*. First, in the argument to the first of the five Epistles which make up this poem, Hayley warns against the 'Danger of a bigoted acquiescence in critical Systems'; he then goes on to defend those poets who 'the inborn vigour of [their] soul defend'. Both the dismissal of a passive allegiance to old systems and the advice to turn to what nature has implanted in man find their climax in Hayley's solution to a major eighteenth-century critical problem. Could an epic poem still be written or not? Hayley's answer was that it could, but that the model for an epic poem had to be renewed, and this could be done by changing the setting of epic, by turning to a different 'province ' – "Tis the Celestial Sphere, or Fairy Ground'. Imagination therefore had to create a fairyland, or leave the earth on a cosmic journey. The example and antecedent of this new English epic was to be found in Italy: 'Thy daring DANTE, his wild Vision sung,*/ And raised to Epic pomp his native Tongue'.[5] Here not just the words 'Vision' and 'wild', but particularly the word 'daring' is indicative of Hayley's pose. It is as a footnote to this passage (at the point marked by an asterisk) that Hayley translated the first three cantos of *Inferno*, to provide an example of the new 'English' epic poem. Hayley himself does not put his precept into practice so far as epic is concerned, and suggests that Mason – William Mason (1725-97), author of *The English Garden* and another nearly forgotten author in our day – could write such an epic. But in his most popular poem, *The Triumphs of Temper*, Hayley does something very similar in design within a different genre. In this poem we see the actual search for new models.

Hayley begins the 'Preface' to the *Triumphs* by stating that a poet must attempt to uplift 'the dignity of a declining Art by making it ... beneficial to Life and Manners...';[6] and thus he adds to Pope's 'sportive satire' a very overt moralistic purpose. We know that Pope's own poem owes part of its poignancy to the unresolved ambivalence in the significance of Belinda and her world – she is beautiful but her values are shallow; her world is brittle and when it cracks chaos reigns, but at least it is an order of sorts, and hence valuable. Pope leaves the reader to make up his own mind. But Hayley, on the contrary, decides to take much of the power of establishing values out of the reader's hands and to place it firmly within the poem. Accordingly, he chooses a perfect heroine, Serena, who will learn to reject the world of artificial relationships and trivial pleasures and will conclude her poetic career with the episode crucial to eighteenth-century fiction: marriage to a loved and well-to-do, handsome young man. The poem is about the process of learning Serena undergoes and its consequences. According to Martin Price, in *The Rape of the Lock* Pope shows that 'a lovely order composed without consciousness is easily lost'.[7] Hayley seems to have realized this perfectly, but appears blind to the fact that the greatness of Pope's art partly derives from the tension between aesthetic and moral values; as a result, he simply adds the consciousness of the need to avoid evil and choose what is good. The poem therefore limits itself to making clear, at the very opening, that Serena is an example of 'female excellence' and then tracing the systematic strengthening of her consciousness. Hayley's different kind of central character and the more overt moral intent will 'render it [the poem] more interesting to the heart' and 'more noble', but will also add 'an air of novelty' (p. ix).

Hayley's search for novelty, however, takes him a step further. Tassoni, he points out in the 'Preface', is supposed to have 'styled ... a new species of poetry, invented by himself ... . A few partial friends have asserted, that the present performance has some degree of similar merit' (p. vii). Hayley's *Triumphs*, in fact, is styled as a completely new kind of work also through a second innovation – a change in scope: as stated in the preface, the allegorical pictures of Pope's poem, such as the Cave of Spleen, are to be sketched 'on a much wider canvas' (p. vi). Besides being 'more noble' (p. ix), therefore, Hayley's poem is also wider in scope, and this is effected by a very simple process of addition: a canto in the manner of *The Rape of the Lock* alternates with a canto drawn from Dante and Ariosto.[8] This is how Hayley himself put it:

> I wished, indeed (but I fear most ineffectually) for powers to unite some of the sportive wildness of Ariosto, and the more serious sublime painting of Dante, with some portion of the enchanting elegance, the refined imagination, and the moral graces of Pope; and to do this, if possible, without violating those rules of propriety, which mr. Cambridge has illustrated... (p. x).

Hayley's choice of models is unusual not only for the inclusion of Dante. For if Hayley's intention was to write a poem which would be 'beneficial to Life and Manners' of society, he could have turned to Pope's *Dunciad*, where the poet speaks as a moral prophet and where the 'canvas' contains a picture of Hell which is in places very similar to Dante's. He could then have produced a sharp satire by combining the means used by Pope and those used by Dante. But it is to the lighter graces and tone of the *Rape of the Lock* that Hayley turns. This illuminates the scope of Hayley's poetic world, and already suggests the limited way in which Hayley could and did borrow from Dante, his Hell, for example, being only sufficiently frightening to cause Serena to faint.

Turning to an analysis of Hayley's debt to Dante throughout the *Triumphs*, we find that Canto III and V of the *Triumphs* owe a heavy debt to Dante, but the cantos in the manner of Pope (Cantos I, II, IV and VI) also reveal the influence of Dante's poem. The very first canto sets out the plot of the poem, and is sufficient to show how the framework of the *Triumphs* is based on the *Commedia*. Here the reader meets Serena in her daily life and is also introduced to the supernatural machinery of the spirits in the form of the fairy Sophrosyne. The latter has obviously learned from the failure of Pope's Ariel due to Belinda's loss of temper, and therefore informs Serena that to achieve her aim in life – naturally enough, a happy marriage – she must learn the management of her temper. To reach this goal she must experience Hell and Paradise in order to strengthen her moral awareness. Moreover she must pass three tests, consisting of her encounters with three of Spleen's agents:

> "Perchance three prime supporters of her sway,
> The basest of her Fiends, may cross thy way:"   (I 368-9)

The tests and the meetings with the allegorical monsters make a Spenserian knight of Serena. But the situation depicted in these words is that of the Dantean protagonist in the first canto of *Inferno*, who encounters three beasts, representing sins, but is helped by a guide. In the *Triumphs*, Sophrosyne introduces herself as Serena's 'guide' who will help the heroine to overcome the three Dantean beasts, which appear in three of the cantos in the manner of Pope. Hayley therefore reduces to a very functional and restricted level the complex moral scene of Pope's poem; and he conflates it with the quest of heroic romance and with the basic situation of the first canto of Dante's *Inferno*, which are similarly reduced in significance and range.

Canto III of the *Triumphs* is the descent of Serena into Hell, and it follows the general plot of the third canto of Dante's *Inferno*. Serena goes through Hell's gate, which bears above it an English version of Dante's frightening inscription; and having entered, she is enveloped by the darkness and noise that Dante's protagonist faced. Then she comes across a train of people, and the river with Charon and his boat. The spectacle of sinners and their punishment concludes, as in Dante's third canto, with the protagonist fainting at the sound of a bugle. In Dante, this enabled the writer to transport the protagonist to another canto and another place, and in Hayley Serena is transported to her bedroom.

Besides retracing the third canto of Dante's *Inferno*, Hayley's canto continues further into Hell and takes Serena to 'icy crags' and a 'dreary plain' where she can see 'The ghastly Tyrant of the gloomy waste' (III 528). We therefore proceed further into the depths of Hell and Dante's thirty-third canto; in this case, however, the tyrant of Hell is not Dante's Satan, but Misanthropy, son of Pride and the Gorgon Disappointment. We are in Dante's Hell, but it turns out to contain Pope's Cave of Spleen, and a very Spenserian one at that, full of allegorical monsters. Nevertheless, *Inferno* is the major source and is specifically referred to; Hayley's inscription over Hell's gate is accompanied by a footnote with the quotation of the Italian original and the specific canto and line number. Also, Serena's fears are said to be worse 'Than those, which erst the Bard of Florence felt' (III 181) when he was separated from Virgil by the devils. Furthermore, there are similarities with Dante in this canto of Hayley's in the form of specific details, as well as more general features.

As far as details are concerned, Toynbee has pointed out four passages from Canto III of the *Triumphs*, eight to fifteen lines long, which are direct imitations of specific passages from Canto III of *Inferno*,[9] and many more cases can be isolated. For example, there are single lines of direct translation: 'Pass! and regard them not!' (III 517) is the advice of the guide Sophrosyne to Serena to ignore 'the envious', echoing Virgil's advice to Dante when they meet 'the lukewarm' in Canto III of *Inferno* (Virgil, however, lets the protagonist look at the souls: 'non ragioniam di lor, ma guarda e passa', l. 51, 'Let us not talk of them; but look and pass on'). Concerning the similarity in general features, one example is that the punishments of the sinners in Hayley's Hell of Spleen are a mocking version of Dante's system of punishments, the 'contrapasso', where the punishment corresponds to the sin. In Hayley, the Lord Mayor of London's 'Glutton Flesh' is torn to pieces by a 'circling group of Fish, and Fowl, and Beast' who over him 'their reunited limbs display: ... See! fifty Turkeys gobble on his Paunch!' (III 390, 394, 398). This passage was, in fact, cut out in the second edition of the poem, but still other similar examples such as the punishment of Xantippe were retained:

> Mark...
> The fierce Xantippe flaming in the van,
> The vase, she emptied on the Sage's head,
> Hangs o'er her own, a different shower to shed;
> For, drop by drop, distilling liquid fire,
> It fills the Vixen with new tropes of ire.   (III 371-375)

What these examples show is that the indebtedness to Dante is pervasive as well as overtly stated, but it does not run deep – in fact, it is in itself mocked, and we face a parody of the horrors of Hell. It is not here that Hayley's didactic purpose is most evident. In fact if the function of poetry is to instruct and to amuse, it is the latter that plays the most important role, and to a superficially amusing parody and burlesque we can add a purely literary game. Dante's Hell is also Pope's Spenserian Cave of Spleen, and is in fact more up to date than that; one only has to read Sophrosyne's description of Hell as 'The Gulph of Indolence' (III 110) to realize that the world of Spenser and the language in which it is pictured is that of eighteenth-century Spenserian poems such as Thomson's *Castle of Indolence*. The eighteenth-century literary scene is present in other guises; the final episode before the sounding of the bugle, which closes the canto, is the daily offering by Misanthropy's 'High-priest', who turns out to be 'the shade of Swift'. In a passage 60 lines long, Swift appears in the company not only of his Yahoos and 'Horses' but also of the fiends 'Derision' and 'Perverted Ridicule' (III 619, 633).

Hayley's Hell, then, is a transformation of Dante's Hell. Hayley creates a mixture of different models, adding burlesque and changing the scale of the created world. The combination destroys Dante's realism and the personal relevance of the journey for the reader, and turns the created world into one which has a strong element of romance and fairy tale.

Hayley's Purgatory and Paradise in Canto V of the *Triumphs* very strikingly exemplify the same transformation – from a poem of typological and prophetic significance to a fantastic romance. The transformation is gradual, and, in fact, at the beginning Sophrosyne's flight with Serena to her realm in the sky seems very serious in significance and tone, and is close to Dante. When Sophrosyne reaches the sphere where she resides, she may be compared to Leah or Matilda in Dante's earthly Paradise at the top of Mount Purgatory. The initial resemblance, however, is only superficial, and it would be easy to imagine other sources for the imagery, such as the Bible, or allegorical pageantry which enlivened Italian as well as English cities in the Middle Ages and which is reflected in the works of Spenser and later of Bunyan. Soon, however, Sophrosyne turns more clearly into Beatrice leading the pageant of Revelation in *Purgatorio*. The public triumph of Beatrice includes her arrival on a cart led by a griffin and enclosed by four biblical animals.[10] Hayley gives Sophrosyne a similar public triumph, also on a chariot:

> These figures, pencill'd with a touch so light,
> That every image seem'd a heavenly Sprite,
> Breathe on the car; whose light enchanting frame
> Four wheels sustain, of pale and purple flame;
> For no fleet animals to earth unknown
> Bear thro' aetherial fields this flying throne.   (V 83-88)

The wheels of flame and the animals come from the book of Ezekiel, or Revelation; but the description of the chariot, and the absence of the griffin, specifically mentioned (which very logically explains the need for four wheels whereas Dante's cart, pulled by the griffin, had two wheels), point to Beatrice's 'carro ... triunfale' ('triumphal car'). Hayley, however, turns Dante's complex image of God's revelation into a 'light enchanting frame' more worthy of the world of Belinda – or even Cinderella – than that of Dante's spirits.

Another feature that Hayley lifts from Dante and transforms is that of the circling spheres:

> ... three Orbs, that in yon Crystal sphere
> A separate system in themselves appear.   (V 125-6)

The knowledgeable reader of Dante is immediately reminded of more than one important image of the *Divina Commedia*. As Serena rising upwards sees the circling orbs, so Dante's traveller sees Paradise as concentric spheres – the 'eterne rote' Beatrice intently stares at (*Paradiso*, I, 64). Hayley also refers to this traditional picture of the heavens when he mentions the 'Crystal sphere' – corresponding to Dante's crystalline heaven. This could just be a reference to a conventional term, but a closer similarity is that between the three circles in Hayley and the final vision of Dante, the revelation of the Trinity. Dante's 'tre giri/ di tre colori e d'una contenenza' (*Paradiso*, XXXIII, 116-7, 'three circles/ Of three colours and one circumference'), like Hayley's three orbs which 'a separate system in themselves appear', pictures three circles which form a single unity. But Dante's complex final image of the *Commedia* is used by Hayley in a quite different manner.

One of the spheres in Hayley is the residence of the goddess of this heaven, Sophrosyne; it is her palace, where her triumph takes place. Another sphere is the nether sphere, a world in which

> ... these Beings dwell
> Who wanted Soul to act or ill or well
> Who saunter'd thoughtless thro' their mortal time
> Without a Care, a Virtue or a Crime.   (V 139-142)

This is a paraphrase of Virgil's description of 'the lukewarm' in Dante's third canto ('l'anime triste di coloro/ che visser senza infamia e senza lodo', III, 35-6, 'the wretched souls of those/ who lived without infamy and without praise'). Inserted between the triumph of Sophrosyne and the rest of the journey in heaven this is a strange interruption in Hayley's fifth canto. Dante places his 'ignavi' or 'lukewarm' in the ante-hell, as unworthy of even the notice and position damnation would bestow on them, and it was towards them that he was urged to show the same scornful indifference that Sophrosyne tells Serena, in the third canto of the *Triumphs*, to show to 'the envious'. The world of the 'lukewarm', and the guide's words to the protagonist are two elements of the encounter in Dante's third canto which Hayley separates and uses in different parts of his poem, the fifth and third canto respectively. This indicates that, as far as his own poem is concerned, Hayley's interest lies in the effective phrase or remarkable episode of Dante, rather than what is most significant. The strange inclusion of this ante-hell could then be explained as the adaptation of an element of Dante to Hayley's world in the *Triumphs*. The 'lukewarm' or inane in this second sphere are in a kind of castle of indolence, where 'Indifference' and 'Oblivion' use the charm of the poppy to induce a 'sluggish state'. This fits in with both the fabulous aspect of Hayley's heaven and the compatible features of Spenserian true and false Paradises, which had become so popular again in Hayley's time. The presence of the 'indolents' and Hayley's choice of Spleen as the spiritual enemy indicate that indeed Hayley should have mentioned Spenser as a fourth model and Thomson and his *Castle of Indolence* as a fifth. Hayley's third sphere contains his version of Purgatory and Paradise, and, like his nether sphere, also draws from Spenser and the late eighteenth-century poets.

Naturally enough, the protestant Hayley does not lead Serena through the purification of Purgatory – which she does not need anyway – but takes her straight to a place similar to the top of Dante's Mount Purgatory, the earthly Paradise. Rather than a state of achieved purity, however, Hayley's Eden is very earthly indeed, more earthly even than the gardens painted by Virgil and Statius in their poetry. When these poets see the beauty of Eden on Dante's Mount Purgatory, they recognize what they had dreamt of and written in their poetry (see *Purgatorio* XXVIII 139-147). The Heaven Serena is faced with in her progress towards a happy marriage is a perfect garden worthy of the Golden Age, a 'plain' in which one can find 'all the flowers that bloom' (V 199). But the god in control of the 'verdant ground' is Love, so that we soon realize that, far from being in a Christian or even a classical Eden, we are in a world more like Arcadia.

Love, in Hayley's Eden, is called 'the mighty master of the revels' (V 233), and Serena witnesses the formal revels of courtship at a lord's residence. Knights and damsels are concerned only with wooing and being courted, and the hope of becoming worthy of God is here replaced by other pleasures. The blessed enjoy 'fluttering hope' and 'rapturous desire' in what is clearly the world of courtly love. This garden is not a false Paradise such as Spenser's Bower of Bliss, and its queen is not as ambiguous and artful as Spenser's bathing maidens, but still Serena is meant to recognize in this queen a possibility of womanhood which must not be imitated:

Thro' her thin vest her heighten'd beauties shine;
For earthly gauze was never half so fine.
Of that enchanting age her figure seems,

...

And just between the woman and the child.   (V 213-215, 220)

This figure is clearly presented as a mirror image of Serena. The similarity is not only a question of age; the clothes the queen of the garden wears are very similar to Serena's mask for the ball, 'the robes of Ariel' which she was wearing for the dance she was forbidden to attend in the previous canto (Canto IV), and which she will wear in the next (Canto VI).

But in Canto VI it becomes evident that her experience in the garden has taught Serena something, since her dress 'to the nymph recalls/ Those disappointments that may yet befall' (VI 155-6). This refers to the course of events in Hayley's garden of love. Its shallow pleasures are subject to what one feels justified in calling Mutabilitie, since after the description of flowers, meadows, and courtiers wooing a change occurs: a speck in the sky becomes a cloud, which grows until

Sudden from hence the sound of anguish flow,
And joy's sweet carols end in shrieks of woe:
The wither'd flowers are fall'n, that bloom'd so fair,
and poison all the pestilential air.
From the rent earth dark demons force their way,
And make the sportive revellers their prey.   (V 253-8)

Soon joy returns, shadows flee, and 'the gentle ruler of the changeful land' resumes her place. Serena learns by example, but again the literary game takes over, and the mock-heroic enters and touches even Serena when she cries, '"Blest be this hour! for now I see Rousseau"' (V 340).

Serena's reference to Rousseau marks a turning point in the fifth canto; for prior to this the poetry had moved through alternating narrative and descriptive passages such as those quoted, and seemed to simply feed and rely on its own variety. But now the mocking tone, which is used to describe Rousseau, the listening crowd and Serena, takes over completely, and turns Hayley's Paradise into a burlesque. Serena sees a Heaven for oppressed females, who had been victimized by brothers, sisters, and particularly parents. One of three groups of the highest of the blessed is a group of women who have ignored 'injurious mockery, and coarse contempt', satisfied at having fulfilled their duty, even if they have to make do with 'the name of ancient maid'.[11] The burlesque is entertaining; and the Heaven pictured is appropriate, because it is complementary to a Hell dominated by Misanthropy and the spectre of Sterne. But Hayley's Heaven is absolutely external to Serena's journey, since the existence of this Heaven might offer consolation for Serena's aunt Penelope, but hardly for Serena herself. And from this point onwards Hayley's Paradise becomes too different from Dante's for similarities to occur.

It is true that one can still point to specific phrases which are copied from Dante, such as Hayley's exclamation of his inability to describe the climax of Serena's journey: 'how may human speech/ Thy heavenly raptures in this moment reach?' (V 475-6). Occurring as this does at the climax of Serena's beatific vision, it seems parallel to Dante's stress on the impossibility of expressing the inexpressible. But though these and similar possible echoes occur, they are only external borrowings that do not establish links between the two pictures of Paradise, which remain fundamentally different. The beatific vision Serena is granted is a case in point, for Hayley's God is a Goddess – in fact, a mother and almost a fertility figure: Benevolence, 'a mild maternal form', who 'Embrace'd Serena with a smile as warm/ as the gay spirit Vegetation wears/...' (V 470-1). Hayley may be sketching his heroine along the lines of Sophia in *Tom Jones*, as a young and beautiful girl in the hands of an inept father and silly aunt, with no living mother to serve as an example; and this points to a common feature of this canto – the interweaving, again, of literary allusions. Favourites in Paradise are 'The song of Anstey and the tale of Sterne' (V 598), but the major bard is Cowper, and the blessed's pursuit must be to repeat 'the task of Cooper (their own task)...' (p. 102). In fact, at this point references to the English scene become more obvious than in the previous cantos, and accordingly I now turn to a consideration of Hayley's pervasive debt to English models.

The reference to Cowper is particularly interesting; it did not appear in the first edition of the *Triumphs*, but was added in a later edition, after the appearance of *The Task* in 1785. This testifies to Hayley's familiarity with the literary and cultural scene of the age and the impact this has on his poem. The *Triumphs* is like a map of the eighteenth-century English scene, and in spite of its lack of vividness, it has remarkably wide-ranging references to real events and the culture of the age. Serena's courage in the face of Scandal is supported by Chesterfield's speech in defence of 'the violated stage';[12] the invitation to the masquerade that she receives is pencilled by Cipriani, which is a reference to Gianbattista Cipriani, a Florentine painter and engraver who moved to England in 1755; the reference to Anstey creates a parallel between Paradise and the fashionable world of Bath, depicted in Anstey's *New Bath Guide* (1766).[13] Moreover, in her disappointment at her father's command to retire Serena is pictured

> As the proud dame, whose avaricious glee
> Built golden castles in the rich South Sea,
> Gaz'd on the broker, when he told her first

> Her wealth was vanish'd, and the bubble burst;   (II 384-7)

which is as literal a reference to the South Sea Bubble (which burst in 1720) as one is likely to find in literature.

That the poetry is not more realistic is due to the formal diction and prosody, which is again part of Hayley's allegiance to the eighteenth-century mock-heroic style. In the *Triumphs*, the heroic couplet, at times closed, often extending into longer sentences, but always moving in steady and balanced steps, is occasionally condensed in concise, sharp lines characteristic of the eighteenth-century satire, as when Serena's father is charmed by his daughter:

> In that glad moment he at once forgets
> His empty stomach, and the country's debts   (II 85-6)

This is only a pale reflection of that balance and antithesis that Pope was a master of, but follows the same pattern. Perhaps more successful is a couplet describing Serena's rich and fashionable suitor, an 'early peer' who adopts the latest small talk and sprinkles it with foreign terms:

> Thus our young lord, with fashion's phrase refin'd,
> Fineer'd the mean interior of his mind: (II 143-4)

Here the point is sharper, and the metaphor works. Nothing could be more strikingly different from this style than the poetry of Cantos III and V – the cantos in the manner of Dante. The openings of both cantos provide an eloquent example:

> Canto III
> Ye kind Transporters of the excursive soul!
> Ye Visions! that, when Night enwraps the Pole,
> The lively wanderer to new worlds convey,
> Escaping from her heavy house of clay,
> How could the gentle spirit, foe to strife,
> Bear without you this coil of waking life?   (III 1-6)

> Canto V
> Why art thou fled, o blest poetic time,
> When Fancy wrought the miracles of Rhyme;
> When, darting from her star-encircled throne,
> Her poet's eye commanded worlds unknown;
> When, by her fiat made a mimic God,
> He saw Existence waiting on his nod,
> ...
> Who, at his bidding, thro' the wilds of air,
> Rais'd willing mortals far from earthly care,
> And led them wandering thro' his wide domain,
> Beyond the bounds of Nature's narrow reign;   (V 1-6, 11-14)

In the place of a realistic world of politics, parties and society, we have the solitary nocturnal musings of the bard, who, with his visionary poetry, leaves the earth on a cosmic journey, from which he brings back lessons of the infinity of the universe, and the smallness of humanity. This is the voice of Gray's bard, or that of the poet of Young's *Night Thoughts*, with Serena in the role of Lorenzo. In the place of the neoclassical diction and argumentative ironic voice, we have here the expansive and imaginative unboundedness of what has been seen as the eighteenth-century imitation of Milton's sublimity and paragraph units.

The eighteenth-century pseudo-Miltonic style is, it seems to us today, a persiflage of Milton's 'organ voice'; his inversions and Latinate words became a grand celebratory style, full of resonant phrases. This style, moreover, came to be applied to less public themes, and spoken by protagonists of lesser import than a Satan or an Adam; and thus the speaker of the visionary journey is one of the major differences between the original and the imitation. From being the language of the highest theme that could be sung, and appropriate because it issued from the mouths of the greatest possible heroes in religious history, Milton's sublime becomes, so it seems, the forced, exclamatory utterance of a frantic and over-energetic speaker, who leaves the enclosure of his study to expose himself to nature and its most extreme phenomena with a vengeance.

Hayley does not adopt the most extreme form of this pseudo-Miltonic style, but Cantos III and V of the *Triumphs* follow the basic pattern. Hayley's attempt to include within his poem the two most characteristic styles of his time (the mock-heroic and pseudo-Miltonic) is certainly an interesting experiment, and he saw it as such – experiment is the very word he himself uses in his 'Preface'. The names of Gray and Young, or Thomson and Spenser, do not occur there, but it is obvious that Hayley was deliberately adopting their style in his cantos in the manner of Dante. Indeed, he does say that one of the novelties of his poem is 'the manner of connecting the real and visionary scenes ... in alternate Cantos' in order to 'afford a strong relief to each other, and keep the attention of the Reader alive, by an appearance particularly diversified' (p. 11). The words 'real' and 'visionary' are a good summary of the nature of Hayley's experiment.

Hayley's protagonist, Serena, does not strike the reader as having an 'appearance particularly diversified'. She is portrayed in different cantos as a young woman dressed like a sprite, and remains throughout the poem what she was at the beginning: an example of 'female excellence'. Even when she dresses up as Ariel in 'an azure tissue, and silver gauze' this 'light attire' is meant to be 'her robe of triumph, and a spell to love' in a very pure and innocent manner. And even when, at the ball in Canto VI, she inspires feelings which belong to earth and not heaven – 'The gay Serena every eye allur'd; the hearts her figure won her face secured' (VI 294-5), she is presented as untouched: 'A tender sweetness still the nymph maintained' (VI 296). Significantly, when Serena herself recognizes the similarity between her appearance and that of the queen of love in the garden of Canto V the effect on her is not satisfaction, but anxiety.

But although Serena herself is presented consistently as an example of 'female excellence', some ambiguity attaches to her figure in that she is one of three reflections of young womanhood in the poem. Serena is the innocent counterpart not only of the queen of love but also of a third figure, who appears in the recollections of Serena's father. The memory of the 'worthy knight' goes back to a party

> "When Ch – h's charms amaz'd the public sight;
> When the kind Fair one, in a veil so thin
> That the clear gauze was but a lighter skin,
> Mask'd like a Virgin just prepared to die,
> Gave her plump beauties to each greedy eye!
> On that same night . . .
> I danc'd around her in a Devil's mask;
> And idly chaunted an infernal ode,
> In praise of all this Female temptress shew'd.
> The jocund crowd, who throng'd with me to gaze,
> Extoll's my unpremeditated lays,"   (VI 86-98)

All three figures are very young, they appear dressed in similar clothes, and have the same alluring effect on the spectators in the poem.

Like the jocund crowd, the average reader might find amusement in such verses which sing the praises of this 'Female temptress', but what can the more serious reader do with this passage within the context of the didactic and moral purpose of the poem? One might, indeed, note that 'greedy eyes' had intruded themselves also into Spenser's Bower of Bliss (*The Fairy Queen*, Book II, Canto IX, stanza 64), and so the 'Female temptress' could be the infernal version of Serena, Hayley using traditional biblical imagery. However, such an interpretation, stressing the moral purpose of the passage, is contradicted by the evident entertainment element of the passage, which is never negated.

Yet one cannot doubt the seriousness of Hayley's attempt to make his poem 'more noble' than Pope's. Rather than simply juxtaposing the poetry of wit with the poetry of prophecy, he attempts to bridge them. The juxtaposition in setting shows that Hayley realized that the daytime world of satire was substantially different from the nocturnal musings of the inner soul; but at the same time this juxtaposition is bridged by the natural division into three days divided by two nights, in a person's life. What we are finally faced with is the dual aspect of people's lives, with their commitments to society as well as their reflections upon the daytime world. The two eighteenth-century modes Hayley uses are, it seems, complementary, in that they can give voice to different aspects of man. Hayley's experiment, moreover, is not as new as it might appear, since it follows a tradition: his *Triumphs of Temper* is an eighteenth-century *L'Allegro and il Penseroso*.

Hayley's poem is, therefore, undeservedly forgotten by the critic and by the student of the history of literature, since it is a literary document which exemplifies the forces at work at the time. The allusions themselves recreate the eighteenth-century scene, with music, the figurative arts, philosophy, the theatre, fiction and poetry all being present, and with Swift's work constituting a vision of Hell and Cowper offering possible redemption. The juxtaposition of styles – and the worlds they express – can work for the student as a cross-commentary. For Hayley's smooth heroic couplets show the exhaustion of a medium which had been developed to its full potential: the neoclassical diction and the continuous flow of the heroic couplet, which were used for purposes of satire, were worn to threads, and needed to be renewed. Similarly, the visionary world of Young, with its solitary protagonist and flight into fancy and space, had become a 'manner', an established medium one could imitate with ease. But both modes could be renewed – through the addition of the 'sublime painting of Dante', for example.

To sum up, the poem draws from a number of established models of English poetry, introducing into the poem thereby a range of features, such as the compression of the Popean couplet and the expansion of the Youngian cosmic journey. Hayley uses these features to add variety to his poem. But the combination of these familiar features with the new presence of Dante's voice gives them a renewed appearance in the eye of the reader. The use of allusions to the eighteenth-century scene works in a similar way: they do not point outwards or lead the reader towards a particular insight, but end in themselves. In other words, they essentially strengthen the readers' familiarity with their own literary and historical world. The only exceptions are the references to Dante, which would be mostly unfamiliar to readers of the time and thus lead them out of the world they already knew. Dante, therefore, is responsible both for the new elements which Hayley adds to renew poetry, and also for the references which can prompt the reader to look at his world with different eyes. So the question of the models Hayley used and the nature of the variety in his poem inevitably bring us to the effect they both had on the course of Dante's fame in England.

The basic fact about the effect of the *Triumphs* on current ideas on Dante is that very few readers indeed would have been able to recognize either Hayley's general or specific debt to Dante. They would not, therefore, themselves be in a position to compare Hayley's references with the original. But they were informed in preface and footnotes of the use that was made of Dante in the poem. Thus, when they came to read Dante, they would read his poem through the medium of the expectations which Hayley's *Triumphs* had raised. In terms of the models Hayley used, the effect on the course of Dante's fame in England is obvious. Hayley includes direct references to *Inferno* and adds footnote quotations in his third canto – the descent of Serena into Hell. This would contribute to the current view, initiated and sustained by other aspects of the eighteenth-century literary scene, that Dante was the poet of Hell. Other obvious similarities to Dante occur in this same canto – the only canto, in fact, in which Toynbee, for one, notices similarities. The borrowings we noticed in the cantos in the manner of Pope are less direct, and so it is in one of the visionary cantos that Dante is more overtly present.

Thus, the reader who read Dante under the influence of Hayley's poem would be prepared for the fact that Dante was not a writer of satire, or of poetry immediately relevant to real life. If *Inferno* is not satire and is not neoclassical, the alternative offered by Hayley is the poetry of Young and Thomson. The *Commedia*, then, becomes a visionary poem of a solitary soul lost in space, and of the cosmic journey with its expansive language – with both the setting and the language being of the sublime.

The *Triumphs*' strong element of romance and fairy tale would equally be extended to expectations concerning Dante's poem. Since the romance in the *Triumphs* concentrates on Serena and her good marriage, it takes us away from the issue of the models used, and leads on to Hayley's particular goals in creating a character offering a model of morality more positive than Pope's.

Assuming that the reader of Hayley was unable to recognize the limits of the latter's indebtedness to Dante, it follows naturally that he would include features characteristic of Hayley's poem in his expectations concerning Dante's poem. In Hayley, the stress is very obviously on the protagonist and her acquisition of a measure of moral awareness. A reader would not necessarily transfer the perfection of Serena onto a different protagonist, but he would probably extend the more general situation of Serena to Dante's poem. The protagonist of *Inferno*, then, would be expected to be the centre of attention, and the action of the poem would be directed to his education and the strengthening of his moral fibre. As in the case of Serena, the protagonist's journey into Hell would teach him to shun evil and follow goodness.

It goes without saying that readers of Dante's poem approaching it in terms of Hayley's poem would see their expectations disappointed. For there is little sublimity, either of scenery or of language, in Dante's Hell; nor is there development of moral clarity, let alone the achievement of perfection, in the protagonist, who does not even appear as the centre of the action in the poem. Such disappointment is confirmed by the recorded responses of readers of the age. For disappointment well summarizes the reactions of those readers that we examined in chapter three, who, by virtue of their position in society as well as the popularity of Hayley at the time, may reasonably be assumed to have read Hayley's *Triumphs*. Of these readers, Anna Seward can be taken as an example of someone who is cultured and well-read. Yet, once she actually approached a translation of Dante's poem, she was struck by the egotism of the protagonist and the horrors of the scene, and missed the sentimental story, the moral graces, and the sublime painting she had been led to expect (see p. 41 above). Many other readers of the age who were equally or less well cultured, and would also have been familiar with Hayley's *Triumphs*, would surely have had a similar response.

Hayley's translation of Dante

One would expect Hayley to be less free with the original when producing a translation of Dante than when using a selection of features for his own poem. Comparing him with the translators that had preceded him, Leigh Hunt comments favourably on Hayley's closeness to the original in his version of Dante, 'which if far beneath the majestic simplicity of the original, is at least, for spirit as well as closeness, much above the mouthing nonentities which have been palmed upon us of late years for that wonderful poet.'[14] Hayley's intention to reproduce his original faithfully seems immediately confirmed by two features of the translation. First, the English text appeared side by side with the original, and this is the first time a part of the *Commedia* longer than a few lines appeared in England in the original. Secondly, Hayley was the first of the eighteenth-century translators to use the *terza rima* of the original. However, he thought that no other English poet had used this measure, and so his choice could be due less to a desire to remain faithful to the original than to a desire to offer the reader 'some pleasure from its novelty', as he puts it himself. Yet Hayley's use of the *terza rima* is instrumental in determining the nature and spirit of his translation, and therefore some attention will be given to it here.

Reading the opening of Canto I of Hayley's translation we find that the lines follow one another smoothly and the reading moves forward with no awkwardness:

> In the mid season of this mortal strife,
> I found myself within a gloomy grove,
> Far wandering from the ways of perfect life;   3
> The place I know not, where I chanc'd to rove,

It was a wood so wild, it wounds me sore
　But to remember with what ills I strove:　　　　6
Such still my dread, that death is little more.
　But I will tell the good which there I found.
High things 't was there my fortune to explore:　　9
　Yet how I enter'd on that secret ground
I know not to explain; so much in sleep
　My mortal senses at that hour were drown'd.　　12
But when I reached the bottom of a steep,
　That rose to terminate the dreary vale,
Which made cold terrors thro' my bosom creep,　　15
　I looked on high, where breath'd a purer gale,
And saw the summit glisten with that ray
Which leads the wand'rer safe o'er hill and dale.[15]

A danger of translating in *terza rima* is that often a choice must be made between an accurate phrasing and an effective rhyme. Hayley avoids this pitfall. The rhymes are not strained here, but almost pass unnoticed, and one cannot pinpoint any part where the translator had to perform the tricks of a contortionist to square up his rhymes.

Still the total effect of the verse is quite at variance with Dante's intended effect. The apparent smoothness of Hayley's lines is due to the fact that he pads them out, not only in order to produce the required rhyme endings but also to maintain the iambic pentameter. Hayley pads the lines out by using longer and more formal phrases or individual words – 'within' rather than 'in', 'Far wandering' rather than just 'Wandering', 'terminate' rather than 'close' or 'end', and by consistently adding adjectives to his nouns – 'valle' becomes 'dreary vale', 'paura' 'cold terrors', 'cor' 'struggling spirit'. More formal and more elaborate, the language is also slightly archaic, employing such expressions as 'wounds me sore', for example, in the passage quoted. This padding was a feature of eighteenth-century imitators of Spenser.

These phrases are not quite the 'mouthing nonentities' Leigh Hunt complains of in other translations, but to the modern ear they come dangerously close to it. What saves Hayley's verse from this criticism is the fact that the heavy hand of the writer in this case serves the important function of distinguishing the voice of the poet from that of the protagonist. Probably the most significant aspect of Hayley's translation is that there are two different, contrasting movements at work in the verse. The smooth flow of the lines, the elaborate words, and the sound patterns underline the presence and activity of the writer; but the clustering of lines in units different from the original and with varied syntactic linking underlines the mental experience of the protagonist.

In *Inferno* the tercets are generally self-contained units of thought:[16]

Nel mezzo del cammin di nostra vita
   mi ritrovai per una selva oscura
   che la diritta via era smarrita.   3
Ah quanto a dir qual'era è cosa dura
   esta selva selvaggia e aspra e forte
   che nel pensier rinova la paura!   6
Tant'è amara che poco è piú morte;
   ma per trattar del ben ch'io vi trovai,
   dirò dell'altre cose ch'i' v'ho scorte.   (I 1-9)[17]

Dante's three lines make a unit in terms of both syntax and sense, and the thought simply opens, develops and draws to a conclusion within the three lines. This creates a balanced, controlled pattern, sustained by the way in which sentences – and therefore tercets and lines – are linked. For example, in the third tercet quoted, line seven establishes how affecting the memory of the journey is; lines eight and nine add that in order to be able to tell of the good discovered during the journey, the speaker will tell of all he saw; the 'ma' in line eight contrasts the fear of line seven with the decision in lines eight and nine, while the structure 'per trattar.../dirò' ('to treat of ... I will speak of ...') connects the purpose stated in lines eight and nine, with the effect of the decision in line ten. The lines proceed in very logical steps evenly set out.

Hayley's punctuation is more varied. Lines seven, eight and nine in Hayley's opening of *Inferno* quoted above stand each on their own in terms of the thoughts expressed. Moreover, line seven is the first of the whole passage which is closed by a full stop, and it is presented as a summary of the previous six. Thus, in Hayley a paragraph of seven lines is followed by two lines which are single units of thought. By making the lines stand on their own, Hayley leaves out the logical steps in Dante's argument. Rather than the measured pace of Dante, here we have a more emotional, personal verse-patterning, which is revealed particularly in the syntactic links connecting the lines. In Dante we find a 'ma' ('but') in line eight and another 'ma' in line thirteen. Hayley adds a third 'but' in line six, and a 'yet' in line ten. So while he eliminates a logical patterning, he also doubles the internal oppositions between thoughts, thus creating, by means of complicating the balancing and contrasts of the ideas, what sounds like the tentativeness of a speaking voice. The regular, thoughtful control of the original becomes more varied and uncertain, as if the speaker was attempting to put his thoughts into words there and then. This tentativeness, as opposed to the elaborate and controlled rhyming pattern and language of the writer, introduces the voice of the protagonist.

Hayley therefore reflects in his version the dual presence of the writer, with his control over the prosody of the verse, and of the protagonist, with his mental uncertainty. Clearly Hayley was aware of the presence of two personas, and, as will be shown using Canto II as example, he employed it extensively in his version of Dante. But this does not mean that Hayley also reproduces the different nature of the experience and vision of the two personas. Neither does it mean that Hayley's closeness to Dante as far as prosody is concerned is reflected in a closeness to the original in other senses; both the nature of the created world, and the figure of the protagonist are substantially different from Dante's.

The experience of the protagonist disappears in the obviously allegorical picture Hayley presents to the reader. 'This mortal strife' for 'nostra vita' ('our life'), or 'the ways of perfect life' for 'diritta via' ('straight way'), for example, substitute a mental landscape of moral choices for the literal experience which Dante so vividly created. In this respect Dante's poetic world is replaced with that of Spenser. The persona of the protagonist, however, is no Spenserian knight, but the hero of an eighteenth-century drama or romance. The alliteration characteristic of Spenser's poetry is turned by Hayley into the service of the expression of the passions and sensibility of the protagonist:

> Such sad oppression seized my sinking frame,
> Such horror at these strange tremendous sights

These lines describe the effect on the protagonist of the approach of the wolf, and they are a confession of weakness, exhaustion and fear no epic hero would have stooped to. More importantly, it is not what Dante's speaker reported:

> questa mi pose tanto di gravezza
> con la paura c'uscía di sua vista   (I 52-3)[18]

Dante's wolf is here physically oppressive: even the verbs 'mi pose' and 'uscía' ('placed on me' and 'issued from') indicate weight and movement. The first line quoted specifically shows that the protagonist feels the effect of the wolf in his very body; Hayley's protagonist is fainting not because the 'oppression' is heavy, but because it is 'sad'. The stress is on the extreme emotional state of this figure: words like 'horror' and expressions like 'strange tremendous sights' are the exclamations of the sensitive protagonist of a gothic novel faced with the monstrous. Similarly, in the opening lines of the poem the adjectives Hayley had added either described an extreme emotional upheaval in the protagonist ('cold terrors' and 'struggling spirit') or sketched a frightening setting ('dreary vale'), and the language continues to be used in this way throughout the translation.

In fact all the features of the story seem to serve the function of revealing the reactions of the protagonist's sensibility. The appearance of Virgil is a case in point. Dante's

dinanzi alli occhi mi si fu offerto
chi per lungo silenzio parea fioco.   (I 62-3)[19]

compresses in two lines a number of ideas. The suddenness of the apparition is
similar to the manner in which the three beasts present themselves to the
protagonist, and reminds us of the nature of the poem's opening – what we are
shown is really a vision, but presented as action. The choice of the word 'fioco'
('faint') has been seen as inevitable,[20] since Dante would here be trying to express
distance and therefore depth of perspective, in terms of the weakness of the voice
as well as of the weakness of the light illuminating the figure. This all makes the
image doubly effective: it suggests the physical effect of distance, but it also fits
in perfectly with the allegorical implications of Virgil as reason, whose power over
the protagonist at that point is faint. Hayley has

> A manly figure my glad eyes survey'd,
> Whose voice was like the whisper of a lute.

If the first line suggests a rescuing knight, the second adds to this image the
pastoral figure of a shepherd-poet. In any case, the emphasis here is less on the
appearance of the new figure than on its effect on the protagonist. He finds in
Virgil two sources of comfort: manly strength to reassure him, gentleness to
soothe his sensitivity. Moreover, the scene establishes a contrast between Virgil
and the protagonist which turns the latter into an almost feminine presence.
Certainly from his very first speech the protagonist reveals his nature as one given
to extremes of language and passions, and not at all Dantesque:

> Art thou that Virgil? thou! that copious fount
>   Of richest eloquence, so clear, so bright?
>   I answered, blushing at his kind account;   81
> O thou! of Poets the pure guide and light!
>   Now let me profit by that fond esteem
>   Which kept thy song for ever in my sight!   84
> Thou art my Master! thou my Bard supreme,
>   From whom alone my fond ambition drew
>   That purer style which I my glory deem!   87
> O! from this Beast, so hideous to the view,
>   Save me! O save me! Thou much-honour'd Sage!
>   For growing terrors all my power subdue. – [21]

The eloquence and exclamatory appeal are not those of a hero of drama, but of
the passionate night-musings of Edward Young's speaker, facing apocalyptic
prophecy of perdition, in his *Night Thoughts*. But the blushing appeal to the manly
figure for preservation from the Beast goes too far to resemble the pattern of the
hero of even the most sentimental fiction, and places the speaker in the feminine

role of a heroine of a gothic tale or other romance, in the grip of the typical villain – the gothic version of Beauty and the Beast.

Such is Hayley's protagonist, and though he is different from Dante's, he remains consistent throughout the translation. Hayley attributed to him a particular role, manner and way of speaking and maintained it throughout his version. For example, whereas alliteration is used for the speech of various characters (and thus in Canto II, where Virgil reports Beatrice's words to him, she urges him to teach Dante wisdom 'with thy soft soul-soothing speech'), the exclamatory style is reserved throughout the three cantos for the protagonist's voice, and helps distinguish it from the narrator's voice.

On the basis of the distinction I have outlined between Hayley's protagonist and narrator, the opening of Canto II must be spoken by the latter. In Dante, this opening passage is considered to be the beginning of the poem proper, after the prologue of the first canto, and it does, in fact, include a number of features central to the whole poem. A comparison of the original with Hayley's translation will be sufficient to confirm Hayley's awareness of the dual presence in the poem, and it will show how, in spite of this awareness, Hayley was unable to produce a version close in spirit to its original, both because of his own limitations as an artist, and because of the state of Dante scholarship at the time:

> Lo giorno se n'andava, e l'aere bruno
>   togieva li animai che sono in terra
>   dalle fatiche loro; e io sol uno   3
> m'apparecchiava a sostener la guerra
>   sí del cammino e sí della pietate,
>   che ritrarrà la mente che non erra.   6
> O muse, o alto ingegno, or m'aiutate;
>   o mente che scrivesti ciò ch'io vidi,
>   qui si parrà la tua nobilitate.   (II 1-9)[22]

The experience of the protagonist and of the writer is summarized in line three, where 'io sol uno' ('I myself alone') stresses not just the loneliness of the protagonist, but also his unique mission – and consequently the fact that he becomes the only human being on the journey, and therefore our representative and our eye-witness. Lines six and seven move us smoothly from the experience of the protagonist to the work of the narrator. It is remarkable that Dante here does not invoke a specific Muse such as Urania, or a more Christian muse, but three powers of man: his own 'alto ingegno' ('high genius'), human memory which was considered to be unerring, and the 'muses' which, in this context, simply mean the artist's skills and knowledge.[23] The invocation, therefore, is to the man as poet and not to any supernatural force. So both protagonist and narrator are specifically introduced in these lines, and the interplay between the two figures is quite complex, as a brief look at the tenses used will show.

In the first four lines, the past tense is that of the protagonist's experience: the day waned, and Dante prepared himself for the journey. Line six looks to the future from the perspective of the journey: memory 'ritrarrà' ('will report') what happened. Line seven is in the present tense, because the narrator is invoking the support of all his powers for the present task of writing: 'or m'aiutate', 'help me now'. These present and future tenses link up with line nine, 'qui si parrà' ('here will be shown'), since the unfolding story will demonstrate the skills of the poet – but between lines seven and nine we have two past tenses, 'scrivesti' and 'vidi' in line eight ('wrote' or 'recorded' and 'saw'), jerking us sharply back to the past experience of the protagonist and his 'real' seeing. It is therefore a complex patterning of tenses, underlining the separateness of the two moments in time, but also the fact that both protagonist and narrator have to face a struggle and that they are unified by this unique mission.

Hayley seems to have read Dante's lines carefully, and to have understood some of his most important effects:

The day was sinking, and the dusky air
 On all the animals of earth bestow'd
 Rest from their labours. I alone prepare   3
To meet new toil, both from my dreary road,
 And pious wish to paint in worthy phrase
 The Unerring Mind, and his divine abode.   6
O sacred Muses! now my genius raise!
 O Memory, who writest what I saw,
 From hence shall spring thy ever-during praise!

The passage moves with a rhythm similar to that of the original. In particular, Hayley reproduces Dante's first person singular in 'I alone', and places it in a position similar to Dante's, so that it receives considerable emphasis, and initiates the sentence and the thrust which will be completed by the following tercet. Moreover, he clearly recognizes and underlines the presence of two separate moments in time. Two points in the translation of this passage indicate this. Both are, in fact, mistranslations, and therefore show even more clearly in which direction Hayley's thoughts were moving. First, in line eight, Dante had said that memory 'recorded what I saw', with the two tenses referring to seeing and writing both in the past, since the act of writing referred not to the poet's activity but to the faithful recording by memory of what the protagonist saw. Hayley, however, translates these two past tenses with one present – referring to the writing – and one past tense – referring to the seeing: 'writest what I saw'. Secondly, in line five, Dante's protagonist had prepared himself to face a dual struggle: with the journey and with the 'pietate' (the pity, the sorrow and sympathy he would feel for the damned), both being aspects of the protagonist's experience. Hayley, on the other hand, translates the dual struggle in such a way that it refers to two different ideas: the journey and the writing. Hence the toil is 'both from my dreary road,/ and pious wish to paint in worthy phrase...', where the first line stresses the protagonist's task and the second the writer's. The recognition of two moments in time and two different activities, however, does not enable Hayley to realize that there are, accordingly, two different realities, or two perspectives on reality. In Dante, the journey is a realistic story, but also important for the pattern of love it will reveal; in Hayley, the journey is more allegorical – a 'dreary road' – and its recording in writing becomes a poem with a moral – 'pious', 'worthy'.

What this all seems to show is, in the first place, that Hayley can be a good reader of Dante, but as a writer he is either unable to create vivid images of reality, or simply did not aim to do so. Secondly, it shows that Hayley channels his insights within current ideas – in this case the idea that Dante's poem is allegorical and didactic. In fact it is easy to show that Hayley's version is determined by a variety of current set ideas and prejudices about Dante. In the passage above, for example, Dante is calling upon all his powers to assist him in the difficult task ahead – his memory, his high intellect and all his knowledge and art. Hayley does, in line 8, correctly translate 'mente' as 'memory' rather than, as the word would be understood in modern and eighteenth-century Italian, 'mind'. But he does not do the same in line 6, where 'mente che non erra' ('unerring memory') is translated as 'Unerring Mind'. Clearly, in the first place, Hayley did not know that the memory was simply believed, in Dante's time, to be an instrument which automatically recorded what it met, and, secondly, he assumed that in Dante's religious and medieval world only God was unerring, and that Dante must have been referring to His mental faculties, not his own. Hence Hayley translates the phrase with a capitalized 'Unerring Mind', and since he must pad out his line he adds 'and his divine abode', definitely introducing the presence of God.

The difference is not a minor one. For, in the first place, the stress in Dante on the powers of memory and their accuracy implies that the journey actually took place in reality. Secondly, the introduction of God and heaven at this point goes counter to Dante's careful planning, which keeps God mostly out of his poem about Hell. And, most important of all, Dante's lines centre the powers of the writer in the man himself; no outside force dictates his words and even the muses are as it were internalized, since 'o alto ingegno' seems a paraphrase of 'o muse'. Dante, it must be noticed, is not expressing excessive personal pride, as Sapegno correctly points out in his commentary, since memory simply was believed to be unerring. He is, however, in this passage clearly placing the man, the poet, at the centre of the creating process – at least for the poetry of Hell. But, if you only see Dante as a man of the barbarous Middle Ages, the correct reading of a passage such as the one under consideration is an impossibility, and therefore those emphatic lines which claim such an important role for the poet remain quite inscrutable to Hayley. So, even a translator who had proved himself sensitive to some elements within the poetry becomes fettered by the common ideas current in the culture of his time.

An analysis of Hayley's rendering of Canto III confirms the nature of his protagonist, and adds a clearer picture of his version of Dante's world; moreover, it highlights Hayley's inability to move away from English models in his rendering of Dante's foreign poetry. This last aspect of Hayley's translation will be looked at first, and again the opening of the canto provides sufficient material for the analysis. These famous lines from the *Commedia* are more than the stern warning to the entering soul they are usually taken to be:

PER ME SI VA NELLA CITTÀ DOLENTE,
PER ME SI VA NELL'ETTERNO DOLORE,
PER ME SI VA TRA LA PERDUTA GENTE.   3
GIUSTIZIA MOSSE IL MIO ALTO FATTORE:
FECEMI LA DIVINA POTESTATE,
LA SOMMA SAPIENZA E 'L PRIMO AMORE.   (III 1-6)[24]

The second tercet has been seen as a fundamental statement of belief on which the whole structure of the *Inferno* is based. This tercet explains the nature of the relationship between God and Hell, and is subdivided into two subordinate thoughts: that the Maker was moved by justice, and that Hell was built by the power of the Father, the wisdom of the Son and the love of the Holy Spirit. To a modern mind both thoughts are difficult to accept. That perfect justice should have created punishments such as those one finds in Dante seems a contradiction in terms; similarly, that the creation of Hell does not just demonstrate God's power, but is also a reflection of his wisdom and love does not make sense, now that these two latter words are taken to have more to do with mercy than with punishment.

Hayley's translation rearranges these elements, and eliminates the distinction between the reason for the existence of Hell, that is perfect justice, and the powers of the Trinity the creation of Hell is a proof of:

"Thro' me you pass to Mourning's dark domain;
Thro' me to scenes where Grief must ever pine;
Thro' me, to Misery's devoted train.   3
Justice and power in my Great Founder join,

And love and wisdom all his fabrics rear;
Wisdom above controul, and love divine!"   6

In fact Hayley changes the rhythm, the tone, and the meaning of Dante's lines. In the original he finds poetry of reason rather than passion, and in this case Hayley cannot but turn to Pope and write with the tone of the critic who tries to persuade, rather than of the prophet-poet who states a tenet of faith. Dante's straight, almost catechistic statement of a concept, a formula of belief, becomes, in Hayley's translation, an expression of clear, energetic judgement. The second tercet almost acquires the ring of a heroic couplet, since the third line ('Wisdom above controul, and love divine'), neatly divided into two parts, only repeats the ideas of the second line ('And love and wisdom all his fabrics rear'). The repetition itself suggests a thinking mind, clarifying a previous statement. There is more here of the eighteenth century and of Pope than of Dante.

However, the speaking voice, which is here measured and controlled, has, very inconsistently, opened the canto with a different tone. The very first tercet introduced, it must have seemed to Hayley, the setting and the people of Hell, and he accordingly inserts in those specific points phrases picked from the language of allegory and romance which he consistently uses for the setting, and the crowd of the damned. Thus, Dante's 'città dolente' ('woeful city') becomes 'Mourning's dark domain', and simple words like 'dolore' and 'gente' ('grief' and 'people') become 'pine' and 'train'. Dante's tightly-knit unit of verse above Hell's gate becomes split, in Hayley, by the use of two different modes, and so, between the poetry of judgement and persuasion on the one hand, and the poetry of romance on the other, Dante is lost. This pull between extremes seems to be a characteristic of Hayley; it is not just a question of his translation, since what we see him doing here is exactly what he had already done in the *Triumphs*.

Thus, in spite of his insights, and partly because of the varied and different models he turns to – Spenser, Young and Pope – Hayley distorts Dante considerably. The meaning of the original is misrendered also in less important ways, which, nevertheless, still affect the character of the protagonist as well as the world he finds himself in. Only a few lines further down from the passage just considered, in Canto III, the traveller, having crossed Hell's gate, is encircled by the cries of the sinners:

Quivi sospiri, pianti e alti guai
   risonavan per l'aere sanza stelle,
   per ch'io al cominciar ne lagrimai.   24
Diverse lingue, orribili favelle,
   parole d'odio, accenti d'ira,
   voci alte e fioche, e suon di man con elle   (III 22-27)[25]

> There sighs, and wailings, and severest woes,
>   Deeply resounded through the starless air;
>   And as I first advanced, my fears arose.   24
> Each different cry, the murmuring notes of care,
>   Accents of misery, and words of ire,
>   With all the sounds of discord and despair,   27

In some ways this is a literal translation; line 26, for example, 'accents of misery and words of ire', follows the original closely, though with an odd inversion. But Hayley completely disregards Dante's stress on the strange languages and pronunciations, the unintelligible noise which must be so disturbing to a poet, and only stresses the sorrow and anger expressed. He cuts out line 25, and also the vivid description of the range of high and low sounds and the clapping of hands, and what remains are 'cry', 'notes of care', and 'sounds of discord and despair'. The stress on sorrow and even despair would lead one to surmise an emphasis on the protagonist's feelings, but this is not the case. Before the noise is described, we are immediately prepared for the protagonist's reaction, which is quite different from that of Dante's protagonist. The latter is moved to sympathize, the former is only frightened by it all: 'ne lacrimai' ('they made me weep') becomes 'my fears arose'. This simplification of Dante's protagonist becomes a central failure of Hayley's protagonist. In Canto III Dante begins a psychological sketch of the protagonist which he will change and develop in the course of the journey through Hell. His initial pity, aroused by the depth of sorrow and number of sinners he witnesses, will slowly be corrupted by the experience of Hell. Hayley's portrayal clearly reveals his lack of response to Dante's complex picture.

Throughout the rest of the third canto, so important in *Inferno* because it introduces poet, damned souls and Hell itself, the same is true. Hayley stresses the sensational, the gothic terror and the ranting of passions, reinforced by his underplaying of any thoughtful element of the poetry. The description of the crowd of sinners and their meeting with Charon is a case in point. Dante's measured rendering of the Virgilian simile of the autumn leaves to describe the sinners (ll. 112-118) is a moment of stillness in the noisy and busy scene of Canto III; the fall of the leaves in autumn is touched with the feeling of personal loss, when the branch of the tree is personified as it sees all its leaves lying on the ground. In Hayley, however, the branch relinquishes its leaves 'to the whirlwind'. In Dante, Charon's address to the souls is, after all, a factual description of his task:

> io vengo per menarvi all'altra riva
> nelle tenebre etterne, in caldo e 'n gelo   (III 86-7)[26]

Hayley's rendering is more in tune with the gothic horror of the scene:

> I come to waft you to a different lot;
> To Torture's realm, with endless horror dark:

Hayley adds the idea of torture and the word 'horror'; even a plain 'disse' further down ('said', l. 91) must be enlivened into 'In wrath he cried'. These changes suggest a more horrific scene, but also a less concrete one. In the original we sense the existence of an alien setting – eternal, dark, with extremes of heat and cold. But Hayley's setting is the frightening kingdom of Torture, and the river bank becomes abstracted into the place of doom. In fact, Hayley's world is so vague and mental that the protagonist is not directly affected by it, and the language contributes to the creation of distance between place and central character.

The conclusion of Canto III shows how uninvolved Hayley's protagonist is in the physical world he finds himself in. In the original, Virgil explains Charon's task, and an earthquake follows:

> Finito questo, la buia campagna
>   tremò sí forte, che dello spavento
>   la mente di sudore ancor si bagna.   132
> La terra lacrimosa diede vento,
>   che balenò una luce vermiglia
>   la qual mi vinse ciascun sentimento;
> e caddi come l'uom che'l sonno piglia.   (III 130-136)[27]

The earthquake has an immediate, automatic effect on the protagonist's very body; the red lightning causes him to faint. In Hayley, the protagonist feels at one remove:

> He paus'd; and horrors of approaching ill
>   Now made the mournful troop to stand aghast,
>   Their fears yet strike me with a deadly chill!   132
> The groaning earth sent forth a hollow blast,
>   And flash'd a fiery glare of gloomy red!
>   The horrid scene my fainting power surpast: 135
> I fell, and, as in sleep, my senses fled.

The hostile presence of the 'buia campagna' ('murky countryside') disappears and is turned into the sinners' anticipation of a worse destiny. The protagonist's fear is a reflection of theirs, and a fairly pale reflection at that, since the phrase 'deadly chill' sounds very much like a stock response. The generalized descriptions Hayley uses distance the experience further. In Dante, the light makes him faint, and the grammatical link between phenomenon and person is direct – '[the wind] flashed a carmine light/ *that* left me utterly insensible' (emphasis added). In Hayley, on the other hand, there are two aspects of language which distance the event from its effect. First of all, the description of the phenomenon is wrapped in adjectives which makes it less visual ('fiery', 'gloomy'). Furthermore, there is no direct link between the lightning and the fainting, for the whole passage, with fears, anticipations and blasts is summarized as 'the horrid scene', and it is this summary that overwhelms the protagonist. Together with the lack of a physical setting more than one feature of language contributes to the lack of vividness in the world of Hayley's Hell, and, as a consequence, to the nature of the protagonist's experience.

For his translation of Dante's cantos Hayley uses different models and styles. The latter part of Canto III is more gothic than the opening of the canto, and more gothic than Cantos I and II, the gothic being the style Hayley selects as most appropriate for Charon, the spectacular setting of Hell, and the damned. In fact the gothic style is usually merged into the more encompassing visionary style as used by the eighteenth-century Miltonians such as Young. In specific instances, Hayley also adopts the manner of Pope. What is particularly striking about all this is the deliberateness of Hayley's selection and application of a particular style – the same deliberateness noticed in the *Triumphs*. In both his own poem and the translation from Dante Hayley attempts to build up a whole from many parts, to find a unifying perspective, to write a poem which can hold together the many different strands of the poetry of the day.

The ultimate failure of Hayley's verse in terms of greatness is probably due exactly to this deliberateness. For Hayley saw with great clarity and objectivity the nature of eighteenth-century English poetry, and his was a critical rather than creative mind. In fact, Hayley's most lasting contribution to the fortune of Dante in England resides in the central position he had on the literary scene and within the critical movements of his age. For the discussion of the previous pages has shown that, beyond the distortions pointed out, Hayley understood some basic issues from Dante – as he understood some contemporary poets like Cowper and Blake, and some poets from the past such as Milton. In one of the few references to Hayley in recent years Joseph A. Wittreich makes an important statement:

> Though greatly misunderstood by neoclassical poets (and some modern ones), the Milton tradition was comprehended at the end of the eighteenth century by William Cowper and William Hayley and was relayed to Blake by them. Together Hayley and Cowper sharpened Blake's comprehension of Milton and of the tradition that he shaped....[28]

The Miltonic tradition the critic refers to is the tradition of visionary poetry which combines epic with prophecy. It makes a revolutionary use of previous traditions, which in itself sets in motion a new emerging tradition followed by poets like Shelley. The analysis of Hayley's poem and his translation from *Inferno* show that Dante offers to the eighteenth-century reader and writer a framework and a mythology that can make English poetry new. The last stage in the process of confrontation between Dante and English poetry, when integration takes place, occurs in the work of William Blake. It is in the discussion on Blake – the las analytical section of this study – that the contribution of Hayley to Dante's presence in English literature will become fully clear.

6

Charles Rogers

A collector of books and art objects, Fellow of the Society of Antiquaries and of the Royal Society, author of *A Collection of Prints in Imitation of Drawings*, and a friend of Sir Joshua Reynolds, who painted his portrait, Charles Rogers (1711-1784) published his translation of *Inferno* – the first English translation of the complete *cantica* – anonymously in 1782, the same year as Hayley's version of the first three cantos. Hayley himself had been urged to produce 'an entire translation of Dante', but had been doubtful as to how interesting that would prove to the public, his uncertainty and caution being illustrated by his remark that 'perhaps the reception of these cantos may discover to the Translator the sentiments of the public'.[1] As it turned out, Hayley produced no further translations of Dante, and this suggests that the reception of his three cantos was not favourable. This is only speculation; but Rogers' translation certainly met with a cold, or at least indifferent, response. Surveys of translations include the name of Rogers only as a footnote. Also, there seems to be no extant review of this translation, and no references to it in the correspondence collected by Toynbee. Toynbee himself quotes a comment, in which an unnamed contemporary of Rogers claims on his behalf that 'he chiefly attended to giving the sense of his author with fidelity; the character of a Poet not seeming to have been the object of his ambition'. But Toynbee himself strongly disagrees with this evaluation, claiming that, in addition to being 'entirely devoid of any spark of poetry, [the translation] has not even the merit of being faithful...' (*DEL* 383, *Dante Studies* 294-5). Lines 1-24, and 88-142 from Canto V – respectively the description of Minos and the encounter with Francesca – follow as examples. Since Toynbee adds no comment to explain what he means precisely, we must ourselves read these passages in order to discover to what extent both Rogers' presumed claim and Toynbee's comment are correct.

A comparison of Rogers' version of the Minos passage with the original certainly brings out minor divergences. I remain with Toynbee's example:

> Cosí discesi dal cerchio primaio
>   giú nel secondo, che men luogo cinghia,
>   e tanto piú dolor, che punge a guaio.   3
> Stavvi Minòs orribilmente, e ringhia:
>   essamina le colpe nell'entrata;

giudica e manda secondo ch'avvinghia.   6
Dico che quando l'anima mal nata
  li vien dinanzi, tutta si confessa;
  e quel conoscitor delle peccata   9
vede qual luogo d'inferno è da essa;
  cignesi con la coda tante volte
  quantunque gradi vuol che giú sia messa   (V 1-12)[2]

From the first Circle we descended down
To that which was of a more narrow space,
Where Pain from ev'ry one excited cries.
Horribly grinning Minos, standing there,
Examines at their entrance each one's crime,   5
Tries them, and passes judgement in their turns.
Whenever a guilty Soul before him comes
It all confesses: He the proper place,
Well, knowing, that of Hell's to be their due,
So many times his Tail around him twists,   10
As the Degrees to which he'd have it cast.[3]

The initial paradox Dante had made between the 'men luogo' and 'tanto piú dolor' ('a smaller space' and 'so much more of pain') is missing here; also, there is no mention, in line 6, of Minos' way of making clear to which circle the sinner must go by wrapping his tail round himself a certain number of times, corresponding to the number of the circle to which the sinner must go – 'secondo ch'avvinghia', ('according as he girds himself'). But many translators, Sisson for one, also omit this clause, probably because it is a detail which is described more fully in the original in the subsequent lines. These Rogers translates faithfully.

He also translates faithfully the exchange of words between Minos and the travellers which follows immediately after. Here one may regret that Rogers can produce nothing better than 'For who would do this, can do whatever he wills./ More obstacles it is not fit to raise' (ll. 21-2), as a rendering of Dante's concentrated 'Vuolsi cosí colà dove si puote/ ciò che si vuole, e piú non dimandare' ('It is so willed where all is possible/ if it is willed: and ask no more'). But this is a question of manner rather than matter – lack of poetry, rather than of faithfulness.

In the Francesca episode similar minor divergences stand out immediately. Rogers' Francesca describes the 'aere perso' ('darkened air', where 'perso' is a mixture of purple and black) as 'azure'; also, she does not wish, as Dante's Francesca does, that she could pray for the traveller's peace, but more plainly 'for you'; and she does not just admit that the damned souls in her circle had painted the world with blood, but adds that they 'defiled' the world, and with their own blood.

Alongside these minor differences there are grosser mistakes, and one occurs in Francesca's famous threefold reference to love. The first such reference in particular is muddled by Rogers.

> "Amor, ch'al cor gentil ratto s'apprende,   100
>   prese costui della bella persona
>   che mi fu tolta; e 'l modo ancor m'offende."   (V 100-102)[4]

Three points mistranslated by Rogers can be isolated. First, in Dante Francesca speaks, as is well known, in terms which are deliberately impersonal. Secondly, she stresses that Paolo fell in love with her beauty – that is, her appearance. Finally, the last phrase in the quotation is a point of discussion among critics: many take it to mean, as Sisson does, that the manner of her death still hurts her feelings; while others – Sapegno among them – take 'modo' to refer to the intensity of the passion, and therefore take the phrase to mean that Francesca still feels the power of that love. In Rogers' version all three points are rendered differently:

> "Love, which possesses soon a courteous breast,
> "Seiz'd on my handsome Paramour, whose loss
> "I yet lament, reflecting on the act:"   (V 89-91)

This is more personal than the original, since Francesca here reflects and laments, and introduces her lover with a phrase appreciative of his appearance. Rogers has misread the original, and assumes that Francesca is referring not to her own, but her lover's beauty. Consequently the loss mentioned becomes Francesca's loss of Paolo – in spite of the obvious fact that they are still together.

The next gross departure from the original occurs towards the end of the episode. Francesca recounts how she and Paolo were reading the story of the love between Lancelot and Guinevere, how it was this reading that led them to reveal their love to each other, and how, as a result, she and Paolo did not read on, but were themselves carried away by the passion expressed at that point of the story. It is here that she interrupts her tale to inveigh against the writer of love stories, and against the book they were reading, which, like the intermediary Gallehault in the story of Lancelot and Guinevere, made them reveal their love for one another:[5]

> "Galeotto fu il libro e chi lo scrisse:
>   quel giorno piú non vi leggemmo avante."   (V 137-138)[6]

Again Rogers produces an ambiguous version, probably because he could not make out what the original said:

"The Writer, Galeotto, nam'd the Book.
"But from that day we never read in't more."   (V 123-4)

In Dante Francesca's exclamation is something between a literary allusion and a curse, and this accords well with the rhetoric of her speech. Rogers makes of the exclamation a plain statement, so that 'Galeotto' seems to refer to the actual name of the writer of the book, or perhaps its title. In either case, Rogers has misread the original and produced a version which means very little, so that one remains in doubt as to what opposition the following 'but' introduces.

One must admit, therefore, that Rogers does distort the original considerably in places; but there are two more observations to be made. First, most of the divergences are not a question of choice, and of an eighteenth-century free attitude to translation, but seem due to poor knowledge of fourteenth-century Italian, and therefore are real errors. Secondly, the lack of faithfulness observed in the Minos and Francesca passages has been established on the basis of the original, and this is somewhat unfair to Rogers. A more correct and realistic procedure would be to compare Rogers' version with the versions of Dante which had already appeared on the English scene. Checking Rogers' version against the deliberate changes which Hayley brought to the first cantos, and which the other translators brought to the Ugolino episode, shows that Rogers' version is, relatively speaking, accurate. A few examples will suffice.

In Canto I, Hayley had dramatically changed the tone of the protagonist's speech to Virgil (see above p. 97, also for the original and its translation in note). Rogers' protagonist is certainly frightened, and asks for help, but his speech is not turned into the address of a gothic or dramatic hero, as was the case with Hayley's version:

"Are you that Virgil, You that copious spring   70
"Of Eloquence, which many streams supplies?
"O Light and honour of all other Bards,
"Regard the study, and the ardent love
"With which I have attended to your works.
"You are my Master; you are only He   75
"On whom I've formed that beauty of my style
"Which fame and honour to my verse has brought.
"Behold the Beast who caus'd me to turn back;
"Defend me from her with your counsel sage,
"For my whole frame yet trembles at her sight."   (I 70-80)

This speech is closer to the original than Hayley's, being more subdued. Moving to Canto II, we have already observed that in the opening passage Hayley introduced the power of God as inspiration for the poet, whereas the original had listed three powers of man (see p. 100 above). Rogers' version follows the original more closely:

> O Muses, O my lofty Genius join'd
> With Memory, to transcribe what I saw,
> Assist: so shall your pow'rs immense appear.   (II 7-9)

Here Rogers also maintains the idea of the writer as a scribe copying from the book of memory, and therefore shows considerable understanding of some possible implications of the original. In the same passage, Hayley made a distinction between the seeing of the protagonist and the writing by the author, but neglected to mention the pity for the souls. Rogers keeps the distinction as it is in the original:

> When I alone prepared to sustain
> The great fatigues of a laborious way,
> And those in torments to commiserate;   (II 3-5)

Similarly, in Canto III Hayley stressed the fear of the protagonist and left out the pity for the damned; he also stressed the frightening cries of grief, and left out the strange languages (see p. 103 above). Rogers' version is literal in both cases:

> There Sighs, and Cries, and horrid Howlings mix'd   20
> With Shrieks, re-echoed through the starless air,
> Which frequent *tears of pity* from me drew.
> *Varieties of tongues*, reproaching Taunts,
> Words grief expressing, Accents full of ire,
> Voices both loud and hoarse, and clapping Hands   (III 20-25,emphases added)

In the very opening of the same canto, Hayley changed the catechistic statement of the creation of Hell by the three persons of the Trinity, which were listed one by one in the original, and produced, instead, a persuasive reasoning (see p. 102 above). Rogers' version is similar to the original:

> "With strictest justice is this portal made,
> "By Power, Wisdom, and by Love divine."   (III 4-5)

Leaving the first three cantos and the comparison with Hayley's version of Dante, and moving to the Ugolino episode, we see that Rogers does not add colour or gore to his Ugolino:

> His mouth this Sinner from the fell repast
> Withdrew, and wip'd it with that hair he'd torn
> From the head's hinder part; then thus began: (XXXIII 1-3)

The same restraint is maintained throughout the tale, and continues on into the curse of Pisa.

Clearly Toynbee was inaccurate in his attack on Rogers' faithfulness to the original, neglecting to take into account some necessary historical perspective. Rogers' version might indeed deserve to be forgotten as a poem in its own right, but it still possesses some merit, and, for two main reasons, is of importance for this study. First, its publication means that by 1782 there was a complete version, however inaccurate in places, of the basic 'matter' of *Inferno*. Passages such as the base action of Dante's protagonist towards Fra Alberigo were available to the English reader in a plain English version:

> "But now you should extend your hand this way,   145
> "And ope my Eyes." This I did not perform:
> To be a Knave to him was acting right.   (XXXIII 145-7)

This plainness is not only a feature of the language used, but also of the matter presented, which has no sensational additions; and so Rogers' translation introduces, for example, the first plain Ugolino to the English reader.

The second reason why Rogers' version is relevant to this study is that it left very little trace and was, we must therefore conclude, unpopular in its own time. The interesting point here is that Rogers' stance as a translator – his attempt to provide a literal version of a past work – and his choice of blank verse create a connection between his *Inferno* and Henry Francis Cary's translation of Dante's *Commedia*, published as the *Vision* in 1814. But Cary's work became a classic within the translator's lifetime. The contrast is very striking. Cary's version can, at this point, serve as a term of comparison which is useful for clarifying not only the nature of Rogers' presentation of the protagonist and of the world of *Inferno*, but also the nature of Rogers' achievement. This is the opening of *Inferno* in Rogers' and in Cary's version:

> When in my middle Stage of Life, I found
> Myself entangl'd in a wood obscure,
> Having the right path miss'd: but to relate
> The horrid wildness of that rugged wood
> Renews a dread, which that of death itself   5
> Can scarce exceed: yet I will first recount
> Those things I met with, ere I shall declare
> The salutary good I after found.
> How I came in it I can't well explain,
> So much had Sleep my faculties of mind   10
> Confus'd, when I abandon'd the true way.
>   Arriving at a Mountain's foot, whose base
> Bounded the valley which had fill'd my heart
> With fear before unfelt, I looked up,
> And saw its top cloathed with shining Rays
> Of that bright Planet which the right way shews.   (Rogers)

In the middle of this our mortal life,
I found me in a gloomy wood, astray
Gone from the path direct: and e'en to tell
It were no easy task, how savage wild
That forest, how robust and rough its growth,   5
Which to remember only, my dismay
Renews, in bitterness not far from death.
Yet to discourse of what there good befel
All else will I relate discover'd there.
    How first I enter'd it I scarce can say,   10
Such sleepy dullness in that instant weigh'd
My senses down, when the true path I left,
But when a mountain's foot I reach'd, where clos'd
The valley, that had pierc'd my heart with dread,
I look'd aloft, and saw its shoulders broad   15
Already vested with that planet's beam,
Who leads all wanderers safe through every way.[7]   (Cary)

In Cary's version, one soon notices, the language used is somewhat more elevated than in Rogers' version. In line 14 of the passage above, Rogers' 'fear' is Cary's 'dread', and the former's 'looked up' becomes 'look'd aloft'. Similarly in line 15 Rogers refers to the top of the mountain as 'its top', but Cary adds personification and metaphor in 'his shoulders broad'.

Rogers writes in a manner which is relatively plain, as other passages throughout the translation show. Individual instances of this simplicity cumulatively contribute to the nature of Rogers' presentation of the protagonist, his drawing of the setting, and their coming together in the action of the story. I shall briefly look at each of these three features in turn. The passage following the one just quoted provides a good example of Rogers' presentation of the protagonist:

As he who, just recover'd from a storm,
Near Breathless from the sea, attains the shore,   20
Turns back to view the per'lous waves escap'd;
My mind, while yet I ran, oft on the road
Reflected, in which none were left alive.
My body having with some rest refresh'd,
I took my way along the barren Strand;   25
The foot supporting me being still behind.
    From the Hill's first ascent a Panther rush'd,
Both light and nimble, with her spotted hide: (I 19-28)

From the simile which opens the passage emerges a protagonist who presents himself in steady stages. Rogers makes a clear juxtaposition between 'My mind' and 'My body', opening respectively lines 22 and 24, and his protagonist emerges from these reflections upon himself, steps onto the scene, and comes into action – 'I ran', 'I took', and then, suddenly, the first beast appears, and the action continues. In Cary's version, the mind and body of the protagonist become 'my spirit' and 'my weary frame', and introduce a passage in which fear and tiredness colour the bare action with feeling.

Rogers' protagonist, therefore, is immediately present on the scene. The scene itself, moreover, is described in plain terms which create immediacy:

> 'Twas now the early Morn, and the Sun rose
> Among those Stars which him accompanied,   (I 32-33)

Cary's language is more elevated, and therefore the description is more distant and mediated:

> The hour was morning's prime, and on his way
> Aloft the sun ascended with those stars
> That with him were...   (I 35-7)

Rogers' plainer protagonist and setting meet in an action which is also direct. The appearance of the animals is a case in point; Rogers' panther 'rushed' on the scene in the very first line of a passage where each line adds a fact to the story. Cary's panther 'appear'd' in the third line of his version of the same passage, in which the words are structured so as to produce a rhetorical effect. In Rogers, it is the plot that matters, and the experience of the protagonist that is solely on the stage. In Cary, it is the activity of the writer that strikes the reader most. The arrival of the second beast, the lion, provides a further example. In Rogers, the lion enters the scene in a manner which is similar to the panther's: '... soon engag'd my fear/ A Lion tow'rds me running...' (ll. 39-40). Both protagonist and animal are solidly present, facing each other, on Rogers' stage, and the lion is really frightening as it runs and rages. Again a comparison with Cary brings out the greater immediacy of Roger's scene, for in Cary everything happens at one remove: '... in view/ A lion came, 'gainst me, as it appear'd...'. Here the last phrase distances the appearance of the animal, whose presence is really only seen as a reflection in the fear of the protagonist, and therefore is mostly a tool the writer uses to add effect to his tale.

The analysis of Rogers' translation up to this point has shown that its main features are a relative faithfulness to the matter of the original, and both immediacy and conciseness in the presentation of the protagonist and world of Dante. The claim made on behalf of Rogers, that he was interested in the matter and made no pretence of being a poet, seems valid in this respect. Yet Rogers uses the blank verse paragraph, whose lines are iambic pentameters, and he uses inversions of the normal word order and enjambments. All these are some of the more mechanical aspects of the Miltonic style, as it was understood by some practitioners in the eighteenth century, and they are also used by Cary.

A closer look at Rogers' use of these features, however, shows that Rogers' application of the pseudo-Miltonic style was particularly limited. His blank verse paragraph, for instance, follows closely the narrative movement of the story. So, in the opening of *Inferno*, Cary starts a new paragraph when the speaker begins to describe his experience, but Rogers joins this passage to the previous description of the speaker's uncertain state of mind, and begins a new paragraph when the speaker begins to describe the hill, the valley, and the time of day. The rest of the translation is also divided into paragraphs according to the narrative of what happens in Hell rather than according to rhetorical or emotional statements (the speech by Ugolino, for example, being uninterrupted until the protagonist's curse on Pisa).

As for the iambic pentameter, Rogers' lines are regular in so far as each line has, generally, ten syllables, and Rogers varies his spelling in order to make the count regular. So, in the opening passage, line 8 ('How I came in it I can't well explain') has the short form for 'cannot', and 'looked' and 'clothed', in lines 14 and 15, maintain the full spelling (rather than the usual form with the apostrophe) so that each line has ten syllables. But such manipulations are very simple, compared to the padding with elaborate words as used by Hayley, and have little effect on the sense of the line. Moreover, although the lines can be scanned fairly regularly, it seems slightly artificial to do so, since many of the lines (line 8 just quoted being a case in point) retain a conversational, informal sentence stress, the plain diction contributing to this effect. In Rogers, therefore, the iambic pentameter retains much of its basic speech-rhythm. Cary's opening lines, by way of contrast, are very carefully worked out. So, his first line opens with two trisyllabic feet (or anapaestic feet), and his lines 3, 6 and 8 open with an inverted iamb (or trochee) – these being the two standard variants of the basic iambic pentameter line (see above pp. 112-3 for the text). Cary, that is, works as a versifier, while Rogers is content to use only the most basic framework of the blank verse and to keep his lines as close to speech as is compatible with verse. The inversions and enjambments in Rogers' verse follow the same restrained style. In comparison with Cary's, the inversions are far fewer, and the enjambments increase the narrative movement, rather than vary the rhythm of the lines.[8]

Yet Rogers is definitely using a form of the eighteenth-century Miltonic style, and this becomes clear in those passages which an eighteenth-century reader (or translator) would consider 'purple passages'. Whenever the story reaches a climax, or a character steps into the foreground, or whenever a great person such as Virgil or a mythological figure speak, Rogers' diction and tone take flight and become more formal and majestic.[9]

Rogers' verse confirms an observation made on the basis of an analysis of Hayley's translation; for it shows the extent to which the Miltonic style had become an inert manner, which any practitioner felt he could adopt and reproduce whenever required, and which could even be broken up into its basic elements, that could then be reassembled as desired, or used in isolation. His verse also confirms the observation that, although a few critics and poets, like Cowper and Hayley, understood the Miltonic tradition in poetry as meaning chiefly a revolutionary use of previous traditions linking epic and prophecy, the late eighteenth-century practitioners and versifiers saw the legacy of Milton as consisting mainly of a style which could be easily imitated. Rogers' translation of Dante taken as a whole is also significant, in that it suggests observations on the course of English translation practice in general, and of Dante translations into English in particular.

To a certain extent Rogers' stance as a translator is mixed – he tries to reproduce literally poetry from the past, but at the same time he attempts to find a contemporary analogue of Dante's sublimity in some aspects of English poetry. In this respect, Rogers is operating fully within the eighteenth-century convention of separating matter – the world of the poem, which the translator must take as it is from his original and reproduce faithfully – from manner, that is the language, which must of necessity be that of an eighteenth-century writer. This is the stance which Pope had adopted for his *Iliad*. But within this convention, Rogers takes up an extreme position in his pursuit of literalism. Rogers' extraction of some aspects only of the Miltonic style indicates that his rendering comes as close to a prose translation of Dante as the eighteenth century could envisage.

Yet he uses the blank-verse paragraph with some features of the pseudo-Miltonic style, and this indicates that the process of the selection of a contemporary language to dress a poem of a different time, language and culture, was moving in a particular direction. The translator, rather than making a journey from the past, or into the past – asking himself how Dante would have spoken if he were an eighteenth-century Englishman, or what kind of English would be comparable to medieval Italian, remains in the present and in England, and asks himself what would be the contemporary analogue corresponding to the language of the poem.

Furthermore, Rogers attempts to produce a version of Dante that retains the appearance and some features of poetry, is worded in plain language, remains close to speech rhythms, and launches into the sublime only where the original does so (in the eyes of the translator). By avoiding the recreative attitude of the poet/translator, by following the original when it rises to a grander style, and by including variety between plain and more elevated diction Rogers is, in fact, reproducing a contemporary analogue of Dante's poem.[10]

Nine years after the publication of Rogers' *Inferno*, William Cowper published his translation of the *Iliad*, in the introduction to which he discusses the possible English models both for the translator and for the poet. In the case of Rogers, we have no record of the views from which his practice resulted, but his choices and practice would appear to exemplify precisely those views on the models available to the English poet that were to be brought into the foreground by Cowper. Accordingly, I return briefly, at this point, to a discussion of Cowper's ideas on translation expressed in his prefaces to his versions of Homer, as voicing a standpoint comparable to or even, probably, shared by Rogers.

In particular, I mentioned earlier in this study (pp. 34-5) that Cowper seems to put into practice what De Sua had called a 'new vision' of translation developed by the Romantic translator, whom De Sua distinguishes from the eighteenth-century translator who tried to create a new original, 'regardless of how it reflected the qualities of the model'. But Rogers' version of Dante shows that such an eighteenth-century attitude to translation was not universal, and also that the more Romantic translation, which produced an analogue of the original in manner, could appear earlier than De Sua proposed, in the eighteenth century.

Any critic who aims to isolate the predominant method of a particular age, and contrast it with earlier or later methods, must be careful to analyse all the available texts, without ignoring some by labeling them in advance as worthless translations. More importantly, he must use, alongside the translations themselves, other available evidence. In this case, Cowper's 'Preface', and the success (or lack of it) of the translations under consideration offer further necessary material for study. It is probably true that in the nineteenth century a new view of translation developed. But the evidence of Cowper and Rogers seems to point to the fact that it is not a question of a new attitude on the part of the translator, but of a new taste on the part of the reader.

For the unpopularity of Rogers' Dante is also observable in the 1791 version of Cowper's Homer, so much so that Cowper was soon persuaded to revise his text. In the 'Preface' to the second edition, Cowper says what he has changed, and why.[11] First of all he sacrificed the variety of his lines which he had created by the use of pauses in the blank verse (p. xviii), and secondly 'the occasional use of a line irregularly constructed' (p. xix). Moreover, he expunged many epithets, 'retaining ... the most eligible only, and making less frequent use of these'. Cowper made these changes 'though unconvinced ... of their propriety' (p. xix), and because he found that 'some readers much disliked them' (p. xxi). This giving in to the expectations of the reader is very different indeed from Cowper's attitude to this matter voiced in the previous preface. In 1791, Cowper had firmly stated that he was quite unconcerned with the approbation of readers, and in fact was sceptical as to the purity of their taste, since they seem to 'account nothing grand that is not turgid, or elegant that is not bedizened with metaphor' (1791, p. xvi).

Pressure from readers and his publisher was reinforced by Cowper's own change of mind in matters of diction.[12] Cowper was himself dissatisfied with his 1791 version of his translation, since the diction seemed to him 'not sufficiently elevated, or deficient in the grace of ease' (p. xix), and he quotes the established precedent of Pope as authority (p. xx). He had, previously, devoted a whole paragraph to acknowledging the support of a very different authority, Fuseli – a painter of sublime and even gothic subjects, on whom he had relied for his understanding of Homer as well as for comments on his own version of the *Iliad*.

Cowper goes back on his attempt to reproduce the characteristics of Homer's lines – harmony (through blank verse) and energy (through diction). In order to better understand Cowper's change of mind, one should remember that the second edition of Homer was completed only three years before his death, and produced in the worst years of Cowper's depression. In this context, his attempt to revise his original version into a more 'eighteenth-century' style translation (as defined according to the criterion of a critic like De Sua) goes to show that this attitude to translation originates not in the translator's preference, but in the desire, or even need, to please a reading public whose taste was shaped by the traditional classics. When, in 1833-4, Robert Southey prepared his edition of Cowper's works, he preferred the 1791 edition of the *Iliad*; and even earlier, in 1818, Cary's Dante became popular, even though Cary's attitude to translation, and in particular his attitude to reproducing the manner of the original, is similar to that of Rogers. So by 1818, readers' taste had shifted to such an extent that approval for this manner of translating had become the norm.

Although, taken out of its historical context, Rogers' translation is marred as a careful rendering of the original by the many errors, when considered within its historical context and in terms of the moment in time when it appeared it is of considerable importance. It shows, first of all, that the antiquarian taste of a man of culture like Rogers regarded Dante's work as a kind of collector's item, something to be imported into England. Secondly, Rogers' interest in the basic matter of the poem enables him to provide an objective, concrete product, in which the story is what matters, and in which the experiences the story tells have more vividness and solidity than in Boyd's and Cary's later translations. Moreover, his avoidance of the turgid diction of the grand style enables him, occasionally, to produce passages which are as readable and accurate as other versions of the same passage – the opening of *Inferno* being a case in point. Another example of this is the version of Vanni Fucci's curse of God – a blasphemous gesture, difficult to present to eighteenth-century readers. Rogers' Vanni Fucci retains some vestige of a gesture:

> Al fine delle sue parole il ladro
> le mani alzò con amendue le fiche,
> gridando: "Togli, Dio, ch'a te le squadro!" (XXV 1-3)[13]

> When thus the Thief had spoken, he his hands
> Lifted aloft with mocking signs, and cried;
> "See these, Oh God, for pointed they're to you."

Cary's version follows the original very closely, but as far as the actual gesture goes, he can do no better than follow Rogers' rendering:

> When he had spoke, the sinner raised his hands
> Pointed in mockery, and cried: "Take them, God!
> I level them at thee...."

The comparison of Rogers' and Cary's versions of Dante has highlighted Rogers' stress on the narrative aspect of the poem, which would have facilitated the reading of the poem, by keeping the story constantly in view, and by avoiding the problems of a protagonist who is inactive and unsympathetic. However, the stress also suggests the distance from the poem of a translator who was primarily an Antiquary and collector, and the absence on his part of any involvement in the deeper issues at work there. This distance may help to explain why Rogers decided not to acknowledge the book, but to have it published anonymously. Rogers' status in the society of the age would hardly have guaranteed approval of the work, but it would most probably have secured for it at least a significant readership, instead of the very small one it did receive. Rogers' authorship would have enabled his translation to contribute more than it did to making the world of Dante familiar to the English reader, this necessary first step of exposure and response being, it seems, in itself more useful than the nature of that response, whether favourable or unfavourable. In fact, the lack of popularity of Rogers' *Inferno* may well have been the single most important aspect of this translation which had some influence on the course of English translations of Dante. For the very fact that Rogers' stress on plain matter proved unpopular may have suggested that any future attempt at a translation of Dante should follow a different approach.

7

Conclusion to Part I

The survey and analysis of translation of Dante in the eighteenth century spans the movement from the rendering of a short episode, in 1719, to the rendering of a complete *cantica*, in 1782.

The first observation to be made is that each of the various translators adopts a different style, and, occasionally, several different styles. Besides the prose renderings of the Wartons, translators try out couplets (sometimes modified, as in the case of Huggins), *terza rima*, and blank verse. Also, they turn, in their search for a model, to different literary forms and concepts – drama, opera, northern primitivism, and the cosmic journey. But, whatever the difference in form and style, all the models are of a similar nature: they all attribute a greater role to imagination than to judgement, placing more emphasis upon the sublime and pathetic than upon logic and statement. The absence of other literary forms – social satire, didactic and conversational verse – confirms that Dante's poem was seen as the product of the image-making faculty. Hayley's split poem, the *Triumphs of Temper*, sets out the choice in its starkest contrast: Dante's work is a 'visionary' poem, a cosmic journey, initially directed downwards into the recesses of the earth, and then directed upwards to the stars. For a visionary poem of prophecy, or for the dramatic speech of Ugolino, the sublime style of expression was perceived as the most appropriate, as shown by the preference for Miltonic diction and blank verse. Both aspects of the Miltonic tradition (the belief that poetry can give new shape to man's destiny and reveal his future state, and the view that the best means for this kind of poetry are verbal sublimity and the openness of blank verse) are incorporated within the growing tradition of translations of Dante.

If, instead of asking oneself what models the translator of Dante adopted, one turns the question around, and asks why Hayley chose Dante as the model for the 'visionary' sections of his poem, one has a question whose answer can further clarify both the views on Dante and the contribution that translations of Dante made to English studies. When Cowper decided that the right way to render Homer into English was in blank verse he felt that he had to argue his decision strongly, the point being that Homer was a great classic, with a tradition of translation behind him, and that to go against the established pattern of translations of the classics, as established in particular by Dryden and Pope, took vision and courage. But Dante was not a classic, and that very fact enabled writers to be experimental and creative when translating his poem.

It is not simply a matter of respect towards the original, for Homer had even been rendered in burlesque. But what is significant here is that burlesque itself is an accepted mode, with a respected tradition behind it. Poems which leave the earth and social intercourse to launch into space and the imagination, and which even envisage the afterlife or the end of the world could have turned, apart from Dante or the Miltonic tradition, to another model – Pomfret's poems of apocalyptic vision, for example. But Pomfret used the Pindaric ode, a literary form which, although it appears very irregular, is in fact finite and has rules of its own. The Pindaric ode is, furthermore, a classical literary form well established in the eighteenth century. Hayley's choice, highlighting the motivations of other poets and translators, is precisely the avoidance of classical genres and styles.

What we see in the case of translations of Dante is the redirection of the search for models into English native traditions. Milton includes both the more inward-looking sublimity he inherited from Spenser and even Shakespeare, in which history and mythology accept the spiritual and the supernatural in ways closer to the modern sensibility, and the flexibility of blank verse, a form which is not enclosed, but open, and which, to use Cowper's idiom, has 'variety' and 'energy' (surely two of the aesthetic norms of early nineteenth-century poetic discourse). Dante's greater closeness to the spiritual landscape of modern man, his use of a mythology of Christianity, his pathetic sublimity, and the very fact that he is not an established classic of literature mean that the translator can make him speak in various voices, and that the poet can use his work to further experiment with one strand of the contemporary native tradition – the Miltonic vision of fall and redemption.

PART II

THE FIRST TWO COMPLETE
TRANSLATIONS OF DANTE'S COMMEDIA

8

Henry Boyd

The reputations that Henry Boyd and Henry Francis Cary, the authors of the first two complete translations of the *Divina Commedia* into English, gained from their work could not appear to be more different from each other. For Boyd's translation has been ignored, while Cary's, though little read nowadays, was acclaimed as a great achievement and established itself as a classic; and Boyd's name has been relegated to a footnote, while Cary's is inscribed on his grave in Westminster Abbey as 'the translator of Dante', an honour which should, if only based on chronology, go to Boyd. The reasons for the difference in the reception of the two translations are obvious. Boyd departs considerably from the original, contracting and expanding it continuously, and occasionally changing even the facts of the story; moreover, his style is not consistent, and moves to the extremes of eighteenth-century taste. Cary's blank verse, on the contrary, is steady, regular, and consistent throughout the poem and reproduces the original more literally line per line.

However, Boyd and Cary do share a basic approach to Dante; they both see his poem in terms of the eighteenth-century Miltonic tradition, and they both use this tradition as their context. But while Boyd was more ambitious and aggressive, more exploratory and probing – and hence more revealing of the possibilities and limitations of the Miltonic tradition, Cary restricted himself to the imitation of one range of this tradition's established manner. As a result, the legacy of Cary has been more obvious and recognized because his work fits into the accepted canon. But his translation was, as will be seen, less dynamic and fruitful than Boyd's in terms of transmitting and incorporating – through Dante – eighteenth-century poetic values into those of the following period.

An Irish Anglican priest who spent most of his life in Ireland, Henry Boyd (1750-1832) was a writer of poetry and translator of Italian poetry.[1] His version of *Inferno* was published by subscription in 1785 in Dublin, and was also issued in London by Dilly. It was relatively well received at the time, and achieved some status, since it was used for the quotations accompanying the *Compositions by John Flaxman from the Divine Comedy of Dante Alighieri* published in 1807 (this being the English edition of Flaxman's illustrations published originally in Rome in 1793). Certainly, Cary's fame must not blind us to the fact that, before the publication of his version, and for some years after that, Boyd's version was well known. For example, Hayley, for one, had subscribed to seven sets of the two-volume translation of *Inferno* (1785), published in Dublin. One of these sets he gave to Anna Seward. He may have given another to Blake, who in any case possessed, read and annotated a copy of Boyd's *Inferno*. Byron also knew it.[2]

Less is known of readers' reactions to Boyd's translation of the complete *Commedia*, which was published in 1802. References in correspondence all seem to refer to the *Inferno* published in 1785. As a matter of fact, the readers of this translation whose comments have survived in private letters disliked the translation, but reviewers were more favourable, and certainly accepted the changes Boyd made. As the reviewer in the *Gentleman's Magazine* points out, Boyd's changes caused the version to 'please an English, more than an Italian, reader, who compares it with the original'; but the same reviewer still finds that 'This version is in general correct and spirited ...'.[3] More recent commentators, on the contrary, have branded Boyd's version as a free paraphrase, and hence of no value to the modern reader of Dante. In their opinion, free paraphrase is not just bad translation, but is, in fact, not translation at all. As a result of this point of view Boyd loses the claim of being the first translator of Dante.[4]

These strictures are accurate, but the conclusions that are drawn from them are much less so. Critics such as De Sua state that, like most eighteenth-century translators, Boyd distorts his original, first of all because he has no high regard for it, and secondly because of his desire to embellish poetry which is too stark for current taste.[5] Such critics seem to disregard or be blind to a number of important issues: for the fact that Boyd's is the very first translation of the complete *Divina Commedia* (and that his version of *Inferno* comes after the little regarded Rogers translation) has its effect on the translation itself, which must be evaluated on that basis. Moreover, rather than the requirement for embellishments, it is the absence of a morally valid model, as will be shown later, that affects Boyd's text, in which Dante's protagonist becomes something of a *pius Aeneas*. One could say that Boyd is attempting to secure his readers' approval of the protagonist and enjoyment of the sublime setting. This in turn will ensure their willingness to read on and to respond to the poem as a total text. Just as Pope had made his Homer more majestic and solemn in order to rescue the text from the burlesque tradition which had distorted it, so Boyd attempted to rescue Dante from the neglect and disapproval which had hitherto prevented his reception in England. This attitude guides Boyd's choice of models, particularly in *Inferno*, and is clearly stated in the essays which precede the translation.

Boyd's *Inferno*

The text of Boyd's translation begins on page 185 of his first volume. It is preceded by a substantial apparatus to introduce and explain the work: 'A Summary View of the Inferno of Dante. From Warton's History of English Poetry', 'A Comparative view of the Inferno with some other Poems, relative to the original principles of *Human nature*, on which they are founded, or to which they appeal', a 'Historical Essay on the State of Affairs in Florence...', and an 'Introduction'.

It is particularly in the 'Comparative view' that Boyd openly attempts to redress the course of the fame of Dante in England. Most of the reasons given, even in our day, for the course of Dante's fame in England are already mentioned in this essay, and it is interesting that Boyd should contrast an appreciation of Dante with the preference for the poetic values upheld by the French:

> The venerable old Bard who is the subject of the present enquiry has been long neglected; perhaps for that reason, because the merit of his Poem could not be tried by the reigning laws of which the author was ignorant, or which he did not chuse to observe: He always indeed was a favourite with such as were possest of true taste, and dared to think for themselves; but since the French, the restorers of the art of criticism, cast a damp upon original invention, the character of *Dante* has been thrown under a deeper shade.[6]

It is first the poet Dante himself who interests Boyd, and this he uses to initiate acceptance of the poem. At this point, Boyd is keen to establish Dante as a 'gloomy and romantic bard, whose genius [is] ardent, melancholy, and sublime...'. The word 'bard', repeated twice in the same paragraph, already suggests what image of the poet Boyd is creating. He brings together the names of Dante and Shakespeare, both being 'unfettered by rules' and distinguished 'by bold original strokes of sublimity and pathos' (p. 28). Alongside the word 'bard', therefore, one must place words such as 'original invention', 'genius' and 'sublime'. By using the particular diction publicized by Young in his *Conjectures on Original Compositions* (1759), Boyd presents Dante as a poet of imagination.

When he moves from the person of Dante the poet to the poem, however, Boyd stresses not only the passions expressed but also the moral values communicated. Boyd begins by making of *Inferno* a drama in the Greek sense when he says that 'it abounds with powerful appeals to the strongest of all passions, Terror and Pity'. But even these passions, he claims, merely serve to communicate basic principles on which *Inferno* is based – 'the sense of right and wrong, the innate love of virtue and justice, and the influence of conscience' (p. 63). Both the protagonist and the world he finds himself in are viewed by Boyd as proceeding from these principles. The protagonist's fate is '*the Conversion of a Sinner by a spiritual guide, displaying in a series of terrible visions the secrets of Divine Justice'* (p. 30); and the world he finds himself in is one which is full of 'sublime imagery', where landscape, descriptions of suffering (which are more 'sublime than Milton's', p. 66), and the appearance of the souls are all more 'inward' (p. 33) than concrete and corporeal. So, for example, the horrible punishments of the damned are meant as 'an allegorical description of the pangs of mind arising from the consciousness of having degraded their nature' (p. 68). In his stress on moral principles, Boyd turns what had been seen before as horrid physical punishments in Dante's Hell into 'the sufferings of the mind' (pp. 67, 69).

This concern with conscience and mind makes Dante's poem, according to Boyd, of value for contemporary readers; and he stresses that readers should be quite capable of actively responding to Dante's poetry, particularly when rightly understood, and to Dante's world. 'We sympathize with the sufferers, as they are neither Demons nor imaginary beings, but our fellow-creatures' (p. 63); moreover, 'The modes of life, and even the opinions which we meet with in *Dante* are, if not familiar to us, at least allied to our own by a very near affinity' (p. 65). Hence, Dante's poem is good for the reader, since it 'must produce the most salutary of all effects, that moral effect, which all Laws tend to produce...' (p. 63). In claiming that Dante's poem offers pragmatic moral teaching Boyd follows the eighteenth-century concern with ethics, which is expressed most clearly, probably, by Samuel Johnson, and Boyd's generalized statement on the moral effect of 'all Laws' is very Johnsonian indeed.

There then follows a comparison with Homer and Virgil, which brings out the greater closeness of Dante to the contemporary English world, and the consequent value of its moral message. Boyd draws the essay to a close with the admission that he may have toned down the admiration due to Homer, but, he concludes, 'This was the more necessary, as Dante had fallen into a degree of obscurity far below his genuine deserts' (p. 73).

There are a number of conclusions to be drawn, and a number of points to be isolated which can be of use to the analysis of the actual translation. The first conclusion to be drawn is that Boyd's main concern is to make Dante known and accepted, even if this means stressing Homer and Virgil's weaknesses. Secondly, Boyd is certainly highlighting not the sensational quality of Hell, but the ethical significance of the poem. Thirdly, it must be pointed out that Boyd does not see Dante as the greatest Bard – he is a 'Bard of a secondary magnitude' (p. 73), with a 'want of art in the composition'. This last phrase does not mean a lack of skill in writing poetry, or poverty of language and versification, but refers to the dull 'uniformity' of his subject (p. 66). Compensating for this uniformity, however, is the variety in the presentation of human character.

The major point of interest for my ensuing analysis is Boyd's view of the protagonist in relation to all the damned. Their punishments make up the bulk of the work, but 'the very introduction of a living man among them, who, exempt from their sufferings, views all their torments at leisure...' (pp. 67-68) is a key feature of the poem. For while we sympathize with the damned, we identify with the protagonist's experience – in that we, too, are moved to shun vice and follow virtue.

How is Boyd going to present the English reader with an *Inferno* which has as its main purpose the conversion of its protagonist through visions of the consequences of vice? He makes a very definite choice, and both in versification and in the picture presented he picks up and develops the Spenserian elements often used by eighteenth-century poets, and also by Hayley in his translation:

> When life had laboured up her midmost stage
> And, weary with her mortal pilgrimage,
>> Stood in suspense upon the point of Prime;
> Far in a pathless grove I chanced to stray,
> Where scarce imagination dare display,
>> The gloomy scenery of the savage clime.
>> II
> On the deep horrors of the tangled dell,
> With dumb dismay, the pow'rs of mem'ry dwell,
>> Scenes, terrible as dark impending fate!
> Yet tell, O muse! what intellectual store
> I gleaned along the solitary shore,
>> And ring in louder strains the heavenly freight.
>> III
> Whether entranced, I left the central path
> 'Rapt in a vision, to the vale of death,
>> (Such slumbers seal'd my sense) is all unknown:
> Yet down the glen, that filled my soul with fright,
> I straied: – when lo! on hill's aerial height,
>> Vested with glory, met the rising sun.[7]

Four major features of Boyd's opening passage, which in fact are present throughout the translation, deserve attention: the choice of diction, metre and versification, the disappearance of the figure of the narrator, the nature of Boyd's protagonist, and finally the nature of the world around this protagonist and his experience of it.

Some of the features noticed in the Hayley translation can be found in Boyd's version. Adjective-noun constructions abound – 'pathless grove', 'savage clime', 'tangled dell', 'solitary shore'. The words used are chosen consistently from the vocabulary of the poetry of romance, and to the words just quoted we can, for example, add 'glen', rendering the simple 'valle'. Not just the words singly, but the language in general also belongs to the poetry of romance, and is elaborate and ornate in that manner, so that Dante's 'tant'era pien di sonno' ('I was so full of sleep'), which Hayley had rendered as 'so much in sleep /My mortal senses ... were drowned', becomes here 'Such slumbers sealed my sense'. This last phrase illustrates a further feature in common with Hayley, the recurrent use of alliteration. Boyd's translation, therefore, displays all the features noticed in Hayley which linked that version with Spenserian poetry and the neo-Spenserian taste of the eighteenth century. It does not, however, have any of the features which in Hayley created a contrasting tone – there is no evidence of a mind at work here, of a speaker working out his lines, of judgement unfolding, and no echo of the heroic couplet. In fact, one such feature of Hayley's verse mentioned on page 102 – the line split into two parts elaborating the thoughts of the previous line – is employed in a very different manner, as illustrated in line three – 'Stood in suspense upon the point of prime', which is split into two parts in terms of alliteration, as in Old English verse forms.

Boyd looks back to the past also in his choice of rhyme scheme and stanza form. Dante's tercets are in *Inferno* mostly closed. The linking middle line of each tercet in the pattern of *terza rima* (aba bcb cdc etc.) counteracts and balances this start-stop effect, creates continuity throughout the canto, and facilitates reading. Boyd seems to attempt to maintain part of the *terza rima* structure by splitting his stanzas into two sets of three lines each, with a linking third and sixth rhyme: aab ccb. Moreover, usually he either expands one tercet into one six-line stanza, with considerable padding, or simply has two tercets in one stanza. Some connection is therefore maintained between the original tercet and the six-line stanza. Yet the difference from the original is still considerable, particularly since the stanza form has a very noticeable effect both on the pace of reading and on the nature of the experience presented, and it is this effect that Boyd must have been aiming for. Boyd's stanzas stand isolated, each presenting a picture, a focus of its own; and Dante's slender but effective connection of rhymes and lines is not just diminished, but vanishes in the absence of a chain, in the layout of the separate stanzas on the page, and in the new unit of rhymes within the stanzas. Although the stanza form and the rhyme scheme are not the same as in Spenser's *Fairy Queen*, the movement of Boyd's stanzas is very similar, and this, added to the nature of his diction, indicates that Boyd was trying to ensure that the reader saw a similarity between Dante's poem and the only major poetic allegory in English.

The same model is used for the protagonist and the world of *Inferno*; both belong fully to the world of medieval romance and Spenserian allegory. Dante's first lines had contrasted the general import of the journey ('*nostra* vita') with the individuality of the protagonist and his experience ('*mi* ritrovai'). In Boyd, this tension is lost in the distanced personification of human life which 'labours', 'is weary', and 'stands in suspense'. The protagonist himself appears, in Boyd's version, only in the fourth line and then only briefly. Also, 'I chanced to stray' seems, in two respects, a very inappropriate reproduction of the protagonist's state. First, the reader will not form the impression that this protagonist has sinned, as the original clearly suggests, since guilt and chance would seem mutually exclusive. Secondly, the phrase introduces, even if in a limited way, a movement, a process, which implies a moment preceding the loss of the right way. But Dante's protagonist suddenly found himself in the wood; both the reason for the situation ('la via era smarrita') and the description of the coming to an awareness of his state ('mi ritrovai in una selva') are sudden. Dante's opening scene is like an abrupt awakening, with no trace of a process, a movement, a plot. The steps of the development of a story taking place are deliberately left out by Dante.

The impact of the appearance of Dante's protagonist is lost in Boyd. Moreover, having fleetingly appeared in line four, this figure is immediately drowned in further personifications, of 'imagination' and 'the powers of memory'. The protagonist, therefore, is not vividly placed at the centre of the scene, but is distanced by personifications of human powers. The other aspect of the central figure in the poem, his function as the narrator, which is also introduced and developed in Dante in the very first lines, in Boyd disappears completely. In his third line and the second and third tercet of the poem, Dante establishes not only that the present tense is that of the telling and not of the living of the experience, but also that the narrator finds his task difficult and distressing. The different tenses highlight this tension, which Hayley, in his own way, had reproduced, but which in Boyd disappears. Moreover, while Dante's narrator had taken upon himself the task of recounting everything that, as protagonist, he had seen, whether good or evil, Boyd introduces a muse (which of the muses exactly is left to the reader's imagination) who will sing in her own voice. Her task is certainly not to inspire the poet-traveller. He, in fact, is struck into 'dumb dismay', and thereby loses completely the powers of speech. The central figure of Dante's poem is thus turned into a passive puppet. As a traveller he seems to be in the hands of chance or fate, and as a poet in the hands of the muse.

It is no wayfarer-poet that the reader is introduced to in Boyd's first lines, but a passive Everyman who understands and controls very little of his experience. And while Dante maintains the consistency of the first, literal layer of meaning of his story, Boyd bridges the literal and anagogic when we are informed directly that life is a mortal pilgrimage. *Inferno* is *Everyman*; the wayfarer is here firmly placed in the world of Christian allegory, and the reader is therefore given directions to interpret what he reads as an allegory, rather than as a combination of the real experience and vision of a protagonist.

This effect is increased further by the very nature of the pictures presented. The poet wanderer, having been reduced to just a wanderer, seems to take his first steps into Hell as a (Red Cross) knight. This is the encounter between the protagonist and one of three beasts in Dante:

> Ed ecco, quasi al cominciar dell'erta,
>   una lonza leggiera e presta molto,
>   che di pel macolato era coverta;   33
> e non mi si partía d'innanzi al volto,
>   anzi impediva tanto il mio cammino,
>   ch'i' fui per ritornar piú volte vòlto.   36
>
> . . .
>
>   sí ch'a bene sperar m'era cagione
>   di quella fera alla gaetta pelle
>   l'ora del tempo e la dolce stagione;   (I 31-36, 41-43)[8]

The leopard is suddenly on the scene. In fact there is not even a verb which might suggest the movement of its coming. As in the first lines of the poem, so here the situation is presented in terms not of action but of a sudden appearance. Dante again maintains the apparent realism of the story: his leopard is not presented as a malignant power but as a wild animal. Its description is very brief and detached: it is light and quick, and covered with a speckled skin, which later the wayfarer, soothed by the vision of the rising sun and by the 'sweet season', even calls bright and beautiful. Its attitude is not described as aggressive: for the leopard simply places itself right in front of the traveller, so that he cannot go further.

Boyd's rendering of the same passage is as follows:

VI

When lo! A Panther in the op'ning straight
couchant, with gleaming eyes, expecting fat,
  All formidable gay, in speckled pride.
Suspense, I sought to shun the dubious war,
But the grim tyrant of the woods afar
  Still opposite, his prey malignant ey'd.

...

VIII

The cheerful morn, and spring's benignant smile,
New hope inspired, to seize the gaudy spoil,
  And with the speckled hide my limbs invest;
But other cares the childish hope withheld,
For other thoughts the rage of combat quelled,
  and the warm instinct of my soul suppressed.

Boyd's version pictures a knight facing a threatening, malignant power, clearly more than a mere animal – it is the tyrant of the woods, and it is eyeing its prey. On the one hand the picture has something of the static composition of an emblem, since the leopard is 'couchant', in a heraldic pose of inert menace; but on the other hand the verses move to the climax of a personal combat, since the animal has placed itself in a narrow opening, and is malignant. In fact, the animal is analogous to the monster that the Red Cross Knight has to slay, and Boyd just stops short of calling it Pride, but does so indirectly by referring to its skin as 'speckled pride'. Then, facing the monster Pride, Boyd places not a lost wanderer but a combative knight, who at first tries to avoid a fight – although only because the odds are against him, but hopes soon to possess himself of the 'gaudy spoil'. This not only changes the character of the protagonist, but makes nonsense of the Christian allegory in Dante, where the light of God's love inspires the poet with hope, one of the three attributes of the Christian man which are necessary to overcome the darkness of sin. But Boyd's hero, on the other hand, seems only to hope that he may cover himself with the 'speckled pride' of the beast.

Around the two figures in their respective attitudes Boyd pictures a backdrop which is also different from Dante's Hell. Dante's 'selva' and the other features of the landscape in that first scene paint a very bare landscape, merely sketched in its basic contours: besides the 'selva selvaggia e aspra e forte' ('wood wild and rough and vigorous'), mention is made only of the 'pié d'un colle' ('foot of a hill'), the valley beneath the hill, and the sun above. The reason for this is made clear in the second tercet, which, as indicated earlier, establishes that the poem contains, as one important element, the telling of a story. Dante says, 'Ah quanto a *dir* qual'era è cosa dura' ('Oh how hard it is *to tell* of that wood', emphasis added), and the emphasis is on the difficulty of expression, on the search for the right words, so that the list of three adjectives that follow suggests the attempt to find the right one. It is not only the forest, but also the language that is wild, rough and vigorous. The adventure is not only that of the traveller who has lost his way, but also of the poet who has to find a way to create a language and compose a poem, as Dante had to. The next tercet confirms this: 'per trattar del ben ch'io vi trovai /dirò dell'altre cose ch'i v'ho scorte' ('But to treat of the good I found there,/ I will tell of the other things I saw there') means that the seeing is the necessary prerequisite for the purpose of telling.

Boyd's landscape is only slightly more detailed than that of his original, but its difference could not be more striking. All the features are described with emotionally loaded words referring to the distress of the traveller ('gloomy', 'savage', 'horrors', 'solitary', 'impending fate'). Moreover, height and depth are increased by Boyd, whose picture stresses the distance between 'the deep horrors of the tangled dell' and 'the hill's aerial light', creating a depth and a darkness which oppress the small figure of the protagonist. The spaciousness, darkness and fateful doom are those of Milton's Hell, and Boyd's second stanza resembles less the description in Dante than that of Milton in Book I of *Paradise Lost*:

> The dismal situation waste and wild:
> A dungeon horrible, on all sides round,
> As one great furnace, flamed; yet from those flames
> No light, but rather darkness visible
> Served only to discover sights of woe,
> Regions of sorrow, doleful shades, ...
> ...
> As far removed from God and light of heaven,   (I 60-65, 73)[9]

Boyd is clearly looking at Dante through Spenserian and Miltonic lenses. From Spenser he takes the moral significance of spiritual allegory, and from Milton the sublimity of setting, which often accompanies Miltonic sublimity in eighteenth-century poetry. Both these elements remain features of Boyd's translation throughout, so that the stress on 'the pathetic' and 'the sublime' for moral purposes is characteristic of this version of *Inferno*.

Occasionally, it is true, specific passages seem to adopt the sensationalism and colouring of the gothic. In Canto V, the lines which precede the episode of Francesca borrow the diction of the gothic:

> XIII
> There screaming flits along *Eliza*'s ghost,
> That on herself reveng'd her lover lost:
>   Then Aegypt's wanton Queen ascending soars.
> Next I beheld the Spartan Dame appear,
> The common pest of many a rolling year,
>   While mutual slaughter dy'd Scamander's shore.

Only the first line of this stanza, however, contains a real gothic image. This suggests that the gothic is a secondary model, whose function is occasionally to support or enliven the description.

The important encounter with Ugolino (like the encounter with Fra Alberigo, briefly mentioned on p. 137) confirms Boyd's primary concern to stress the sublime setting, the pathos, and the moral soundness of the protagonist:

> I
> SLOWLY the sinner left his bloody meal,
> Then, gazing upwards from the depths of Hell,
>   He smooth'd the clotted hair, and thus reply'd:
> "Mortal! thou bid'st me recollect my doom,
> An horrid scene! that lives beyond the tomb,
>   And stops my speech with sorrow's whelming tide."

Apart from calling Ugolino's meal 'bloody', nothing is added to the horror of his action; in fact, Boyd seems to stress the surroundings rather than the figure of the sinner. Ugolino does not raise his head from the horrid meal, but gazes 'upwards from the depths of Hell'. His story is not of a 'disperato dolor', but a 'horrid scene', and Dante's 'lacrimar' becomes 'sorrow's whelming tide'. These phrases show how Boyd here moves away from the character's inner life, and objectifies it by turning it into his surroundings.

The same happens towards the end of the Ugolino episode. The curse uttered by the protagonist, that Pisa might be punished with a flood, is not, in Boyd, an outburst of anger, but is turned instead into the description of the actual landscape under a deluge:

> Ahi Pisa, vituperio delle genti
>   del bel paese là dove 'l sí sona,
>   poi che i vicini a te punir son lenti
> muovasi la Capraia a la Gorgona,
>   e faccian siepe ad Arno in su la foce.
>   sí ch'elli annieghi in te ogni persona!   (XXXIII 79-84)[10]

XVII

> ...
> – Ye tow'rs of Pisa! May GORGONA's strand
> With lofty mounds, the coming flood withstand,
> And send it foaming down to whelm thy shame

Extracted in this way, and isolated from its context Dante's passage is a powerful indictment of human injustice, contrasted with an impersonal but just, apocalyptic act of natural forces. The curse on Pisa, which is here a collective name for her people and their moral corruption, consists of a visionary scene in which two islands move to block Arno's estuary, thereby causing a flood which no one will survive. Dante avoids descriptive terms, the islands only being mentioned by their name, as if they were characters, so that the reader needs a footnote to tell him what they actually are. Similarly, the river is simply 'Arno', and there is no mention of flood or tide but specifically of the death of all of Pisa's inhabitants.

Boyd's version loses the upheaval of nature, since the island's high hills are an obstacle in the way of a seemingly natural flood. Also, the landscape retains its physical appearance: Pisa is a city pictured with its towers, Gorgona is a 'strand' with 'lofty mounds'. At the same time, rather than the specific Arno, there is a generalized but impressive 'coming flood', described as 'foaming', a word which adds sublimity but remains, to the modern reader, inert and stereotyped. And rather than an apocalyptic destruction of human life, the protagonist's curse more mercifully calls for the annihilation of Pisa's 'shame'.

Surrounded and enclosed by this landscape of generalized sublimity are the two figures of Ugolino and Ruggieri, and their presentation is also coloured, in Boyd, by aspects of eighteenth-century English literature. Ruggieri is touched up with strokes borrowed from gothic fiction, and Ugolino becomes a figure of pathos.

Dante briefly identifies the gnawed skull as 'questi é l'arcivescovo Ruggieri' ('this is the Archbishop Ruggieri'); but his position in the church is not mentioned again, because Ruggieri is being punished as a traitor, his sins being those of a corrupted politician. In the dream he only appears as the master of the hunt. But Boyd's Ugolino introduces Ruggieri as a 'curs'd Prelate', and repeats the word 'Prelate' in stanza four; while in the dream Ruggieri appears as an 'infernal Priest', adopting a characteristic role in a gothic novel. Ugolino himself is furious and passionate rather than an automaton or a beast. In his very first words he turns to his victim to address him with the rhetorical 'Yes, Traitor, thou! it was thou thy friend accus'd' (stanza IV). Moreover, when he sets his teeth in the skull again he does so 'with malignant look, and furious haste,/ Like a staunch blood-hound to his savage game'. This stress on passion and pathos leads Boyd finally to invert Dante's meaning at Ugolino's death. In Dante it was hunger or famine – the power of animal appetites – that killed Ugolino. In the *Inferno* of 1785 Boyd has as cause of Ugolino's death 'want, with grief combin'd' (st. XV), and in the 1802 edition it is grief alone that kills Ugolino:

> XVI
>
> "...
> Gaunt famine long had try'd its pow'rs in vain;
> But mortal grief at last reliev'd my pain,
> ..."

Boyd's reading of Ugolino is similar to Reynolds' rendering of the episode in his picture exhibited at the Royal Academy in 1773. In both cases the stress is on sublimity and pathos, and probably both reflect not only the current way of viewing Dante, but also the only way of reproducing Dante which would please the reader or spectator. Horace Walpole certainly felt that in no other age 'were paternal despair and the horrors of death pronounced with more expressive accents than in [Reynolds'] picture of Count Ugolino' (1780, 'Advertisement' to *Anecdotes of Painting in England* vol. 4, *DEL* p. 339). A more recent observer would, as Ellis Waterhouse says, probably comment 'that Reynolds showed "a rage for sublimity ill-understood"'.[11]

The same phrase could be used by the present day reader to describe Boyd's distortion of the original. But it is not true to say, as De Sua does, that Boyd's translation deserves to be forgotten by the present day reader because it has lost all connection with recent poetic values. That would be to deny, for one thing, the extent to which the past may illuminate the present, which is one of the ideas this study is at pains to illustrate. Boyd's translation was clearly written for the audience of the age, at a particular moment in time, and was a particular step in the course of translating Dante into English. Charles Rogers' translation had created a version of Dante's poem which obviously did not please the reading public. In order to rescue Dante from neglect, therefore, Boyd had to take into consideration the proven taste of the contemporary reader, who, as we have seen in Chapter 3, enjoyed the pathetic story of Ugolino, but objected to the lack of sublimity in Dante's landscape, and particularly to the lack of moral stature of Dante's hero. These are the features which Boyd focuses on. He highlights the pathetic, and adds the sublimity of darkness, space and loftiness, together with the characteristic sublime imagery. Furthermore, having turned the protagonist into a Spenserian knight, he ensures that no action should spoil this picture. Hence, his curse on Pisa is more merciful, and, more strikingly, his reaction to Fra Alberigo is completely changed:

XXVIII
...
"Far be the task profane!" the Mantuan cry'd.
Mute I obeyed my unrelenting guide,
    And darkling follow'd to the depths below.

The responsibility for this cruel act is attributed unequivocally to Virgil, and the protagonist continues with his passive, but spiritually pure, role – not without a respectful but disapproving comment upon Virgil's act.

Boyd's *Inferno* fulfils the primary need of an early translation of a neglected author – to adapt it first to contemporary taste, and only secondly to the original.

Boyd's *Purgatorio*

The one major problem faced by the translator of Dante's second *cantica* into English at the end of the eighteenth century was the reader's utter rejection of the basic fiction used as a framework – the idea of a Purgatory through which a protagonist could journey on the way to salvation, and around which a poet could write a sublime poem of spiritual conversion. It is precisely this problem that Boyd tackles in the 'Preliminary Essay on the Purgatorio of Dante', a text of fifty-five pages mainly dedicated to a justification of the idea of Purgatory to protestant ears.[12] Boyd begins by very cautiously expressing the hope that he may be allowed the liberty to defend Dante, and he does this by stressing the fictionality of the idea of Purgatory. Even to Dante, Boyd states, Purgatory did not actually exist, but was only an allegory of the trial the soul goes through on earth.

To support his statement Boyd brings in various arguments based on the text. First, he points out how, once in Paradise, even though Dante meets a number of blessed, he never 'asserts that they had passed through' Purgatory; instead, reference to their 'probation ... is entirely confined to THIS LIFE' (p. 8). More specifically, Boyd refers to a particular passage from Canto VIII where 'a singular phenomenon is introduced, which is not easily accounted for...' (p. 5), this phenomenon being the appearance of the Tempter who, in the shape of a serpent, approaches a group of souls singing an evening prayer, but is chased away by an angel. The explanation for this strange occurrence in Purgatory is, according to Boyd, that 'This is so natural a representation of the devotions of an evening, and the vigilance of Providence, which we implore to repel the phantoms of the night ... that it appears somewhat like a presumptive evidence of the allegorical hypothesis' (p. 6), a hypothesis which is further confirmed by the words of the hymn the souls sing once Satan has been chased away.

A less serious, but still substantial problem for the translator of Dante is represented by the souls' repeated prayer that the protagonist should intercede with God in their favour. This is a Catholic belief in intercession which Boyd describes in the same essay as having 'first introduced a lucrative branch of commerce.' Boyd justifies the souls' prayer, somewhat weakly, as representing a symptom of reformation and 'an allegorical representation of our present state of moral improvement' (p. 7).

Again, therefore, Boyd seeks to stress the relevance of the *Commedia* for the contemporary reader, and the value of the poem as an instrument of spiritual education. He puts forward, in this essay on *Purgatorio*, a view of man as being in need of education, which he sees as a process requiring both rewards and punishments. He disagrees with Shaftesbury's view that 'rewards are derogatory to genuine goodness'. Shaftesbury himself, says Boyd, was a good man, and he judged others by himself – he therefore made the mistake of going 'from *particulars* to *universals* without regard for logic or experience' (p. 44). Boyd obviously believes that he is not committing this same mistake when, assuming a very typically eighteenth-century stance, he surveys both man's history and the current habits and beliefs of far away peoples, such as the Chinese, Japanese and savage tribes like 'the KAMSCHATKADALES' (p. 18), in order to prove that everywhere and always fear of punishments, religious terror, and superstition have actually been used by Providence as the means of moral progress, contributing to the education not only of the moral but also of the religious sense. Purgatory answers a natural idea of justice which is universal and which requires both rewards and punishments.

Boyd's purpose is to defend the idea of Purgatory, but in the process he expresses views which reveal his reading of Dante's second *cantica*. There seem to be three major views to be extracted from the essay. First of all, Boyd notices the importance, in this second *cantica*, of descriptions of nature. It is quite true that in Dante's *Purgatorio* the souls are not yet fully committed to the afterlife – they still feel connected to their families on earth, and, though with detachment, remember places and experiences (in particular, the moment of their death) more vividly than either the damned or the blessed. The Mount of Purgatory itself, the sea surrounding it, the shore and its reeds, the sun and stars in the southern hemisphere, and the similes they call up in the poet's writing all combine to create an interweaving of landscapes. Boyd notices the 'strong analogy between real phenomena of this life,' and Dante's descriptions of nature in *Purgatorio* (p. 8). Here we find 'scenes of great turbulence or deep tranquillity', and such scenes have an 'agreeable effect upon the mind' (p. 14). In addition to the importance of nature, Boyd continually stresses an allegorical reading, which reveals the moral significance of the events described beyond their literal interest as parts of the plot. Thirdly, which in a way includes the other two, there is the view that *Purgatorio* is filled not so much with serenity or expectation of future bliss, but with strong passions.

These three views are intertwined, and on closer examination they not only provide us with a means of unravelling Boyd's system of thought but can also lead us to discover a way of evaluating his translation. For these comments on *Purgatorio* set out a scale of values, or a chain of human powers. Highest of all is morality and the moral sense. But morality is fed by the mind, and is dependant on mental energy (p. 10); and since Dante's punishments 'produce mental exertions' (p. 8) they are instrumental in building up the reader's moral sense. However, although it is true that the activity of the mind takes place 'in subordination of the leading power of Reason' (p. 9), the nature of this activity is more connected with a different human power: 'the true activity of the mind is sympathy' (p. 12). The moral sense proceeds from the mind, in particular from its feelings of sympathy. In its turn, sympathy is the highest form of a less elevated aspect of human experience – the exercise of passions. For the writer of poetry, 'to include the excesses of any of the passions, when they are exerted in the utmost exacerbation, seems nothing else but the natural activity of the mind, struggling too late against a legion of invading foes, which, by its own passiveness and neglect, it had suffered to enclose around' (p. 15). To sum up, passions, the mind, and the moral sense are the path education has to follow to affect man. It therefore follows that a poem which includes descriptions of 'scenes of turbulence or serenity', and which is an allegory of man's conversion will effectively lead its reader from the lowest level of awareness to the highest.

This is the system which Boyd envisages. It is clearly based on the current aesthetics of sensibility, which the eighteenth-century reader must to some extent have shared. This ladder of learning – from passions and fear, through inner or mental activity, to the attainment of moral and religious values – is lost to us. Modern readers are often trapped in the eighteenth-century metaphors of rhetorical language, of sublime landscape, or even of gothic gore. Consequently they are often unable to see that, rather than simply satisfying a widespread but somewhat infantile taste, the excesses of rhetoric and imagery are part of a complicated scheme – the lower rung of a ladder of significance which an eighteenth-century reader, recognizing the code embedded in the metaphors, would have understood. Modern readers, then, will censure the vehicles of the metaphor, remaining unable to grasp their 'tenor' and unable, therefore, to translate them into values with vital links to their own fears and hopes.

There are two lessons to be learned from Boyd's discussion of *Purgatorio*. The first concerns the primary limitations of translation. However willing the translator might be to reproduce the original, often his willingness cannot be transposed into the words on the page, without distortions. He must express the significance of the original's narrative in a new code which his own readers will interpret. The second lesson is one for the modern reader, or critic. To compare a translation by, say, William Boyd with Dante's original poem and notice discrepancies is a useless enterprise if it is the only basis for an evaluation of a translation. Any evaluation of and attempt at understanding must rely not only on an awareness of the historical temper of the period, including its science and philosophies, but in particular on a familiarity with the metaphors of the period, through which language gives shape to man and his world and communicates significance. For these metaphors change: so that today we censure the rhetorical excesses of Restoration drama and smile at the simplicity of gothic gore only because we have lost the key to their interpretations. The change, however, is not sudden. The patterns of significance Boyd uses in the essay under consideration are extremely useful in allowing us to see the continuity in values from the eighteenth to the nineteenth century.

At first sight Boyd seems to be yet another eighteenth-century writer who is unable to express himself, except in terms of the movement from particulars to universals or the Johnsonian method of surveying mankind 'from China to Peru' – which he uses for the purposes of the moral education of the reader. Indeed, the basic elements of Boyd's arguments are typical of eighteenth-century thought and are particularly reminiscent of Johnson. But beyond this conservative context one can distinguish elements characteristic of the Romantic imagination. So, although Boyd's concern with the education of the reader appears characteristic of the eighteenth century, particularly as it is expressed by Johnson in, for example, the *Vanity of Human Wishes*, the choice of Dante's poem as a tool for the education of the reader, and the scale of values in Boyd's essay reveal a shift towards Romantic thinking. For, first, the basic metaphor for progress – the attainment of (or progressive approximation to) happiness or a vague but ultimate human goal – is seen by Romantic thinkers as embodied in the myth of the fall and redemption of man. Poets like Wordsworth, Shelley and Keats, and philosophers like Schelling, Hegel and Fichte all adopt this story as the metaphor for their ideas, turning myth into the language of thought and philosophy. Secondly, two aspects of the poets' and philosophers' adaptation of this story are significant here: it is the individual who must pass through the experiences of creation, fall and redemption; and it is in this life that he must pass through them.[13]

Redemption becomes, in the view of these thinkers, not the reconciliation with a God above, but a process of self education, and of an increasing consciousness of both the self in nature and the self as the integration of its cognitive and moral constituent parts. It is remarkable that, in spite of being a priest and therefore committed to the transcendental pattern of redemption, in which Providence and Grace are indispensable, Boyd should stress to such an extent the redemption of man in this life, the action of Providence through the history of mankind, and particularly the need for man to move from error, through suffering, to a redeemed moral sense by reading a prophetic poem such as Dante's.

The very choice of this poem is a sign of the movement towards the myths characteristic of Romantic literature, which, as M.H. Abrams has said, is '"a literature of movement", in which the protagonist is a compulsive wanderer' and in which 'especially common is the story of the pilgrimage or quest', a story which, in addition, 'may be literal and realistic, with the progress of the individual pilgrim represented as typical of all artists, or all philosophical minds, or all mankind; or [the story] may be cased in an allegorical or symbolic mode ...'.[14] In his stress on the closeness of Dante's world to his own and on the allegorical mode used by Dante, Boyd also underlines the vital links between *Purgatorio* and those values in contemporary poetry that were coming to the fore at the time.

Turning to Boyd's rendering of *Purgatorio* we see that this well illustrates how the translator adapts his original to the metaphors, language and images which his readers would be able to respond to. In order to stress the redemptive pattern in the *Commedia*, Boyd reduces the role of the protagonist as an active agent so that he becomes a mere witness, but heightens the exemplary value of the figures the protagonist meets and the dramatic power of the stories they tell. To the same end Boyd adds sublimity to the landscape and to the language. The style is Miltonic – very visual and epithetic, thus stressing the English tradition within which Dante is placed. Indeed, in the final cantos of *Purgatorio* the arrival of Beatrice and the pageant of the Scriptures are presented not only in terms of the Miltonic sublime style, but in terms of images borrowed directly from Milton's poems.

Dante's *Purgatorio* opens on a scene of deep tranquillity, where, after the darkness and oppressiveness of Hell, the description of sea, sky, the island and its shore (in which Dante washes away the blackness of Hell and plucks one of the many reeds to tie round his waist) breathes freedom, spaciousness and serenity. It is not until Canto III that Dante (the protagonist) and the souls who have arrived on the shore suddenly turn to the Mount Purgatory towering above them. It is at this point that Dante's hard climb begins. The contrasting landscapes of sea and shores, rivers and valleys, and mountains, which have already played a significant role in *Inferno*, recur continuously in *Purgatorio*, not only in the natural landscape of the setting, but also in the stories told.

Boyd had noticed the tranquillity of the initial landscape of stars and skies, and renders it accordingly, but still he adds some personifications and one or two references to the past 'Stygian gloom', which suggest the lingering presence of the terrible sublime. Also, the landscape is not as vivid and striking in its contrasts as in the original, because the attention is focused more on the figures whom Dante meets. The encounters with Manfred in Canto III and with the souls who repented at the last moment in Canto V are a case in point.

This is the encounter with Manfred:

> Io mi volsi ver lui e guardail fiso:
>   biondo era e bello e di gentile aspetto,
>   ma l'un de' cigli un colpo avea diviso.   108
> Quand'i' mi fui umilmente disdetto
>   d'averlo visto mai, el disse: "Or vedi";
>   e mostrommi una piaga a sommo 'l petto.
> Poi sorridendo disse: "Io son Manfredi,"   (III 106-112)[15]

Manfred's gentle, smiling countenance is that of forgiveness experienced, but also that of Christ offering proof of God's pattern of redemption to Thomas. The reader who compares this with Boyd's version cannot but be initially shocked:

> ### XXI
> I turn'd me round, and mark'd his noble air,
> The gentle Vision wav'd his golden hair,
>   And inborn dignity his feature show'd,
> As when the honours of the world he wore;

But half his manly face was steep'd in gore,
Which from his wounded brow incessant flow'd
                    XXII
... at length his bosom, gor'd
by mortal steel, the mighty Phantom bar'd;
"See MANFRED here!..."

Boyd's distortion of the original is twofold: first, he adds the notion of 'might' and of 'the honours of the world', and secondly he adds an almost gothic flow of blood. In both cases Boyd is trying to do two things: to inform the reader as to the historical truth of the character, while at the same time attempting to recreate for the reader the meaning which the original embodied. For Dante's Italian reader knew full well that Manfred was at the time a symbol of the historical and political redemption of mankind. But to the English reader Manfred would at most have been a minor king of Naples, who was reported to have been a dissolute epicurean, eventually excommunicated by the Church. Thus Boyd's addition of a whole line ('As when the honours of the world he wore') and of the word 'mighty' serves to establish Manfred's reputation in Dante's time. Then, by creating a contrast between the honour bestowed on the man first and the 'mortal steel' that killed him in the end, Boyd reproduces something of Dante's pattern of redemption. For Manfred's story illustrates the brevity of worldy success, and also shows that conversion brings a heavenly reward that will not end. However, Boyd feels that he must justify Manfred's future reward in Paradise, and this leads him to his second distortion – the addition of gothic gore.[16] Manfred goes on shedding blood in Purgatory, where his expiation still continues. Boyd's distortions serve to underline the visionary quality of the apparition: Manfred becomes a vision of an apocalypse and an example from history.

The vision of blood that Boyd's Manfred introduces is not totally created without reference to the text, but is in fact transposed from Canto V, where Iacopo del Cassero and Buonconte da Montefeltro tell the story of their death and thus introduce into the text 'due visioni, due ossessioni' ('two visions, two obsessions') of blood.[17] Two warriors, each like Manfred, their stories form a unity with his, this unity being underlined by the similarity of the landscape in which their last moments take place. In Dante the three characters and their stories form a total vision, especially since Manfred was the hero of Dante's own political party, while Buonconte fought against Dante face to face in the battle of Campaldino. Manfred and Buonconte's similar fate, with their bones dispersed by the wind and rain, underlines the futility of political partisanship before the divine pattern of the individual's redemption. The history of Florentine battles is too distant from England in the eighteenth century for Boyd to be able to use it. But what he can do is underline the similarity in the destiny and conversion of these souls. Boyd is at pains to create links between the episode in Canto III and that in Canto V, first by picturing Manfred stained with the blood which so strikingly emerges from the stories of Iacopo and Buonconte, and, secondly, by having Jacopo introduce the group of souls in Canto V with the same words Manfred had used in Canto III: 'Behold these wounds!'

The encounter between Dante and the penitents of the last hour in Canto V opens with a comparison between the arrival of the souls, running like a troop with loose rein, and lightning:

> Vapori accesi non vid'io sí tosto
> di prima notte mai fender sereno,
> né, sol calando, nuvole d'agosto,   39
> che color non tornasser suso in meno;
> e, giunti là, con li altri a noi dier volta
> come schiera che scorre senza freno.   42
> "Questa gente che preme a noi è molta,
> e vegnonti a pregar," disse il poeta:
> "però pur va, ed in andando ascolta."   45
> "O anima che vai per esser lieta
> con quelle membra con le quai nascesti,"
> venían gridando, "un poco il passo queta.   48
> Guarda s'alcun di noi unqua vedesti,
> sí che di lui di là novella porti:
> deh, perché vai? deh, perché non t'arresti
> Noi fummo tutti già per forza morti"   (V 37-52)[18]

The visions of sky described briefly in the initial comparison are bright, but serene and peaceful. They also refer to sights which are simple and belong to common earthly experience. In particular, both the visions of sky and the sight of the souls assume vividness and probability because they are viewed by the poet/protagonist: 'vid' io' ('I saw') stresses that the experience really took place, and also brings together physical sensations on earth and the sights in Purgatory. So, indirectly, the personal vision of the poet/protagonist which justifies the experience and orders it becomes central. His vision is one of speed and movement, in which he joins. The souls appear as courteous and gentle, though eager.

Boyd disregards the clear serenity of the scene:

> VII
> In Autumn's windy close, a shooting Star
> Glancing across pale Ev'ning's umber'd car,
>   Or the short glimpses of a Summer's Sun,
> When 'gainst the driving rack he seems to ride,
> Are dull and tardy to the living tide,
>   That round in gloomy bands were seen to run.
> VIII
> Besieg'd we stood, by many a wond'ring soul;

Too eager far, they seem'd to bear control:
  "Repress your fears," the gentle Poet said;
"They're suppliants all, nor mean you any harm:
Listen to what they say, without alarm;
  Nor let your arduous journey be delay'd."
               IX
"OH THOU! that bear'st thy high distinguish'd clay
(A guest stupendous) to the realms of day,
  A moment check thy haste", they cry'd aloud:
"Mortal! contemplate these wan files, and try,
If any known resemblance meet thine eye,
  Oh! stay, and gratify a suppliant crowd!
              X
"Behold those wounds! we all in battle fell,"

The most striking difference with the original is certainly in the opening comparison with its descriptions of sky, which in Dante introduce an earthly landscape. Boyd leaves out the personal vision, which suggests the reality of the sight, and he makes the simile more classical by introducing forces with mythological trappings: Evening is made to move on an 'umbr'd car' which is clearly the counterpart of Phoebus' chariot. In addition, Boyd interprets the ignited vapours as a shooting star, and changes the month of August into late Autumn.

Had Boyd wished to reproduce the natural world with some vividness, he could have turned to English models, such as parts of Thomson's *The Seasons*, where close observation produced detailed descriptions which are vivid and maintain a link with the natural world.[19] But at this point Boyd is not trying to reproduce the original in contemporary terms. Rather, the close verbal similarity suggests that he was not translating Dante directly, but through Milton's imitation of Dante in Book IV of *Paradise Lost*:

> ... swift as a shooting star
> In autumn thwarts the night, when vapours fired
> Impress the air, ...   (IV 556-58)

Boyd is trying to make the reader see that Dante's poem belongs to the tradition of Milton's epic, and he will continue to do so by the repeated use of words such as 'autumn' and 'vapours'. And here Boyd's technique goes further than a simple adoption of the eighteenth-century Miltonic diction, and attempts to establish a literal link with Milton's poem.

Boyd further changes the original by adding a sense of danger and alarm rather than serenity, so that the protagonist needs Virgil's repeated assurances. The protagonist's fears keep his character consistent with that of the passive observer of Boyd's Hell, the recipient of what takes place rather than a participant. In addition to his alarm, other features of Boyd's translation contribute to placing the protagonist in the background of the action. The initial simile and the arrival of the souls are made vivid, in Dante, by the viewpoint of the poet/protagonist, the 'I saw' underlining the personal experience which is the basis for the fiction. Moreover, when the souls press around him, they are eager to speak to Dante, who is the centre of the scene, because he is a welcome link with earth. But in Boyd, Iacopo, the soul who speaks first, does not mention anything about intercession on earth, and so Boyd not only leaves unexplained the reason for the souls' eagerness, but also minimizes the role that the protagonist plays in the episode. And while the protagonist is placed in the background of the action, the other souls are pushed to the foreground; Iacopo addresses the protagonist in formal and elaborate language, and takes over the stage totally. Also, instead of having died violently, the souls in Boyd 'all in battle fell', so that the encounter becomes one with high-born princes and warriors, and Iacopo's courtesy then seems due to his knightly code rather than feelings of friendliness and a nostalgia for earthly affections.[20]

The world recalled in the simile, the situation of danger, and the speech of Iacopo all distance the poem as a record of lived experience, and stress its weight as a written narrative. The impressions drawn from the short passage examined are confirmed by a reading of the rest of the canto. To begin with the protagonist, he retains his exemplary but passive character. So, when he answers Iacopo that he cannot recognize anybody, Boyd adds the line, 'and yet a noble semblance all display'. This phrase suggests the courtesy of the knight, but it also diminishes the urgency of the issue at stake – the help he could provide. This effect is reinforced when, later, Boyd leaves out Buonconte's words 'io dirò 'l ver, e tu 'l ridil fra i vivi' ('I tell the truth: and do you tell it again among the living:'). Clearly, then, Boyd's protagonist does not serve as a recounter of truth on earth, and in his comment on the souls' 'semblance' he simply underlines their outward nobility.

But Boyd is at pains to stress the great worth of these souls, as we have already seen in his version of Manfred, and this intention continues to guide Boyd's hand. Buonconte had revealed his identity to Dante by saying 'Io fui da Montefeltro, io son Buonconte' ('I was of Montefeltro: I am Buonconte'), placing pride in his family name firmly in the past. Boyd, on the contrary, ensures that the English reader should realize that this new soul is also worthy to be the hero of an epic story, and has him say 'I boast the blood of MONTEFELTRO's line'. Dante's protagonist, we know, appeared too passive to the English reader, and so Boyd makes sure that other figures in the poem will appear to be worthy of attention.

For the same reason, Boyd also increases the narrative interest in the stories of their deaths which the two souls tell, and in particular in the description of the storm which follows Buonconte's death. Both Iacopo and Buonconte die after a long flight, which traces a similar course – from a mountain and down a valley along a river. Iacopo reaches some marshes, and becomes entangled in the mire and the reeds. He dies as he sees his own blood form a lake. Buonconte flees on foot with a shaft in his neck, "nsanguinando 'l piano' ('bloodying the plain'), and dies at the point where the river flows into the Arno, his solitary flight showing the loneliness of the sinner at his death. But Boyd makes the obvious plight of these men even more distressing, by heightening in both stories the urgency of their flight. In both cases the pursuers are mentioned: so, when Iacopo gets entangled, he sees that 'they [his pursuers] hemmed me round', while Buonconte was 'by terror chased', both clauses being additions.

The mention not only of the pursued but also of the pursuers is an apparently gothic touch, which would probably please the reader of gothic fiction, but it also underlines the horror of these men's deaths in contrast to the nobility and courtesy of their lives, and justifies, by contrast, the dignity of their state in the afterlife. Boyd therefore stresses the difference between their worldly, and their spiritual destinies. In the case of Buonconte, for example, he concludes:

> "...
>   And, 'reft of sight and speech, my limbs repos'd.
>   XVIII
> "In MARY's name, I breathe'd my latest pray'r;
> Releas'd, my soaring Spirit wing'd the air
>   ..."

The last verse, introducing a feeling of freedom, is a complete addition, and contrasts the release of the spirit with the oppression of the body. In these lines the adjective 'latest' is also added to refer to his prayer, obviously in order to justify, to protestant readers, Buonconte's heavenly reward. For the word 'latest' implies that Buonconte had not repented only at the last moment, but had turned to God before. The sense of sublime space introduced at this point is continued in the description of the storm that breaks loose at Buonconte's death.

Just as in Canto V of *Inferno* Francesca's passion had found its natural correspondence in the stormy winds which carried the souls along, so here the storm and the other passages of description picture a landscape of fallen man, where wars and storms rage. In Canto V of *Purgatorio*, the storm is caused by a devil's anger at seeing Buonconte's soul snatched away by an angel as a consequence of that single prayer. In Dante this devil, called briefly 'quel d'inferno', is a very medieval creature, simply the opposite of the good angel fighting for a soul, and brings the storm on all by himself. In fact, when he does so, he is called 'quel mal volere' ('that evil will') who combines will and intellect.

The upheaval of nature is caused by this abstract definition of evil – depraved will and intellect. He is a force, rather than a figure, which one cannot visualize on the basis of the text alone, although no doubt the medieval reader would have been able to fill in the gap on the basis of those few words, which would call up any images of the devil he might already have stored in his mind.

Boyd, however, leaves little to the imagination:

XVII

"...
Releas'd, my soaring Spirit wing'd the air;
  Aloft, an heav'nly Pursuivant was seen,
Commission'd from the sky: but soon below,
A swarthy Claimant, from the world of woe,
  Rose, with funereal yell, and rush'd between.

XIX

"'How dare you seize my right?' aloud he cried;
'Is it because a tear was seen to glide
  Down his wan cheek, before he breath'd his last?
Must that an endless fount of bliss supply? –
– Yet not in peace the Caitiff's corse shall lie,
  If yet I rule the rude aerial bast.'

XX

"Those vapours that usurp the ambient skies,
Till to the frigid element they rise;
  That checks their pride, and sends their livid stores
In rainy deluges; the Demon caught,
And in long range his gloomy squadrons brought,
  To pour their stormy rage on ARNO's shore.

XXI

"From APPENNINE the cloudy veil he drew,
Till PRATOMAGNO's plains were lost to view;
  While sullen EVE was seen, with dusky hand,
To add he texture of her STYGIAN loom;
The sky put on a formidable gloom.
  And ruffling winds obey'd his stern command."[21]

The description is laden with periphrases and elaborate, ponderous language. Each noun has a descriptive adjective, and these usually enlarge the scale and intensify the awfulness of the thing described – 'proud', 'bloody', 'soaring', 'heav'nly', 'swarthy', 'funereal', 'endless', 'rude'. At times, the adjective doubles the meaning of the noun, as in 'rainy deluges', or 'stormy rage'. In this setting, painted with the colours of the terrible sublime, a devil appears like an actor on a stage. In the place of Dante's abstract force, here we have a figure: we are informed of his dark complexion, and he steps on stage shouting and rushing between the two other figures. Colour, sound and movement all contribute to the shaping of this figure. And he is not just any devil, but Satan himself. In the second stanza quoted he utters a full speech, and concludes it with a statement of his power: 'If yet I rule the rude aerial blast.' Clearly a self-magnifying, self-dramatizing Satan, Boyd's devil has hellish troops at his command. He calls upon his 'gloomy squadrons' to cause the upheaval in the sky. The forces in nature are also magnified and turn into personified powers; the vapours 'usurp' the sky and possess 'pride' and 'rage'. The notion of 'pride' is referred to again twice in the following stanzas, once in the combination 'proud and majestic', referring to the flood. This picture of evil is directly linked with Hell through the reference, absent in the original, to the 'Stygian loom' of evening. Some of the words used, the presence of Satan, and the awful sublimity of the picture are not mere features of the eighteenth-century sublime style, and are more direct references to Milton's *Paradise Lost*.

The pageant of Revelation and the arrival of Beatrice that form the closing section of *Purgatorio* confirm Boyd's attempt to stress the moral relevance of the lesson in *Purgatorio*, and confirm his choice of Milton as the model and the tradition which can best give shape and voice to Dante's poem and foster the reader's acceptance of it.

The arrival of Beatrice is introduced, like the encounter with Iacopo and Buonconte, with a comparison – to dawn, in this case, rather than sunset:

> Io vidi già nel cominciar del giorno
> la parte oriental tutta rosata,
> e l'altro ciel di bel sereno adorno;   24
> e la faccia del sol nascere ombrata,
> sí che, per temperanza di vapori,
> l'occhio la sostenea lunga fiata: 27
> cosí dentro una nuvola di fiori
> che dalle mani angeliche saliva
> e ricadeva in giú dentro e di fori,   30
> sovra candido vel cinta d'uliva
> donna m'apparve, sotto verde manto
> vestita di color di fiamma viva.   (XXX, 22-33)[22]

'Io vidi' – 'I saw' – introduces the description of a sky at dawn, which is the natural scene corresponding to the supernatural apparition of Beatrice. This apparition is prepared throughout the tercets, which move to the climax of line 32. The natural description is peaceful and soothing; and even the brightness of the sun is veiled by clouds, so that it does not overwhelm man's sight. The supernatural description is of angels scattering flowers. Only at line 32 does Beatrice appear, like a vision – her olive crown a sign of peace and wisdom, and her clothes the colours of hope, faith and charity. At this initial point, Beatrice seems to be purely an emblematic picture and the symbolic link between the natural and the supernatural, presented in obviously Christian terms.

Boyd, however, tones down both the natural and the divine:

VI

While Earth was clad with FLORA's spoils below,
Sudden the East, with corresponding glow,
   Seemed to reflect the blushing tint afar:
So have I seen, o'er Ocean's wavy bed,
The Sun ascend, celestial rosy red,
   When vapours paint his flaming Car.

VII

Ruddy as Phoebus, in AURORA's Bower,
A radiance, veil'd amid the fragrant shower
   Of falling roses, seem'd, with umber'd glance,
To rival Day's fair Lord; and soon display'd
Thro' the deep cloud of sweets, a matchless Maid
   Seem'd thro' the plausive Squadrons to advance.

VIII

A snowy veil she wore; with olive bound,
A green stole far behind her, swept the ground;
   Beneath, a tunic like AURORA's vest
Her decent limbs embrac'd with cincture bright:

The original's merging of the natural and the supernatural here disappears. The former is obscured and abstracted in the wealth of mythological names and attributes, among which we find some of Boyd's favourite expressions – the car, the vapours, autumn. As for the supernatural, religious and ceremonial expressions are erased: the hands throwing flowers are not angelic, and the figure of the woman appears as the mythological figure Aurora. Further on in the poem she is called 'The Fair', and the 'Nymph' who guides men to Elysium. Her emblematic power is also distorted: for, first, she does not appear suddenly, as in a vision; and secondly, rather than a 'lady', it is a 'maid' who slowly advances. Above all, the changed details must have reminded the English reader of a different female image altogether, since Boyd's additions – the 'cincture', the decent covering of the limbs, the robe flowing to the ground – correspond to a specific literary figure:

    Come pensive Nun, devout and pure,
Sober, stedfast, and demure,
All in a robe of darkest grain,
Flowing with majestic train,
And sable stole of cypress lawn,
Over thy decent shoulders drawn,   ('Il Penseroso' 31-36)

This woman in Milton's 'Penseroso', upon which Boyd draws, immediately strikes one as the absolute opposite of Hayley's temptress 'Ch – h' in *The Triumphs of Temper* (see p. 90 above). Even more than Hayley's pure Serena Milton's devout nun is the true opposite of the 'whore of Babylon' – the two forming what Frye calls the 'apocalyptic' and 'demonic' versions of the same image.[23]

This pervasive biblical image joins notions of temptation and salvation (and of the dual significance of apocalypse) within the image of marriage, for the whore suggests the violation of the marriage covenant in the form of sexual infidelity or whoredom, while the virgin hails the coming of a new heaven and a new earth in the union of Christ and the heavenly city, his bride. English literature has made full use of this complex system of images, and of the significance and iconography implicit in them. The eighteenth century's pervasive concern with the theme of marriage, and of the role of the woman in marriage and in society, naturally assumed the biblical typology as its context. Hence, Pope, in his disguise as Esdras Barnivelt, comments on his own *Rape of the Lock* that Belinda can be seen as a type of the whore of Babylon.[24]

But Boyd, unlike Hayley, avoids such direct references. When, in *The Triumphs of Temper*, Sophrosyne had assumed the role of Beatrice on the car, Hayley had added to her figure a feature, the crown of twelve stars, from Revelation 12:1:

> From her fair brow a radiant diadem
> Shone in twelve stars, and every separate gem
> Shot magic rays ....   (1804, V, p. 83)

Hayley therefore inserts a specific emblem to establish the significance of this spirit. Boyd, however, secularizes the image of Beatrice on the car, or at least turns it into an image which is linked directly with an image in earlier English poems, and only indirectly to the common source of both images in biblical texts. The link is not only with Milton, but also with Spenserian romance. In Dante's *Purgatorio* the revelation that Beatrice brings is for mankind, but also specifically for Dante, her beloved. Dante is back in the earthly Paradise, but as a result of the experience of the journey his state is spiritually more elevated than that of man before the fall. In the original the protagonist is again smitten by love for Beatrice – but this love is called 'l'alta virtu' ('high virtue'), so that one can immediately see the divine love behind the earthly love. Here a return to higher morality and wisdom is expressed in language similar to that of Dante's earlier love poetry; the very sentence 'Donna m'apparve' fits in both with the emblematic context and with the language of the *canzoni* of the *Vita Nuova*. What Boyd does here is to stress, appropriately enough, the personal feelings, but also to change the recognition of high virtue into the outburst of a courtier: "T was my first love!' (VIII). Boyd's language, moreover, takes on a vague aura of Spenser in such moments as the following transition from one sentence to the next:

> VII
> ... and soon display'd
> Thro' the deep cloud of sweets, a matchless Maid

Seem'd thro' the plausive Squadrons to advance.

This deliberate echoing of a Spenserian atmosphere of romance is suitable for rendering the poetry of friendship and of love, which plays a role in *Purgatorio*, beginning with Casella's song and finding its climax in the arrival of Beatrice. And the combination of Milton and Spenser as the medium through which Boyd translates Dante's poetry means that the reader can approach Dante through the language and metaphors of familiar authors. In the case of biblical echoes, the pattern of redemption will appear secularized, and the tension between Dantean and biblical typology will also be mediated through English poetry. The readers will then experience Dante's poem as less foreign, and will be in less danger of misunderstanding the significance of the images, which they would read in Protestant terms. In addition, in Boyd's view, they will probably be able to respond more directly to the moral instruction, which Boyd is at pains to underline.

Clearly *Purgatorio* was seen by Boyd as a poem in the tradition of Milton and Spenser, and as an instrument of moral instruction: and Boyd's version of the closing moments of the pageant of Revelation finally confirm these conclusions. The pageant continues in Canto XXXII with the attack on the cart by a fox, an eagle and a dragon. The dragon pushes his tail through the floor of the cart, destroying part of it. Dante hardly describes the dragon, again relying, probably, on the reader's familiarity with the iconography he is using. Boyd makes the image more precise by describing a 'serpent' who 'drew his fatal spires, and spread his dragon wings'. Resembling more and more Spenser's and Milton's embodiments of evil, the serpent then destroys the cart, which is twice called the 'Sacred Seat' – clearly a Miltonic phrase. The use of Miltonic imagery and vocabulary continues to the end of the episode. The transformation of the chariot into the beast of the Apocalypse with seven heads is translated literally by Boyd, who, however, adds that the heads 'with baleful accents breath'd revenge and war', echoing the key words of Satan and the devils' debate in Book I of *Paradise Lost*.

The canto, and the pageant, close with the vision of the harlot and her lover, a giant – emblems of the corrupt church and conniving empire. His jealousy inflamed by the harlot's glances towards the protagonist, the giant drags her into the wood. In his version, Boyd distances the apocalyptic images and keeps his protagonist in the background. Had Boyd translated the original literally, the eighteenth-century English reader must have interpreted the figures of the whore and the giant as representing the church of Rome and the pope (the antichrist) respectively. But Boyd turns the harlot into an 'adulteress', and her lover into her 'consort'. Thus Boyd's version of these two figures still suggests the demonic image of the biblical marriage, and turns Dante's allegory into a plausible representation of sinfulness in Christian terms. Boyd keeps the character of the protagonist consistent by keeping him constantly in the background, and by continuing to stress his purity. In the original, the whore looked insistently at Dante himself (whose name has been mentioned by Beatrice in Canto XXX), thereby stressing that this revelation is directed at him. But Boyd's adulteress is made to cast her general glance around her, and Dante becomes just a witness rather than a protagonist.

The reader who knows Dante's poem will miss much in Boyd's translation of the significance of the final cantos of *Purgatorio*, which are among the most poignant and at the same time most difficult. It is here that Dante's imagination succeeds best, perhaps, in combining, in a unique and indissoluble narrative, the story of a man's life in its most personal and deeply felt moments with a view of the universal redemption of mankind. Much of the subtlety and complexity of Dante's poem is inevitably lost in Boyd's translation, whose contemporary reader would find it difficult, if not impossible, to envisage Beatrice as Christ, or as the sacrament of the Eucharist, and would consequently be unable to discover the intricacy behind the simplicity of Dante's design. But it would be unrealistic and wrong to expect the first translation of Dante into English to be able to reproduce all these patterns of significance. And Boyd's achievement in his translation of *Purgatorio* is really quite considerable, weaknesses being balanced by strengths.

One could, for example, find much to criticize in Boyd's version of the protagonist. But in spite of his passivity, this figure remains consistent throughout the translation, and his character seems to solve the problems which readers of the age appear to have found in Dante's protagonist. As for the moral instruction which is the motivation for many of Boyd's changes, a stress on moral judgement is not inappropriate in *Purgatorio*, where the reader repeatedly and very obviously feels 'il severo giudizio del poeta', and 'il carattere morale dell'ispirazione dantesca' ('the poet's stern judgement' and 'the moral character of Dante's inspiration').[25]

Boyd's awareness of the importance of earthly landscape is translated into a geographically accurate world. The indirect references, in the original, to places or names scattered in many of the stories which are told, such as those of Iacopo and Buonconte, are paraphrased by Boyd with accurate geographical terms and names. So 'tra Romagna e quel di Carlo' becomes ''twixt Romagna and th'Apulian coast', and 'in grembo alli Antenori' becomes 'by Po's resounding flood'. In Boyd's 'a stream descends,/ By Camaldoli's walls its current bends,/ Till in proud Arno's wave its name is lost', 'Camaldoli' translates Dante's 'l'Ermo' correctly. In the first two examples the name of a family or a person is replaced with the corresponding geographical area. Certainly this diminishes the impression created by the original, where the landscape is linked by name to the men who live and lived there. Boyd's version also cuts down the number of names of people and families requiring explanations, perhaps tedious for the contemporary reader, and provides in their place further strokes with which to sketch the sublime landscape of coast and river characteristic of *Purgatorio*.

While to add sublimity to the landscape of Hell might be a mistake, to add it to *Purgatorio* is possibly more appropriate, since some modern critics see its landscape in terms which correspond to eighteenth-century sublimity.[26] And since the eighteenth-century sublime is not simply meant to provide the reader with a pleasurable *frisson*, but also to lift up the mind and soul towards the divine, it is certainly appropriate in a poem which, after perfecting his moral sense, carries the protagonist to God.

Perhaps more importantly, Boyd's attempt to relate *Purgatorio* to *Paradise Lost* in terms of vocabulary corresponds in fact to the original's choice of imagery and symbolism, which are often derived, as di Pino pointed out in his reading of Canto X, from the symbols surrounding the story of the fall.[27] Thus snakes, flowers, angels, the name of Eve, and the exile from Paradise create a pattern of reference very different from that of *Inferno*, where man had rejected redemption. To the modern reader, Boyd's mythological references, the personifications, and the abundance of adjectives and phrases which increase the import and awfulness of the actions and descriptions seem forced and excessively rhetorical. This resonant pseudo-Miltonic style is certainly unable to adequately render the lyrical and elegiac tone of most of the *cantica*, though, in some moments, Boyd does turn to the language of Spenserian romance in an attempt to vary his style and introduce the tone and diction of courtly and love poetry. In addition, the style of Spenser and Milton would display a sense of the antique, and a quality of religious tradition in literature. In this sense, the Miltonic style does correspond to the stern medium in the passages describing the allegorical pageant in the original, where Dante 'used a language which had for himself and his contemporaries the traditional solemn authority of vision and inspiration'.[28] The Miltonic style seems to have had the same solemn authority for Boyd's contemporaries. Thus, by extending the use of this style throughout the poem, Boyd is therefore turning the whole of *Purgatorio* into a poem of vision and inspiration. The direct links with poems such as the 'Penseroso' and in particular *Paradise Lost*, the increased sublimity of the descriptions, and even the gothic touches all contribute to this same effect.

Boyd's *Paradiso*

Boyd's choice of diction and the more specific echoes of Milton's poems place Dante's *Commedia* within the tradition of English prophetic poetry, which was established by Spenser and Milton, represented somewhat freely by Thomson and Young in the eighteenth century, and inherited by Blake and Wordsworth in their own different ways. This is a mainly Protestant tradition, which adopts as a major source the Bible, and in particular the Book of Revelation. Italian writers of prose or poetry in the Middle Ages also drew much of their language and many of their metaphors from the same biblical texts. To take a small example from Dante, the repeated 'io vidi' is a sign which belongs to the mode of visionary literature; upon it depend not only the organization of the material (as successive visions), but also the role of an autobiographical self as witness, suggesting on its own the basic typological view of past and future, which includes recorded history and revealed afterlife. Boyd's version of Dante's *Inferno* and *Purgatorio*, however, seems contradictory in its relation to the Bible. Boyd is at pains to introduce the poems as belonging to the tradition of English prophetic literature; yet at the same time he changes Dante's images drawn directly from the Bible into the Spenserian and Miltonic versions of the same images, and he tones down Dante's direct allusions to the Book of Revelation. So, as we have seen, he takes away from the protagonist the role of witness and of link between the revealed truth and those for whom the revelation is meant, a change which is indicated, for one thing, by the disappearance, in places, of the mode of personal vision – the 'io vidi'.

This might suggest that the nature of Boyd's translation is due less to deliberate choice than simply to the ready availability in England of a native tradition which seems to accommodate, in a perfectly natural fashion, a journey into Hell and a flight into space towards the divine, and which is in fact highly imitable. But Boyd was in fact aware of the key role played by the protagonist in the original, as is shown by his stress on the function of the protagonist in his preliminary essay to *Purgatorio*. Further confirmation that Boyd read Dante's poem as a poem of vision is provided in the 'Preliminary Essay on the Paradiso of Dante'.

Boyd's introductory essay opens with a direct statement of the theme he has chosen for discussion, which he must, therefore, see as central to *Paradiso*:

> In this Essay I shall confine myself to the illustration of an opinion which often occurs in this part of DANTE's Poem, ... probably learned from Saint Augustine ... the idea of seeing all things in God.[29]

Boyd continues by explaining this view, according to which the nature of true vision would be the perception of objects of sense in the ideas which exist in the mind of God; and he adds that 'the premises are arguable, but ... so captivating to the fancy that a Poet may easily obtain pardon for having adopted a system, which formerly was defended by the gravest Philosophers ...' (p. 5). These philosophers seem to be Dr Reid, Bishop Berkeley, and especially Malebranche and Plato. The rest of the essay is mainly taken up with an exposition of the views of Malebranche, as being so similar to Dante's that a closer examination is considered necessary.

What Boyd highlights in Dante's poem is the fact that the notion of 'vision' includes the shift from the sight of concrete objects of perception to the abstract vision 'of the most sublime intellectual truths'. Boyd's choice of this as the theme of his discussion illuminates the very centre of Dante's third *cantica*, in which indeed the idea of sight – the limitations of mortal sight, the difficulty of describing the sights of Paradise, and the final failure of sight which is however redeemed by vision – summarizes the progress of the protagonist and the reader in their journey from Hell to Paradise. Boyd's choice of themes proves to be even more perceptive when the preliminary essay is followed by an 'Extract from the Symposium of Plato – the Speech attributed to Socrates, on the Means of acquiring the Love of God, or the First Good'. The extract selected focuses on the idea of love. Love and the idea of sight, therefore, are established as the two basic issues in Dante's *Paradiso*, which in turn means that Boyd's introductory apparatus to the *cantica* guides the reader to see the whole *Commedia* as a poem centred upon love and structured around the idea of vision.

Vision as prophecy is also strongly highlighted in the extract from the *Symposium*. Here, the narrative is meant to be the teaching of 'DIOTIMA, a Prophetess' to Socrates, and the mediated passing on of this lesson by Socrates to his friends, the other guests of a banquet.[30] This framework in itself introduces the basic ideas of revelation and instruction. Moreover, the issues Socrates recounts assume a particular significance in the context of Dante's *Commedia* and its introduction into England in the early years of the nineteenth century.

Love, according to Diotima, is 'desire for some inseparable good', and includes love of beauty as well as of immortality, both being necessary for the fulfillment of the lover's chief desire – to bring forth progeny. There is a progeny of the body, but also a progeny of the mind, and 'Poets, in this respect, may be called parents' (p. 25). Indeed, the spiritual offspring of poets or legislators is 'truly immortal, and to be preferred to all others' (p. 26).

Socrates is presented as being in need of both 'instruction' (p. 24) and 'inspiration' (p. 22), and at this point Diotima promises that she will assist him with all her power so that he may be able to produce 'such an offspring'. What follows is an initiation into the mysteries concerning the notion of love. The revelation of the mysteries proceeds in a series of steps. First the lover falls in love with one particular person; he will then move through a succession of stages of love – beginning from love of physical beauty, and moving afterwards to love of the 'Beauty of the Mind'. Next he will proceed to 'moral duty' and a 'Love of Virtue'. Having comprehended ethics and contemplated the Sciences, he will 'not only see, but feel' the power of the mind: 'Lost in the contemplation of Beauty, as in a boundless ocean, he will then be able to contemplate the wonderful fabric of all philosophy in all its proportions, various in its relations, but uniform in its tendency' (p. 27). Here metaphors of spatial sublimity support the expression of a 'passion' for the sublimity of the spiritual, emphasized by the repeated use of phrases such as 'utmost ardour' and 'ineffable transport'. Having moved from ethics to this 'passion', the lover may then achieve a vision of the divine, described by Plato (in Boyd's translation) in these terms:

> The great uncreated *self-existent Being*, who not like other beings a mixture of perfection and defect, unites in himself all perfections; he that sees him, does not see as here below, a fading image of moral excellence, but VIRTUE itself in visible form (p. 27).

The final words of the extract describe the felicity of the man who sees absolute beauty in its essence. Having brought forth pure goodness, such a man will be loved by God, and will become himself 'immortal' (p. 28).

By recalling this passage in the introduction to *Paradiso* Boyd guides the reader to notice the similarity of some of its features with the final vision of *Paradiso*. I am not arguing for a direct indebtedness of Dante to Plato – something which might well be true, but which falls outside the scope of my own competence here. What is very important in the present context is to see how thoroughly Boyd tries to present Dante as a philosophical writer whose poem reveals truth, setting out in the complete poem a scale of values – from the corporeal, to ethics, to the ultimate vision of beauty.

But it is equally important to notice how tentative and cautious Boyd is in his stance. The names of British thinkers and the ideas of Malebranche and Plato build around Dante's poem a context meant to establish his status as a writer of philosophical and instructive poetry, a writer moreover who might choose to achieve his aim occasionally through gothic or melancholy gloom. Yet Boyd is still uncertain whether an emphasis such as this will be well received, and his caution appears in the very fact that he does not explain his reasons for including the passage from Plato. He provides the reader with the combination of the two texts, Plato's and Dante's, and hopes the reader will do the rest for himself. Thus, in the introductory essay, he does not commit himself totally to this view of Dante, and he is even more hesitant in his translation of *Paradiso*.

Boyd does stress, in his translation, the role played by sight, the philosophical nature of the poem, and the mystic vision which concludes it, but he does not dare or choose to put into practice all that he shows he has perceived. The final vision, in particular, has little of universal love, and the visionary powers are restricted to the figure of the poet. It is as if in his introductory material Boyd plants a seed which he hopes will bear fruit in the readers' awareness of the nature of Dante's poem. But that this seed did not germinate is proved by Dante's status, in England in the first half of the nineteenth century, as the melancholy poet of Hell. The lack of response to Boyd's introductory essays is further shown by his failure to later publish them all separately from the translation and in a more worked out form, as he had intended. Still, his translation of *Paradiso* is very interesting as a text in its own right, because it is the first version of the *Paradiso* in English, and because in it Boyd pursues his efforts to find a language and images with which to render the world of Dante into English. As we shall see, Boyd not only continues with his reliance on Miltonic sublimity, but adds variety to the style, and attempts to insert more subtle poetic effects in the manipulation of sounds. He also continues with his presentation of a passive protagonist, but presents the poet as a bard who achieves vision. Boyd's *Paradiso* is a poem of vision, has a stress on narrative movement, and contains within it a morally valid model of conduct.

The very opening of Boyd's third *cantica* immediately indicates his choice of a definite English model, and his departure from the original:

> La gloria di colui che tutto move
> per l'universo penetra e risplende
> in una parte più e meno altrove.   3
> Nel ciel che piú della sua luce prende
> fu' io, e vidi cose che ridire
> né sa né può chi di là su discende;   6
> perché appressando sé al suo disire,
> nostro intelletto si sprofonda tanto,
> che dietro la memoria non può ire.   9
> Veramente quant'io del regno santo
> nella mia mente potei far tesoro,
> sarà ora matera del mio canto.   12
> O buon Apollo, all'ultimo lavoro
> fammi del tuo valor sí fatto vaso,
> come dimandi a dar l'amato alloro.   (I 1-15)[31]

Dante introduces immediately the presence of God, but not in an anthropomorphic form. God is known by his effect upon the observable movement of the universe; and on the basis of his own visit to Paradise the poet can add that God's light shines in different degrees according to the merit attributed to the particular place – an idea which will be developed in later cantos. The fourth tercet introduces the distinct figures of the protagonist and of the poet: the two possessive adjectives (ll. 11 and 12) refer in a first moment to the memory of the past experience, and in a separate, second moment to the present of the recounting ('sarà ora matera del mio canto'), on the basis of which the poet hopes he will be crowned with the bays. A further obvious point of Dante's lines is the controlled presence of light and movement, represented by single words or verbs – 'luce', 'penetra', 'risplende' ('light', 'penetrates', 'shines').

All these features – God, the poet, light and movement – are present in Boyd's version in heightened form:

> His Glory, who, with solitary hand,
> Launches thro' boundless space the stellar Band,
>   And shines effulgent, or involves his Throne
> In darkness, as he wills, in daring strains
> I sing, admitted to the lofty planes,
>   Fill'd with the Glory of th'ETERNAL ONE.
>   II
> There saw I things beyond Creation's bourne,
> Which some who from her flaming bounds return
>   Can tell, when soaring Thought is launch'd so far
> In Being's vast Abyss, that Mem'ry fails,
> Nor dares pursue, altho' with crowded sails
>   She tries the Voyage o'er th'eternal Bar.
>   III
> But some small remnant of that heavn'ly Spoil,
> From that strange Voyage won with arduous toil
>   To her dear native soil, the Muse shall bear;
> If the bless'd Pow'r of Inspiration deign
> To breathe his Spirit thro' my latest strain,
>   And make it worthy of the wreath I wear.

God is on the scene here in person, as it were, in the image of his 'solitary hand', and also in the description of his actions, which are not the basic motions indicating his control of the universe, but are rather spectacular and visual as he 'launches' the stars on their course, and shines or wraps his throne in darkness. Light and darkness, as in Genesis, divide space, which is itself extended to the limit and beyond in the 'lofty soaring' and the 'vast Abyss'. These phrases belong to the Miltonic sublime, but the language and style are closer to the eighteenth-century version of the mode. Essentially, Boyd turns to the boundless darkness of Young's cosmic voyage in 'Night the IXth' of the *Night Thoughts*, a voyage performed in order to witness a revelation of human destiny (in general as well as in its particular application to one particular individual, this being, in Young, Lorenzo). So, Boyd adds the word 'voyage' to the original and in fact repeats it twice in his version of this passage. The descriptions and the movements from one scene to another in *Paradiso* are consistently rendered by Boyd in this vein.[32] Partly it is an inescapable choice, since the poetry of Young was the obvious English model for a poem which centred upon the idea of revelation through a cosmic journey. But, nevertheless, it implies that Boyd was searching for an equivalent of Dante's poem which would be familiar to the English reader.

Boyd's recreative approach to the original is paralleled by a recreative approach to his models, for he also modifies the characteristic poetry of Young's *Night Thoughts*, shaping it according to his ideas on Dante, which often coincide with more recent developing views in English poetry. It is true that Boyd continues with the heavy predication characteristic of the Miltonic sublime: his translation is laden with general, indefinite adjectives – 'solitary', 'boundless', 'stellar', 'daring', 'lofty', 'flaming', 'soaring', 'crowded'; and some of the nouns these adjectives modify express vague spatial concepts – 'space', 'planes', 'bounds', 'Abyss'. But alongside these more conservative elements, three changes must be pointed out. First, the abstractions, personifications and mythological references are fewer than in Young's version of the Miltonic sublime. The stress is on the 'strange Voyage' rather than on 'thought', so that, even though the objects presented are not truly visible, they still suggest the possibility of vision. Secondly, Boyd's language departs from Young's conservative stress on the abstract and super-natural, and moves towards the more physical 'hand', the more personal 'hearing' and 'seeing', the more human-related 'power' and' spirit', which all suggest human response to scene.[33] Thirdly, Boyd's lines are full of verbs indicating action in a manner quite unlike Young's verses, where verbs are proportionally few. As in the figure of God launching the stars, Boyd's stress on movement, action in place of state, and expanded space emphasize the role played by setting and action in the original, and therefore add a narrative interest which can be found throughout this *cantica* in Boyd's version.

It is, therefore, through his imitation, rather than slavish copying, of Young and Thomson's Miltonic style that Boyd creates his version of *Paradiso*, one in which description and narrative become much more prominent than in the original – although the descriptions are of general sublimity. A further example, this time from Canto VII, will confirm that the greater prominence given by Boyd to description and narrative is sustained throughout. Beatrice explains the fall of Adam, and in Dante her story is somewhat abstract and generalized:

> "Per non soffrire alla virtú che vole
> freno a suo prode, quell'uom che non nacque,
> dannando sé, dannò tutta sua prole;   27
> onde l'umana specie inferma giacque
> giú per secoli molti in grande errore,
> fin ch'al Verbo di Dio discender piacque   30
> u' la natura, che dal suo fattore
> s'era allungata, uní a sé in persona
> con l'atto sol del suo etterno amore."   (VII, 25-33)[34]

In Boyd this becomes a sequence of events and separate actions:

"Created free to chuse the unborn man,
When to his lordly will the reins were giv'n,
Turn'd a proud rebel in the face of Heav'n,
And led to HADES all the human clan.
V
"Deeply they plung'd beneath the deadly shade
Of mental Night, that her broad wing display'd
Thro' many a dark age o'er the slumb'ring Soul;
Till from disclosing Heav'n th'omnific Word,
With soul-renewing grace their strength restor'd,
And with new light illum'd the dusky Pole.
VI
"Lost man, to Demon-guidance long resign'd ,
That left each character of Heav'n behind,
He seized, as, driving down the tide of Time,
He sail'd before the stream, and form'd anew
To that first pattern which their Maker drew,
When first they breath'd in EDEN's happy clime."

In Boyd's version, Adam was given physical control, as it were, of his own destiny and that of mankind; but subsequently he 'turned rebel', and 'led' man to Hell in a succession of separate events spread out over the course of time – and time markers are added and emphasized in Boyd's text. In addition, Dante's general and static 'onde l'umana specie inferma giacque/ giú per molti secoli in grande errore' ('so that the human race lay sick/ down there for many centuries in great error') becomes the Miltonic plunge 'beneath the deadly shade of mental night'. The story becomes animated by obvious literal references to Milton's *Paradise Lost*, so that Adam assumes the movements and experiences of Satan. At this point in Boyd the tone, the language, and the very life of Dante's *Paradiso* are all lost. In Dante not a single reference to darkness, or night, or gloom is to be found; while the visible, on the contrary, is characterized by an unprecedented variety and gradation of luminosity. Boyd diverges so greatly from the original that occasionally, as in the case of the last stanza quoted, it is difficult to see if Boyd is translating by paraphrasing lines from Dante, or adding some of his own.

Yet, alongside such drastic distortions and the pastiche of the style of Young, one also finds in Boyd's *Paradiso* a strongly contrasting literalness in the translation, and a diction which is bare and controlled. Some of the passages most literally translated are those which describe sight as knowledge, Boyd here following the theme of his introductory essay. Two examples of this literalness will suffice. The first is from Canto I:

Beatrice tutta nell'etterne rote
fissa con li occhi stava; ed io in lei

le luci fissi, di là su remote,   66
Nel suo aspetto tal dentro mi fei
    qual si fe Glauco nel gustar dell'erba
    che 'l fe consorte in mar delli altri dei.   (I 64-69)[35]
                    XVI
As if she meant to watch in museful mood
The mighty mundane wheel, absorbed she stood;
    I watched her look with unaverted eye,
    Still wond'ring, and still changing as I gaz'd;
    Like Glaucus, by the magic herb amaz'd
    When first he long'd new elements to try.

And again in Canto II:

Beatrice in suso, e io in lei guardava,
    e forse in tanto in quanto un quadrel posa
    e vola e dalla noce si dischiava,   24
giunto mi vidi ove mirabil cosa
    mi torse il viso a sé; e però quella
    cui non potea mia cura essere ascosa,   27
volta ver me, sí lieta come bella,   (II 22-28)[36]
                    V
Fix'd on the stars the Virgin kept her eye,
And I in her, as though the ample sky
    Swift as an arrow from the sounding yew
I wing'd my flight: but soon, disclosing wide
A wond'rous prospect drew my eyes aside;
    Soft smil'd the Maid, for all my thoughts she knew.

In fact, Boyd's interest in sight becomes excessive in places, in that it leads him to introduce the concept even when it is not in the original. So, in the third canto, Piccarda's 'I' fui nel mondo vergine sorella' (l. 46, 'In the world, I was a virgin sister') becomes 'When from yon Earth I viewed the circling sky/ One of the holy sisterhood was I'. In these cases Boyd is often consistent with his introduction, and is attempting to highlight the Platonic echoes. For example, Dante's recognition of Piccarda's features, in spite of her greater beauty as one of the blessed, is brief and concise: 'ma or m'aiuta ciò che tu mi dici,/ sí che raffigurar m'è piú latino' (ll. 62-3, 'but now what you say helps me/ so that I can make you out much more clearly'). Boyd turns the recognition into a clearly recognizable Platonic process: 'Taught by your voice ... the waken'd soul/ Beams in your eye with recollect'd pow'rs.'

In the sections where sight occurs, or some clear statement is made, the diction is not as heavily 'sublime' as in the passages of description. And at times Boyd's stanzas in this *cantica* open with a Popean couplet:

Contemplate him as made by Heav'n design;
His nature, form and semblance seem divine: (VII, st. VII)

Degenerate Man, of every good bereft,
Since Eden first, and happiness, he left, (VII, st. XVIII)

No pearly cincture then the vest secur'd,
No meretricious ornaments allur'd. (XV, st. XX)

None then, to distant Gaul, by lucre led,
His Consort left to fill a lonely bed. (XV, st. XXIV)

This device is particularly used in order to render Dante's more logically connected, reasoning tercets. Two of the couplets quoted come from the Cacciaguida Cantos, which, together with the canto setting out the story of St Francis, are seen by some critics as the basic narrative in *Paradiso*, building up towards the full statement of the mission of the protagonist. In the case of St Francis, Boyd's version is literal and controlled, but its effect of directness is diluted by his heavy footnotes, which attempt to defend Dante to a Protestant audience.[37] In the Cacciaguida Cantos, Boyd's translation follows models and uses techniques which owe more to Goldsmith and Crabbe than the Young of the *Night Thoughts*. It seems that heightened imagination is only necessary in order to load descriptions of space with emotion, and that the enclosed, small world of a rustic community has sufficient emotional content to require little further colouring:

"Your city, then, no further spreads its bound
Than where the solemn bell, with iron sound,
  Warns you of wasted hours..." (XV, st XIX)

This is the early Florence of Cacciaguida's memories, and the poetry of these passages is the nostalgia for a life of familiar virtues, and for the loss of the beauty and purity of affections:

XXIV
"None, then, to distant Gaul, by lucre led,
His Consort left to fill a lonely bed;
  The Mother pleas'd the child with many a strain,
(the genuine product of their native tongue,)
the distaff dancing to the simple song,
  While ancient tales amus'd the rustic train."

This last stanza joins together lines 106-7 and lines 121-125 of the original, leaving out the intervening references to local families. Boyd, therefore, still cuts or changes the original in these Cacciaguida Cantos, but is at great pains to maintain the effect created.

At this point, as elsewhere in similar passages where human affections are described, rather than the sublime it is the elegiac that Boyd highlights, and one of his basic techniques in such cases is the reintroduction of a technique he had used in *Inferno* but had dropped in *Purgatorio* – the manipulation of sounds. In the passage quoted, the effects are various. Simple alliteration is used in the last line but one ('the distaff dancing to the simple song'), where the effect is hardly Spenserian, but rather echoes the meaning of the line, reproducing a kind of sing-song. Boyd establishes a close connection between the first and the second line through the repetition of the 'l' sound. The second line in particular ('His Consort left to fill a lonely bed') is very effective, because the words roll along in a line of connected consonants ('s', 'f', 'l' and 't') until the final word, a monosyllable, which is unconnected to the preceding words in its consonant sounds. This isolation reinforces the effect of the word (an addition to the original), which is to check abruptly the elegiac regret with its solidity. The whole of this elegiac passage has sound effects which are, occasionally, more subtle than a simple alliteration, as in the slowness of 'Warns you of wasted hours'.

Subtle sound effects are used occasionally by Boyd throughout the translation. Reading aloud the opening passage, for example (quoted on p. 159), brings out its great variety of syntax, rhythm and diction. The three stanzas follow smoothly one from the other, being logically connected, and the passage closes with the last line of the third stanza: 'And make me worthy of the wreath I wear'. Here the alliteration rounds off the passage, and confirms the truth of the statement made in that line by underlining, through the use of alliteration, the activity of the poet. In another passage quoted (on p. 162), Boyd connects the first two lines of a stanza through sound : '... to watch in museful mood/ The mighty mundane wheel ...'.

Such effects increase towards the end of the last canto of *Paradiso*, where some of the more important moments are highlighted by the manipulation of sound. Here, alliteration is used within single lines – 'When Sun's eclipse the holy semblance stains', 'Like setting splendours in the Ev'ning Skies', 'It shakes my soul like Heav'n's aethereal stroke' – and sometimes it divides the line into two units – 'O tune my tongue with that seraphic strain', or 'More from the Mind on that distinguished day' (from stanzas X, XII, XII, XVI, XXI).

The sound effects contribute to the changed movement of the stanzas, which seem to hang together more, to group themselves into longer units, rather than present individual pictures as in *Inferno*. Perhaps Boyd had noticed that, in *Paradiso*, Dante made extensive use of repetition of sounds. Mario Marti points out how internal rhymes in Dante's *Paradiso* create a rhythm opposed to that of the tercets, a rhythm which lengthens the discourse, connecting more tercets into one unit.[38] This is not exactly the effect of Boyd's technique, but is very similar to it.

It is difficult to say why Boyd should return to this manipulation of sound in his *Paradiso*. It could be part and parcel of the development in style and models which Boyd uses for his translation. For while many features of Boyd's *Inferno* help to build up a picture of a Spenserian poem, in *Paradiso* the stanza form, the Miltonic sublimity accompanied by the conciseness of Pope, and even the more subtle sound patterns are all closer to the poetry of Byron's *Cain* than to that of Spenser's *Fairy Queen*; and in these respects, therefore, Boyd looks forward rather than backward. Partly, also, the manipulation of sound could be explained in terms of Boyd's attempt to reproduce an aspect of the style of the original, and therefore to create a poem which is an analogue of the original in the effects it creates. This points to the basic paradox in Boyd's translation: in strict comparison with the original Boyd's version is a betrayal of Dante's poem, but, taken within its context and historical moment, his version remains an astonishingly careful attempt to reproduce certain aspects of the original. The same is true of some important features and moments of the poem, such as the figure of the protagonist, and the climax and conclusion of the whole poem in the vision of God. I now turn to Boyd's version of these two aspects of the *cantica*, beginning with the figure of the protagonist/poet.

In the previous parts of his version of the *Commedia* Boyd had drowned the protagonist in his story – in part by diminishing the occurrence of personal pronouns – and had turned the speaker into the author of written poetry. In his *Paradiso*, however, the 'I' and all the adjectives or pronouns which contribute towards stressing a personal presence are maintained. Yet Dante as protagonist is still kept in the background, and the building up of Dante's prophetic mission is somewhat toned down. As a consequence of this, and as a consequence also of the strong presence of the figure of the poet in the verse, the 'I' comes to refer to the bard Dante rather than to the Florentine Dante Alighieri.

The historical mission of Dante, who will return to Florence and report his encounters with so many figures of his time, revealing their true destiny, is described in the narrative of the *Commedia*, which is made up of the structured, graded ascent of Dante the protagonist towards the vision that unifies him for a second with God, turning him into Dante the prophet, the composer of the book. The episodes in *Paradiso* are all steps which increasingly make of the protagonist not just a man who has known Hell and has been purified in Purgatory, but a man and a poet worthy and capable of vision; and the reader must see and follow this rising above humanity, the 'trasumanar' mentioned in the first canto. The Cacciaguida Cantos are the climax of the process the figure of Dante undergoes in *Paradiso*, since there he meets his forefather who gathers together the hints thrown at the protagonist in Hell and Purgatory, and prophesies his expiating exile and his mission.

In Boyd's version of this important episode, Dante's mission is toned down, the presence of the poet is stressed, and the appearance of Cacciaguida gives Boyd the opportunity to pick up and develop further a dimension of the original which he had already emphasized in the previous *cantiche*: Boyd presents the figures of the forefather and his descendant as knights, or warriors. Dante's Cacciaguida is described as a 'star', a 'jewel' that 'seemed like fire behind alabaster' ('astro', 'gemma... che parve foco dietro ad alabastro', XV 20-24). But Boyd presents Cacciaguida in these terms: 'Like a bright Warrior clad in arms of Fire,/ The Phantom ran, and gilt the gleam of Night'. And whereas the original continues by comparing Cacciaguida and Dante to 'the shade of Anchises' who recognizes, simply, his son ('figlio' l. 27) in the Elysian fields, Boyd's Cacciaguida is a 'sacred Shade/ [who] With pious love his warlike Son survey'd' (XV, stanzas IV and V). This stress on warriors continues a similar emphasis in the encounter of the protagonist and souls in Purgatory, but takes it a stage further, because now these warriors truly belong to an army of heaven, being saints, servants of 'pious love', and therefore take to its highest plane the world we had already found in Boyd's *Inferno* and *Purgatorio*.

But although the protagonist does become, with Cacciaguida, the focus of attention, he assumes neither an active nor a prophetic role. In the original Cacciaguida first greets his descendant with the words

> "O sanguis meus, o superinfusa
> gratia Dei, sicut tibi cui
> bis unquam coeli ianua reclusa?"   (XV 28-30)

The question of to whom Paradise was ever opened twice is obviously answered with the name of St Paul. The Virgilian echoes here also recall Aeneas,[39] and the passage also echoes the very beginning of the *Commedia*, where Dante, doubting his worthiness, says 'Io non Enea, io non Paulo sono' (II 32, 'I am not Aeneas, neither am I Paul'). Then, a few lines further, Cacciaguida, answering one of Dante's questions, begins with the affectionate words 'O fronda mia in che io compiacemmi' (l. 88, 'O my branch, in whom I was well pleased'), clearly echoing the words of God the Father on the baptism of Christ. Even the well known pride of Dante Alighieri could not have produced an identification of himself with Jesus Christ in an autobiographical sense: instead Dante is creating an autobiographical protagonist who will be a poet only after the final vision – the poem as a whole being written after the return.

In Boyd, it is only the figure of the poet that moves closer to vision and to writing poetry which, like Virgil's, is 'heav'n inspired'. Cacciaguida's first words are not in Latin, but in English, and his question is furthermore deprived of resonance: 'To whom did Heav'n her beamy valves display/ twice but to thee?' (st. VI) might make Dante unique, but does not prepare the reader for his prophetic and apostolic mission. There is no clear echo of the opening of the poem, and as a consequence the identification of Dante with Paul fails. As protagonist, therefore, Dante loses much of his significance as a prophet of truth. What remains is the identification of Dante with Aeneas, so that this episode becomes, as it were, the subject matter for Dante's composition as the encounter of Anchises and Aeneas had been the matter for Virgil's poem.

The reason for the lack of vitality of Boyd's protagonist may be the fact that the autobiographical mode was perhaps used in a more literal manner in eighteenth-century England, and so even if Boyd had recognized this aspect of the poem, he would not have been able to bring into England at the turn of the nineteenth century a Roman Catholic Italian poet as a figure of Christ, as inevitably this would have seemed blasphemy. But probably Boyd had not perceived the distinctness of the two personas.

The continuation of the presentation of the protagonist as a passive figure, and the failure of the Cacciaguida episode to place the protagonist at the centre of the action continue to strengthen the presence of Dante the poet, so that the personal pronouns and adjectives, which often appear in this *cantica*, come more and more to refer to this figure of Dante. Indeed, the poet certainly reaches the last stage of vision in the Platonic order that Boyd had quoted in his introductory essay; and the translator continues, though indirectly, to stress the tradition of visionary poetry.

That Dante's *Commedia* is a visionary poem is finally confirmed by the conclusion of the poem (the final vision which is granted to Dante) in Boyd's version. Here, the stress is more and more on language and writing and also sublime views and the power of sight, until the tension starts building up towards the final vision:

XXVI
Three Splendours seem'd their Glories to unite,
And then diverge amid th'abyss of Light,
    Each catching in their turn the running Blaze;
As if three colours of the show'ry bow,
With bright alternate hues, were seen to glow,
    For ever bending in a radiant maze.
XXVI
The central Glory seem'd a rising Fire,
Darting on either side his flaming spire! –
    Alas! how poorly do my words express
Ev'n the faint Picture that my Fancy drew!
And that, how far beneath the wond'rous View!

It were abuse of words to call it less.
XXVII
Thou self-existent Beam, where all to come,
Present and past, within the ample womb
  Of deep Duration held, to being spring
At once, I saw you with unbounded joy,
As if a second dawn illumed the Sky,
  Soaring to catch thy sight with flaming wing.[40]

To begin with the first stanza, Dante had 'tre giri/ di tre cerchi e d'una contenenza' ('three circles/ of three colours and one circumference'), and though the words
do not specify limited size, still the modern reader reassembles them into a
definite geometrical shape. Boyd's initial picture is without contours, like patches
of brightness of varying hues merging into each other, the hazy colours in the
'Abyss of Light' suggesting the sublime of Burke, and even of Turner.

In the second stanza, the word 'glory' (used for the three colours in the first
stanza) is repeated with reference to the central fire, whereas Dante had simply
used words like 'giri', 'colori', 'iri' ('circles', 'colours', 'rainbows',). Boyd heightens
the formality and solemnity of the moment with his use of words like 'glories' or
'splendours', but perhaps he is also attempting to reconnect the conclusion of
Paradiso with its beginning, where the word 'glory' is the first we come across.
And in spite of this addition, Boyd is trying, in this second stanza, to follow Dante
step by step. Dante's rhyming-words had been 'si spiri', 'foco', 'ch'i' vidi', 'poco',
and, with the addition of two extra lines in the middle, Boyd uses words similar
in meaning and/or form for his endings: 'Fire', 'spire', 'View', 'less'.

More importantly, this stanza introduces the presence of the 'I', which at this
point, with his reference to the difficulty of expression and to 'Fancy', cannot but
be the poet. This is the figure that remains central in the third stanza. The stanza
is split into two parts; the first part defines the Light in terms of time, while the
second part adds description and narrative. There is movement and action as the
poet sees the vision 'with unbounded joy ... Soaring to catch [the] sight with
flaming wing.'

In the stanza that follows the poet remains on the scene: he is 'under a spell',
'in delicious trance' at the sight of a 'human God'. Boyd is describing the trance
of the mystic, and the stress on the 'I', his 'unbounded joy' and his 'soaring' give
a particular colouring to Boyd's 'human God', so that it seems that, in Diotima's
words, the poet has here become immortal. A further point in the translation
suggests the same idea. In Dante, the second circle (which is the Son, created
'light from light') seemed painted with 'our effigy' (l. 131, 'nostra effige'). At this
point in Dante the mystery of the incarnation is presented in its meaning of Christ
as redeemer of every man, and as such of Dante as well. Moreover, the 'our

effigy' here echoes the 'our life' of the opening of *Inferno*, so that the implied
suggestion is that Dante, as our representative, sees his effigy reflected in the Son.
Boyd makes this less poignant but more obvious by turning the circle of light into
a 'sun-bright Mirror', which, at the approach of the soaring poet, shows him 'A
radiant Form, that seem'd a human God'. As he looks into the mirror, the poet
recognizes his own transformation.

This vision of joy and immortality, and of matter and mind united that Boyd
paints in his last stanzas appears only in the background in the very last stanza,
which is concerned with God, but in a manner very different from the original.
Dante's final line, 'l'amor che muove il sole e l'altre stelle' ('the love which moves
the sun and the other stars'), brought to a mystic conclusion Dante's own love
story, and presented the revealed value of the various examples of love shown in
the three *cantiche*. The repetition of the word 'stelle' also linked the three
cantiche together. But what remains with the reader at the end is a particular
image, with a specific associated rhythm: the circular motion of man's will and
desire for knowledge, which, when they are unified with God, move in a circle like
a wheel.

In Boyd, however, there is no mention of love, and the movement of the
protagonist/poet's will and desire, turning along the wheel of God's will, are also
absent. Boyd closes his version with a prayer of obedience to God's will:

> But ill could mortal Sense this sight explore
> Until a lucid Hand, extended o'er
>   My straining eyes, the Miracle display'd,
> Bright as empyreal Noon, which Heav'n denies
> To paint! – O may his Will, that rules the Skies,
>   In this and all, be evermore obey'd![41]

He has not here added or superimposed, but rather selected. For Dante had
placed love as the prime power, making it subsume will and desire for knowledge;
while Boyd selects will as more appropriate to the eighteenth-century view of
wisdom than either of the other two human faculties. Also, this final gesture of
subjection comes across as more celebratory than the original, and more formally
Christian in the sense that it suggests the presentation of an ethically valid model
of conduct. Finally, whereas Dante celebrated God as the power of love in the
universe, Boyd's celebration of God is more obvious and traditional. For he adds
visual images – the hand of God and noon brightness – and traditional phrases
('Miracle', 'rules the Sky').

On page 168 I suggested that the repeated use of the word 'glory' was an
attempt to draw *Paradiso* to a close by echoing the same word that had been used
at its opening. The attempt to produce a complete, circular vision in this last

cantica is probably the reason why Boyd also adds, at the end of *Paradiso*, the same image he had added at its opening by depicting again the hand of God, which at this point is not 'solitary', but 'lucid'. The stress on painting, on the sublimity of the skies and the revealing hand of God add to this final stanza in Boyd an image which belongs to the eighteenth-century view of the sublimity of Michelangelo.

Many things could be said which would indicate the failure of Boyd to reproduce the original adequately, in modern eyes; many passages could be chosen to illustrate divergences from the *Commedia* in his translation. But the sum total of these would not say anything about Boyd's contribution to the introduction of Dante into England, which is the main concern here. All one would learn is that, certainly to the modern reader, Boyd's Dante is not Dante. A more balanced analysis of what takes place in Boyd's text and of what his professed views were, however, brings to light some of the ways in which Dante came to be known to English readers, including artists and poets.

To begin with, Boyd provides us with factual information and the benefit of his research and scholarship, both in his essays – in the form of a life of Dante and history of Florence – and in the text of his translation and the associated footnotes. In the latter Boyd gives the basic facts about some of the figures the protagonist meets, and in general underlines the historical interest of the poem (when he mentions, for example, that from the Cacciaguida Cantos a great deal of information about the early days of Florence can be learned). In the text itself, Boyd's scholarship is evident when, in *Purgatorio*, he substitutes the names of families with the appropriate place names.

The historical scholarship is, however, of secondary importance; Boyd's chief concern throughout is with ethics, philosophy, religion. Both the gothic and the sublime colouring are only the metaphors by which the supernatural and higher realities are intimated and embodied in figure and scene. Of the two, the gothic only appears, in Boyd, in certain words – 'phantom', 'dread', 'wails', never fully extending to a complete episode, and even his version of the Ugolino episode is relatively restrained. The sublime plays a fuller role, not only in that eternity, infinity, and darkness seem the dimensions of all three realms of the after-life, but in that the two aspects of the broad sense of sublimity – a way of understanding and a language – both inform Boyd's poem.

As a language, the sublime of Thomson and Young directly descends from the Miltonic Latinate and Italian style, and reflects the efforts to elevate and heighten thought and feeling in poetry concerned with elevated topics – specifically, the poetry of vision. Boyd's rendering of Dante's poem in terms of this tradition in poetry is thorough as well as penetrating. For Boyd varies the emphasis in the selection of his models, and by so doing he in fact passes on to the English reader a *Commedia* whose development traces the complete course of the Miltonic tradition up to that point. He presents *Inferno* in terms of *Everyman* and Spenser's Christian allegory, *Purgatorio* in terms of the language and images of *Paradise Lost*, and *Paradiso* as a combination of the sublime of Young with the elegiac poetry of the loss of a humble way of life. So the historical progress of that tradition in English poetry is all contained in Dante's *Commedia*.

The *Commedia* is therefore naturalized through various models. Thereby, access to Dante's poem for the English readers is made easier. At the same time, the appearance of a poem such as Boyd's *Commedia* would reinforce the identity and growth of the English poetry of vision.

But Boyd's language also exposes how fixed, how imitable the language of the eighteenth-century Miltonic sublime had become. It is against this language and against the eighteenth-century version of the Miltonic tradition that a poet like William Blake had to react. To be a poet of prophecy Blake felt he had to recreate language, the imagery, a whole mythology; for what came to his hand had become drained of significance by the exhaustion of the rhetoric of the sublime, which was the aspect of the Miltonic tradition exploited by the eighteenth-century Miltonic poets. Boyd's version exactly indicates the tiredness and emptiness of the old codes.

Yet two significant aspects of the Miltonic tradition as it is passed on by Boyd must be pointed out. First, that it is possible, indeed necessary, to vary and add to it, to make it grow and develop – in Boyd, by the infusion of the elegiac, of philosophy, and of nostalgia for the loss of simpler ways of life. Secondly, for a poet of prophecy like Blake, Milton remained both the antagonist and the touchstone; for beyond the legacy of language distorted and drained by excessive use, Milton was the epitome of the poet who tried, in his poetry, to create out of different traditions a total view of man and his destiny.[41] In this sense, the sublime of Milton is also a poetic stance, and one which Boyd integrates within his translation. Boyd often reduces the concreteness of Dante's world, while highlighting its allegorical dimension. He therefore stresses the spiritual significance of this world, which is what the poet's vision reveals.

In fact, the conclusion of Boyd's version of the *Commedia* presents a poet who has been granted vision and has therefore seen the truth. The introductory essays to *Inferno* had introduced a 'bard' who worked not by rules, but by his sublime genius, and who had produced a poem concerned with basic religious and ethical matters – and in particular, the notion of salvation through the experience of the self. Boyd's conclusion shows this very bard in the fulfilment of his journey of the mind, and rewarded with redemption and immortality.

Only if one is prepared to question the absolute validity of some of the criteria used to judge translations (such as, for example, that a translation which is mostly paraphrase is not worthy of attention), and only if one takes into consideration as much as possible of the context of each work, will it be possible to identify and recognize the dynamics by which literature renews itself, and finds new metaphors and a new mythology, which are so vitally required by writers and readers alike.

9

Henry Francis Cary

The poetry of vision

Henry Francis Cary (1772-1844) first published his version of *Inferno* in 1805-6, and his version of the entire *Commedia* in 1814. In the preface to this 1814 edition of his translation Cary says: 'In one or two of those editions [other editions of the *Commedia* which he has examined] is to be found the title of "The Vision;" which I have adopted as more conformable to the genius of our language than that of "Divine Comedy"'.[1] It is certainly true that the use of the word 'vision' had become more common than before, and titles of poems reflected this. William Blake had published his *Visions of the Daughters of Albion* in 1793 and Southey's *A Vision of Judgement* appeared in 1821, followed one year later by Byron's parody of this poem in his *A Vision of Judgement*. And Byron's *The Prophecy of Dante* (1821) was also called, by Byron himself, *The Vision of Dante*.

Henry Boyd's reading of *Paradiso* in terms of vision – and, in particular, of vision not as sight of real objects but as 'seeing all things in God' – reveals the ambivalence of the word 'vision', an ambivalence explored and examined in the poetry of the eighteenth century. Since both Boyd and Cary use the notion of vision, and since I am particularly concerned in this study with the visual, it is appropriate at this point to briefly survey the role which optics, the sense of sight and mystical vision play in English poetry in the eighteenth and early nineteenth century.

That sight was considered in the eighteenth century as the sense through which knowledge is most directly acquired is well known; equally well known is the preponderance of visual images in poetry of nature, so that the narrative line of a poem often consists of what the eye sees. Newton's *Opticks* (1704) exerted a great influence throughout the eighteenth century, and indeed the rapidly developing science of optics provided a fertile source of new and striking imagery:

> The lively diamond drinks thy purest rays,
> Collected light compact; that, polished bright,
> And all its native lustre let abroad,
> Dares, as it sparkles on the fair one's breast,
> With vain ambition emulate her eyes.
> At thee the ruby lights its deepening glow,

And with a waving radiance inward flames.
From thee the sapphire, solid ether, takes
Its hue cerulean; and, of evening tinct,
The purple-streaming amethyst is thine.
With thy own smile the yellow topaz burns;
Nor deeper verdure dyes the robe of Spring,
When first she gives it to the southern gale,
Than the green emerald shows. But, all combined,
Thick through the whitening opal play thy beams;
Or, flying several from its surface, form
A trembling variance of revolving hues
As the site varies in the gazer's hand.   ('Summer' 142-159)[2]

As a consequence of the discovery of the prism, the concept of whiteness acquires connotations of the divine, containing as it does all other colours, and reverberates in verses through the use of words like 'bright' or 'shining'. In fact a fondness for colour is characteristic of eighteenth-century poetry, and appears, for example, in poems as different as Pope's 'Eloisa and Abelard' (with the description of the pheasant), Thomson's 'Spring' (in the list of flowers), and, later, Cowper's *The Task* (where there is a similar list of flowers).[3] But alongside the scientific eye of the botanist, and his sometimes minutely detailed observations, in the poetry of the eighteenth century there is also to be found the description of what is seen by other eyes – the creative eye of the poet, the eye of the philosopher, and the prophetic eye of the visionary poet.

Visionary poetry is not new to the late eighteenth century. Pope, for one, produces visions of chaos and disorder in his *Dunciad* (as well as visions of order in *An Essay on Man*), and often leaves the world of social satire to offer a vision of possible or future restoration of the natural order, as in the 'Epistle to Richard Boyle'. But as the century progresses the poetry moves further and further away from a picture of contemporary society and into nature (as viewed by the contemplative mind of the poet). The poet himself becomes more clearly the seer who brings revelation to the reader.

Thomson and Cowper can be taken as examples of an early and later eighteenth-century poet respectively whose poetry contains examples of the visual. For the purposes of the present discussion, only a few features of these poets' use both of the modality of sight and of the mechanics of vision will be brought forward as examples; much of the subtlety of their poetry and many of the differences between the individual poets will be set aside as irrelevant to this context.

To begin with Thomson, there is immense variety in his use of the visual, particularly in *The Seasons*. Here nature is often scanned by the careful eye of the botanist. In fact Thomson has been praised for the sudden sharp details which make his descriptions vivid and for his attempt to create a diction which combines poetic language and scientific classifications.[4] But the sense of sight can also fail and confuse the viewer, as when, in 'Summer', 'A faint erroneous ray,/ Glanced from the imperfect surfaces of things,/ Flings half an image on the straining eye'. Then the various forms of nature 'are all one swimming scene,/ Uncertain if beheld' ('Summer' 1687-8, 1692-93).

In addition to physical sight (whose information, however, is not always clear), man also has an inward sight, with which he can recreate in his imagination the landscapes he reads about, or create pictures of his own, or even lose himself in dreams:

> There let the classic page thy fancy lead
> Through rural scenes, such as the Mantuan swain
> Paints in the matchless harmony of song;
> Or catch thyself the landscape, gliding swift
> Athwart imagination's vivid eye;
> Or, by the vocal woods and waters lulled,
> And lost in lonely musings, in a dream
> Confused of careless solitude where mix
> Ten thousand wandering images of things,　　　('Spring' 455-463)

But not all men can abandon themselves to the power of imagination without danger. Thomson distinguishes between the 'benighted wretch' who wanders bewildered , 'full of pale fancies and chimeras huge' ('Autumn' 1145 ff.), and the 'man of philosophic eye' ('Autumn' 1133), whose understanding is not restricted to the appearances he sees, but who enquires into their 'causes and materials'. It is, however, the poet who can use his creative imagination best to see through nature into the divine. This movement to the divine can be made under the guidance of Melancholy, who leads the poet to see with 'the mind's creative eye', taking him to 'devotion raised/ To rapture, and divine astonishment' ('Autumn' 1016-19). This is the sublime that leads to prophecy:

> Oh! bear me then to vast embowering shades,
> To twilight groves, and visionary vales,
> To weeping grottoes, and prophetic glooms;　　　('Autumn' 1030-33)

In practice Thomson seems to prefer the less gloomy and more peaceful landscapes, but here, too, 'the regulated wild' will teach 'gay fancy' to 'correct her pencil to the purest truth/ Of Nature' ('Autumn' 1055, 1058-9). From nature, however, the 'I' will move higher into revelation, and the conclusion to 'Autumn' summarizes the course of the poet's sight:

> O Nature! all sufficient! over all
> Enrich me with the knowledge of thy works;
> Snatch me to heaven; ...   ('Autumn' 1352-54)

The tension characteristic of Thomson's poetry derives from the alternation of the various possibilities – night, for example, is 'the visionary hour' appropriate for musings ('Summer' 556), but is also characterized by lack of light and colour, and so it is 'one universal blot' ('Autumn' 1143), with loss of beauty, variety and distinctness.

Cowper's viewing of nature takes forms less ambiguous than Thomson's. Like Thomson, Cowper is fond of adding colour, contour and form to his descriptions. Moreover, he, too, is fascinated by the 'multiform inventions to which the mind resorts'; and he, too, is suspicious of dreams and fancies, in which 'all are wanderers, gone astray,/ Each in his own delusions' (III p. 150). But Cowper is more suspicious of the detailed observation of a 'botanist' than Thomson is:

> Brutes graze the mountain-top with faces prone
> And eyes intent upon the scanty herb
> It yields them; or recumbent on its brow,
> Ruminate heedless of the scene outspread
> Beneath, beyond, and stretching far away
> From inland regions to the distant main.
> Man views it and admires, but rests content
> With what he views. The landscape has its praise,
> But not its Author. Unconcerned who formed
> The paradise he sees, he finds it such,
> And such well-pleased to find it, asks no more.   (V p. 195-6).

Cowper mistrusts the modality of the visible. Man must look beyond nature rather than through it, for nature cannot possibly give man any final answer. Science can heighten man's physical sight, and show him through a telescope worlds 'else/ Not visible', but it can never 'Discover Him that rules them'. Cowper's view is that only revelation from above can provide man with a final answer. God's word can 'reveal truths undiscerned but by that holy light,/ Then all is plain. Philosophy baptized/ In the pure fountain of eternal love/ Has eyes indeed' (III, pp. 152, 153). The contingent appearances of nature will not distract the man who has this sight, who will be pleased by all seasons – 'though winter had been none had man been true,/ And earth be punished for its tenant's sake' (VI p. 203). And it is the poet who is endowed with this higher sight, as well as with the gift – in fact the urge – to share whatever is revealed to him:

> Sweet is the harp of prophecy; too sweet
> Not to be wronged by a mere mortal touch;
> Nor can the wonders it records be sung
> To meaner music, and not suffer loss.

> But when a poet, or when one like me,
> Happy to rove among poetic flowers,
> Though poor in skill to rear them, lights at last
> On some fair theme, some theme divinely fair,
> Such is the impulse and the spur he feels
> To give it praise proportioned to its worth,
> That not to attempt it, arduous as he deems
> The labour, were a task more arduous still.   (VI pp. 212-3)

This task is certainly performed by this particular poet – the 'I' of 'one like me' – who proceeds indeed to the vision of the regained Paradise, preceded by the Apocalypse:

> Haste, then and wheel away a shattered world,
> Ye slow-revolving seasons! We would see
> (A sight to which our eyes are strangers yet)
> A world that does not dread and hate his laws,
> And suffer for its crime: would learn how fair
> The creature is that God pronounces good.   (VI p. 214)

In Thomson nature offers proof of the existence of the divine and can lead to prophecy; in Cowper only divine illumination can bring revelation. But both poets – like Collins, or Smart, or Gray in their different ways – attempt to analyse the possibilities and limitations of the sense of sight, are worried by the dangers of subjectivism, and conclude by recognizing the role of the poet in the discovery of truth through a sight higher than the purely physical one. A poet can, it is true, be a prophet in many different ways: like Gray's bard, unheeded and despairing, or like Young's teacher, who requires the darkness of night (with its lack of daylight reason and distracting colour) to be inspired by the ray of Newtonian light, and to see beyond the present world. Most visionary of all is Blake's 'I', who discovers shapes, forces and movements within and beyond the visible world, and who sees the fall of man as a contraction of the human eye into 'a little narrow orb, closd up & dark/ Scarcely beholding the Great Light; conversing with the ground' (*Jerusalem*, 2:49 ll. 34-5),[5] so that

> The Visions of Eternity, by reason of narrowed perceptions,
> Are become weak Visions of Time & Space, ...   (ll. 21-22)

Paradise regained, accordingly, is to Blake the recovery of the 'fourfold vision' of Divine Imagination (sense perception, moral vision, creative vision, and, transforming these three, mystical ecstasy):

> Now I a fourfold vision see
> And a fourfold vision is given to me
> Tis fourfold in my supreme delight
> And three fold in soft Beulahs night

> And twofold Always. May God us keep
> From Single vision & Newtons sleep[6]

Restored to this perfect vision, men will transcend and transform reality:

> And they conversed together in Visionary forms dramatic ...
> Creating Space, Creating Time according to the wonders Divine
> Of Human Imagination,...   (*Jerusalem*, 4:98, ll. 28, 31-2)

In their different ways, Coleridge and Wordsworth both inherit the visionary sight which had been developed by the Miltonic poets of the eighteenth century. Wordsworth in particular adopts the role of the prophet, and in the 'Prospectus to the Excursion' he invokes (as Milton had done before him, and Dante even earlier) the 'prophetic Spirit' that lives 'in the hearts/ Of mighty Poets', in order that he may receive the gift 'of genuine insight'. He will then

> ... with the thing
> contemplated, describe the mind of man
> contemplating; and who, and what he was –
> The transitory Being that beheld
> The Vision; ...[7]

Wordsworth's own contribution to the poetry of vision – one which adds to Thomson's and takes Cowper's a step further – is the focus on the mind viewing. Wordsworth had personal experience of such revelation. Like Blake, he felt he had been given a vision; and his poetry was the attempt to be true to it. Nature, recollections of one's personal past, but also Classical and Christian myths shape his attempts at communication. His, moreover, is a vision not of Hell, but of Paradise: Wordsword states that 'Our Minds, the Mind of Man' will see not 'Chaos' or 'Erebus', but 'Paradise, and groves/ Elysian, Fortunate Fields' (ll. 35-48). Paradise lost and Paradise regained – as in Cowper's reference to the fall, or Young's vision of the Apocalypse – remain the myths through which poets communicate their visions.

Cary's *The Vision of Dante*

Clearly the word 'vision' and the notion of vision (whether it means the ordinary faculty of sight or a mental insight) are central to the poetry of the time, and in fact explain Cary's choice of title for his version of Dante's work. The title-page of Cary's translation bears the general title of *The Vision; or, Hell, Purgatory and Paradise of Dante Alighieri*, but each *cantica* bears only a shortened form of this title, namely *The Vision of Dante*, and this is the form which is occasionally used by critics for Cary's translation. In comparison with the original title, it suggests a greater role on the part of the author, who is also the protagonist, and also greater distance between the real world on the one hand, and, on the other, the world of the poem, which loses its objective reality and is absorbed within the poet's imaginings. The title, therefore, seems to refer purely to a dream-vision of the poet Dante.

Cary's stress on the person of Dante is heightened by the fact that his only introductory essay to his translation is a 'Life of Dante' (with no separate introduction to the poem itself).[8] Here, the history of Dante's life (pp. v-xxv) is followed by a description of his face, manners and character, with Cary losing no opportunity of establishing links between the story of the poem and its author:

> He spoke seldom, and in a low voice; but what he said derived authority from the subtileness of his observations, somewhat like his own heroes, who
> Parlavan rado con voci soavi.
>   – spake
> Seldom, but all their words were tuneful sweet.   *Hell* IV (p. XXVI)

We are further informed that the poet is supposed to have been very good at 'the art of designing', and that this seems confirmed by the variety and accuracy of his presentation of objects. Next follows a survey of Dante's works, in which the *Vita Nuova* is twice described as a vision ('somewhat mystical', 'a marvellous vision', p. xxix). Interestingly, this is not said of the *Commedia*; Cary points out that 'some have termed it an epic poem; and others, a satire' but adds that a definition hardly matters.

> It suffices that the poem seizes on the heart by its two great holds, terror and pity; detains the fancy by an accurate and lively delineation of the objects it represents; and displays throughout such an originality of conception, as leaves to Homer and Shakespeare alone the power of challenging the pre-eminence or equality (p. XXXIV).

Cary's mention of terror and pity in preference to prophecy seems to indicate that, far from stressing the visionary power of Dante as poet, Cary is secularizing the divine nature of Dante's comedy of man.

Cary's motivation for studying Dante when still at Oxford in the early 1790's was a personal enthusiasm which many friends found 'eccentric and objectionable', and which Cary's biographer, King, goes so far as to call 'worship'.[9] At that time, Cary tried to convince Anna Seward of the beauty of the *Commedia* by sending her his translations of short extracts – but to little avail, as Seward's answers show. Cary must have felt that he was the only repository of knowledge on Dante, and that it was up to him to provide access to, and set the record straight about, the Italian poet. The method he used to gather knowledge well illustrates Cary's view of Dante, which, from the very start, was very different from that of a visionary poet:

I am infinitely delighted with Dante, as an historian of his own time; so that I am collecting
anecdotes, so plentifully interspersed among his work, for my amusement.[10]

This was the beginning of a life-long study. Over a period of years Cary collected
anecdotes and illustrations of Dante, which 'grew into a large Commonplace book
filled with notes and extracts from all manner of authors in half-a-dozen
languages, carefully classified under various heads' (King, p. 74). By the time he
came to translate *Inferno*, his scholarship on Dante was extensive. Cary's
references to the *Convito* and the *Vita Nuova* in his 'Life of Dante', the
introductory essay to the translation, reflect a familiarity with the contents of
these books, and perhaps he was familiar also with the *De Vulgari Eloquentia*.
Moreover, the last paragraphs of the 'Life' are dedicated to an evaluation of the
'four chief commentators on Dante, namely, Landino, Vellutello, Venturi and
Lombardi ...' (pp. xxxviii-xl). Furthermore, references in the essay and in the notes
show that he had also consulted general works on Italian literature by Tiraboschi,
Pelli, Perticari, and Frescobaldi, and the lives of Dante by Boccaccio and
Leonardo Aretino. Cary's *Vision* is a milestone mainly for his emphasis on
scholarship, which is equally well illustrated by another feature of Cary's work.
His first edition of *Inferno* in 1805-6 was accompanied by the Italian text, and this
was the first time any part of the original *Divina Commedia* had been published
in England.

Cary's *Inferno*, in two volumes, appeared in 1805-6, but, although it was
favourably reviewed, it did not sell. Eight years later, in 1814, after completing the
whole *Commedia*, Cary was unable to find a publisher for it. Undeterred, he went
ahead and published it himself, in three small volumes in very small print; but
these, too, received some attention from reviewers but none from buyers.

Fame came suddenly both to Cary's Dante and Dante himself after Cary had
met Coleridge in 1817 and lent the poet a copy of his translation. Coleridge
praised it highly in his letters and conversations, and began to quote and mention
Dante repeatedly as a central point of comparison with English writers in his
lectures on Milton and Shakespeare. Coleridge also mentioned Dante a few times
in his *Biographia Literaria* (1817), where he refers to Dante in order to support
his own statements with the authority of a well established poet.[11] In 1818, he
went so far as to devote part of a lecture to Dante, quoting both the original and
Cary's translation, and sales of Cary's translation followed 'almost instantaneous-
ly'.[12] The fact is that Coleridge, with his references to Dante, and Cary, with his
translation of the *Commedia*, both do the same thing – they present Dante's
Divine Commedia as a classic, which must be studied, commented on, looked up
to.

Cary's translation was praised, in its own day, for its fidelity to the sense of the original, for its closeness to the language of the original, and for its style.[13] Coleridge praised 'the learned simplicity of the diction' and 'the peculiar character of the Blank verse'. This has 'the variety of Milton without mere Miltonisms', and its effect is 'so Dantesque that to those who should compare it only with other English poems, it would, I doubt not, have the same effect as the Terza Rima has compared with other Italian meters'.[14] Very similar claims have been made for Cary's version of Dante in our own day, and it is useful to briefly reconsider the extent of the accuracy of these views: the fidelity of the translation, the effect of the blank verse, and the use of the Miltonic style.

Cary's translation is certainly closer to the text of the original than Boyd's, and more accurate than Rogers'. De Sua expresses the right amount of agreement with nineteenth-century critics when he says that

> In short, Cary considerably alters the tone of the passages by rendering them in circuitous, diluted and, at times, elegantly prosaic language not unlike that of his 18th century predecessors, even while he avoids their gross mistranslations and liberties with the sense. Still, as a complete translation, Cary's was by far one of the most distinguished, careful and, despite lapses into monotony, sustained versions of the 19th century (p. 36).

The monotony of Cary's verse, which De Sua mentions only in passing, will actually prove to be of very great import also as far as the transmission of the sense of the poem is concerned.

As for the second of the established views on Cary, concerning his blank verse, De Sua agrees fully with Coleridge and labels Cary, accordingly, as a 'Romantic' translator, who is at pains to produce a text which creates an aesthetic effect similar to that which the original work has in Italian (see also pp. 34-5 above). There can, indeed, be no doubt that the creation of an analogous aesthetic effect was becoming a very important feature of translation, and Coleridge's words support this view. That in practice the result of this view is very different from the results of previous views of translation can, however, be doubted, if Cary's version is an example to go by. De Sua believes that he is demonstrating Cary's new attitude to translation when he quotes an important passage from his 'Life of Dante':

> The phraseology [of Dante's original] has been accused of being at times hard and uncouth; but if this is acknowledged, yet it must be remembered that he gave a permanent stamp and character to the language in which he wrote, and in which, before him, nothing great had been attempted; that the diction is strictly vernacular, without any debasement of foreign idiom; that his numbers have as much variety as the Italian tongue, at least in that kind of metre, could supply; and that, although succeeding writers may have surpassed him in the lighter graces and embellishments of style, not one of them has equalled him in succinctness, vivacity, and strength (p. XXXVI).

Cary certainly mentions the nature and effect of Dante's language, whereas Boyd says very little specifically on this subject. But Cary's view of Dante is very similar to Boyd's, describing him, as he does, as 'the most sublime and moral, but ... obscure writer in any language'.[15] Cary's primary stress is still on sublimity and on the moral principles which Dante's *Inferno* illustrates. And although the quotation above proves that Cary does notice stylistic and semantic features like energy and conciseness, Cary's version of the *Commedia* shows either that he did not attempt to reproduce them or that he was utterly unable to do so. I use here the opening of *Inferno*, but extracts from other *cantiche* would illustrate the same points equally well:

> In the midway of this our mortal life,
> I found me in a gloomy wood, astray
> Gone from the path direct: and e'en to tell
> It were no easy task, how savage and wild
> That forest, how robust and rough its growth, 5
> Which to remember only, my dismay
> Renews, in bitterness not far from death.
> Yet to discourse of what there good befel,
> All else will I relate discovered there.
>   How first I entered it I scarce can say, 10
> Such sleepy dulness in that instant weigh'd
> My senses down, when the true path I left,
> But when a mountain's foot I reach'd, where clos'd
> The valley, that had pierc'd my heart with dread,
> I look'd aloft, and saw his shoulders broad
> Already vested with that planet's beam,
> Who leads all wanderers safe through every way. (I 1-17)

The word order, enjambments and continuous inversions do not create an effect of succinctness and vivacity, but of complexity; they weigh down the lines in an obscurity and slowness of pace which continue throughout the first canto and further. The Italian usually follows a word order which is quite natural and colloquial, and often, with the substitution of a word and the modernization of a spelling, one could express oneself in modern Italian in a similar way. Cary's language, on the contrary, is not English as it is or ever was spoken – the first tercet in the original and the translation being a good example of this.[16] His diction is obviously not as 'strictly vernacular' as he notices Dante's to be. Neither is Cary 'succinct', as many of Dante's words receive the addition of an adjective, while phrases are lengthened and embellished: 'pien di sonno' becomes 'Such sleepy dulness ... weighed my senses down' and 'spalle' becomes 'shoulders broad'. The phrase 'struggling with terror' in line 25 is an addition. Later, 'la bestia' is 'that fell beast', and 'altri poeti' 'all the tuneful train'. Neither does Cary follow Dante, or Cowper for that matter, in imitating the 'rough and uncouth' lines, but in fact varies, for example, his diction: Dante's 'paura' – an important word, hammered into the reader three times in the first 15 lines, and then soon after repeated twice – is rendered first with 'dismay' and then twice with 'dread' and twice with 'fear'. Clearly, therefore, Cary rejected Dante's succinctness and vernacular language for the more elevated neoclassical idiom of the time; and in fact Rogers' version was (in terms of attitude to the words of the original, if not actual accuracy of reading) more 'literal' than Cary's.

Therefore, the difference between Cary and Boyd is only a question of degree: Cary assumes the same attitude as Boyd, only with more restraint and control. Moreover, Cary also changes his original, particularly through the use of the sublime style.

Accordingly, I now turn to the third of the established views on Cary's translation – the consideration of Cary's use of the Miltonic style, which must begin with the authoritative views of Havens. In his study of *The Influence of Milton on English Poetry*, Havens discusses the Miltonic style of Cary's translation as one of the highest points of the mode:

> The terseness, the restraint, the concentrated power, of the Divine Comedy are admirably reproduced in a style that achieves dignity with ease and without pomposity. ... Miltonic they are, but so unobtrusively, so naturally ....[17]

He goes on to add that Miltonisms are not occasional but pervasive, and 'woven into the very fibre of the style', repeating Coleridge's view. This is surely correct up to a point, and it underlines the nature of Cary's indebtedness to Milton, which is mainly a question of the choice of a few basic features of the Miltonic style. But the modern reader cannot totally agree with Havens. Does the paragraph which opens the poem have 'dignity with ease'? Are the Miltonisms 'unobtrusive'? The modern reader, at least the present reader, must answer no to both questions. As already indicated, the word order is too insistent and regular to produce, in the long run, any effect but monotony. All the inversions are very heavy, but some, like 'astray/ Gone', sound almost perverse, since the line could well have borne the length and syllable quality of 'Gone/ astray' – or was Cary attempting to keep some remnant of rhyme by having 'astray' 'dismay' 'say' in lines two, six and ten respectively? There is another true rhyme in the same first fifteen lines ('tell'/'befel'), and if one then starts examining the line endings more closely one wonders if 'weighed'/'dread' or 'closed'/'broad' are supposed to sound or to look like approximate rhymes. But these sounds do not create a noticeable rhythm which enriches the paragraph. Cunningham is probably correct when he points out that Cary chose not to reproduce the music of Milton's lines.[18] These approximate rhymes are hardly heard in a reading aloud of the poem, and no connection between rhyme and sense can be found, making these rhymes seem gratuitous. The inversions in Cary's verses, furthermore, do not contribute to a stately, solemn tone, but rather create monotony and a halting pace. A similar effect is created by that other aspect of the eighteenth-century Miltonic style – the use of enjambments.

Critics have noticed Cary's enjambments, and pointed out that they are an attempt to create variety, adding that the three lines of a tercet are rendered either by two and a half, or by three and a half lines.[19] This is, in a way, a misrepresentation of the rhythm of Cary's lines. The main point is that, while in Dante a sentence or clause generally corresponds to one or more lines, with the beginning of the sentence being the beginning of the line, in Cary most of the sentences begin and end in middle line, creating a curious misplacement:

> questa mi pose tanto di gravezza
>   con la paura ch'uscía di sua vista
>   ch'io perdei la speranza dell'altezza.   (I 52-4)[20]

> ... . She with such fear
> O'erwhelm'd me, at the sight of her appall'd,
> That of the height all hope I lost. ...   (I 48-50)

Since the idea of being overwhelmed and appalled are not in the original, a comparison of the translation with the original makes one think that Cary pads out his lines merely in order to begin and end in the middle of a line. This seems to be the one guiding rule of Cary's lines and sentences, and the attempt to do it consistently becomes, in the long run, so noticeable and regular that it creates an effect of monotony.

Similarly the Miltonic inversions follow one another with excessive uniformity, since each phrase ends, as in the lines above, with the verb (or verbal phrase): 'o'erwhelm'd me', 'appall'd' and 'lost'. The effect created is one of slowness and heaviness. Dante's pauses were at the end of each line (and of each phrase, the two being one and the same). But in Cary the end of the line – which always entails a slight pause, however brief – must be added to the end of the clauses, which occur in mid-line and often on slow-sounding words, and this creates a very halting rhythm. The feeling of 'wandering on and on' that Coleridge had praised in Cary's translation – and which De Sua correctly calls very inappropriate to render Dante's well organized movement (which pushes the poetry on in even steps and makes of the *Commedia* one of the most fast reading of all poems) – seems in fact based on a silent, visual reading, since a reading aloud brings out a starting and stopping pace which considerably slows down the reading process.[21]

The *Divina Commedia* needs to be read continuously; the swiftness of the pace moves the reader on so that he can manage long units of poetry. But, more importantly, if the reader is moved onwards it means that he cannot pause long over one meeting or one character. The encounter with, say, Farinata is a pause in the journey, because the episode itself takes up a number of lines; but it is interrupted by Cavalcanti's words, and soon followed by other meetings. It is the course of the whole experience that produces the strongest impact on the reader. -Slowness of pace and monotony, therefore, also affect the sense of the poetry, and in particular the creation of a concrete world in which the protagonist moves.

Because of the great influence Cary's Dante has had on the course of Dante in England (many poets, including Blake and Shelley, having read Dante mainly in this version), I intend to analyse this translation in more detail than Boyd's, also in comparison with the original. Some of the claims which have been made for Cary's version (of fidelity to the text and to the language of the original, and of the harmony of his Miltonic style and blank verse) continue to be assessed on the basis of Cary's text, whenever appropriate. Moreover, I attempt to place the translation within the context of the poetry of vision, in order to see to what extent Cary's choice for the title of his version of the *Commedia* reflects a concern, worked out in the text, with the modality of the visual and with the power of the visionary poet.

Cary's *Hell*

In his lecture on Dante (Lecture X, 1818) Coleridge very specifically lists Dante's seven 'chief excellences as a poet'. The first has to do with language:

> I. Style – the vividness, logical connexion, strength, and energy of which cannot be surpassed. In this I think Dante superior to Milton; ...[22]

The reference here is to that 'passion and miracle of words' of medieval Italy which 'gave an almost romantic character, a virtuous quality and power, to what was read in a book'. This is, in itself, a 'sublime' view of language. In fact, all the other 'excellences' recognized by Coleridge have to do either with the sublime or with the visual. These other excellences listed are Dante's images (II); the 'profoundness' of the third canto of *Inferno*, which produces 'a total impression of infinity', 'an inner feeling of totality, and of absolute being' (III); the 'picturesqueness', in which Dante cannot be surpassed and which brings him close to 'Michel Angelo' (IV); something closely related to this, namely the topographic quality of Dante's journey through Hell (V); the pathetic, of which Francesca and Ugolino are the highest examples (VI); and, finally, 'the endless subtle beauties of Dante', which seem to include particularly felicitously phrased images. However, Coleridge's lecture is not all praise of Dante; it contains towards the

end censure of Dante's presentation of some specific pictures. Following his list
of excellences, Coleridge regrets the lack of space for a comparison of Dante with
Milton, and limits himself to pointing out 'Dante's occasional fault of becoming
grotesque', in particular in his picture of Lucifer as compared with Milton's Satan.
All this goes to show, first, that Coleridge's view of Dante's poetry is clearly
limited to a consideration of the poetry of Hell (it will therefore be discussed in
this section devoted to Dante's *Inferno*), and, secondly, that the aspects of Dante's
poetry of Hell which Coleridge values are limited to passages and moments which
have to do with the visual and with the sublime – including the gothic and
pathetic.

The combination of Cary's translation and Coleridge's comments on Dante
greatly increased Dante's fame in England. To see, therefore, how Cary and
Coleridge presented Dante's 'excellences' to their readers and audience I will
focus, in the analysis of Cary's translation of *Inferno*, mainly on the two features
of the visual and the sublime. Cary's presentation of the protagonist shows no
striking departures that can immediately point to a specific view of this feature of
Dante's poem, so that this aspect of Cary's version emerges only slowly in the
translation. Whenever relevant, the discussion will focus on this feature of the
poem. The examples are drawn from three of the four episodes Coleridge
referred to, and from which he quoted in his lecture using Cary's translation:
Canto III, the episode of Ugolino, and the figure of Lucifer.

The canto where visual presentation really begins is the third canto of *Inferno*,
which includes descriptions of large spaces, of crowds, and of individuals, one of
these being the protagonist, whose psychological growth is made the focus of
attention. Coleridge mentions this canto twice in his list of Dante's 'chief
excellences', and makes an interesting distinction:

> Consider the wonderful profundity of the whole third Canto of the Inferno and especially
> of the inscription over Hell gate: 'Per me si va,' etc.... I say profoundness rather than
> sublimity; for Dante does not so much elevate your thoughts as send them down deeper (p.
> 408).

It would, indeed, be contrary to the total experience of Hell as prison of the spirit
for the protagonist to be elevated by sublime sights or feelings; an eighteenth-
century reader of gothic stories would see Hell as the subterranean vaults of a
gothic cathedral, rather than the 'forest' of the cathedral itself, which in its vertical
lines uplifts the mind of the onlooker. Coleridge's words express a clear insight
into the poetry of Hell. For although the text does not contain a specific picture,
it does creates an image indirectly. The reader is led to see the gateway into Hell
as a squat broad opening, for in this case the eye can be immediately attracted to
the writing over the gate, and this is the only clue given to suggest the function

and shape of the door. Certainly this is the way the gateway into Hell is seen by most authoritative scholars on Dante in this century. Guido Mazzoni puts this very clearly in his reading of the third canto in *Letture Dantesche*:

Siamo alla porta dell'Inferno. Non è sottile e alta o a sesto acuto, ne è ornata di arditi pinnacoli, quali piacevano ai contemporanei di Dante nelle loro chiese, come per elevare fin dalla soglia l'aspirazione dell'anima verso Dio; ma invece è larga molto, e schiacciata in basso; e il poeta ha subito attratto l'occhio dalle parole 'di colore oscuro' che stanno in un' iscrizione al sommo di essa.[23]

Coleridge at his point in time is a good reader of Dante, since he has recreated in his thought the shape suggested by the text and all it implies. He realizes that Hell is a prison, but also that its darkness and restricted visibility suggest aspects of the sublime such as infinity and eternity, and therefore he uses the word 'profundity', a word current in contemporary critical vocabulary, denoting a notion similar to the sublime, but opposed to it in terms of the direction of the physical movement.[24]

Indeed, the place beyond Hell's door, in spite of its immensity, is far from sublime. We are not shown walls, cliffs, crags, or sky; instead, the eye is directed to the ground – the horizontal line being the only one that becomes visible. If lifted up or turned from side to side, the eye meets darkness. Through the darkness a flag is seen, and behind it a crowd running. The crowd itself is hardly described, but we are told of the worms and blood collecting at their feet; then, beyond them, the ground becomes a shore and, further on, a lake. So while the vagueness and darkness suggests an immense landscape, the effect is not of depth, but of distance and continuing oppression, and the very elements often involved in the creation of the sublime assume the opposite function.

The general features of the picture and the movement within it are faithfully reproduced by Cary – though this proves little about Cary's stance, since only a translator who wanted to alter the original drastically would change features such as the blood and worms gathering on the ground, or the shore with a lake beyond.[25] Cary translates these settings literally, but misrepresents the one feature of the canto which offers the translator the opportunity for a striking picture. Instead of framing Hell in terms of the same low, horizontal lines used in the course of the canto, Cary turns the entrance into the tall entrance of a gothic church:

Such characters in colour dim I mark'd
Over a portal's lofty arch inscrib'd: (III 10-11)

The misunderstanding of the visual picture is not, however, a distortion peculiar to Cary. Most illustrators, constrained by Dante's manner of making us see, must interpret what is given and can only do so on the basis of personal vision or contemporary ideas. Thus Blake's watercolour of Hell's door is really 'sottile e alta' and 'a sesto acuto', in Mazzoni's words. In Blake's picture, the eye must surely be attracted rather by the flaming layered space beyond the door than by the writing above its high arch. Blake's depiction of a grave in his illustration for Blair's *The Grave*, its square opening made to appear lower by the squat beam above it, would have been closer to Dante's vision. Cary repeatedly proves willing to add sublimity to his pictures, just as he does in his diction, while at the same time avoiding touches of the more sensational gothic. Accordingly, he adds space and height in his lofty arch, but does not heighten, for example, the horrid appearance of Charon.

His picture of the ferryman is more restrained than the versions of many later translators.[26] Certainly Cary does not develop the potential wildness in the famous pictures of Charon's eyes – 'che 'ntorno alli occhi avea di fiamma rote' (l. 99), and 'Caron dimonio, con occhi di bragia' (l. 109), ('around whose eyes were wheels of flame', and 'the devil Charon, with eyes of glowing coals'). Cary renders these phrases as 'Around whose eyes glared wheeling flames' and 'with eyes of burning coal' – very much a controlled translation, though the 'wheeling' adds a movement which could be seen as inappropriate. Dorothy Sayers' 'his eyes like a burning brand' is flatter and less direct, since the burning of the eyes becomes a mere simile. But this follows her 'Only his flame-ringed eyeballs rolled a-glower', where she seems to revel in a gothic rolling of eyes.[27]

Cary's control and avoidance of passion also occurs in the portrait of the protagonist. One example will suffice. There are two readings of line 31: 'E io ch'avea d'*orror* la testa cinta', and 'E io ch'avea d'*error* la testa cinta' ('And I who had my head circled with error', or 'with horror', emphases added). Many editors prefer the reading 'orror', probably because of the Virgilian echo (Aen. II, 556 'At me ... saevus circumstaetit horror'), and many translators follow in the track of these editors – Ciardi, Bickersteth and Sayers being three examples. Charles Singleton chooses 'error', basing his choice on the authority of Petrocchi's scholarly edition of Dante.[28] Cary was clearly familiar with both readings, because he mentions both in a footnote, but, very interestingly, for his translation he chooses 'error', thereby underlining the intellectual dimension of the journey. Possibly Cary is only too keen to tone down the more extreme 'pathos of passion' as Coleridge calls it.

Cary's version of the Ugolino episode illustrates a number of the observations to be made on this translation – Cary's inability to render the vividness of experience and his stress, as a result, on the poem as written artifact, the lack of concreteness and variety in his presentation of the physical world, and the attempt to heighten the sublime and tone down the gothic and the expression of passions. In the Ugolino episode, however, Cary is perhaps at his best.

This is the opening of Canto XXXIII in Dante:

> La bocca sollevò dal fiero pasto
> quel peccator, forbendola a' capelli
> del capo ch'elli avea di retro guasto.   3
> Poi cominciò: "Tu vuo' ch'io rinovelli
> disperato dolor che 'l cor mi preme
> già pur pensando, pria ch'io ne favelli.   6
> Ma se le mie parole esser dien seme
> che frutti infamia al traditor ch'i rodo,
> parlare e lacrimar vedrai inseme."   (XXXIII 1-9)[29]

As in the opening of the poem, so here there is a specific function for each tercet, the one following the other by a more than chronological necessity. The first tercet establishes as it were the movement of the two heads. We have remarked earlier on the slow movement suggested by those first lines and on the gradual raising of the sinner from animal to human (see p. 72 above). The second tercet, accordingly, is a quiet, tentative awakening to words: Dante the protagonist has called Ugolino back from beastliness to memory of his past life, and the movement continues from the 'disperato dolor' of his mind to the renewed grief of his heart and then to the words to be found. In the third tercet the voice gradually rises in tone until, at the end of the second line, it reaches a climax in the harsh repeated sounds of 'traditor ch'i rodo',[30] while the third line lowers the tone again into the quiet intensity of Ugolino's recounting.

This is Cary's version:

> His jaws uplifting from their fell repast,
> That sinner wip'd them on the hairs o' th' head,
> Which he behind had mangled, then began:
> "Thy will obeying, I call up afresh
> Sorrow past cure; which, but to think of wrings   5
> My heart, or ere I tell on't. But if words,
> That I may utter, shall prove seed to bear
> Fruit of eternal infamy to him,
> The traitor whom I gnaw at, thou at once
> Shalt see me speak and weep. Who thou mayst be   10
> I know not, not how here below art come:
> But Florentine thou seemest of a truth,
> When I do hear thee. Know I was on earth
> Count Ugolino, and th' Archbishop he
> Ruggieri ..."

While Dante's opening three tercets make up an orchestrated effect of mounting tension, Cary gives us instead the preparation for a dramatic monologue. The very movement of Ugolino's head in Cary's first three lines is structured to introduce the forthcoming speech: 'His jaws uplifting, ... then began:'. The second group of three lines is divided into a number of phrases and is full of punctuation, and therefore of pauses. But instead of rendering hesitation, the whole suggests formal, determined speech. And the crescendo pointed out in the third tercet of the original becomes more formal and rhetorical: 'Le mie parole' ('my words') becomes 'words,/ That I may utter', and Dante's climactic phrase becomes in Cary the smooth 'to him,/ The traitor whom I gnaw at' – a phrase in which so much care appears to have been taken to make it syntactically correct, balanced and polished that the reader cannot but wonder if the action referred to could really be the gnawing of a skull.

Cary's biographer, W. King, discusses Cary's translation in the last chapter of his book, and points out how 'by a strong infusion of vigorous native turns of expression, derived from poets of the Elizabethan age or of earlier periods, ... Cary succeeded in simplifying the somewhat cumbrous Miltonic Style, and so adapted it for reflecting the brevity and vivid directness of Dante's manner' (p. 302). First of all it must be remarked that it is difficult to identify what aspects of his own diction Cary borrowed from the Elizabethans rather than Milton, since Milton himself borrowed from the Elizabethans. Thus King mentions Chaucer, Spenser and Shakespeare as sources for Cary's diction; but Havens mentions the very same three names as sources for archaic words which are one characteristic of the Miltonic style as seen in the eighteenth century. Also, imitation of traditional 'turns of phrases' from past literature hardly ensures the achievement of simplicity.

Formality and correctness go hand in hand, in Cary's version, with a lack of sudden shifts in setting. But Dante's poetry in this episode moves in paragraphs, and Ugolino's story in stretches of narrative which differ from each other – even, sometimes, in setting. 'Io non so chi tu se" (l. 10) opens one movement, in which Ugolino points to the position in Hell of himself and his 'neighbour'; 'Breve pertugio' (l. 22) takes us suddenly into the tower of famine, and into the past of Ugolino's death. There is a clear, abrupt pause before each shift.[31] The dream entails a further shift in setting, which is introduced, however, with less sharp a break. But Ugolino's awakening from the dream introduces yet another violent change in setting, opening a new stage in the story and, as it were, a new paragraph in the poetry; and so on. In Cary all these openings occur in middle line, and this affects the rhythm of the reading, the flow of the language, and the abruptness of the breaks. In the long run, this cannot but increase the impression of continuity.

While elsewhere in the poem (in the opening passages, for example) Dante had followed a straightforward word order, here he often uses inversions (which can, in any case, be quite natural in Italian) and even, occasionally, run-on lines, to increase the tension. It accordingly seems odd that, while Cary had elsewhere added these devices to his version of the original, he should avoid them here, and, therefore, deviate from Dante precisely when Dante is closer to Milton. An instance of varied word order occurs where Dante says 'pianger senti' fra 'l sonno i miei figliuoli' (word per word, 'crying I heard in their sleep my children', where 'crying' refers to the children), with the mention of the children coming only at the end, to give a further turn of the screw to the sound of sorrow. The pause on the final word, 'children', is made more haunting by the lengthened form Dante uses ('figliuoli' rather that 'figli'), which is a kind of affectionate diminutive, introducing overtones different from the non-lengthened form. Cary does not follow Dante's word order, with the verb 'crying' placed at the beginning and 'children' at the end, missing the powerful effect that Dante had achieved. Furthermore, 'amid their sleep I heard/ My sons (for they were with me) weep and ask /For bread' is far too reasoned, formal, and elaborately constructed (with that parenthetic insertion) to have much dramatic effect. An example of the run-on lines occurs when Ugolino first gives way to his grief – or rage:

> "Come un poco di raggio si fu messo
>   nel doloroso carcere, e io scorsi
>   per quattro visi il mio aspetto stesso,
> ambo le man per lo dolor mi morsi;"   (XXXIII 55-57)[32]

Clearly this is a unit of four lines, the fourth providing the climax to the crescendo of the first three. The crescendo of Cary's lines is less effective, but it does have poise and rhythm:

> " ... When a faint beam
> Had to our doleful prison made its way,
> And in four countenances I descry'd
> The image of my own, on either hand   55
> Through agony I bit, ..."

The movement here is controlled, and though it does not mount up to a climax as powerfully as in Dante, still there is variety, some rhythm, and tension – for 'the image of my own' in particular has a gripping slow movement to self-aware-ness. There are other moments in this same episode which make a genuine contribution to English poetry:

> " ... ; the mind
> Of each misgave him through his dream, and I
> Heard, at its outlet underneath lock'd up

> The' horrible tower: whence, utt'ring not a word,   45
> I look'd upon the visage of my sons.
> I wept not: so all stone I felt within.
> They wept: and one, my little Anselm, cried;
> 'Thou lookest so! Father, what ails thee?' Yet
> I shed no tear, nor answer'd all that day   50
> Nor the next night, until another sun
> Came up upon the world. ..."[33]

This is quiet, restrained, and very tense. The pauses here do not split up and interrupt the flow of the story with excessive punctuation or parenthetic remarks, but add variety, vigour and power to the thoughts expressed. In particular, that slow, drawn out 'The horrible tower' followed by a substantial pause and short, quiet clauses, is dramatic. Cary at times follows the line openings of Dante and at times does not, but here it does not matter, because the language – its movement, sound and rhythm – corresponds to the character and his story and, without being over-pathetic, Cary communicates the setting, the fears, and all the possibilities inherent in the situation of Ugolino and his sons in prison. Perhaps Cary's control and understatement suits the taste of a modern reader better than pathos, sublimity and gothic touches, which are certainly reduced in his translation:

> .... Thus having spoke,
> Once more upon the wretched skull his teeth   75
> He fasten'd like a mastiff's 'gainst the bone
> Firm and unyielding. Oh, thou Pisa! shame
> Of all the people ...[34]

The language of the whole episode is firm and strong, and Ugolino rises to measured blank verse drama. However, it is purely verbal drama, and, along with sudden breaks, shifts in setting and pathos, Ugolino's animal hate, passion and very physical presence have all disappeared behind the story. The solidity of the statue – or even of a man – is absent from Cary's Ugolino. Furthermore, in Dante, the man and father, at the end, regresses again to the beast: Ugolino 'Quand'ebbe detto cio, *con gli occhi torti/* riprese 'l teschio misero co' denti' ('When he had said that, *with his eyes bulging,/* he again seized the miserable skull with his teeth', emphasis added). But this is glossed over by Cary who leaves out the rolling of the eyes. In judging Cary's 'fidelity', therefore, one must not only look at his, admittedly restrained, additions in language and sublimity; one must also consider the fact that he reduces the horror of Hell by cutting out, occasionally, a phrase.

The last canto of *Inferno*, and in particular the colossal shape of Lucifer towering over it, illustrates the aspects of Cary's translation already isolated – his elimination of the experience of the protagonist, his stress on the poem as written narrative, his addition of sublimity, and the toning down of the physical solidity of Dante's world:

> How frozen and how faint I then became,
> Ask me not, reader! for I write it not,
> Since words would fail to tell thee of my state.
> I was not dead nor living. Think thyself   25
> If quick conception work in thee at all,
> How I did feel. That emperor, who sways
> The realm of sorrow, at mid breast from th' ice
> Stood forth; and I in stature am more like
> A giant, than the giants are his arms.   30
> Mark now how great that whole must be, which suits
> With such a part. If he were beautiful
> As he is hideous now, and yet did dare
> To scowl upon his Maker, well from him
> May all our mis'ry flow. Oh, what a sight!   35
> How passing strange it seem'd, when I did spy
> Upon his head three faces: one in front
> Of hue vermilion, th' other two with this
> Midway each shoulder join'd and at the crest;
> The right 'twixt wan and yellow seem'd: the left   40
> To look on, such as come from whence old Nile
> Stoops to the lowlands. Under each shot forth
> Two mighty wings, enormous as became
> A bird so vast. Sails never such I saw
> Outstretch'd on the wide sea. No plumes had they,   45
> But were in texture like a bat, and these
> He flapp'd i' th' air, that from him issued still
> Three winds, wherewith Cocytus to its depth
> Was frozen. At six eyes he wept: the tears
> Adown his chins distill'd with bloody foam.   50
> At every mouth his teeth a sinner champ'd,
> Bruis'd as with pond'rous engine, so that three
> Were in this guise tormented. But far more
> Than from the gnawing, was the foremost pang'd
> By the fierce rending, whence ofttimes the back
> Was stript of all its skin ...   (XXXIV 22-56)[35]

The opening of the passage in the original is clearly meant to remind the reader of the dual nature of Dante in the poem, and does so by using the same devices employed at the very beginning of *Inferno*: again we have two 'io''s and two tenses, one past and one present – 'com'io divenni' ('how I then became'), and 'ch'i' non lo scrivo' ('for I do not write it'). The protagonist feels the harrowing effect of the sight of Lucifer; the writer will not, he says, attempt to describe these feelings. Words – 'parlar' – are inadequate to communicate feelings. What the writer is able to put down on paper is the description of the sight, which encodes the feelings of death-in-life of the protagonist. This is one of the moments when the writer openly refers to the active role his reader has to take: the reader must imagine for himself what it feels like to be without death and also without life, and if a reader has 'fior d'ingegno' ('any wit') he will indeed be able to recreate the protagonist's feelings at the sight of Lucifer on the basis of the description of the latter's appearance.

The description of Lucifer moves from an initial sketch of the general shape of Dis to a gradual filling in of details. Dis first appears as a machine, an automaton, since he represents denial of humanity. He also embodies immobility, and the only movement he has is mechanical. Paradoxically, he is lifeless but also cannibalistic. In the original, the details which eventually fill in the general picture do not describe a horrifying devil, nor do they depict a grotesque monster, rather this Lucifer seems a complex symbol, being an absolute inversion of God. For he is called emperor, as God often is in the *Divina Commedia*, and painted as a physical, monstrous trinity.

In Cary's version, the controlled tone of recollection, the careful organization of the description, the attempt to indicate the size of Lucifer, and the unemotional description of the latter's features are direct and clear. The translation reflects the text's creation of Dis as, in Cary's excellent rendering of 'a guisa di maciulla', a 'pond'rous engine'. Lucifer's lack of movement (apart from mechanical movement) reflects his lack of human emotions, so nothing could be further from Dante's Dis than Milton's rendering of the tripartite division of the face of his Satan: 'each passion dimm'd his face/ Thrice changed with pale ire, envy and despair' (*PL* IV, 114-5). Similarly, the freezing wind which issues from the wings causes what is in Dante's vision a very great sin – cowardice or inaction. The movement of these wings is therefore of a very different nature from Milton's depiction of Satan who spreads 'his sail-broad vans/ ... for flight' (*PL* II, 927-8). Cary himself quotes these passages from Milton in his footnotes. He does not comment on them, nor does he attempt to paint his Dis with Milton's colours; he has seen the difference in the pictures and has rejected Milton's expressions as inappropriate representations of Dante. Here, therefore, Cary is not just translating literally a descriptive passage, but he is making a conscious choice based on an understanding of the original.

This is not just speculation; for Cary does, indeed, occasionally bring in small variations and additions, both to the figure of Dis, and to the setting, and so, had he found it appropriate, he could easily have changed more details, or echoed Milton more closely. For example, Cary calls Dis 'That emperor, who sway'd/ The realm of sorrow', where Dante's 'lo 'mperador del doloroso regno' is much flatter; also, the wings of Dis are, in Cary, 'mighty' and 'enormous', while in Dante they are just 'due grand'ali' ('two great wings'). Further on, Dante's 'Non era camminata di palagio' is indeed rendered by Cary literally with 'it was no palace hall', to which, however, he adds 'lofty and luminous'; and later a 'tomba' becomes a 'vaulted tomb'. Cary, therefore, repeatedly introduces words which suggest space and grandiosity. Dis himself is here and there touched up, and a few details are added to the description. So where Dante briefly mentions Dis' 'vellute coste' ('hairy sides'), Cary prefers 'shaggy sides', which the travellers descend 'from pile to pile'. And while in the original Dis 'ne fe scala col pelo' ('made a ladder for us with his hair'), Cary has 'whose shaggy pile we scaled', where the vocabulary is almost Wordsworthian and increases the size and awfulness of the form.

The consistent additions to Dis' sublimity are explained by the fact that, though Cary obviously was aware of the nature of some aspects of Dante's pictures, he was unable to respond to them intimately and, on the contrary, saw them as strange and even ridiculous. He practically says this much in the 'Life of Dante':

> His solicitude, it is true, to define all images in such a manner as to bring them distinctly within the circle of our vision, and to subject them to the power of the pencil, sometimes renders him little better than grotesque, where Milton has since taught us to expect sublimity. But his faults, in general, were less those of the poet than of the age he lived (p. xxxvi).

Cary's words indicate a reading of Dante very close to that of the many readers mentioned in the first section of Chapter 2: the barbarous middle ages guide Dante's pencil. Accordingly, what Cary is aiming to do in his translation is improve his original with a few injections of sublimity – an attitude which is not so dissimilar from Boyd's.

It is not only Cary who sees Dante's images as lacking sublimity, but also Coleridge – in fact, Cary's version seems to be putting into practice Coleridge's views. Comparing Dante to Milton, Coleridge says:

> And in this comparison I should notice Dante's occasional fault of becoming grotesque from being too graphic without imagination; as in Lucifer compared with Milton's Satan. Indeed, he is sometimes horrible rather than terrible (p. 409).

At this point, Coleridge is fettered by the labeling of aesthetic responses which were current at the time, and expresses his reading of Dante's and Milton's figures of Satan in terms which are inseparable from Burke's analysis of the sublime and beautiful and from Ann Radcliffe's views on the sublime and gothic.

The emotion of terror is the very foundation of Burke's aesthetic system of the sublime ('whatever is in any sort terrible, ... is a source of the *sublime*; that is, it is productive of the strongest emotion which the mind is capable of feeling').[36] Burke also uses the word horror, but without distinguishing it absolutely from terror. He says, for example, that 'delight' (which derives from privation of fear) is produced by 'a sort of delightful horror, a sort of tranquillity tinged with terror' (IV 7), and that astonishment is 'that state of the soul in which all its motions are suspended with some degree of horror' (II 1). Burke's references to terror and horror are developed by Ann Radcliffe, who asserts that the two are opposites, since terror expands the soul, while horror 'contracts, freezes, and nearly annihilates'. This means, therefore, that Ann Radcliffe sees terror as coming from without, and engulfing us in the sublime and in infinity, while horror is understood as coming from within and causing us to sink downwards into dread and obscurity.[37] Coleridge, we know, did not think highly of Burke's treatise, but the views by which he assesses the figures of Satan derive from it, and also seem consonant with Radcliffe's. For Coleridge practically defines horror as 'grotesque', 'too graphic' and 'without imagination', which means that an object of horror is not sublime because it is neither obscure nor vague – that is, it does not fit in with Burke's categories for the sublime. Moreover, in Ann Radcliffe's terms, Dante's Dis does not expand the soul through imagination, whereas Milton's Satan, which has the sublimity of terror, does.

Both Cary and Coleridge, therefore, see Dante's Dis as 'too graphic', drawn with 'the power of the pencil', and do not see the symbolic nature of the picture. It is not, accordingly, that Dante's picture is inadequate, but that Dante's readers, at the moment in time under consideration, lack the kind of imagination needed to read the implications of the picture. At the opening of the canto, the poet had stated that he would not write the feelings inspired by the sight, but would only describe the sight itself, and had called on his reader to 'think for himself' and imagine what such feelings would be. Perhaps, therefore, one must conclude that the early nineteenth-century readers did not have the same kind of 'fior d'ingegno' that Dante expected in his readers; otherwise they would not have dwelled on the details of the shape and seen them as excessively specific and unnatural, but would have recognized the image as signifying the inversion of the trinity as well as absolute existential fear.

Cary's main failure in his rendering of *Inferno* is his inability to read Dante's pictures as Dante had expected his readers to do, as signs for ideas, and this is not only a matter of the description in Canto XXXIV but of the whole of the *Commedia*. Obviously Cary cannot be blamed for a failure which he shares with a poet like Coleridge, and an artist like Blake, and which simply proceeds from their expectations as educated readers of Dante. Still, the fact must be pointed out because it does, in effect, determine the nature of Cary's translation. Cary's attempt to add sublimity goes hand in hand with the other fundamental feature of his translation: the monotonous pace at which it moves. The nervous speed of the tercets in *Inferno* (throughout the *cantica*, but in this case in Canto XXXIV) is absolutely necessary – to prevent the attention from being focused too long on the monstrous details of Dis' features. For it is this speed that leaves the reader with a powerful impression to which each individual feature contributes.

Cary's blank verse, therefore, is instrumental in communicating a vision of Dante which is less solid, more spatial, more sublime (though in a controlled manner), and more 'literary' – a 'classic' of literature, with the sharp points smoothed down. It is Cary's scholarship and the weight of the whole edition – footnotes included – that are his major achievement. But Cary also demonstrated the ability and intelligence to make use of his scholarship. In this respect, De Sua is belittling Cary's achievement when he says that his mistranslations are the common misreadings of his age; for, as in the case of the choice between the two readings 'error' and horror', so also elsewhere Cary goes well beyond the current common knowledge of Dante. For example, Boyd's portrait of a protagonist who wanted to kill the leopard and wear its skin (see p. 00 143) could be justified on the basis of the scholarship then current; but Cary not only translates this passage in terms of the scholarship available even today, but adds a footnote, mentioning the alternative reading preferred 'by all the commentators, whom I have seen'. Moreover, he also refers the reader to a passage in the sixteenth canto of *Inferno* which might support this alternative reading – and yet he finds his own choice more in accordance with the text in its totality. Cary's translation, and the legacy he leaves behind, seems already characterized by these two aspects noticed in his rendering of *Inferno*: the very substantial scholarship, used with diligence as well as intelligence, and his particular kind of distortion of the realism of Dante's world and of the voice describing it.

Cary's *Purgatory*

When Cary decided to work on a complete translation of Dante's *Commedia*, he started with *Purgatorio*, on January the 16th, 1797, and by March he had already finished the first five cantos. Then he laid the enterprise aside for over two years, and started again, with *Inferno*, on May 23rd, 1800. The reasons for the initial delay, and for subsequently beginning with *Inferno* are not clear;[38] the possibility that Cary found *Purgatorio* harder to translate than he had anticipated, however, seems confirmed by the fact that even as it now stands Cary's *Purgatory* is in many ways a weak text and a faulty translation of the original, much more, and more fundamentally so, than his *Hell* is.

In *Purgatory*, as in *Hell*, the language is twisted into forced patterns, and Cary also continues to add grandiosity and solemnity.[39] Even Cary's scholarship seems weak in his translation of *Purgatorio*; and while in his translation of *Inferno* it goes hand in hand with an applied knowledge of Italian and some sensitivity to the nature of the total text (all of which led Cary to choose a particular reading at a given point), in his translation of *Purgatorio* precisely the opposite seems true. The simile at the opening of Canto VI exemplifies all this:

> When from their game of dice men separate,
> He, who hath lost, remains in sadness fix'd,
> Revolving in his mind, what luckless throws
> He cast: but meanwhile all the company
> Go with the other; one before him runs,   5
> And one behind his mantle twitches, one
> Fast by his side bids him remember him.
> He stops not; and each one, to whom his hand
> Is stretch'd, well knows he bids him stand aside;[40]

This is a *comparatio domestica* – one of the many in *Purgatorio*, where they call up in plain language feelings or images which will awaken in the reader familiar memories. In this case, the Florentine reader of the fourteenth century would have been reminded of the game of *zara*, forbidden by the republic but extremely popular nevertheless; even the modern reader, however, will respond to the feeling of loss, the going over in one's mind of past decisions to see what went wrong and how one could do better next time. Cary does at least notice, as he reveals in a footnote, that 'there is something very natural in this', but adds 'but whether the sense can be fairly deduced by the words is another question' (n. 2, p. 188). The original in fact is not complicated, and the words are fairly clear: in Dante's 'a cui porge la man, piú non fa pressa' ('each to whom he reaches his hand, presses on him no longer'), 'porge' implies giving rather that just stretching, and suggests that the winner gives something to this or that person to stop them pressing him.

Cary's translation goes against what the Italian implies. It also goes against the secondary material available. Cary quotes in a footnote a certain Archdeacon Fisher who 'pointed out to me a passage in the *Novela de la Gitanilla* of Cervantes, ed. Valentia, 1797, p. 12, from which it appears that it was usual for money to be given to by-standers at play by winners; and as he well remarked "Dante is therefore describing, with his usual power of observation, what he had often seen, the shuffling, boon-denying exit of the successful gamester"' (n. 3, p. 188). Fisher himself seems very inconsistent, since first he quotes a reference to Cervantes in which boon-paying is recognized as a custom, and then concludes that in Dante we have a boon-denying winner. Cary is equally inconsistent, and his learning seems here forced and in fact gratuitous. Why should he quote Cervantes, if he will then agree, rather, with the interpretation of the text of Archdeacon Fisher, and present the reader with a 'boon-denying winner'? In addition to lack of understanding of the Italian, and carelessness with secondary comments, Cary also shows misunderstanding of the spirit of the poetry. The simile describes the situation in which the protagonist also finds himself, pressed by a crowd of souls who ask to be remembered to their dear ones on earth, so that they can pray for them. The community of prayer, the union of the living and dead in the love of God is one of the issues often referred to in *Purgatorio*, so that the protagonist as denying winner is absolutely monstrous in this context. Cary simply has not stopped to think what the poetry is about, and has misread the scholarship that could have guided him in that direction. Probably Cary was uncertain of the real meaning of the lines and tried to cover up, first by being vague in his actual translation (in a manner very similar to Rogers' in comparable circumstances) and, secondly, by relying on someone else's interpretation in his footnotes.

The analysis of Cary's version of *Purgatorio* leads to three main observations. First, Cary's landscape lacks vividness and solidity and, although Cary is careful to reproduce the sublimity that he read in the original, still the landscape does not reveal the spiritual and visionary significance of the visible. Secondly, Cary stresses the figure of the writer Dante, but the experience of the protagonist disappears. Thirdly, by using the same style throughout the *cantica* Cary further deprives *Purgatorio* of the spiritual significance that the world of Dante and the figure of the protagonist/poet can communicate. In order to illustrate and explore these aspects of Cary's translation I shall focus on two aspects of his *Purgatory*: the descriptions of landscape, and the reunion of Dante with Beatrice.

The descriptions which Dante sketches in the opening cantos of *Purgatorio* depict the sky, the island which forms the basis of Mount Purgatory, the sea which extends horizontally as far as the eye can see, and the mountain, which is, however, first mentioned only in Canto III. The first sight to greet the pilgrims as they reach Purgatory is that of the pure air, a clear sky full of colour:

> Sweet hue of eastern sapphire, that was spread
> O'er the serene aspect of the pure air,
> High up as the first circle, to mine eyes   15
> Unwonted joy renew'd, soon as I 'scap'd
> Forth from the atmosphere of deadly gloom,
> That had mine eyes and bosom fill'd with grief.
> The radiant planet, that to love invites,
> Made all the orient laugh, and veil'd beneath   20
> The Pisces' light, that in his escort came.
>   To the right hand I turn'd, and fix'd my mind

On the' other pole attentive, where I saw
Four stars ne'er seen before save by the ken
Of our first parents. Heaven of their rays   25
Seem'd joyous. O thou northern site, bereft
Indeed, and widow'd, since of these depriv'd.
   As from this view I had desisted, straight
Turning a little tow'rds the other pole,
There from whence the wain had disappear'd,   30
I saw an old man standing by my side
Alone,...[41]

A number of words are added – 'unwonted', 'attentive' – and the setting is more diffuse and less solid than Dante's, since Cary places his protagonist not under the constellation of the Pisces, which takes shape solidly in the sky (though shaded by Venus), but under the Pisces' 'light', and this is made to contrast sharply with the more haunting 'atmosphere of deadly gloom' – Cary's translation of the original's plainer but physical 'aura morta' ('dead air'). Cary's inversions ('To the right hand I turn'd' and 'As from this view I had desisted') diminish the directness and almost barrenness of the movements described by Dante, so that character and movement become secondary, while the language and diction the writer chooses acquire greater importance.

But the greatest distortion which Cary makes in relation to the original is to superimpose infinity on the pictures. In the opening of the poem, the sweet hue of oriental sapphire 's'accoglieva nel sereno aspetto', that is, 'it was gathered together' within the serenity of the blue sky. Tommaseo points out how 'altri avrebbe detto spandeva, ma nell'immensità il nostro vede unità' ('others would have said "was spread", but in immensity our writer sees unity').[42] Cary's 'was spread' translates what 'altri' would have said, but not what the text says. Cary takes the eye outwards, while Dante lets it embrace the whole. In the very next line, the air was 'puro insino al primo giro' ('pure right to the first circle'), a phrase which establishes the boundary of the sky, and draws as it were a sphere of pure air enclosed by the *Primum Mobile*. Cary's 'High up as the first circle' stresses the height, rather than the enclosure. The modern reader of the original soon notices how Dante's space seems organized and enclosed, contained by the infinity of God. The various constellations are made to circle in the sky around the observing eyes of the protagonist, but, rather than bright visions of infinity, they are the beautiful elements of a complex system of spheres which all obey God's power and reveal the harmony of his works. Possibly, Cary could not but read infinity into descriptions of sky; but more probably, it is the style he chose that carries with itself, almost unnoticed by its user, suggestions of infinity.

Descriptions next focus on the island:

Questa isoletta intorno ad imo ad imo,
  là giú colà dove la batte l'onda,
  porta de' giunchi sovra 'l molle limo   (I 100-102)[43]

Very little is said about the island, but stress is laid on the shore line which is mentioned three times: 'intorno', 'ad imo ad imo' and 'dove la batte l'onda' ('all around' 'about the base' 'there where the waves are always beating on it'). The reader is made to rest on this point, rather than move on quickly; first he sees the shore line, then the stretch of the island extending towards it ('ad imo ad imo'), and then the stretch of the sea as it touches it. Along this stressed boundary between water and earth, the 'molle limo' sketches an area between solid and liquid, a muddy water or soft ground, where the only vegetation which can survive the buffetings of the water grow – and the underlying significance is perfectly integrated into the realistic landscape. Cary translates literally, but there seems to be very little care or awareness of what the original begins to suggest:

This islet all around, there far beneath,   100
Where the wave beats it, on the oozy bed
Produces stores of reeds ....

The addition of the word 'stores' suggests that there is plenty for Dante to gird himself with, and 'far beneath' is more vague and distant than the original; the original's continuous stress on the boundary line, and the moral meaning of the bending reeds are both diminished. The splitting of the lines into smaller units, and the addition of commas slows down the pace of the poetry, giving a tone more casual and less focused than in the original.

Cary clearly has not realized how central to Dante's picture boundaries are at this point, sketching, as they do, a kind of threshold between states of being. When, further down, Virgil cleans Dante's face, he wets his hands on the grass, just at the edge where 'the dew strives with the sun' ('la rugiada pugna col sole') – again a boundary, this time between wet and dry. This stress on boundary lines is lessened in Cary, who is also less precise and definite in his translations of the views of the sea which encloses the island.

Descriptions of the wide expanse of sea, such as one in Canto II which describes the approach of the boat of souls guided by a shining angel – one of Shelley's favourite passages – are characterized by detailed observation (though what is seen is often unclear), plain language, and tentativeness in the description of the sights.[44] The plain language and exact description of whatever is seen, even if it is vague like 'a something white' which later turns out to be wings, result in an emphasis on the experience of the viewer, that is, the protagonist. Cary, on the other hand, stresses the writer's recognition of the beauty of the view, and his attempt render it into controlled language. The picture of the immense expanse of sea at dawn ('through the thick vapours Mars with fiery beam/ Glares down in west, over the ocean floor') captures Cary's eye more than the inner motions of the protagonist.

Cary's renderings of sky and sea indicate that also in this respect he read the original in terms of Burke's sublime in nature. Burke had said, 'A level plain of a vast extent on land, is certainly no mean idea; the prospect of such a plain may be as extensive as a prospect of the ocean; but can it ever fill the mind with any thing so great as the ocean itself?' (II 2). In fact, it is even probable that Dante's descriptions, and the protagonist's reactions both at this point and throughout these first cantos, confirmed Cary's reading of them as examples of the sublime in nature. The effects of the sublime, again in Burke's words, are astonishment (the main effect), 'admiration, reverence and respect' (II 1).[45] Such are, in the original, the reactions of the protagonist, and of the other souls, to the sights they meet. In Cary's version, the souls are 'astounded with the place' on reaching the shore, and the sight of Dante makes them grow 'pale with wonder'. The word 'maraviglia' and the feelings of astonishment and surprise it suggests occur repeatedly in these first cantos. According to Singleton, these words indicate the mental state of the pilgrim who has been brought to freedom and the promised land, but they might have helped to suggest to Cary the presence of sublimity in Dante's world.[46]

Cary, then, could hardly have seen anything other than Burke's sublime in Dante's *Purgatorio*; the result of this reading, however, is not a heightening of sublimity in the text, but a blindness to other aspects of the original. In particular, Cary removes the protagonist from the scene by eliminating his uncertainty of sight and tentativeness of expression. In the original the mechanics of sight, in particular, very specifically point to the presence of the protagonist, a good example being Dante's first sight of the sea in the first canto:

> L'alba vinceva l'ora mattutina
>   che fuggía innanzi, sí che di lontano
>   conobbi il tremolar della marina.   (I 115-117)[47]

Cary's translation is literal, but static:

> The dawn had chased the matin hour of prime,
> Which fled before it, so that from afar
> I spied the trembling of the ocean stream.

The original gives a picture of a process taking place before our very eyes: 'Fuggía' ('was running') suggests a movement that is taking place there and then. Cary gives us a static description of a completed process, since the dawn 'had chased' the night away and was, presumably, in total control. Also, 'ocean stream', like all phrases drawn from neoclassical diction, calls attention to itself – that is, to poetic language as artifact – and therefore distances the realistic visual impression of the waves just visible because of the trembling light.

Contrary to what happened with protagonists of eighteenth-century poems or novels watching a sublime landscape, nature here is not an outer reality inspiring certain reactions in the human observer. Accordingly, the reactions of the protagonist are not added to the description. In *Purgatorio* the reaction *is* the object seen; the landscape is described in terms of the inner movements of the mind and heart. So in this tercet, in the words of Torraca, *'di lontano* pare un grido di ammirazione alla vista inattesa di spettacolo stupendo; *tremolar* dipinge e insieme anima la pittura col suono' (*'from afar* seems a cry of wonder at the unexpected view of a beautiful sight; *trembling* paints and at the same time enlivens the picture with sound').[48] In other words, the cry of wonder becomes a concrete and intimate part of the total scene – as opposed to being a reaction of a viewer, with both the reaction and the viewer distinguished from the landscape and not unified with the landscape in a total scene. This is proven by the word Dante here uses for sight: 'conobbi' ('I knew', or perhaps 'I recognized') the trembling of the sea. Cary's 'I spied' loses the overtones of inner motion. Earlier, Dante had similarly expressed the fact of seeing with phrases such as 'alli occhi miei ricominciò diletto', and 'puosi mente ... e vidi' (I 16, 22-3, 'restored to my eyes the touch of pleasure', 'I fixed my mind ... and saw').

The same device is used at the beginning of Canto III, when suddenly the eyes of the protagonist are turned upwards to the mountain:

> la mente mia, che prima era ristretta,
> lo 'ntento rallargò, sí come vaga,
> e diedi 'l viso mio incontro al poggio
> che 'nverso il ciel piú alto si dislaga.
> Lo sol, che dietro fiammeggiava roggio,
> rotto m'era dinanzi alla figura,
> ch'avea in me de' suoi raggi l'appoggio.   (III 12-18)[49]

Again the landscape is mingled with the inner world of the protagonist: it is first the mind, then the face which is turned upwards – the rising of the mountain is the rising of the mind, as the lingering by the water was the lingering of the soul, not yet ready for the difficult ascent of purification. Yet at the same time the redness of the sun and the solidity of the protagonist's body add definition to the scene.

Soon the mountain itself assumes solidity and is described, with even more precision than sea or sky, in terms of specific geographical references:

> Noi divenimmo intanto a piè del monte:
> quivi trovammo la roccia sí erta,

> che 'ndarno vi saríen le gambe pronte.
> Tra Lerice e Turbia, la piú diserta,
> la piú rotta ruina è una scala,
> verso di quella, agevole e aperta.　　(III 46-51)[50]

The region referred to is not far from the mountains through which Emily, St. Aubert and Valancourt travel and meet death, fear and experience in Ann Radcliffe's *The Mysteries of Udolpho*. Their fear of the 'banditti' is counterbalanced by their feelings of awe at the grandeur, the stupendous height and fantastic shape of the mountains. The presence of God is continuously felt by Emily. The happy ending of that story is summarized in a comparison: 'they were, at length, restored to each other – to the beloved landscapes of their beloved country'.[51] Indeed the Italian mountain landscape was, to the English viewer, too grand for comfort; and the nineteenth century came to see that very landscape as the seat of poets, and the setting for romantic literature. It was at Lerici that Shelley set up his last house, and on one of the beaches that here and there interrupt the steep cliffs of those mountains that his body was washed ashore. In Cary's day, therefore, this area of Italy became the epitome of the landscape of romance and death. When, much more recently, Umberto Eco was looking for an appropriate setting for the monastery of his neo-gothic novel, he picked on 'il dorsale appenninico, tra Piemonte, Liguria e Francia (*come dire tra Lerici e Turbia*)' ('the mountain range of the Appenines, between Piedmont, Liguria, and France (*between Lerici and Turbia, so to speak*)', italics added).[52] But the modern reader who looks at descriptions of the mountain in *Purgatorio* sees very little romance or sublimity, but perhaps rather the difficulty of climbing it, as expressed in realistic physical descriptions, and the recollection of familiar places near the protagonist's own home.

The difficulty of the climb is often stated in the original, and the reference to high hills and crags near Florence create a parallel between the life of Dante the man and the present experience of Dante the protagonist; we are told in colloquial language that 'the most deserted, the most broken scree, compared to that,/ Is an open and convenient stairway', and that

> Vassi in Sanleo e discendesi in Noli,
> montasi su in Bismantova in cacume
> con esso i pié; ma qui convien ch'om voli;　　(IV 25-27)[53]

Brief, plain and very colloquial the tercet concludes with a phrase which is in fact an exclamation; only in a second moment, in the next tercet, is this outburst connected to the higher meaning it acquires here: 'dico con l'ale snelle e con le piume/ del gran disio' ('I mean with the swift wings and plumage/ of great desire'). The two dimensions of the landscape – its solidity, and its moral significance – are, in this case, divided into two distinct moments, each of which has its own vividness. Protagonist and narrator share the stage, as it were.

Dante's direct equation of a broken ruinous path with a staircase becomes more grand, more rhetorical in Cary:

> ... Meanwhile we had arriv'd
> Far as the mountain's foot, and there the rock   45
> Found of so steep ascent, that nimblest steps
> To climb it had been vain. The most remote
> Most wild untrodden path, in all the tract
> 'Twixt Lerice and Turbia were to this
> A ladder easy' and open of access.   50

Words like 'deserted' and 'broken ruin' become here the more unreachable and dangerous 'remote' and 'wild'. Through the addition of the 'untrodden path' and of the phrase 'in all the tract', and through the positioning of the geographical names in the middle, rather than at the beginning, of the sentence, Cary gives more prominence to the broken landscape than to the actual comparison with a ladder. Dante's ladder is as real as the mountain – 'è una scala', while Cary distances both by turning the ladder into a figure of speech – 'were to this a ladder'. Similarly, what follows becomes far too grand as a reproduction of the protagonist's speech:

> ... On Sanleo's road
> Who journeys, or to Noli low descends,
> Or mounts Bismantua's height, must use his feet;   25
> But here a man has need to fly, I mean
> with the swift wing and plumes of high desire,

Here it is mainly the inversions which create a formality which is not in the original; but, in addition, the completeness of 'a man has need to fly' diminishes the impression of an exclamation, while the fact that the allegorical meaning of the comparison follows in the same line, without a physical break in the verse, merges the two, rather than establishing the reality of each.

In the original the landscape of the mountain appears occasionally friendly and even comforting, because of the use of comparisons with lowly, familiar occupations, in a language and style which are not just colloquial, but homely:

> Maggiore aperta molte volte impruna
>   con una forcatella di sue spine
>   l'uom della villa quando l'uva imbruna,
> che non era la calla onde salíne
>   lo duca mio, ed io appresso, soli,
>   come da noi la schiera si partíne.   (IV 19-24)[54]

The reference is to the habit of blocking any holes in the hedge around a vineyard with a few thorny branches. This is another instance of a *comparatio domestica*, because the style is low and humble, and it serves, as Sapegno points out, to add naturalness to the poetry of the journey.[79] Cary reduces the homely overtones:

> A larger aperture ofttimes is stopp'd,
> With forked stake of thorn by villager,
> When the ripe grape imbrowns, than was the path,   20
> By which my guide, and I behind him close,
> Ascended solitary, when that troop
> Departing left us. ...

The second line is enough to destroy the tone of the original. 'Forked stake' hardly translates 'una forcatella' – 'a little forkful', which almost suggests the movement involved; similarly, 'of thorn' is general and abstract when compared to 'di sue spine' – 'of his thorns'. Dante's peasant could almost be seen at work, while Cary's version becomes abstract and formal, particularly as a result of the passive structure of the sentence, which closes with the mention of a general 'by villager'. Moreover, as Cary often seems to do, here also he eliminates all articles in the phrase, in a misplaced imitation of Milton's Italianate style. Cary simply has not caught the basic tone of much of *Purgatorio*, which is one of human feelings of nostalgia for the earth and particularly its more humble memories. On the contrary, he often adds overtones which are the reverse of those in the original. So, in another description of the mountain, he adds the word 'lofty' and translates 'superba' (which, in the context, simply means 'steep') as 'proudly rising'.[55]

The landscape in the original is solidly real, and at the same time intimate and spiritual, suggesting self-reflection and recognition; it is phrased in simple, colloquial language, suggesting nostalgia for home. Cary reduces all these elements to the single effect of sublimity in nature and language, and turns the feelings of nostalgia of Dante the man into references to the historical world of Dante the writer. Cary's stress on Dante himself and his particular version of the landscape of *Purgatorio* will have repercussions on later poets like Blake and will be related to readers by critics like Ruskin; it is therefore important to realize the extent of Cary's distortion of the original. In the encounter with Manfred and with the penitents of the last hour we have a repetition of features of the landscape of Purgatory. When Manfred's bones are taken out of the protection of a mound and cast out in a river 'di fuor del regno' ('outside the kingdom'), the reader begins to connect the details of Manfred's death with the political theme, and the notion of security or lack of it in earthly kingdoms. When Jacopo del Cassero dies in the marshes and the reeds, the modern reader should begin to see the subtle, pervasive significance of features of landscape: a juxtaposition is made between the 'palude' ('marshes') of Jacopo's death and the 'molle limo' ('soft mud') around the islet of Purgatory's mountain, and between the 'giunchi' ('rushes') of Dante's salvation and the 'cannucce' ('reeds') of Jacopo's death. The difference is between the earthly landscape of the fall and the landscape of God. Similarly, the mention of the names of rulers and powerful families goes beyond an inescapable involvement in Florentine politics by the writer Dante, and stresses the difference between these kingdoms or states and the kingdom of God.

In effect Cary altogether tones down the role of the landscape in the poetry. Since, furthermore, his additions of sublimity are restrained and limited, his version is likely to communicate the spiritual significance of natural features less than Boyd's, where stress is placed on the contrast between the power of Manfred or Buonconte on earth and their dramatic deaths. To quote but one example, in the original Buonconte's 'Io fui da Montefeltro, io son Buonconte' contrasts the worldly power of a family, which is identified with the territories the family controls, with the intimate truth of the individual. Cary's 'Of Montefeltro I; Buonconte I:' is extremely painful as an English phrase, besides failing to render the deeper sense of Dante's contrast. In fact, Cary avoids the identification between place and character throughout his rendering of such instances.[56]

All the features discussed up to this point cumulatively indicate that the writer is on the scene, not the protagonist. In the original text the mountain is compared to places near Florence, familiar to Dante in the sense that they are close to home and have the attributes of affection and simplicity. In Cary the descriptions are purely autobiographical references, leading the reader's attention out of the poem and into the history and geography of fourteenth-century Florence. In other words, the geographical names become not references to places where a man – in this case, Dante, whose life is the 'literal' level of the allegory – experiences the hardships of climbing a steep mountain, but references to the world of Dante the Florentine writer. The consequence of this for the role of the figure of Dante in the poem is that, rather than this real man with his life-history being turned into a specific dramatis persona, whose life within the poem illustrates the potential future of every man, the references to real places seem to be used by the writer to embellish and add effect and variety to the writing. These references, therefore, do not add value to the creation of the persona, but receive value from being connected to Dante, the writer of a classic work of literature.

Turning to the protagonist and the world of Purgatory in later cantos, we see that in the original the poetry of the encounter between Beatrice and the protagonist in the earthly Paradise is subtly different from the poetry of the hard climb of purification on the mountain. Cary's language and style, however, remain the same. Furthermore, whereas in the original the change in the nature of the poetry is highlighted by the change in the landscape, in Cary's version the landscape also remains essentially similar throughout the *cantica*, and therefore fails to offer indications of the very different state of the protagonist. Thus, when Dante is led by the seven ladies into the shade of some trees, Cary adds touches of sublimity:

> ...so paus'd
> The sev'nfold band, arriving at the verge
> Of a dun umbrage hoar, such as is seen,
> Beneath green leaves and gloomy branches, oft
> To overbrow a bleak and alpine cliff.   (XXXIII 106-110)

Words like 'dun', 'gloomy', 'bleak' and 'hoar' are quite enough to justify a reading of these lines which suggests the terrible sublime – and indeed a later reader of Cary's Dante, John Ruskin, quoted these very lines to support his contention that Dante had an absolute dislike for mountains and 'never mentioned them but in bad weather, or snow'.[55] But in actual fact just one of these words appears in the original:

> le sette donne al fin d'un'ombra smorta,
> qual sotto foglie verdi e rami nigri
> sovra suoi freddi rivi l'Alpe porta.   (XXXIII 109-111)[57]

Here the comparison is with the muted shade in mountains, and their cold streams, a shade dim in comparison with the dark forest, and muted because the sun, which has in fact just been mentioned, does reach it by filtering through the leaves and branches of the trees. There is absolutely no mention of a cliff, bleak or not. The seven ladies are the ladies of the pageant, who lead Dante out of Purgatory, and the lines immediately following those quoted should make clear how the comparison with the mountain introduces ideas of rest and refreshment, rather than gloom and unpleasantness:

> Dinanzi ad esse Eufratès e Tigri
> veder mi parve uscir d'una fontana,
> e, quasi amici, dipartirsi pigri.   (XXXIII, 112-114)[58]

The appearance of two rivers, which are in fact Lethe and Eunoe, is therefore prepared in the comparison to the mountain scenery, and the words 'fontana' ('spring'), 'amici' ('friends') and 'pigri' ('slow in parting') here suggest a landscape which is far from unfriendly. The spring from which the two rivers flow is the goal of the seven ladies, who make Dante drink its water. The effect on him is such that he wishes he had more space to describe 'lo dolce ber che mai non m'avria sazio' (XXXIII 138, 'the sweet drink of which I could never have had enough'). Within the total context of the original, the description of the mountain assumes overtones of refreshing coolness rather than hoary gloominess.[59] The weather is sunny, and the place offers shade and the opportunity for the quenching of thirst.

Cary's translation of the simile just referred to shows that his version of the landscape of *Purgatorio* is the same throughout the second *cantica*, and this in itself is a sign of his misunderstanding of the development taking place within *Purgatorio*. For Cary's version, as King says, 'satisfies the supreme requirement [of a translation] : *it has a style*'. King goes on to add that it is not a style that 'fully reflects every facet of Dante's – his sublimity, his dignity, his tenderness, his astonishing simplicity. Yet ... has an all-round adaptability, a flexibility ... while retaining a continuity and evenness of texture which corresponds as closely, perhaps, as is possible in English to the marble clarity of Dante's form' (p. 307). These extravagant claims for Cary's translation betray King's excessive partisanship for the subject of his biography, as well as his own very limited reading of the original.[60]

That Cary's style has flexibility is questionable, but that it has evenness of texture is beyond dispute, and yet this is partly the problem with Cary's rendering of *Purgatorio*. For the original moves from the poetry of fallen landscape to the poetry (quite different in nature) of the earthly Paradise, while the basis of the symbolism remains the same. It is the very nature of the landscape and the nature of the poetry which suggest the very different spiritual state of the protagonist: having gone through purification on the mountain, Dante reaches the peace and beauty of Eden; and, having left behind the harsh poetry of Hell, the *Commedia* moves towards the poetry of love. Cary's addition of the terrible sublime in his landscape of the later cantos of *Purgatorio*, and the uniformity of his style throughout the poem strongly reduce the suggestion of development in the protagonist's experience. The reunion between Dante and Beatrice is a major climax in this experience, and the poetry which describes it echoes the poetry of the *Vita Nuova*.

The return to the pure vision of Dante's early youth is retraced in various ways, one of them being the encounter with the Provençal poet Arnaut Daniel. Arnaut is the last soul Dante speaks with before facing the wall of fire and the other rites of purification, his entrance into the fire retracing Arnaut's own movement: 'Poi s'ascose nel foco che li affina' (XXVI 148, 'Then he hid himself in the fire that purifies them'). The presence of Arnaut at this point in the protagonist's experience is the climax of the theme of poetry and poets in *Purgatorio*. The poetry of the original is now very different from what it was before the protagonist's purification. Cary's failure to trace the change in Dante's poetry is best illustrated in the passages recounting the departure of Virgil and the encounter with Beatrice.

This episode, which is the conclusion of the pageant of Revelation, opens with the description of a sunrise through clouds, so that the eye can sustain the sight of the sun (see pp. 149-50 above); similarly, says the poet, through a shower of flowers

> sovra candido vel cinta d'uliva
> donna m'apparve, sotto verde manto
> vestita del color di fiamma viva.   33
> E lo spirito mio, che già cotanto
> tempo era stato che alla sua presenza
> non era di stupor, tremando, affranto,   36
> sanza delli occhi aver più conoscenza,
> per occulta virtú che da lei mosse,
> d'antico amor sentí la gran potenza.   (XXX 31-39)[61]

The sentence which begins with line 34 only finishes at the end of line 39, the whole sentence having as its subject 'lo spirito mio'. Indeed, all is spiritual, and the description has little to do with physical sight, which has become useless.

This is Cary's rendering:

> ... in white veil with olive wreath'd,
> A virgin in my view appear'd, beneath
> Green mantle, rob'd in hue of living flame:
> And o'er my spirit, that in former days
> Within her presence had abode so long,   35
> No shudd'ring terror crept. Mine eyes no more
> Had knowledge of her; yet there mov'd from her
> A hidden virtue, at whose touch awak'd,
> The power of ancient love was strong within me.[62]

A number of details are inappropriate: the suddenness of 'donna m'apparve' is lost in Cary, and his 'virgin' is a poetic word very different in use and connotations from 'donna', which is in the manner of the 'dolce stil novo'. The rendering is not grossly inaccurate, but, for one thing, the last five or six lines read like prose – there is no rhythm, no search for particular effects. The complex tension created in the original is quite lost; there, the lines are made to carry more than one suggestion. Lines 34 and 35, for example, are a long statement of the time which has passed since Dante last saw Beatrice, and the very length of the statement enacts the stretch of time it refers to. Placing the negative particle at the beginning of the next sentence, moreover, has the effect of turning the statement of what Dante had not felt in all that time into a statement of what he now feels; and the three successive final words in 'non era di stupor, tremando, affranto' suggest an increasing intensification of feeling.

Cary loses all these effects, and particularly the cumulative suggestion of the lover's feelings; but, what is worse, Cary's description of the lover's feelings comes from the world of a gothic novel, since he mentions the notion of 'shudd'ring terror'. Beatrice arrives here like a ghostly apparition.

Further on in the original Beatrice is compared with an admiral, but the comparison is brief:

    Quasi ammiraglio che in poppa ed in prora
      viene a veder la gente che ministra
      per li altri legni, e a ben far l'incora;
    in su la sponda del carro sinistra,
      quando mi volsi al suon del nome mio,
      che di necessità qui si registra,
    vidi la donna ... .   (XXX 58-64)[63]

Beyond the mention of 'poppa' and 'prora' and maybe 'legni', all the other words used – 'gente', 'ministra', 'a ben far l'incora' – are general, and in fact refer to moral encouragement. Cary picks up the comparison but develops it to excess:

    As to the prow or stern, some admiral
    Paces the deck, inspiriting his crew,
    When 'mid the sail-yards all hands ply aloof;
    Thus, on the left side of the car, I saw   60

Cary carries the simile further than in the original, and goes so far as to add more specific, even technical vocabulary, such as 'deck', 'crew', 'hands', and 'sail-yard'. Moreover, he also stresses the military stance of this admiral, who paces the deck. After this kind of preparation, the figure of Beatrice becomes, in the last two lines, slightly ridiculous. From the comparison with an admiral on his ship she must step back into Eden in the midst of the angelic crowd; not surprisingly, all Cary achieves is the bathos of the phrase 'the virgin station'd'.

Of course, in the original, when the eyes of Beatrice and the protagonist meet, it is not in loving recognition. Beatrice is angry, and reproaches the protagonist. She speaks in tones of "l più caldo parlar', 'the most heated reproachcs'; and her words are, indeed, heated, as the repetition in 'ben son, ben son Beatrice' so well suggests. But her anger and disdain are the result of concern, and, like a mother to her child, she has to appear rash for his own good, as is made plain in lines 79 and 80, where 'pietade acerba' ('stern pity') summarizes the contrast.

This is Cary's rendering:

    Though from her brow the veil descending, bound
    With foliage of Minerva, suffer'd not
    That I beheld her clearly; then with act
    Full royal, still insulting o'er her thrall,
    Added, as one, who speaking keepeth back   70
    The bitterest saying, to conclude the speech:
    "Observe me well. I am, in sooth, I am
    Beatrice. What! and hast thou deigned at last

Approach the mountain? Knewest not, O man!
Thy happiness is here?" Down fell mine eyes   75
On the clear fount; but there, myself espying,
Recoil'd, and sought the greenswerd; such a weight
Of shame was on my forehead. With a mien
Of that stern majesty, which doth surround
A mother's presence to her awe-struck child,   80
She look'd; a flavour of such bitterness
Was mingled in her pity. ...[64]

Cary changes considerably the sustained comparison of Beatrice and Dante with
a mother and her child. Rather than a loving but, when necessary, stern mother,
Cary's Beatrice is an unreachable figure for this child; Cary adds the word
'insulting', and also the exercise of power of a master over a slave. Rather than
heated in her anger, Cary's Beatrice sounds calculating in her bitterness; so it is
not surprising that in the face of her 'stern majesty' this child is 'awe-struck' –
these two phrases being two further additions. None of this was in the original,
in which the maternal and filial love had been mentioned earlier and are repeated
when the protagonist turns to Virgil for comfort 'quale il fantolin corre alla
mamma/ quando ha paura o quando elli è afflitto'. Here even the words used –
'fantolino' and 'mamma' – suggest affection and comfort.

A Beatrice who has been turned into a figure resembling so closely an admiral
pacing the deck, or an insulting slave master, is very different from the lady who
punished her lover by withholding her greeting, and is a good example of Cary's
taking not just the language, but also the spirit and sense of the poetry very
literally. The *Commedia* then becomes something different from the celebration
of Beatrice as foretold in the *Vita Nuova*. The position and role of the protagonist
is then also completely changed, for just as his physical vision of the world he
travels through has been made abstract, so his journey to mystical vision and
revelation is non-existent.

It is in Canto XXIX that the name of Dante is mentioned for the first and last
time in the *Commedia*. This direct reference to the author's real name, identified
here with the protagonist's, would seem to unify the two figures of protagonist and
narrator with the actual author, and pose the question of the autobiographical
dimension of the poem. But this unique mention of Dante's name is not a
moment of pride, but shame: at that very point, Dante sees his reflection in the
water, and has to look away. The question remains, it seems, at the level of
paradox, a further tension adding interest to the poetry. At this point, the mention
of the name and the shame it brings seems to underline that this particular,
historically real man, purified of sin, is still only a poet in the making, and can
himself bring revelation only after the gift of vision. The autobiographical

reference, therefore, briefly brings to light the reality of the literal level in the poem, and it will be the work of the last canto of *Purgatorio* and the whole of *Paradiso* to unite history and revelation. Accordingly, the naming is forced on the writer. Dante says,

> quando mi volsi al suon del nome mio,
> che di necessità qui si registra.   (XXX, 62-63)[65]

The 'mio', in emphatic position, seems to refer to the protagonist, since its effect is to make him act – turn around. The next line states that the protagonist would have preferred not to have his name appear at this point, suggesting the lack of control of the protagonist over the record of his journey, as well as over what is happening around him. Sapegno points out that at this point the name deliberately mentioned by the protagonist is not a sign of pride, but serves to increase his sense of shame;[66] this is true, except for the fact that Dante maintains the ambiguity of who is actually speaking, by using an impersonal construction: *'si registra'* (emphasis added). The narrator, it seems, also disclaims responsibility.

Cary changes both the position of stress, and the impersonal construction:

> Thus on the left side of the car I saw,   60
> (Turning me at the sound of mine own name,
> Which here I am compell'd to register)

Cary might seem to stress the figure of the protagonist, since 'I saw', and 'turning me', clearly referring to the protagonist, attract what follows – 'mine own name' and 'I ... register' – into their own sphere, so that all the phrases are established as belonging to the same voice. However, most of this observation comes as a kind of aside, between brackets, in the middle of the story told, and is therefore a comment made by way of explanation of what the writer is doing, and made at a later moment; it can only be an addition of the writer, and the 'I am compelled' must refer to him. If anything, this lack of control of the writer, who feels forced to include his name, suggests the shame the writer feels at being connected with a protagonist in that particular position, though his integrity as a writer enables him to overcome this. The opposite to a stress on the protagonist therefore happens, so that even the 'I saw' definitely falls under the continuous stress of a story told, where the writer not only pulls all the strings, but is the only figure to receive any solidity and to achieve presence.

Cary's *Purgatory* is clearly a very disappointing translation. It produces a consistent style, which can generally be defined as 'Miltonic', but only in so far as it consists of blank verse paragraph units and has some measure of sublime diction, although this is very controlled. It places a definite emphasis on the poetry as its author's artifact, but the voice of this author is bland, uncommitted, uniform. Cunningham mentions Cowper as a writer whose style Cary approximates.[67] But Cowper's blank verse, though, indeed, controlled, is extremely varied. It can be vividly descriptive, traditionally rhetorical or sublime, highly concentrated, even curt and sarcastic. None of this variety is to be found in Cary. The regularity and lack of variety in the latter's verse indicates his lack of sensitivity to the more subtle effects of the language and rhythm of the original, and also his lack of interest in the poetry's total significance.

Cary's *Paradise*

Paradiso is the restoration of Eden into Paradise, which is, however, a state of being higher than that of the original Eden. It is here that, in Blake's terms, man achieves the 'fourfold vision' and sees himself as the Christ he truly is, and it is here that the poet can renew both place and time, through his 'Divine/ Human Imagination'. As in Blake, so in Dante a protagonist moves from sight to mystic insight. Furthermore, Dante sees this process as requiring first of all a rising of man above his human limitations (a view not very different from Blake's):

> Trasumanar significar per verba
> non si poría; però l'essemplo basti
> a cui esperienza grazia serba   (I 70-2)[68]

But while Blake's visions retain their solidity and simply add the spiritual to the physical, with man retaining his human form, Dante's protagonist encounters sights of single, large shapes (the eagle, the stairs, the rose), some of which are even abstract and geometrical (the cross, the circles). These large shapes are formed by the souls, who are each reduced to a single point of light. The faculty of sight, however, does remains central in this *cantica*, and is also present in the comparisons and similes necessary to convey to the reader the experience of the journey. It is, accordingly, on the rendering of the two meanings of the word 'vision' that the following pages concentrate. But first an initial assessment of Cary's achievement in *Paradise* in terms of the language used must be made.

Contrary to his method in the previous *cantiche* (*Purgatory* especially), Cary's rendering, in his *Paradise*, of individual phrases and brief passages is very careful, well informed, and, often, very readable. In addition, occasionally Cary seems at pains to reproduce the rhythm of the original, musical effects being the very fabric of the verse in *Paradiso*. So, in the description of the sphere of the moon 'the ever-during pearl' reproduces a comparable rhythm to the original's 'l'etterna margarita', and Piccarda's famous words 'and in his will is our tranquillity' echo, with the slow even pace of that last word, the contentment expressed by the original. Cary also seems to be careful and accurate in the selection and repetition of key words; so Cary's translation of the long speech of Piccarda in Canto III maintains the original's repetition of the words 'volere' and 'amore' ('will' and 'charity'). The word 'amore', therefore, appears twice, correctly translated by 'charity', while in the twenty-one verses of her speech 'will(s)' occurs seven times. Both literal sense and more subtle effect of the poetry seem the concern of the translator at this point.

But this is not always the case; for Cary fails to realize that the rhythm of the verse contributes far more to the poetry than occasional felicitous lines, being also, as an alternative to the use of sights and sounds, a means of communicating meaning, as will be seen in the discussion of the visual in Cary's version of *Paradiso*. Furthermore, Cary continues using the controlled version of the Miltonic style he has used before, and he therefore chooses a relatively elaborate, solemn and heavy language and rhythm, which affects both the presentation of the world of Paradise, and of the two figures of the protagonist/narrator. In the address to the readers which opens Canto II, for example, the poet states that he writes *Paradiso* only for 'Voi altri pochi' (l. 10), the 'you other few' who can follow his furrow. Not everyone can follow a prophetic vision, and Dante contrasts his 'legno' with the 'piccioletta barca' of some readers, the former being more sea-worthy; but the contrast is one of inherent virtue.

In Cary's version, the sublime style superimposes adjectives and spatiality on the original: '*proud* keel', '*deep* maze', '*deep* brine' (II 3, 7, 14; emphases added). The poet's vessel in Cary's translation is not more worthy – it is a 'proud keel' which would surely not go far in God's grace. In fact Cary gives us an Odysseus-like figure engaged on an 'adventurous track', but who is himself very passive. So, while in the original the mythological references also suggest that the viewer is guided in his journey by wisdom (Minerva), by poetic imagination (Apollo), and by art (the Muses), in Cary the viewer is described also at this point as just a passive spectator lost in rapture, Cary's addition of the phrase 'to my rapt sight' (l. 10) echoing other similar renderings, such as 'charm'd mine ear' for 'mi fece atteso' (I 77; 'took my attention'). What Cary is mainly concerned with here is to insert Dante into English literature, also by echoing the classical writers. In his footnotes (especially those he added for the fourth edition of 1844) Cary often connects the original to English poems, particularly Milton, often also Chaucer, and in the case of the 'piccioletta barca' he believes to have noticed an echo in Pope's 'Say, shall my little bark attendant sail?' (*Essay on Man*, Ep. iv).[69]

To sum up this initial assessment of Cary's version of the third *cantica* in terms of the language used, it can be said that Cary loses the substantiality of the images, trivializes the use of sound and rhythm in the poetry, and stresses the role of the writer. Also, in his footnotes Cary widens as much as possible the literary allusions of the *Commedia*. In particular, Cary often suggests equivalences between the poem and works of English literature which are fully established in the contemporary canon.

It is with these observations on Cary's achievement in *Paradise* in mind that the analysis of the translation in terms of the rendering of the visual, and also of the protagonist, must be understood. I begin, therefore, with the analysis of Cary's version of the visible in *Paradise*. The analysis focuses first on the opening cantos of *Paradiso*, where the visual is still connected to earthly shapes and the human form, and then move to the later cantos, where what is visible are often large single shapes formed by groups of souls. In these later figures, such as the eagle or the crown of souls, physical sight imperceptibly turns into visionary sight of God, and the analysis will, accordingly, focus on this change.

The sights that appear to the protagonist in the first cantos of *Paradiso* are often indefinite, without contours, fluctuating and receding, and in order to describe them it is necessary to use metaphors. But the author does succeed in making visible a spiritual reality, and of giving it some concreteness which is credible and beautiful. The reader can clearly visualize the appearances of the souls, and he can follow Dante's eyes as they strain not to lose them as they disappear:

> Cosí parlommi, e poi cominciò 'Ave
> Maria' cantando, e cantando vanío
> come per acqua cupa cosa grave.   (III 121-123)[70]

This last metaphor provides an image with substance and weight. Cary's rendering has less solidity:

> She ceas'd from further talk, and then began
> '*Ave Maria*' singing; and with that song
> Vanish'd, as heavy substance through deep wave.   125

Literal it may be, but where is the plain objectivity, in Cary's 'substance' and 'wave', of the original's simple 'cosa' and 'acqua' ('object', 'water')? More importantly, the more one reads, the more one realizes how the significance of the verses is, in the original, portrayed by the music of the lines. The regular rhythm created by the succession of words of similar length and pattern in the last line in the original reproduces the steady movement of the object and its disappearance. This effect is made the more striking by the undulating rhythm of the previous line, where the rhythm of the first word, 'Maria', is repeated in the last, 'vanìo', while, moving to the centre of the line, we have a mirror image and a repeated rhythm in 'cantando' joined by the conjunction. It is not impossible for a translator to attempt to reproduce, in Pope's words, 'something similar, tho' not the same'; Sisson certainly does so, in the contrast between the fragmented, but lengthened sense of loss in the middle line ('...and, singing, vanished') and the regular rhythm of the short words in the following line, which describe a common sight in the plainest terms.[71] Cary's generalized diction and the rhythm of blank verse, as he uses it, do not lend themselves to the suggestions of the more subtle shading in the original. Perhaps more importantly, however, one wonders whether Cary had enough sensitivity to feel the rhythm of the original.

Sound goes hand in hand with sight in these first cantos of *Paradiso*, and in fact it seems to slowly take over. For, though sight is present, it becomes tentative and ambiguous. Sight, in fact, alternates with lack of sight, as when the souls, of which Piccarda is one, appear to Dante looking like reflections in water: 'deeming these/ Reflected semblances, to see of whom/ They were, I turn'd mine eyes, *and nothing saw*;' (Cary, III 18-20, emphasis added). The point is that the original text succeeds in communicating even lack of sight as part of the realistic experience of this protagonist; for he is unable to recognize Piccarda by her features but does so as soon as she speaks – the sound of her voice carrying more meaning, in *Paradiso*, than the transformed face. Cary translates the sentences word for word, but his sustained emphasis on the activity of the writer engulfs also the use of sound within itself, so that it becomes the mere exercise of writing skill rather than a means of indicating a significant shift in the ways of communicating in Paradise.

The features of landscape which appeared repeatedly in *Purgatorio*, namely mountains, rivers and the sea, are also mentioned by the blessed in *Paradiso*. But the physical solidity which characterized their presence in the previous *cantica* undergoes a considerable shift. For mountain, river and sea are mentioned in metaphors, in a manner which highlights the very different nature of the landscape of Paradise, and which, in fact, attributes to each feature of landscape its apocalyptic, revealed significance. The basic story in *Paradiso* is the protagonist's effortless flight to God, while the story in *Purgatorio* was the hard climb of a mountain. In order to explain the nature of Paradise to the protagonist, Beatrice makes a comparison with nature on earth, that is, she contrasts the natural ascent of Dante, purified of his imperfections, to his maker with the descent of a river from a high mountain to its foot. This also means that in a fallen landscape natural movement is downwards and requires effort, whereas Paradise is the very opposite, and its natural movement is upward flight. Also Piccarda's description of man's abandonment to God's will is expressed in a comparison with nature, in this case with the sea:

"E 'n la sua voluntade è nostra pace:
  ell'è quel mare al qual tutto si move
  ciò ch'ella cria e che natura face."   (III 85-87)[72]

The sea where Casella waited for the boat of Purgatory, and where rivers bring their spoils becomes the final resting place of all souls, as it is of their bodies. Beatrice's and Piccarda's references to earthly landscape have two different implications: they enable the reader to imagine for himself the nature of Paradise by comparing it with nature on earth, but they also reveal the hidden significance of fallen landscape, as it had appeared in *Purgatorio*. Cary had not produced, in his version of the world of Purgatory, a landscape which was both real and spiritual; but, had he literally reproduced the clear attribution of significance to features of this landscape in Paradise, his text could still have led its reader to see that the world of the *Commedia* is based on one single, though complex, view and also to recognize that mountains as well as gardens are versions of the complex unity which is God. A reader, that is, could have projected the meaning discovered in Paradise onto the landscape of Purgatory. But Cary's version of the world of Paradise is as inaccurate as his version of the world of Purgatory had been.

Cary's allegiance to the sublime Miltonic style is often apparent in the surface of the text, but is not very deep, and does not, therefore, lead the reader to discover significance in the text. For example, Cary very interestingly renders the natural ascent of Dante compared with the natural descent of a river as 'Thou no more admire/ Thy soaring ... than lapse/ Of torrent downwards from a mountain's height' (I 131-3), where the words 'soaring' and 'lapse' immediately remind the reader familiar with the sublime style in general, and with *Paradise Lost* in particular, of the actions of the fall and of flight as referred to in the action of *Paradise Lost*. Height and depth, and the movement between them, which *Paradise Lost* exploits fully, also have moral significance, of course. But the use of these words at this particular point in Cary's translation is confusing, because it does not correspond to a system of meaning. The word 'lapse' has associations of sin and guilt, perhaps even more so than the word 'fall', which is also associated with the phrase 'fortunate fall'. This does not fit in with the image of the river's downward movement as being natural for a fallen landscape. Similarly, 'soaring' has connotations of sinful pride, and was used for Satan's flight from Pandemonium towards Eden and God. These words, therefore, evoke echoes of Milton at the level of diction, and have little resonance within the sense of the whole. In short, Cary uses words which the English reader would quickly recognize as fully belonging to the familiar vocabulary of his own tradition in literature. The equivalence, however, is a false one in that it establishes a connection at the level of word, but not of meaning. As a result Cary loses the grounding of *Paradiso* in real nature, which forms the basis for the vision of human destiny.

Similarly, the sea, the mention of which in *Paradiso* contains the more factual references to earthly reality it had accumulated in *Purgatorio*, becomes in Cary 'the mighty ocean', where the addition of the word 'mighty' in particular echoes the addition of the same word in Canto I, when Apollo, figure of God, is called 'mighty Sire' by Cary, but 'padre' by Dante (I 28). Again, such additions introduce different connotations, not so much at the level of inward experience, but rather at the level of the writer's chosen style.

What Cary does not see, and his translation therefore misses, is the contrast, particularly central to the first cantos of *Paradiso*, between the visible and concrete (the earthly and human) and what cannot be seen or touched (because it is pure spirit, thought and love). Cary consistently diminishes the prominent place the original gives to earthly experience and turns Dante's precise language into pseudo-poetic images; he thereby emphasizes the activity of the writer.

Remaining with the discussion of Cary's rendering of the visual, I now move to the sights which face the protagonist later in the *cantica*, where the descriptions of the world of Paradise in earthly terms have moved further in the direction of abstract shapes and complex pictures. Yet even at this stage references to earthly sights are made in the original. The souls no longer have any human features, have lost all human appearance, and are pure lights; still, the world of the heavenly spheres is made real to us, and it is not a world of ideas and love, but a surrealistic visionary world. The best example of this world is the description of the movement of the souls after St Peter's invective, before Dante rises to the *Primum Mobile* (Canto XXVII).

The sight of the souls rising slowly upwards like 'frozen vapours' would be nothing out of the ordinary; but in the text the reader is first confronted with a simile which draws a picture of snowflakes slowly drifting down. Then, he is told that in just such a way the protagonist saw the souls moving – but then upwards (ll. 71-2, '*in su* vid'io ... fioccar', '*upwards* I saw [the vapours] flaking', emphasis added). The reader is made, as it were, to first envisage the snowfall, and then invert its direction. 'Fioccar' ('flaking') is repeated to describe the upward movement of the souls, and clinches the connection between the two opposing scenes, at the same time stressing the large number of snowflakes and their slow movement. Followed, as it is, by Beatrice's making Dante turn his eyes downwards, so that he sees the northern hemisphere underneath him – complete with the pillars of Hercules, this is altogether a passage which forces the reader to use his imagination and create images. But Cary's version loses the basic movement by means of which the text guides the reader:

> ... As a flood
> Of frozen vapours streams adown the air,
> What time the she-goat with her skiey horn
> Touches the sun; so saw I there stream wide
> The vapours, who with us had linger'd late,   65
> And with glad triumph deck th' eternal cope.
> Onward my sight their semblances pursued;
> So far pursued, as till the space between
> From its reach sever'd them; ...   (XXVII 61-9)

Is it clear, in Cary, that the movement and number of the souls is each comparable to that of snowflakes? The words 'flood' and 'stream' indicate a different movement, and a different composition. Moreover, Cary omits the 'in su' and the whole upward movement; so, the comparison remains flat and vague, and does not jerk the reader into the visualization of this very different universe.[73] Yet the reader must learn to see with the protagonist, or he will miss much of the poem's meaning. The reader is, as it were, being trained to use his imagination, and only if he learns to do so now will he be able to respond to the final vision in all its complexity. As we slowly approach the orchestrated effects of the last cantos, the poem really begins to move in units which describe both states of consciousness and pictures.

Together with the lengthier descriptions – the abstract shapes of the cross, the stair and the rose – are others, and one of them is the crown of flowers and sparks in the Empyrean. This passage is a good illustration of the manner in which in the later cantos of *Paradiso* the visual turns into the visionary. For physical sights begin to offer glimpses of the divinity, and also the language and prosody guide the reader to identify modes characteristic of visionary literature:

> Poi come gente stata sotto larve
>   che pare altro che prima, se si sveste
>   la sembianza non sua in che disparve,   93
> cosí mi si cambiaro in maggio feste
>   li fiori e le faville, sí ch'io vidi
>   ambo le corti del ciel manifeste.   96
> O isplendor di Dio, per cu'io vidi
>   l'alto triunfo del regno verace,
>   dammi virtú a dir com'io il vidi!   99
> Lume è là su che visibile face
>   lo creatore a quella creatura
>   che solo in lui vedere ha la sua pace.   102
> E' si distende in circular figura,
>   in tanto che la sua circunferenza

sarebbe al sol troppo larga cintura. 105
Fassi di raggio tutta sua parvenza
   reflesso al sommo del mobile primo,
che prende quindi vivere e potenza. 108
E come clivo in acqua di suo imo
   si specchia, quasi per vedersi adorno,
quando è nel verde e ne' fioretti opimo, 111
sí, soprastando al lume intorno intorno,
   vidi specchiarsi in piú di mille soglie
quanto di noi là su fatto ha ritorno.   (XXX 91-114)[74]

This passage is made up of three units, which enact the very growth of the protagonist/poet in *Paradiso*. First comes a simile describing the vision by comparing it with an earthly experience – the sight of masked people taking off their disguise and revealing their true faces. This simile is followed by a prayer to God to enable the poet to 'dir com'io il vidi' (l. 99, 'to say how I saw it'). Finally comes the actual description of the light of God, which is so serene, clear and measured, that it proves the prayer has been answered. The threefold repetition, in final rhyming position, of 'io vidi' (preceded in each case by a phrase with a 'c'-sound, which lengthens the rhyme) lays stress on what the protagonist saw, but also prepares, in an echo of the mode of Revelation, the shift to the inner, mystic vision which is suggested by the external, physical vision. The repetition also creates a tension, which increases the emotional tone of the invocation to God (directly named here), emotion being further heightened by the exclamation, a device more sparingly used in the original than it is by Cary. The tension and the emotion find release in the description of the crown, a description which moves in waves, or, better, in equal, orderly breaths. Each tercet is, as it were, one human breath, and the serenity, contentment and human ideal this suggests go even beyond the words on the page. The rhythm is almost incantatory here; but the choice of the words on the page is in perfect harmony with the rhythm. From 'Lume è' onwards the words and sentences are crystal clear, luminous in their transparency; the balance between 'creatore' and 'creatura', and the slow, deliberate movement of God as a light who stretches himself ('si distende') into the perfection of the circular figure both contribute to the final simile – of the hill being reflected into the lake at its feet. The whole passage contains the features of landscape which have appeared repeatedly in the *Commedia*, and prepares the final vision (of the circles uniting God and man) in *Paradiso*.

Though something must be sacrificed in a rendering of the original, yet in such a long passage a translator ought always to be able to find ways of communicating to the reader the crucial points of the poetry. Cary does not do so, however:

Then as a troop of maskers, when they put
Their vizors off, look other than before,

The counterfeited semblance thrown aside;
So into greater jubilee were chang'd
Those flowers and sparkles, and distinct I saw   95
Before me either court of heav'n display'd.
   O prime enlightener! thou who gav'st me strength
On the high triumph of thy realm to gaze!
Great virtue now to utter what I kenn'd.
   There is in heav'n a light, whose goodly shine   100
Makes the Creator visible to all
Created, that in seeing him alone
Have peace; and in a circle spreads so far,
That the circumf'rence were too loose a zone
To girdle in the sun. All is one beam,   105
Reflected from the summit of the first,
That moves, which being hence and vigour takes,
And as some cliff, that from the bottom eyes
Its image mirror'd in the crystal flood,
As if t' admire his brave appareling   110
Of verdure and of flowers; so, round about,
Eyeing the light, on more than million thrones,
Stood, eminent, whatever from our earth
Has to the skies return'd. ...

Cary has noticed the three movements of the passage, but seems unable to render the change in movement and tone which takes place in the original, except by indenting paragraphs – a technique belonging to prose rather than verse. He misses the simplicity of the references to earthly experiences – the 'hill' and 'water at its foot' become 'a cliff' and a 'crystal flood', and the 'people' with 'masks' become a 'troop' with 'vizors', all of which introduces connotations absolutely extraneous to the original. The plainness of the picture is lost, and so, too, is its symbolic significance: the masks are not identified as 'the looks not their own in which they were hid' (l. 93), but 'the counterfeited semblance' – suggesting deceit, rather than the impossibility of seeing truth on earth. In Cary, the protagonist gazes on God's kingdom, whereas in the original he saw the kingdom of truth, and the original expressed this spiritual concern in a prayer, while the translation phrases its grand achievement in a literary mannerism (l. 99).

   Both sight and vision are therefore reduced in Cary. Perhaps even more important are two more differences. The first concerns Dante's active verb 'si stende', which in the original forces the reader to envisage the light of truth as stretching itself in a circle to enable the creature to see its creator. Cary's rendering – 'in a circle spreads so far' – places the stress on the size of the circle, and employs a verb which (though not actually in the passive voice) suggests a more passive state. The second difference is the fact that Cary misses the repetition of the 'I saw', an omission which encapsulates on its own the nature of

Cary's translation of *Paradiso*: for to reduce the prominence of verbs of seeing corresponds to Cary's reduction of physical and of visionary sight. The protagonist is, in Cary, no plain 'universal man', and he will be no prophet; furthermore, the narrator is deprived of the threefold structure of his discourse, which, with the addition of rhythm, highlights the significance of the words, while at the same time introducing tension.

The threefold repetition of words and the citation of the number three become increasingly prominent in the original text. The tercet, and Dante's handling of it, is naturally useful in highlighting this emphasis:

> Qui vince la memoria mia lo 'ngegno;
>   ché 'n quella croce lampeggiava Cristo,
>   sí ch'io non so trovare essemplo degno;   105
> ma chi prende sua croce e segue Cristo,
>   ancor mi scuserà di quel ch'io lasso,
>   vedendo in quell'albor balenar Cristo.   (XIV 103-108)[75]

The unusual and therefore even more repetitive rhyme is further emphasized by the fact that the name of Christ occurs in what is, more or less, a final position within the syntactic sentence or subordinate clause or phrase. The text gives us one long sentence connected by 'che', 'sí ch'io', and 'ma' ('for', 'so that I', 'but') – a complex sentence, but a single one, which pauses regularly on the word 'Cristo'. Cary's rendering loses the formulaic repetition and becomes a discursive speech:

> Here memory mocks the toil of genius. Christ   95
> Beam'd on that cross; and pattern fails me now.
> But whoso takes his cross, and follows Christ,
> Will pardon me for that I leave untold,
> When in the flecker'd dawning he shall spy   100
> The glitterance of Christ. ...

Here, memory has become a generalized power, the personal 'mia' being omitted and lost, while the more metaphorical 'mocks' and 'toil' are completely absent from the original. The original's automatic, almost inexorable repetition of the name of Christ, moreover, is here placed in varying positions in the line. In Dante, this threefold repetition stresses the importance of the number three, which the tercet, as it were, embodies and emphasizes. Coming after the repetition of 'io vidi' ('I saw'), this new occurrence of threefold repetition begins to impress on the reader the pervasiveness of its significance. In the many different ways in which it is repeated and handled within the lines of a tercet, the number three becomes more and more pervasive as the poem continues to add features, one by one, to the portrait of the *alter Christus*. Indeed, the repetition of the number three adds a tone of incantation, of clear staccato and almost catechistic repetition:

> Quell'uno e due e tre che sempre vive
>   e regna sempre in tre e 'n due e 'n uno,
>   non circunscritto, e tutto circunscrive,
> tre volte era cantato da ciascuno   (XIV 28-30)[76]

Line one lists the three numbers – slowly and regularly, and separating each with a conjunction. Line two repeats the counting in inverse order and places it in the opposite part of the line. The two lines are united in meaning, however, by the repeated 'sempre'. Line three continues to add to the subtlety of the thought, since the negative, 'non', is soon followed by the all-inclusive 'tutto'. The fourth line, which summarizes the preceding tercet, begins with a three and closes with a 'ciascuno'. This is Cary's version:

> Him, who lives ever, and for ever reigns
> In mystic union of the Three in One,
> Unbounded, bounding all, each spirit thrice
> Sang, ...

Cary seems unable to turn anywhere, for a model of mystic language, except to the sublimity of the late eighteenth-century aesthetics – with all its boundlessness. The phrase in the middle line paraphrases, in terms of a religious tenet, the mystery that the original so deliberately displays to the reader in its numerical symbolism. In Cary there is no playing off of one line against another; the two occurrences of 'ever' are in the same first line, and 'unbounded' and 'bounding' are together in the third line, so that, rather than language in tension, we are faced with a paradox which seems already solved. The other repetitions – particularly of the individual naming of each number – are lost.

This has very little to do with lack of clarity or not, since the basic sense of the original is there. What Cary's *Paradise* lacks is a very important element of the original: tension. The absence of precision and definition in the language, and the smoothing down of everything into a sameness of diction destroy the tension in the language. This tension, in fact, is nothing but the reflection of more significant tensions – the tension in the duality of the protagonist and narrator and of their coming together, the tension in the duality of knowledge and revelation, and the final tension, which embraces them all, between the subject and the product of the poetry (that is, the continuous struggle of Dante the writer to bring all the threads of his vision together in poetry written in imitation of God's way of writing). In a way, Cary's *Paradise* is a tired, excessively long conclusion of an already finished story. For the lack of tension in the protagonist's journey through Paradise implies that, in terms of the narrative, he has already reached his goal and there is nothing new to expect. Accordingly, the various steps in the narrative of *Paradiso*

– the celebration of St Francis as a figure of Christ, or the encounter with Cacciaguida and the ensuing declaration of the mission of Dante – are well translated by Cary, but in their lack of movement and tension seem a redundant self-celebration.

The discussion of Cary's rendering of the visible and the visionary in *Paradiso* has already indicated the very limited function which the protagonist, and also the narrator, retain in Cary's translation of *Paradiso*. A survey of a few points arising throughout the poem will, therefore, be sufficient to follow this particular thread and take us to the final vision of the *Commedia*.

Cary tones down any reference to or preparation of a possible mission of Dante as prophet, or a possible role of Dante as *alter Christus*. One of the ways in which this role is adumbrated in the original is in the very fact that the protagonist becomes increasingly more central. He was so, physically, from the start, but as he rises higher in Paradise he does not need, for example, the mediation of Beatrice in order to put questions to the souls – he must do so directly. Moreover, he is even questioned and examined by saints on various issues: the 'trasumanar' of the first cantos is proceeding rapidly. Canto XIV prepares the Cacciaguida Cantos, which occur at the centre of the *cantica* and unify history and revelation in the figure of Dante. It is from Canto XIV that the quotations with the formulaic repetitions were taken. It is here, also, that first person singular pronouns and adjectives become insistent:

> Ma Beatrice sí bella e ridente
> *mi* si mostrò, che tra quelle vedute
> si vuol lasciar che non seguir la mente.   81
> Quindi ripreser li occhi *miei* virtute
> a rilevarsi; e vidi*mi* traslato
> sol con *mia* donna in piú alta salute.   84
> Ben *m'*accors' *io* ch'*io* era piú levato,
> per l'affocato riso della stella,
> che mi parea piú roggio che l'usato.   (XIV 79-87; emphases added)[77]

Perhaps Cary simply thought that these were awkward repetitions of no poetic significance, and this is why he reduces them. As, in a previous quotation, 'la mia memoria' had become 'memory', so here 'mi si mostrò' becomes 'showed':

> ... But so fair,
> So passing lovely, Beatrice show'd,
> Mind cannot follow it, nor words express   75
> Her infinite sweetness. Thence mine eyes regain'd
> Power to look up, and I beheld myself
> Sole with my lady, to more lofty bliss
> Translated: for the star, with warmer smile
> Impurpled, well denoted our ascent.   80

The hammering on the personal pronouns in the original, for example in line 85, is particularly obvious because it is absolutely unnecessary in Italian, where the form of the verb already unambiguously indicates the person; but Cary still chooses to avoid them. Similarly, the last sight, of the reddening of the star, becomes a general descriptive statement rather than a personal observation ('mi parea'). This passage provides a good example of a continuous tendency in Cary, who clearly does not see that the use of personal pronouns and possessive adjectives is a technique for focusing the attention of the reader on the protagonist.

Cacciaguida is one of the souls making up the very first of the abstract pictures Dante creates, that of the cross. The souls appear purely as lights, and one of these lights runs down from the extreme right branch to the centre of the cross, and then downwards. This is Cacciaguida, who addresses his descendant Dante in Latin (XV 28-30; see also above, p. 166). The use of Latin at this point establishes a connection between Dante's poem, the Bible, and classical literature. Accordingly, Cacciaguida's welcoming address means that the protagonist is being accepted in the select group of the blessed, although not yet quite ready for the final vision. In fact, soon the blessed will speak of such deep concepts, that Dante will not be able to understand. Language as a medium of communication is therefore brought into discussion, and one is reminded of the difficulty the narrator has in expressing elevated thoughts and divine concepts in language. Cary's translation is correct, but, unlike Dante, he does not switch to Latin but continues to use English:

> ... "O thou, my blood!
> O most exceeding grace divine! to whom,
> As now to thee, hath twice the heav'nly gate
> Been e'er unclos'd?" ...[78]

At least Cary maintains the literal meaning, where Boyd, for example, had distorted it by saying 'to whom but to thee', thereby losing the implied comparison between Dante, Paul and Aeneas. But since Cacciaguida's question is there to remind the reader of the answer, perhaps even as late as the early nineteenth century Latin would have contributed to suggesting the connection with Virgil's hero, though not with the Bible. The lack of Latin produces a loss of effect, which is further reinforced by a similar loss of effect in the words with which Cacciaguida reveals his identity:

> "I am thy root, O leaf! whom to expect
> Even, hath pleas'd me" ... [79]

In the original, the first line retraces closely the words of God the Father on the baptism of Christ and underlines the attribution to the protagonist of the role of *alter Christus*. But Cary, having already, to some extent, toned down or abolished all preparations for the clear presentation of this role of the protagonist, carries this process even further in his rendering of this affirmation. He loses the word order which would have maintained the echoes of the original, and turns the whole into a mere metaphor.

The loss of this dimension means that all that is left in Cary of prophecy and future destiny has to do with the political fall of Dante Alighieri and his consequent exile. When in the last of the Cacciaguida Cantos the mission of Dante is mentioned, Cary's concern is not with vision as mystic sight, but as the total story to be recounted by the writer, who is, again, in the foreground. In the original Cacciaguida had said:

> "Ma nondimen, rimossa ogni menzogna,
> tutta tua vision fa manifesta;
> e lascia pur grattar dov'è la rogna."   (XVII 127-129)[80]

Here, Cacciaguida expresses his indignation – at those who will feel offended by Dante's revelation of his vision – by comparing these people's resentment to a dog's mange. Cary succeeds in finding a metaphor which maintains the implied comparison with an animal, and also the alliteration of the original:

> "Thou, notwithstanding, all deceit remov'd,
> See the whole vision be made manifest.
> And let them wince, who have their withers wrung."

However, Cary's translation is altogether more elevated in all its constituents: to wince is more genteel than to scratch, the dislocated shoulder of a horse is more acceptable in polite society than the disease of a dog, and the very 'w' sound is less harsh than the Italian 'r' sound, which is also used elsewhere in the poem by Dante to suggest baseness and even bestiality.[81] In addition, the mention of the poet's mission here is very much reduced. First, he becomes a kind of publisher rather than a writer, since he must only see to it that this vision is made public. More importantly, rather than a personal revelation ('tua visione'), Cary mentions a general 'the ... vision'. It is not just a question of the absence of the personal pronoun in this particular instance. Cary has reduced throughout his translation the stress on a personal presence, which includes historical relevance and spiritual progress. Therefore, because of all that has, or in fact has not, preceded it, this vision cannot but signify a flight of fancy, a dream, a story, grounded not in fact, but only in the imagination.

Thus the title of Cary's translation (*The Vision of Dante*) reflects not the prophetic or Messianic role of the protagonist/narrator Dante, but the report of an imaginary experience, and stresses the unreality of the world through which the reader follows the protagonist. This is confirmed by Cary's particular version of Dante's final vision. Before examining the conclusion of the poem, however, two passages occurring in Cantos XIX and XXI respectively are worth considering first, because they shed light on some particular aspects of Cary's version of the last movements of the poem.

In Canto XIX the souls appear to Dante grouped together in the form of an eagle, who speaks to the protagonist in a single voice:

> E quel che mi convien ritrar testeso,
> non portò voce mai, né scrisse incostro,
> né fu per fantasia già mai compreso;
> ch'io vidi e anche udi' parlar lo rostro,
> e sonar nella voce e 'io' e 'mio',
> quand'era nel concetto e 'noi' e 'nostro'.　　(XIX 7-12)[82]

The eagle of God's justice confirms even through the manner of its speech the fact that God's justice cannot but be one for all. In addition, the paradox that 'I' is identified with 'we' reminds one of the original's stress, indicated earlier, on personal pronouns and adjectives referring to the protagonist. Consequently, the passage tells the reader not only that souls have one voice in Paradise, but also that the Dante who approaches the beatific vision shares in that community of spirit. The reader can now begin to read the first set of grammatical units between inverted commas ('I' and 'mine') in terms of the second set ('we' and 'ours'); the protagonist sees and speaks for us, too. Cary's version is less specific:

> ... And that, which next
> Befals me to portray, voice hath not utter'd,
> Nor hath ink written, not in fantasy
> Was e'er conceived. For I beheld and heard
> The beak discourse; and, what intention form'd　　10
> Of many, singly as of one express,
> Beginning: ...

The translator generalizes and summarizes the original's definite reference to specific grammatical units of speech, and therefore fails to provide the reader with the means by which to interpret the language of Paradise. Even if Cary had translated the original word for word, however, much would still have been lost, because he had, in the previous cantos, diminished the original's stress on the first person singular pronouns and adjectives.[83]

The final shape in which, in Canto XXXI, the souls appear to Dante, that of the rose, establishes links with Revelation in a very obvious way. The angels, who sink in the flower and then fly upwards to God in a continuous movement, have faces of fire, wings of gold, and white robes. Cary's version is literal, but his diction seems particularly inert: the 'gran fiore' becomes the 'mighty flower', and the 'fianco' becomes the 'plumy loins', in a periphrasis which, though characteristic of eighteenth-century diction, must have been dead poetic language by the second decade of the nineteenth century.

The whiteness of the angels' robes is reflected in the whiteness of the rose of which the souls are the petals. Whereas in the original this whiteness shows that angels and souls belong to the same community as the people 'arrayed in white robes' of Revelation (robes made white 'in the blood of the lamb'), in Cary the whiteness of the robes becomes 'white as the driven snow'. This commonplace combines with the other instances of turgid diction – which look backwards, rather than forwards – to counteract the significance of the references to the future of mankind according to Christian religion and myth. The footnotes carry only references to poets; Homer, Virgil, Ovid and also Milton are mentioned for having used similar metaphors or mythological references.[84] Thus Cary highlights surface and wording, and is not attempting to produce a version of *Paradiso* which recreates basic features of the original's meaning. Had Cary been concerned with meaning, he might have emphasized (in his footnotes if not in the text) the reference to the concept of whiteness, which was easily associated with God (see p. 174 above).

The final vision of the *Commedia* must communicate to readers at any time and in any place – on condition that they look at what the text says and how it says it – the struggle of man with his limited powers, and of the poet with his imperfect medium. In an initial summary of this dual struggle, Dante prays to the 'Somma luce' to grant him some traces both of memory and of language in order to tell future men what he saw – for both memory and language are intimately bound up with the senses, and therefore must inevitably fail to record or express the matter of God, which is pure mind. But there is one power of man which retains the vision and can express it, and that is emotion. At least twice (ll. 63, 93) Dante specifies that, as he attempts to recapture the vision, he feels a happiness, which is evidence of the reality of his experience. Very simply, he says 'perché piú di largo,/ dicendo questo, mi sento ch' i' godo' (l. 93, 'because when I say this/ I feel my joy expand'). Furthermore, the verses bear in themselves the imprint of emotion, and thus Dante's exclamatory words concerning the weakness of his medium are an emotional outburst: 'Oh quanto è corto il dire e come fioco/ al mio concetto!' (ll. 121-2; 'O how scant is speech, and how faint/ to my conception!'). Here, the simple words echo the faintness of the medium, and enact their own inadequacy in rendering Dante's intention. Cary's 'O speech!/ How feeble and how faint art thou, to give/ Conception birth' is a rhetorical address, clothed in metaphorical language. Rather than reproducing the meaning it expresses, the language denies it. In fact, while Dante is forced to coin new words and insert unusual Latinisms, Cary is never at a loss for words, and continues to use the same diction that has sustained his translation from the very start. The rapidly increasing tension of the original is completely lost in Cary's version.

Alongside the failure of memory to retain Dante's experience and the failure of language to express it, the text of the original repeatedly stresses the difficulty of distinguishing anything by means of physical sight. But the poet is still able to render to human eyes the reality of the vision. Thus, to make the reader fully grasp that the protagonist sees the whole universe enclosed within God, the text compares the universe to the scattered leaves of a book and God to the bound volume. Also, the attempts of the protagonist/poet to describe the actual vision of God is complex, but clear, and does not rely on theological formulae, but on sight:

> Nella profonda e chiara sussistenza
> dell'alto lume parvermi tre giri
> di tre colori e d'una contenenza;   (XXXIII 115-117)[85]

Cary adds even more sublimity than he had used before, both to the passage describing the universe in God as a book and the one just quoted. In the first example, the original's 'giunsi/ l'aspetto mio col valore infinito' (79-80 'I reached with my gaze/ the infinite essence') becomes in Cary 'Hover'd the brink of dread infinity', which is a clear reference to the terrible sublime. In the second example, Cary again flatly follows the dictates of Miltonic sublimity:

> ... In that abyss
> Of radiance, clear and lofty, seem'd, methought,
> Three orbs of triple hue, clipt in one bound:

Cary here contrasts height with depth, and therefore adds 'height' to the original, which only stressed depth. Also, as in the reference to 'hovering' and to 'brink' in the earlier example, here, too, Cary uses words which refer to features of sublime landscape ('abyss', 'orbs'). Cary's addition of sublimity here simply continues the similar addition in the previous *cantiche*, but the form it takes at this point is particularly out of place, introducing into Paradise, as it does, notes of physical danger and of threat.

Cary brings fear into the final moment of the vision in Paradise, which should not have such a feature, but he diminishes the tension of the experience of the protagonist/poet. The progress to salvation of Dante the man finds its point of highest tension in the sight of the 'image in the circle' – this being the second of the three circles, that of Christ, which contains the human joined to the divine. Translating this passage, Boyd had changed the sense of the original, developing narratively what was only suggested, and had presented Dante rising up to the light and being reflected in the image of Christ (see pp. 168-9 above). That was, in Boyd, the appropriate conclusion of his version of the protagonist: appearing in the opening of the poem as Everyman, Dante appears in the end as the human effigy framed in the circle of divinity which is Christ.

In Cary, on the contrary, Dante does not rise above the human in this way, and in fact human presence in general is very much reduced. First, the 'geometer', which the original vividly places before us in person, as it were, becomes in Cary 'one/ Versed in geometric lore'. Further, the counterpointing, in the original, of possessive adjectives and pronouns such as 'his', 'ours', 'mine' is less sharp and definite. Also, the emphasis on the 'I' is very much diluted. In the original 'tal era io a quella vista nova;/ volea veder ...' strongly stresses the 'I', which refers to the protagonist, and strongly stresses that it is the 'I' that is keen to see. The very fact that these two sentences are placed in the initial position of two successive lines greatly stresses the personal presence of the protagonist/poet. Cary's '... e'en such was I, intent to scan/ The novel wonder ...', on the other hand, places the 'I' in a less prominent position in mid line, and, in addition, continues with an adjectival phrase which, syntactically, does not repeat the first person singular, and, semantically, does not express so much the protagonist's desire to see, but rather, less emotionally, his concentration on the act of seeing. Finally, Dante's compact phrase 'l'imago al cerchio', which joins human image to divine form in the most striking tension, is diluted into two separate clauses, and therefore loses much of its vividness and all of its paradoxical meaning. It is slow, loose, and stresses the narrative rather than the human element.[86] In many ways, therefore, Cary reduces the human presence in this part of the poem.

As for the poet, the failing of memory, language, and sight means that he has to struggle against great odds. Communication through 'questi versi' and the image of the volume including the whole universe in its pages make clear, in the original, that poetry and writing as themes are brought into discussion; but this notion comes across with less clarity in Cary. At this point in the poem, in addition to the other faculties, imagination also fails, and this truly signifies that the writing of poetry becomes impossible; the poem must, by definition, end – to continue it would be to deny the reality of the vision. In fact, the statement that imagination has reached its limit opens the final tercet and the final sentence of the poem, in which Dante, his human faculties exhausted, becomes one with God in the circular movement of the wheel. Man has been elevated into the divine, absorbed within the second circle of the Trinity, and the poem acquires the very movement of the wheel of the universe. Both Man and Poem have, therefore, reached perfection. The poem is finished, because the last canto of *Paradiso* is '... the highest point that poetry has ever reached, or ever can reach.'[87]

Boyd had attempted to underline the circularity of the poem, and had highlighted Dante's soaring to divinity. Cary does the very opposite. Having diminished the role and importance of man and his destiny, Cary also diminishes the role and importance of the poem as a perfect artifact:

> Here vigour fail'd the tow'ring fantasy:
> But yet the will roll'd onward, like a wheel
> In even motion, by the love impell'd,
> That moves the sun in heav'n and all the stars.[88]

Cary retains only two of the three faculties mentioned in the original, namely will and love, although he places love in a secondary position, and also in a passive construction. By dropping desire, Cary in fact eliminates the word which suggests the more properly human, as opposed to divine, of the three faculties, and by dropping also the 'mio', which precedes the word desire in the original, he drops the word which referred directly to the protagonist.

In eliminating the personal presence of Dante as protagonist/poet within the poem Cary's rendering of the final vision of God well reflects his total version of *Paradiso*. More importantly, Cary changes the very form and movement of the poem. The self-enclosure of the perfect circle, which in the original becomes the figure of the Trinity, of man, of the universe, and of the poem, assumes a completely different meaning. For Cary gives us a real wheel, rolling on along its unspecified course. Coleridge's reading of Cary's lines is pertinent here: they seem to continue 'wandering and wandering, onward and onward'.[89] In Cary's verses not just the rhythm, but the very sense of the original is turned into a pattern where perfection, completion – in short, the achievement of vision – are not simply denied, but are in fact absolutely non-existent.

Cary was a scholar rather than a creative writer or even a critic, and the version of the *Commedia* he leaves behind is characterized more by the 'Life of Dante' and the learned footnotes than by the interest of the text itself or by a critical commentary which might have presented a particular view of the *Commedia*.

Cary's 'Life of Dante' does present a specific view of Dante himself, and it is a view which has little in common with the figure of the Byronic Dante current between 1800-1840. In his chapter on Dante as the Byronic hero, Ellis quotes from reviews, from Macaulay, Byron, and Hazlitt, down to Carlyle in 1840. Ellis illustrates how the Romantics saw Dante as one of the heroes of their own day, a 'Satano-Promethean hero', whose brow bears the mark of Cain, and whose character is moved by 'gloomy and fiery egotism'.[90] Boccaccio's description of Dante also quoted in Cary's 'Life of Dante' would have contributed to this view.

But Cary's introductory essay to the *Commedia*, his description of the *Commedia*, and his description of the face and figure of Dante in the same essay all build a much more balanced picture of Dante. His summary of the story of the *Commedia* says:

> The fiction, it has been remarked, is admirable, and the work of an inventive talent truly great. It comprises a description of the heavens and heavenly bodies; a description of men, their deserts and punishments, of supreme happiness and utter misery, and of the middle state between the two extremes (p. xxxiv-v).

The emphasis is certainly not on Hell and fire. Similarly, Cary introduces Dante by saying that 'One or two sonnets prove that he [Dante] could occasionally condescend to sportiveness and pleasantry'; and though this seems to us too begrudging, still it is in contrast with a view of Dante who hates levity. Moreover, when he quotes Boccaccio's description of Dante's person Cary cuts out what is not to his purpose:

> Il suo volto fu lungo, e 'l naso aquilino, e gli occhi anzi grossi che piccoli, le mascelle grandi, e dal labbro di sotto era quel di sopra avanzato; e il colore era bruno, e i capelli e la barba spessi, neri e crespi, e sempre nella faccia malincolico e pensoso (his face was long, his nose aquiline, his eyes big rather than small, his jaws large and with the bottom lip sticking out further than the upper. He had a dark complexion, with hair and beard that were thick, black and curling; his expression was always melancholy and pensive).[91]

This is the original and its translation which are quoted in Ellis' book as an example of the evidence that contributed to the current view of the grim Dante. Cary himself omits the last clause, and thus cuts out the only stroke which suggests the grimness of Dante's character.

Cary could only have contributed to the view of Dante as the poet of Hell indirectly and in two ways: because of the monotony of his *Paradise* (which might have discouraged readers) and because of his emphasis, in the text, on the presence of the writer Dante. This emphasis is one of four features of Cary's version which exemplify the nature of this version, the second of which is that Cary highlights the presence of sublimity in Dante's world; in *Hell* he diminishes the potentially gothic touches, but in *Paradise* he adds, at the very end, some strokes of the terrible sublime, thus rendering the two parts uniform in this respect and similar to *Purgatory*. The third feature is Cary's particular version of Beatrice as she appears in *Purgatorio*, in the pageant of Revelation. Since the episode is the culmination of Dante's journey and of the preparation for his flight to a vision, the fact that Beatrice appears as a forbidding, stern and powerful force cannot but introduce a remarkable change in the whole structure of the experience. Finally, the achievement of vision is absent from Cary's version of *Paradiso*. Cary's contribution to views on Dante, to the course of translations of Dante in England, and to the course of the Miltonic tradition can best be considered in a comparison with Boyd's contribution. This comparison forms the conclusion to Part II of this study.

10

Conclusion to Part II

Both Boyd and Cary saw Dante as a sublime poet whose work is grounded in the basic human religious and ethical principles. Neither Boyd nor Cary heightens the potential gothic terror and pathos of *Inferno*, and neither presents Dante as the grim poet of Hell. For, although Boyd calls Dante, at the opening of his 'Comparative View', 'this melancholy Bard', this single reference to Dante is far outweighed by Boyd's stress on the moral purpose of the total poem, on its atmosphere of romance and chivalry, on the vision that takes place in it, and on the Platonic philosophy which forms the basis of *Paradiso*. Cary, too, included in the last fifty lines of the poem two footnotes referring the reader to Plato's *Parmenides* and second *Epistle*. Both these translations, therefore, reveal an approach to Dante similar to that of many readers whose comments on Dante have survived (see Chapter 3 above), an approach in which the horrid gothic plays no role. Such readers saw Dante's poem often as political and historical – a satire of its own day – and also as sublime.

Yet the existence of this consistent view of Dante in the second half of the eighteenth century has hardly been recognized. Sayers identifies the 'discovery' of Dante with the excitement of the horrid gothic, and in effect draws the translations by Boyd and Cary into the same movement. Ellis stresses Boyd's and Cary's contribution to the view of Dante as the grim and unforgiving poet of Hell when he mentions the portraits used as frontispieces for the translations, and the description of Dante quoted also in Cary's 'Life of Dante'. He quotes the passage as it stands on p. 233 above, and overlooks the fact that Cary has manipulated the original, cutting out Boccaccio's single reference to the poet's melancholy temper.

What Boyd and Cary did contribute to the creation of a Romantic Dante is the notion (less ephemeral than the *frisson* offered by the horrid gothic) that it takes an irregular genius to create a sublime poem. To invoke sublimity in a poem means to suggest that this poem is a profoundly significant statement on man's condition. To the extent that Cary evokes sublimity he also suggests such a reading of Dante. But, as we have seen, Cary's text is monotonous, uniform in its use of the sublime, and lacks that tension which might have faced the reader with ambivalent or complex meanings, forcing him to confront Dante's text more closely. Moreover, Cary was unable, as a writer, to integrate sublimity in his very verse. He does not, like Thomson, lay emphasis on the modality of the visible and how this reveals the divine; he does not use Milton actively as a model, something which would have highlighted the religious and prophetic character of the poem; and he diverges from the original in the final moments of the mystical experience of Dante.

Boyd's translation is very different in this respect. No one can possibly see the protagonist, at the opening of the poem, as anything but an Everyman or a Red Cross Knight; no one can miss the echoes of Milton's poems of vision throughout the translation; and no one can miss the soaring of the narrator himself to mystic vision at the end. To say that Dante is Everyman is not very different from saying that he is Universal Man, except that, in the later development of the medieval tradition, Everyman – the protagonist – is not formulated as an abstraction, but rather portrayed as a particular individual. Hence, Boyd's inclusion of historical information about Dante and his times as an introduction is sufficient to guarantee that the literal meaning of the story in his translation can still be taken to be the 'life' of Dante. Yet Boyd's stress on the moral interpretation of the journey, on the atmosphere of romance, and on the visionary experience that it contains can lead the reader to other layers of meaning embedded in the text. This is the first conclusion to be drawn from an analysis of the two translations: Boyd's version offers a real contribution to the transmission of Dante's poem as a poem of vision. There are two more conclusions to be drawn.

Our second conclusion has to do with the ways in which both Boyd's and Cary's translations carry forward the Miltonic tradition. In this respect, the difference between Boyd and Cary could not be more stark: Boyd notices a similarity of approach between Dante and Milton in those passages from the *Commedia* which have to do with sublimity and with the visionary and prophetic stance of *Lycidas*, 'Il Penseroso', and *Paradise Lost*. This awareness of a similarity results in Boyd's manipulation of the verse itself, so that the reader of Dante is faced with a diction, a rhythm of the lines and direct allusions which forcibly remind him of Milton (and other poets of the Miltonic tradition).

Cary, on the contrary, notices similarities at specific points and in given phrases (the simile of the autumn leaves in *Hell* III, for instance, and the 'plumy loins' of the angels in *Paradise* XXXIII). More precise than Boyd, Cary also notices differences between Dante and Milton, as in their portrayals of Lucifer. But neither the similarities nor the differences are allowed to affect the finished verse; they are simply recorded in a footnote. Boyd integrates Milton into his very text, while Cary separates the text from the referential apparatus. Cary, that is, offers learned indications of the debt English literature owes to Dante, whereas Boyd's reader is faced with a text which communicates notions of a bard achieving vision. The different effect of the two translations (also apparent in their handling of the Miltonic tradition) will become clear in the discussion of William Blake below.

Our third conclusion concerns the practice of translations of Dante. The appearance of Cary's translation quite obscured Boyd's work. This probably is due not only to Boyd's lack of fidelity to the original, but also to Boyd's taste for the various eighteenth-century styles, and in particular for a Youngian excess, which quickly fell into disrepute, and certainly finds little sympathy in audiences today. Today, Boyd's style alone would be sufficient to ensure a general rejection of his translation, since the blander Miltonics of Cary are more acceptable to current taste than the extreme of sublimity, the grandiose tone, and the elaborate diction of Boyd. The latter's work on Dante quickly became a closed chapter as an example of translation practice.

Cary's translation had a very different fate. It rapidly became a classic, went through many reprints and new editions in the nineteenth century, and has been republished even in the present century.[1] To give a few examples, the Nonesuch Press collated in a single publication in 1928 the Italian version edited by Casella, the English version by Cary and the illustrations by Botticelli; Cary's *Inferno* was published, with some of Blake's illustrations, in New York in 1931; the Everyman's Library reprinted the complete Cary translation in 1948; and as recently as 1970 the complete translation was again republished, in Geneva, with some of Flaxman's illustrations, in the series 'Books that have changed Man's Thinking'.

One cannot deny Cary's great contribution to establishing the fame of Dante, popularizing the poem to some degree, and making readers familiar with some scholarship on Dante as early as the first decade of the nineteenth century. Even so, it is regrettable that the very fact that Cary's Dante became a classic meant that, rather than measure up to the original, later translators went on working in the tradition founded by Cary. To survey the future of Dante in England after Cary is to see how the vital line of growth and response does not follow translations, but finds a new medium in the use of Dante made by poets in pursuing their own work. It is in the line that moves from Shelley to Rossetti in the nineteenth century, and on to Yeats, Pound and Eliot in this century that Dante becomes a force in English literature. The most recent translators, like Sisson and Mandelbaum, adopt a stance quite different from their predecessors, and Sisson in particular acknowledges as his antecedents a translator like Dryden, and a poet like Eliot. Eventually, therefore, Cary's legacy was to become a burden and a dead end. Cary is the first of that inert and monotonous line – in terms of poetic life – that from him moves through Longfellow and Binyon, to Bickersteth, Ciardi, Sayers, Sinclair, and even Singleton. These are the names of scholars who reproduce a more or less accurate version of a text they look at with reverence, and who measure their skills on Dante's verse. One thing they do not attempt to do is recreate the original in such a way that it will be meaningful and relevant to a contemporary reader. Arguably, Boyd's legacy, as inherited by Blake, will prove to be more significantly influential in this sense than Cary's.

PART III

INTEGRATION INTO ENGLISH POETRY

11

William Blake

Most of the names and issues which are of central importance in the study of the reception of Dante in England in the eighteenth and early nineteenth centuries come together in an account of the life and work of William Blake. As a poet and also painter, illustrator and engraver Blake confronts in his work the role Dante and the *Commedia* played, in England, in these arts. Moreover, Blake's work is a milestone within the Miltonic tradition in English poetry, carrying over aspects of Milton's own achievement (and also features of the eighteenth-century Miltonic poets such as Young and Cowper) not only into the poetry of the great Romantics, whose attitude towards the Miltonic poets is generally one of rejection and opposition, but also into the more general line of imaginative poetry in England. Thus, Blake's use of Dante in his own work and his illustrations to the *Divina Commedia* weave into one pattern the separate threads making up the reception of Dante in England. Furthermore, Blake's work makes visible the implications and consequences of the response of early readers of Dante, of the distorted pictures of Dante created by the translators, and of the possibilities introduced by poets' creative use of the *Commedia*.

Before the brief survey of Blake's position in respect to the painters, poets and translators who have played a part in the growth of Dante's role in English poetry, a further point must be dealt with. Blake's life and work contain also another thread which has appeared in the course of this study (see pp. 8-10 above); for Blake was a republican, whose views of history and whose interpretation of current events form the basis of his prophetic vision as a poet and in fact shape all his work.

Blake lived through the American and French Revolutions, and, more importantly, was fully aware of and sympathetic to the radical movement which inherited and carried on the notions of liberty current throughout the seventeenth century. There is no evidence to show that Blake took an active part in any of the radical societies of the time, but he was well acquainted with many who did.[1] In his apprentice years he worked also for the Antiquaries, and although some of these were mostly pedants, others were moved by a passionate interest in national and popular art, exploring the sources of culture and history in England as well as abroad, and yet many others, like Hollis, were among the more forceful radicals of the age.[2]

Blake's work is evidence enough of his views in these matters. Some of the *Poetical Sketches* (*Gwin, King of Norway*, the dramatic fragments on English kings, *King Edward the Third*), *America* and *The French Revolution* all clearly show that Blake consistently argued against tyranny and for the freedom of the individual, though his republican sympathies were a vision of history and never turned into sectarian activism. In this sense, Blake's stance is very dissimilar from the more obvious radicalism of the early Wordsworth and Coleridge, and lies closer to Shelley's. History provided Blake with a further basis for his mythology, and each revolution, as also each instance of tyrannical oppression, was a metaphor of the other. History, therefore, like the Bible and Milton's work, provided Blake with narrative and iconography; Dante's *Inferno*, as will be seen, did the same, and was read by Blake in these terms.

I now turn to Blake's position at the very centre of the web of names and ideas which have appeared earlier in this study, examining first the painters and illustrators involved, and secondly the poets who provided the models for the translators.

As a painter and engraver Blake was acquainted with the writings of J. Richardson and Reynolds as well as with the latter's paintings. Fuseli and Flaxman, both authors of illustrations or paintings on subjects drawn from Dante, were Blake's close friends. Through Flaxman Blake became acquainted with William Hayley, who eventually became Blake's patron, just as he was already Cowper's. This closeness to Hayley had a number of consequences for Blake's involvement with Dante. Blake was certainly familiar with Hayley's *Triumphs of Temper*, a copy of which he was presented with by the author. It seems, then, very likely that Blake would have been acquainted with Hayley's translation of Dante as well, and with Boyd's translation of *Inferno*, of which, as indicated earlier, Hayley had purchased seven sets; Blake certainly read and annotated a copy of Boyd's *Inferno* around 1800.

All these books would have been in Hayley's library at Turret House, Hayley's residence at Felpham in Surrey. Hayley offered Blake the use of a cottage at Felpham, near his own home, and there Blake spent the years 1800-1803. Hayley's library at Turret House assumes an important role in a study of Blake's work on Dante, not only because of Blake's probable use of it, but also because Blake was asked to paint a series of portraits of poets (including Dante) admired by Hayley, to decorate this very library. For some reason Ellis does not include this particular portrait in his list of Dante portraits, but this is a gap which must be filled. For Blake's portrait appears, when observed superficially, to belong fully to the then fashionable representations of Dante as the grim and melancholic poet of Hell. But by slightly changing elements of the iconography which was already traditionally connected with a portrait of Dante, and by adding features of his own, Blake manages to produce a characteristically personal version of the traditional portrait, and, in fact, to convey a comment on and criticism of Dante. In terms of Blake's own views on Dante, the portrait is of particular importance, since it reveals a definite change in these views – from an endorsement of Dante's vision, to doubt about the truth of this vision.

Blake's work as an artist, and above all as an illustrator, often conveyed a striking comment on and interpretation of his subject, rather than simply being a visual translation of some of its aspects. Certainly Blake's illustrations to the poetry of Milton, Gray, and Blair, to Young's *Night Thoughts*, and to the Book of Job are all either an endorsement or a criticism of these poets' views, as interpreted on the basis of Blake's own vision and expressed in terms of Blake's own iconography. Blake often turned to other visionary poets, in order to compare his own vision with theirs, and to discover parallels. Since Milton was to Blake the epitome of the poet of imagination, revolution, and apocalypse, Milton himself, and the poets writing in his tradition, were naturally the object of Blake's close study. But, as Blake saw it, Milton had not been wholly true to his visionary and revolutionary calling. For their part, the eighteenth-century Miltonic poets had misused and distorted Milton's true legacy, by carrying Milton's style and diction to excess while ignoring the revolutionary impulse of his vision.

Blake's final views on Dante were somewhat similar to these views on Milton. Although Blake always asserted, when asked,[3] that Dante was a genius and a poet of vision, his illustrations to the *Commedia* nevertheless show that he saw the poem as a record of what he called an Orc cycle; for in spite of being on the very brink of Eden the protagonist/poet proved unworthy of his vision, fell back into the state Blake called 'Beulah', did not proceed to redemption, but fell yet further and re-enacted the fall. In a comment written on one of the illustrations Blake makes clear that he saw the poem as founded on lack of vision:

> everything in Dantes Comedia shews that for Tyrannical Purposes he has made This World the Foundation of All & the Goddess Nature Mistress. ... Swedenborg does the same in saying that in this World is the Ultimate of Heaven. This is the most damnable Falsehood of Satan & his Antichrist.[4]

In the most recent study of Blake's illustrations to the *Commedia*, Milton Klonsky quotes these words as expressing Blake's view of Dante's poem. This is perhaps a correct summary of Blake's later views; but it does not correspond to his earlier views. In fact, a closer examination of Blake's use of Dante's work reveals considerable change in Blake's attitude towards it. The illustrations to the

Divina Commedia were the very last of Blake's works. He began the illustrations in 1824, and was still working on them when he died, in 1827, leaving most of them unfinished. But the first direct reference to Dante and use of his work can be found in Blake's early works, dating back to about 1793.[5]

In fact, Blake's use of Dante is a growing concern of his, parallel to the growth of his own art and vision. This study will therefore attempt to throw light on Blake's views on Dante by examining three moments or manifestations of Blake's acquaintance with him: the poetry and pictures of *The Marriage of Heaven and Hell*, written about 1793, the portrait of Dante for Hayley's library, painted around 1801-1802, and the illustrations to *La Divina Commedia*, dating from 1824 to 1827. In considering each of these three moments one must first remind oneself of the sources of Blake's knowledge, and secondly see how Blake seems to have responded to them. By 1824, more material on, and more translations of Dante were available than in 1793; and by 1802 Blake's own art had developed further than in 1793.

Very interestingly, the first two stages of Blake's response to Dante were mainly based on his familiarity with the early translators of Dante, and with Boyd's *Inferno*, a copy of which Blake read and annotated, possibly in 1800 – the exact date is uncertain. For the purpose of producing his illustrations, however, Blake tried to learn some Italian, but still had to rely heavily on a translation, and chose Cary's. He also came to know Cary personally, and is likely to have discussed the *Commedia* with him. Thus, Blake's views of Dante prior to his illustrations to the *Commedia* reflect his reading of Dante through versions such as those by Richardson, Hayley and Boyd, whereas his illustrations were made mainly under the guidance of Cary's work.

The Marriage of Heaven and Hell

As the evidence below shows, by 1793 Blake was certainly well acquainted with passages from *Inferno*, but all the evidence available tends to indicate that he knew very little about *Purgatorio*, and possibly nothing at all about *Paradiso*. The materials he had access to were the various translations of the Ugolino episode, Hayley's translation of the first three cantos of *Inferno*, and Boyd's *Inferno*. Albert S. Roe, author of *Blake's Illustrations to the Divine Comedy* (1953), attaches great importance to Blake's friendship with Fuseli and with Flaxman, who 'both knew Italian and could have read and explained portions of the Divine Comedy to Blake long before the first complete translation appeared', and he therefore concludes that 'Thus we see that Blake in all probability was reasonably familiar with the poem thirty years or more before he undertook his own illustrations' (p. 51). But both internal evidence, based on Blake's work, and also external evidence, based on the availability of material, on the nature of Fuseli's and Flaxman's work on Dante, and on the chronology of their friendship with Blake suggest that Blake's familiarity with Dante at the time was practically limited to *Inferno*.

Roe's assumptions that the three artists must have discussed and probably worked on Dante together are almost certainly correct. This seems borne out by the fact that, when Blake saw Flaxman's illustrations, he claimed that Flaxman had 'stolen' his ideas, something which would be possible only if the two artists had, indeed, at least discussed the poem and perhaps even made a few sketches together.[6] Since Flaxman went to Rome in 1787 and stayed there until 1794, one year after the publication in Rome of his illustrations, any sharing of ideas could only have taken place before 1787, six years before Flaxman's illustrations were published. A comparison of Flaxman's and Blake's illustrations shows that there are, indeed, striking similarities between some of their illustrations, but that all the similarities occur among the illustrations of *Inferno*.

In his anger at Flaxman's alleged theft, Blake had added that 'the Public will know, & Posterity will know', but in fact no one seems to have noticed – either at the time, or since. Indeed, Klonsky denies Blake even the retrospective justice that posterity can provide when he says that 'even now it is hard to detect Blake's hand in Flaxman's austerely classical line drawings, which, while impressive in themselves, are too narrow stylistically to encompass the emotional range and depth of the *Divine Comedy*'.[7] Like the critics who comment on Boyd's or Cary's translation, Klonsky, too, bases his judgement on matters of style alone. But the iconographical devices an illustrator uses, the general composition of the picture, and the precise choice of those passages selected for illustration are also meaningful aspects of the artist's approach. When one takes these additional aspects into consideration, even a relatively cursory look at Flaxman's and Blake's work on *Inferno* is sufficient to show that underlying the clear differences in style, the compositions of a number of the illustrations are in fact similar, and that, in two cases, the similarities are so striking that there must have been some planning together, if not actual copying by one artists of the other's work.

The first illustration is Blake's Plate 10 for *Inferno*, corresponding to Flaxman's Plate 6.[8] Here, both illustrators have selected the moment when Dante has swooned and is stretched on the ground – an unusual choice. Virgil bends (in Flaxman he kneels) over Dante's head, while the souls of the lovers fly away and seem to be flowing, as it were, from Dante's body. This is one of Blake's most imaginative drawings for *Inferno*, in which he interprets the whole passage in terms of his own vision.[9] The poet has fallen, his Poetic Genius guards him, and the souls of the lovers appear as the separation of the poet into the Spectre and its Emanation, which strive for reunion in Eden. All these and other features of the drawing show that Blake saw Dante's vision here as perfectly in keeping with his own. It is, therefore, quite probable that the original choice both of the moment to be illustrated and also of the general composition came from Blake.

The second illustration is Plate 25, the suicides. Flaxman creates a picture in which two images appear which are quite new to Dante illustrations: first, the suicides trapped within trees are pictured through the subtle and effective sketching of figures in the tree-trunks, and, secondly, the harpies perched on the branches are here small, stocky birds, whose small bodies are dwarfed by their big heads, clawed feet, and large breasts. Blake's drawing for the same episode is, in these important features of the illustration, almost identical.

Other illustrations (such as Plates 49, 53 and 60 in Blake, which correspond to Plates 26, 27 and 30 in Flaxman) are also similar, but not to the extent of the two just mentioned. All five of these illustrations exhibiting similarities, however, are from *Inferno*; the illustrations to *Purgatorio* and *Paradiso* show a very great divergence, not only in style, but also in the selection of passages to illustrate, in the interpretation of Dante's text, and in the composition of the picture. Therefore it seems undeniable that *Inferno* had been at least discussed by the artists, as Roe suggests; but it seems very unlikely indeed that there was any discussion or collaboration on the rest of Dante's poem.

As for Fuseli, who, as Roe points out, came back to England in 1780, his own watercolours on Dante are six in total. Five are from *Inferno*, and one from *Purgatorio*, while *Paradiso* is in fact never even mentioned by Fuseli in his many references to Dante's poem. In addition, the paintings Fuseli entered for Royal Academy exhibitions are all of subjects drawn from *Inferno*. Fuseli's own interest in Dante's poem, therefore, seems to have been limited to the first two *cantiche*, and it seems reasonable to assume that, if readings or discussions took place between Blake and Fuseli, these would have been limited to those parts of the poem they knew and were interested in.[10]

Although Blake's familiarity with parts of *Inferno* and possibly *Purgatorio* was also intensified by his connection with Flaxman and Fuseli, he did not follow their reading of Dante (and I will refer to Fuseli's in particular, who occasionally referred to Dante).[11] For Blake, the task of the visionary poet is to be free of political and religious systems and create his own. To what extent, then, could this view have influenced Blake's interpretation of Dante, and to what extent does Blake's interpretation differ from Fuseli's ideas and the translations then available?

We know that Fuseli was critical of Dante's 'moral lapse' as revealed in Cocytus when he does not fulfil his promise to Alberigo. Clearly Fuseli identified the protagonist of the journey with the author of the work, and furthermore saw Dante as being on the side of infernal punishment and vengeance. Some of the then available translations were also based on an identification of the two personas in Dante's poem, without, however, its being taken as far as Fuseli's conclusion. Richardson, for one, had certainly identified the writer with the protagonist, but in Richardson's translation of the Ugolino episode Ugolino himself is made to appear as the suffering victim of others' vengeance and injustice, both priestly and political. The very fact that Richardson and the other early translators had extracted the Ugolino episode from its context contributes to this sympathetic picture of Ugolino. For, seen in context, Ugolino appears initially as a traitor punished in the very bottom of Hell, and pictured in a manner similar to that used later for Satan; but removed from this total context, as he appears in Gray, Carlisle, and Richardson, Ugolino is a figure of pathos, surrounded by his small and innocent children, whose plight cannot but reflect on that of their father.

One feature of the episode which might have led readers to think that it was Dante the writer on the scene and that he endorsed the philosophy of Hell was the curse on Pisa, but this passage was left out in all these versions. This curse was indeed included in Boyd's translation, which, however, softened the very passage Fuseli had isolated as indicating Dante's own 'hellish' moral attitude – his denial of what he had promised Alberigo in Cocytus. As we have seen, Boyd attributed the cruel decision to Virgil, and let the protagonist simply obey. Boyd's Ugolino, moreover, had stressed the punishment of the 'infernal priest' Ruggieri, almost turning the pattern of the passage into one of the suffering Ugolino punishing the archbishop. A further salient feature of Boyd's translation is his depiction of the protagonist. Boyd's initial picture of the protagonist as an Everyman, and his strong use of the visionary tradition as it developed from Spenser, through Milton, to Young may well have introduced *Inferno* to Blake as a book which was meant to show its reader a vision of man's death and possible damnation, in order to lead him to salvation. Blake's early views of Dante seem to be based on this view.

Blake's Plate 16 of *The Marriage of Heaven and Hell* represents a group of five people in prison. Their identity is not specified, but the drawing is very similar to that of his Plate 12 of *The Gates of Paradise*, where the five are identified as Ugolino as his children. In *The Gates of Paradise*, as Erdman points out, the figures are lean and exhausted, and the words accompanying the plate refer to their being the victims of priestly vengeance.[12] Nothing, however, indicates that in Blake's eyes Dante himself was on the side of priestly vengeance. On the contrary, Blake is using for his own purposes, within his own poem, an episode taken from the work of another visionary poet, an episode which, by that time, had become part of the iconography of the English pathetic sublime. Blake is therefore endorsing Dante's vision.

The presence of Ugolino is not an isolated instance of Blake's concern with Dante's work in the *Marriage of Heaven and Hell*. In the first place, the title itself links the poem to the basic concept of Dante's work, since Blake attempts to join the ideas of Heaven and Hell as being both necessary states to revealed human life. Secondly, the poem opens on a scene which is traditional in literature, but which, considered in combination with other aspects of the poem, could be taken to have been drawn from Dante:

> Once meek, and in a perilous path,
> The just man kept his course along
> The vale of death.[13]

Later in the poem Dante is even mentioned by name. In Plate 21 Blake says

> Hear another plain fact: Any man of mathematical talents may from the writings of Paracelsus or Jacob Behmen, produce ten thousand volumes of equal value with Swedenborg's, and from those of Dante or Shakespeare, an infinite number.
> But when he has done this, let him not say that he knows better than his master, for he only holds a candle in sunshine.

At this point Dante is placed on a higher level than Swedenborg, and equal with Shakespeare. The nature of Blake's use of Dante's name, and in this combination, seems surprising. Blake's knowledge of Shakespeare must have greatly exceeded his knowledge of Dante, so that the reference could be ascribed to a modish name dropping, except that it is not Blake's habit to be concerned with fashion. In fact, the rest of the poem indicates that, though Blake's knowledge of Dante is limited in scope, it is based on a clear insight into the nature of *Inferno*.

In *The Marriage of Heaven and Hell* Blake attempts to clarify the meaning of the words of the title, and the function of their opposition. 'Evil is Hell', but it is not something to be avoided and finally judged and rejected. It is, rather, the opposite of Heaven and Good, and, since life proceeds only from the struggle between opposites, both states are necessary. In fact Blake occasionally seems to regard Heaven as the abode of timid and conventional people, who as a consequence have little hope of final true vision, while Hell is the abode of geniuses and artists. Later, Cary's translation of *Paradiso* presented Blake with a literal picture of Heaven as a monotonous, inert state, inhabited by conventional people ruled by reason, but at this point Blake only knew Dante through his poetry of Hell, in which a poet rages against priestly vengeance.

It is in the *Marriage* that Blake says of Milton that he was unconsciously on the side of Satan; Blake is not so definite here about Dante, but he certainly suggests, in his particular use of the Ugolino group, that Dante is on the side of the damned. When, towards the end of Blake's poem, Ugolino and his sons appear, they are not, as in the *Gates of Paradise*, lean and emaciated, but appear like sleeping giants:

> The Giants who forced this world into its sensual existence and now seem to live in it in chains, are in truth. the cause of its life & the source of all activity. (Plate 16)

With their powerful bodies entrapped and sleeping, these figures embody, as Erdman points out, 'the jailing of gigantic potentiality'. In Blake's narrative, these giants are the five senses, and the picture represents what happens to them when soul and body separate. But though they slumber, they can be awakened by altered vision. Since this picture uses an episode from Dante to communicate a basic belief which, in Blake's eyes, is necessary to man's freedom and his progress to vision, it is not a criticism, but an endorsement of Dante's views. In fact, Blake's use of Ugolino is parallel to his use of the idea of Hell, and is based on a logic which is strikingly similar to a method also used by Dante for his *Inferno*:

> But first the notion that man has a body distinct from the soul, is to be expunged; this I shall do, by printing in the infernal method. by corrosives, which in Hell are salutory and medicinal, melting apparent surfaces away, and displaying the infinite which was hid.
> If the doors of perception were cleansed every thing would appear to man as it is, infinite. (Plate 14)

The 'infernal' method which Blake uses for his engravings he also uses to compose his poetry: his acid, apocalyptic words seem destructive, but finally bring revelation. Dante's Hell, which plays an obvious role in the narrative of Blake's poem, could have also suggested this particular metaphor of Blake's method, which is, in fact, the very method Dante is reputed to have used. Two aspects of it may be distinguished: what Dante's poem presents to the reader as its narrative, and the author's method of composition.

The present most widely-known view of the nature of the souls' state of being in Dante's Hell, which was probably first fully explored and discussed by Erich Auerbach, is that in Hell each soul reveals its 'true' reality, making bare the very essence of the nature of the individual.[14] Deprived of their earthly environment, of the possibility of lying, of the confusion created by appearances, the souls reveal their innermost nature. For example, Vanni Fucci, suspected of certain crimes in his lifetime, is in Dante's Hell punished for them, and, in fact, he himself asserts 'Bestial life was what pleased me, and not human,/ mule that I was; I am Vanni Fucci,/ a beast, and Pistoia was the my fitting den' (*Inferno* XXIV 123-6). The punished soul is the 'figure' of the man on earth as he was in his true nature, and the world of Hell is a picture of the earthly world as it really is, when stripped of coverings and conventions, when it stands revealed. This Blake seems to have seen, for Blake's very choice of the infernal method to reveal the infinite to the reader – in combination with his reference to Dante, and also with his specific borrowing of a moment of Dante's poem to express a moment of his own vision – implies Blake's recognition of Dante's own method.

Blake's prophecies stem from one main belief: that if error is given shape and exposed, it cannot but be rejected, and that one day all error, given generated shape, will be rejected. Blake's poetry enacts this very process: the visions in the poems give error a generated shape, and his characters re-enact, in the action of the poem, the cycle of fall and redemption, all of this being in function of the effect on the reader. Dante's dramatic presentation of continuous encounters and contrasts of characters must have seemed to Blake (who always looked for similar visions to his own in those he took to be inspired poets) basically similar to his own poetry.

Dante's technique is indeed very similar to Blake's. Dante's reader is made to react to the protagonist, following the guiding voice of the poet. Dante's *Commedia* requires an active reading; as Charity says, 'the aim is to bring the reader to the point of change, or repentance, and commitment to real Christian existence; ...the poem does aim, and persistently, to provoke the reader into implicit self-criticism'. As the same critic points out, Dante had made all this quite clear in the well known letter to Can Grande, where he specified that his aim was 'to remove *the living in this life* from misery to happiness' (emphasis added).[15] This is the reading of Dante's intention and method which recent criticism has reached – through Singleton, the re-evaluation of the prophetic reading, the re-assessment of the meaning and use of 'allegory' in literature of the Middle Ages.

But Blake had no access to Dante's letter to Can Grande. On the contrary, current views on Dante continued to stress Dante's pride and his stern rejection of levity, the prime example of which was his discourtesy at Can Grande's table, an anecdote reported by both Boyd and Cary, and turned into a painting by Lord Leighton.[16] This being the view of Dante most consistently expressed at the time (by Blake's friend Fuseli among others), it would not be surprising if it had, eventually, influenced Blake. Certainly by 1801-2, when Blake painted the head of Dante, he seems to have moved to a view of the Italian poet and his vision different from that described in the preceding paragraphs.

One further point must, however, be mentioned first. Blake borrows from Dante a scene and a story which perfectly expresses his own vision of man and his redemption. It is a scene which English poets had turned into an icon, and it offers to Blake an image which is universal because it is not only metaphorical and mythological, but also real and historical. For Blake's Ugolino is connected to history at one remove – the history of fourteenth-century Florence – but connects itself to modern history through Blake's own vision, in which Ugolino and his family are mankind under oppression, whether in America, France or England, wherever and whenever such oppression occurs. In the conclusion of *America: a Prophecy* (1793, the year following the writing of the *Marriage* and the same year as the *Gates of Paradise*) the visionary poet redeems history by foreseeing the revolution that will set Ugolino and his children free:

> Stiff shudderings shook the heavenly thrones! France, Spain & Italy
> In terror view'd the bands of Albion and the ancient Guardians
> Fainting upon the elements, smitten with their own plagues.
> They slow advance to shut the five gates of their law-built heaven
> Filled with blasting fancies and with mildews of despair,
> With fierce disease and lust, unable to stem the fires of Orc.
> But the five gates were consum'd, & their bolts and hinges melted,
> And the fierce flames burnt round the heavens & round the abodes of men.

Blake's portrait of Dante

Blake's portrait of Dante is one of a series of heads of poets Blake painted for William Hayley's library in Turret House, a small marine villa at Felpham in Sussex. There is a great deal of uncertainty surrounding practically everything concerning the portraits. Were they originally in tempera? How many of them were there? Were they in fact ever hung in the library? These uncertainties are easy to understand if one considers the history of the series, which disappeared from sight until the second half of the nineteenth century, and was exhibited in its entirety only in 1925.[17] All one can do is describe the surviving series. There are eighteen canvasses in all, some unfinished. They are painted in oil, but might have been a repainting over the original tempera. The heads of Milton and Homer have been given some contrasting colours, but the rest are almost entirely in monochrome. The subjects are equally divided between English and foreign authors, the choice being no doubt Hayley's, reflecting his taste in reading and the contents of his library.

All the canvasses have the same basic design. The head of the poet, surrounded by a garland, is at the centre. To the right and left there are spaces, in which figures, scenes or objects from the author's writings are painted. In the extreme right and left borders there are usually slight fronds, often only in the top corners, which enclose the whole picture. As models Blake used, in some instances, other extant, well known paintings and, in other instances, easily accessible engravings of paintings.[18] The heads are mostly in three-quarter view: in fact, only two are in profile and two (Dante's and Chaucer's) almost in profile, while seven face three-quarter right (among these William Cowper, Pope and Dryden) and seven three-quarter left (including Milton, Shakespeare, Spenser and Tasso). These positions seems to have been determined by the position of the particular painting on the walls of the library.

Blake manages to work considerable variety into this recurrent composition, so that no one picture is very similar to any other. To begin with, the canvasses vary in size. More importantly, the heads are sometimes almost sculpted, sometimes sketched, sometimes fully drawn in detail. The garlands vary greatly: Milton (Fig. 1) has a stiff heavy garland of oak leaves, while the young Tom Hayley has a single sprig of ivy, and Voltaire a garland made of seven different flowering plants.[19] The inset illustrations to the right and left of the head add a further element of variety.

This combination of uniformity and variety is one of the ways in which Blake managed to give Hayley the kind of celebrative portrait that he wanted, while at the same time creating of each an individual piece of art. One of the difficulties of studying the portraits stems from the fact that Hayley, as is well known, liked to collaborate with the artists under his patronage. In the case of these portraits, however, one can distinguish not only Blake's use of traditional iconography (exploited in order to express admiration and celebration of the relevant author), but also the addition of iconographical traits of Blake's own making (or his idiosyncratic manipulation of the traditional ones); and in this way he satisfied his patron while retaining his independent vision.

Blake's portrait of Dante (Fig. 2) seems to reflect the current 'romantic' idea of the poet – grim Dante, his brow bearing the mark of Cain. The head is based on the portrait of Dante by Raphael, to be seen to the right of the earthly group in the *Disputa* of 1511 (in the Vatican), but Blake's model was probably the eighteenth-century engraving by Paolo Fidanza.[20] The grimness of the engraving is toned down in Blake; but certainly we are not given a head of Dante in any way similar to the Botticelli portrait which represents the Dante of the *Vita Nuova*, a portrait not to be discovered until 1840.

When Blake painted his portrait, the iconography of a Dante portrait had become fully established – although discussions on how closely this corresponded to the original 'reality' were rife.[21] Dante is pictured more or less in profile in order to set off his protruding lower lip and aquiline nose; he wears cap and earflaps, and is crowned with laurel. To his model Blake adds the features which enclose the head within a framework. The most obvious feature is the picture to the right of the head, which seems to confirm Blake's unquestioning adherence to the current idea of Dante, since the group sketched there represents Ugolino and his four sons in prison. The space on the other side of the head is empty, except for the heavy masonry of Ugolino's prison, from which hangs a heavy ring and the chain which fetters Ugolino's hands and feet. Dante has been firmly placed within the world of *Inferno*.

But within this entirely traditional convention, Blake introduces innovations. In adding his own iconographical traits, or in slightly changing the traditional ones, Blake attempts to convey a view of Dante, rather than merely a reproduction of his features. Both the composition of the various elements of the portrait, and the way in which the Ugolino group is represented contribute to this. This is Blake's technique not only in the case of Dante, but also, and particularly strikingly, in the case of Milton.

In the *Marriage* Blake had said that Milton was 'a true Poet and of the Devils party without knowing it' (Plate 5); but in later years he came to see Milton's repression of the revolutionary principle in his writings as a betrayal of the artist's task, and proceeded to take up and systematically develop what Milton had repressed. The final achievement in this process is Blake's *Milton*, finished in 1804, in which he brings back the poet to give him a second chance – or, possibly, sees Milton reincarnated in himself. The portrait of Milton for Hayley's library (Fig. 1) is evidence that Blake had reached a clear standpoint about Milton at that time: the poet is pictured as a statuesque bust, and the stiff, large collar underlines the restrictions the poet had imposed upon himself, confirming what the stone-like eyes of the picture indicate – inner blindness. The bust is framed by a very stiff garland of oak leaves, which in Blake suggest Druidic error. In this way – in the articulated composition of many elements – Blake succeeds in combining in the painting the celebrative portrait Hayley would have wanted with a representation of his own critical views.

Considering the importance of Milton in the reception of Dante in England, as well as in the art of Blake, a comparison between the two portraits seems well justified – the more so because Blake intervened in both portraits, turning the heads in the direction contrary to that of the engravings he used as models, in order to have Dante and Milton face each other, since the portraits hung along the far end of the same wall in Hayley's library.[22] A closer study of Milton's portrait will assist in the study of Dante's, particularly because the latter has received no attention whatsoever to this day, while the head of Milton has been cited as an exemplification of Blake's views of Milton, notably by Joseph A. Wittreich.

In his discussion of the head of Milton, Wittreich underlines the great significance of one of the iconographical traits of the portrait – the palm trees which frame it. In his view they suggest iconoclasm, and are the symbol of the pilgrim, 'the wayfaring, warfaring man', recalling Christ's triumphal entry into Jerusalem, and the victorious heroes of the Book of Revelation who, clothed in white, stand with the palm of victory before the throne of God. Wittreich adds that 'In both the Four Zoas and Jerusalem the palm tree and the oak – images of suffering and weeping – stand upon the edge of Beulah .... Under the trees, Albion falls into the deathlike sleep of the oak, which may be troubled by the act of self-annihilation symbolized by the palm'.[23] The argument is perhaps weakened when we see that of the 18 portraits no less that 13 are framed by branches of palm trees, which form one unifying feature of the series. Even the portraits of Pope, Dryden, Voltaire, Otway and Klopstock – poets whom Blake occasionally strongly attacked – are framed by palm branches.

Nevertheless, within this unifying feature differences may be noticed, and perhaps the extent to which the presence of the palm is made more or less imposing conveys meaning. Indeed, in many of the portraits there are only two half-sketched fronds, while in the case of Milton the trees are painted in their entirety and in great detail. The head of Milton is, in general, more carefully worked out than the others in the series.

Milton's head looks more like a bust than a painting; the wreath around it is similarly stiff and solid, heavy and complex. The illustration to the right of the medallion represents the pipes of pastoral, reminding the reader of Milton's early pastoral and lyrical poetry (*Lycidas* and 'L'Allegro'), and is also an image of Paradise; to the left, a harp stands out against the palm trunk and a snake appears with an apple in its mouth, these being clearly emblems of epic and of *Paradise Lost*. In this combination of iconographical traits Blake suggests a complex view of Milton. It is true, as Wittreich points out, that reading the pictures from right to left indicates the chronological progress of Milton's work, from the early pipes of pastoral to epic. But I would add that the emblems and their location also suggest the fall of Milton from Paradise to Paradise Lost – from perfect vision to betrayal of that vision.

The differences between Milton's and Dante's portrait could not be more striking. Dante's head is not statuesque, but on the contrary has all the expression and lining that the engraving suggested; the wreath around it is the most vigorous and wild of the whole series. It is the laurel which Dante aspired to, but it seems to be flowing as in flames, away from the poet. It seems almost as if it is straining to be free from the head it encircles in order to frame Ugolino, and at the right it reaches the palm fronds to arch with these over Ugolino's head, creating a second arch of a very different nature from the heavy arch of masonry underneath it. Something similar happens in the case of the head of Dryden, but there, as suggested by Wells, its purpose could be 'to compensate for the absence of any interest on that side', while in the portrait of Dante it is the left side which is almost empty. If anything, the wreath contributes towards underlining the fullness and richness of the picture at the right.

The Dante portrait is divided into three parts: an almost empty left space, the head itself in the centre, and the Ugolino group to the right. If a reading from right to left in Milton represents the poet's progress, the same is not true of the Dante portrait, or otherwise Dante's poetry has moved from the poetry of Hell, suffering and hope of salvation to an even heavier chain. The chain which fetters Ugolino's hands and feet is lightly traced, but the heavy ring and chain in the empty space on the left side wall is reminiscent of Blake's 'mind forg'd manacles'. All in all, Blake has produced a portrait which conveys two views of Dante: on the one hand the traditional, current bardolatry of the early nineteenth century and of William Hayley, and on the other Blake's own vision of Dante, which suggests doubt and criticism of Dante's achievement as a prophetic poet. This becomes evident in the composition of the Ugolino group.

The execution of this topic is very different both from the compositions of Reynolds, Fuseli and Flaxman, and also from other representations by Blake himself.[24] In the illustration at the right of the portrait of Dante Ugolino appears, in contradistinction to all the other versions (by Blake and others), pictured in profile. This makes Ugolino face the central medallion, and his intense gaze seems fixed on the face of Dante, who appears to stare back. The affectionate, protective embrace of the children, and the varied positions of the five figures and their harmonious limbs, composed into a united group which forms a human circle, combine to make the palms and the overarching wreath more significant for the Ugolino group than for the Dante head: these are indeed the palms which are emblems of Christ's love and forgiveness, and they embrace Ugolino and his children. The dignified and loving group of human beings centred upon Ugolino isolate even more the single, proud head of Dante, who, more than grim, seems alone and uncomprehending. This portrait in all its elements seems to suggest a view of Dante on the part of Blake which is less sympathetic than the view emerging from *The Marriage*, and certainly a kind of confrontation between the values embodied by the poet and those embodied by the experience of Ugolino.

One is strongly reminded of an early poem of Blake's, 'The Couch of Death' (*Poetical Sketches*, 1783). Here, the horrors of the Black Death are redeemed in the communion of mother and son, both of whom will die. The horror of tyranny, disease and death seems to find appeasement and relief in the suggestion of release from that horror in family communion and life after death. Sin is one element of the poem, both mother and son explaining their death to themselves as proceeding from their sinfulness. When, later, Blake came to reject the machinery of sin, punishment and repentance, he retained the iconographical scene of the couch of death – but now to signify a vision of a new world of joy and love beyond the fraud of tyranny, political or moral. The Ugolino group to the right of the portrait of Dante similarly suggests a vision of freedom from tyranny, of love and beauty imprisoned, and of forgiveness and promise of happiness. Just as Blake saw Milton as having fallen short so, it would seem, he came to see Dante as a poet-prophet who has betrayed his calling and who, after wandering through Beulah, does not achieve vision, but falls back into Selfhood.

Blake had begun to notice a flaw in Dante shortly before he started working on the portrait. In his annotations to the introductory essays to Boyd's translation of *Inferno*, dated around 1800, one can trace the way in which this change of view came into being.[25] In his first comments on Boyd's 'A Comparative View of the Inferno' Blake seems to adhere to the sympathetic idea of Dante's Hell that is revealed in *The Marriage*. Boyd had underlined the usefulness of Dante's poem in warning the reader to acquire virtue and shun vice, and had explained the mechanics of moral instruction through poetry in a comparison with *Hamlet*. When a man learns the story of the murder of Hamlet's father, Boyd said, 'he will know the difference from right and wrong much more clearly than from all the moralists that ever wrote'. Blake disagrees strongly with this comment: in his annotation he says 'Poetry is Immoral, the Grandest Characters Wicked, Very Satan'; he adds that 'the Poet is Independent & Wicked; the Philosopher is Dependent and Good', and concludes that 'Poetry is to excuse Vice & shew its reason and necessary purgation'.

That Dante, as Blake saw it, did not have the didactic moral aims his translator underlines, but rather a similar standpoint to Blake's own is confirmed by other annotations. Blake comments on Boyd's words in other passages, in a similar manner to the one above. So when Boyd says 'It [the good poetical character] must have something that ... appeals to the *moral sense*', Blake deletes the words italicized and substitutes 'passions & senses'. Further down, in the sentence 'nothing can thoroughly captivate the fancy ... that does not awake the sympathy and interest the passions *that enlist on the side of Virtue*' the words italicized are deleted by Blake. Then at the very end of the 'Comparative view', on a blank page, Blake attributes the didactic ideas to the translator, not to Dante:

> Every sentiment & Opinion as Every Principle in Dante is in these Preliminary Essays controverted & proved Foolish by his Translator, If I have any Judgement in Such Things as Sentiments Opinions & Principles.

What is notable in all these comments is, first, that it appears obvious that Blake based the observations on his reading and understanding of the poem, which has taken him to views quite different from those voiced by Boyd. Secondly, Blake is not objecting to the translation itself – it is Boyd's comments on it that are criticized. Blake therefore takes objection to a narrow, traditionalist, moral interpretation of the poem, and clarifies, in opposition to this, his own attitudes, which, according to Blake, Dante shares. At the end of the 'Comparative View' essay, Blake still sees Dante as a poet of vision, a revolutionary belonging, like Milton, to 'the Devils party without knowing it' (*The Marriage*, Plate 5).

Doubts about Dante begin to arise in Blake's mind when he reads of the historical events in Florence, and the poet's part in them. Boyd mentions the fact that, when Prior of Florence, Dante 'gave the advice, *ruinous to himself*, and *pernicious to his native country*, of calling in the heads of the two factions to Florence'. Boyd puts it rather strongly; since Dante's decision was not intended as harmful to Florence, and the city suffered from it only in consequence of what society made of that decision. However, the important issue is that Blake italicized the phrases as indicated above, and added:

> Dante was a Fool or his Translator was Not; That is, Dante was Hired or Tr. was not. it appears to Me that Men are hired to Run down Men of Genius under the Mask of Translators, but Dante gives too much to Caesar: he is not a Republican.

Blake begins by being tentative and uncertain, and he is not sure whether to censure the translator or Dante, but the final clause certainly condemns Dante for not being a radical. Then at the top of the page, as a kind of summary or later realization, Blake adds 'Dante was an Emperor's, a Caesar's Man: Luther also left the Priest & joined the Soldier'. This is more precise and critical of Dante's stance, and though it does not suggest anything specific about Blake's views of Dante's poetry and vision, it is nevertheless close to that aspect of his later views on Dante quoted on page 243 above, so that in this context the phrase 'For Tyrannical purposes' in that quotation acquires a greater significance.

At this point, after reading Boyd's translation and his introductory essays, Blake comes to realize that Dante the man and politician was not the heretic revolutionary that so many Romantics believed him to be, though Blake expresses no doubts concerning Dante as a visionary poet. To the end of his life Blake seems to have been of two minds, condemning Dante's lack of radicalism in religion and politics, but still accepting the validity of his vision as a poet. This is more or less what Blake has to say in his conversations in 1825 with Crabb Robinson, who summarized Blake's standpoint thus: 'He [Dante] was an 'Atheist', a mere politician, busied about this world as Milton was' but 'this did not appear to affect his [Blake's] estimation of Dante's genius, or his opinion of the truth of Dante's vision'.[26] This is probably an accurate summary of Blake's views of Dante, although a close look at Blake's illustrations to the *Commedia* show that at times Blake doubted the truth of Dante's vision. Probably these doubts were partly suggested by Cary's translation of Dante, which Blake used at the time of his work on the *Commedia* (1824-1827).[27]

Blake's illustrations and thought

Blake's thought remained remarkably consistent throughout his life and work, so that the views and myths to be found in *The Marriage of Heaven and Hell* also belong to the patterns of Blake's later prophecies. There were, of course, some developments and shifts. Blake's early indictment of tyranny and his insistence on the need for rebellion, using history as a framework, for example, turned into an exploration of the spiritual forces active in this world and in man, and of the ways in which man, in all his complex psychology, can achieve redemption. From Orc we move to Los and Luvah, from Urizen to the rejection of Jehovah/Urizen/Nobodaddy/Satan and the rediscovery of Christ in man. Instead of rebellion and revolution, the Four Zoas and their possible interplay in the different states of being become the characters and the narrative in Blake's visionary poems.

To call a poem visionary means in one sense to attribute it very personally to its author, who has 'seen' the real structure of this world, and has not merely created, in his artifact, an abstract if credible metaphor of the real world. Blake puts it bluntly: '*The Ghost of Abel*, A Revelation In the Visions of Jehovah, Seen by William Blake', where the poet is literally the seer and not only the author. But though Blake's poems are indeed based on the mode of Revelation in the sense that there is a personal witness, they are not presented as a direct recounting of the revelation: the 'I saw' is the basis, but not the mode of the poem. The poem itself, that is to say, is not the recollection by a witness of whatever is left of a flash of revelation in his memory, but the unfolding of the vision itself, in the present (if not always in the present tense) before the mind's eye of the reader. Blake makes things new by giving new names and new narratives to human fears, motivations and desires, and places the reader before an unmediated narrative of myths.

The purpose of the visions (which is to free the reader from restricting intellectual systems and, consequently, to enable the imagination to grow and act) is a didactic one; it is directed towards the benefit of mankind, but at the same time against any system of rules. It seems, then, paradoxical that Blake should have created a system of his own, though he himself recognized the paradox and explained it by admitting that 'I must Create a System, or be enslav'd by another Mans' (*Jerusalem*, 10:20). But the Blakean mythology is not fixed, with each figure or force having one attribute or value only, but is organic and dynamic and often ambivalent, so that each force and each moment in the narrative can be redeeming and damning. Many of Blake's judgements and terms are similarly ambivalent, and should not be taken as prescriptive and normative.

There are three further points in Blake's thought which are relevant to a discussion of his illustrations to the *Commedia* (and I am assuming here that the reader will be familiar with the complex structure of Blake's vision). These issues are Blake's juxtaposition of the classics with the Bible and his choice of the Bible as a model for literature, his view of God and man, and, finally, his view of nature.

Blake's rejection of prescriptive norms means that he rejects classical writers as models for literature, and in fact sometimes strongly attacks them. He saw Homer, Ovid, Plato, and Cicero not as inspired men, but as 'slaves of the Sword' who celebrated war, and were moved not by the Daughters of Inspiration but by the Daughters of Memory ('Preface' to *Milton*). The single book which is inspired and therefore can provide patterns for the imagination is the Bible.

Blake's plots are narratives of creation and fall (the two being, in Blake, one process), redemption, and apocalypse. Rather than secularize the myths of the Bible, however, Blake makes man holy and life a sacrament, each man being Christ. God is in man, and not far away in space; yet he is certainly not in nature. Nature can provide happiness and relief, but it can also be a delusion which enslaves man. In a high state of being (in Beulah, which Blake seems to have identified with Dante's Purgatory) Vala, the female emanation of Luvah, is reunited with her masculine counterpart, and provides restoration in love, or happiness in natural beauty. But in a Fallen World (in Hell, which is our world) Vala becomes a sexually alien Other, which Blake calls the Female Will – a jealous and cruel mistress, who conquers through the wiles of the Whore of Babylon, and makes man a slave to restricting laws, and blind to imagination.

These views (which are here merely indicated to the reader, who will recollect their more complex ramifications) help to explain Blake's censure of Dante, as he expresses it in comments on the illustrations as well as in iconographical elements of the illustrations. They are, however, also views which crystallize the differences between Blake's views and those of another poet, Edward Young – differences concerning the relationship between man and God, the nature of God, and the role of the natural world in the poet's vision. The great importance of Young's *Night Thoughts* in late eighteenth-century poetry and the crucial role it played in offering a native model for rendering the *Commedia* into English poetry find a point of encounter in Blake, who was profoundly influenced by Young, and who, as will be seen, read Dante partly in terms of Young.

Blake's *Illustrations to the Night Thoughts* show that Young's poetry inspired Blake to produce some of his best work, and to find solutions to the problems with which the poetry confronted the illustrator. Blake also learned from Young's visions, and used the icons he discovered there in his own later works. Yet it would be difficult to point to single statements or fundamental issues either in the contents or the form of Young's poetry which could explain Blake's eager acceptance of Young. In fact, the two poets seem to have disagreed on almost everything.

The *Night Thoughts* are didactic in the literal manner Blake abhorred, and the message of the poem is the importance of a rejection of pleasure and social life and a withdrawal into contemplation, an attitude which Blake rejected as one of subservience to moral law, which leads to inaction. Furthermore, the divine in Young is the very opposite of Blake's: Young's God is a distant Father, an 'Almighty, [who] from his throne, on earth surveys/ Nought greater, than an honest, humble heart' (VIII, 475-77), whereas Blake's God declares 'I am not a God afar off, I am a brother and a friend' (*Jerusalem*, 4:18). Young's God, moreover, is not only a God of mercy but also of vengeance; for Young, divine vengeance

> ... thunders; – but it thunders to preserve;
> It strengthens what it strikes; its wholesome dread
> Averts the dreaded pain; its [Hell's] hideous groans
> Join heaven's sweet hallelujahs in thy praise,
> Great Source of good alone! how kind in all!
> In vengeance kind! Pain, Death, Gehenna, save. (IX, 475-480)

What is more, the basis of Young's revelation is Nature. Although everyday sense perceptions fall quite outside the field of experience presented in the poem, nevertheless it is the flight into boundless stellar space which transports the speaker, and consequently Lorenzo, to emotional conviction – the basis of it all is Nature:

> My song but echoes what great Nature speaks.
> What has she spoken? Thus the goddess spoke,
> Thus speaks for ever: – "Place, at nature's head,
> A sovereign ..." (IX, 2022-2025)

Like Thomson, Young seems to accept that the very existence of nature postulates its creation by a God, and therefore observation of nature leads the observer to belief.

It is equally true to say, however, that Young's poem sees man in a perspective which is purely religious, placing him in a setting the bounds of which are infinite, and in a context of immortality and redemption. Young's model is the Bible, and his poem follows in the tradition of apocalypse and prophecy – the tradition of Spenser and Milton, that is, the poetry of vision, not of wit. Young's allegiance to the poetry of vision seems to be the overriding factor which makes Blake respond to the poetry creatively, and neither the purpose of the poem, nor the philosophy behind it, nor the grandiose language and the images drawn from nature, nor even the poet's stated allegiance to reason rather than imagination are sufficient to negate Blake's response.

When, therefore, a critic identifies an obvious and even openly-stated disagreement between Blake's views and Dante's, the example of Blake's Young should make him think twice before he goes so far as to conclude that Blake rejected Dante's vision.

Blake's illustrations for the *Commedia*

There are 102 plates of Blake's illustrations for Dante's *Commedia* (72 for *Inferno*, 20 for *Purgatorio* and 10 for *Paradiso*), and seven engravings. All of these, after Blake's death, came into the hands of Linnell, who had commissioned Blake to produce the work, and, after Linnell's own death, were in the possession of his family. Their existence was known by scholars, and was first recorded by William Michael Rossetti, who put them into order and assigned them titles when asked to produce a catalogue for Gilchrist's *Life of Blake* in 1862. But the plates were neither exhibited nor printed for many decades, and Blake's images were not, therefore, readily accessible.[28] It was not until 1893 that twenty-nine of the drawings were exhibited at the Royal Academy, and not until 1912 that another exhibition was held of twenty drawings (ten of which had been in the previous exhibition). In 1918 all the drawings were sold at Christie's to various museums and institutions, but before they were finally dispersed in 1922, a limited edition of collotype reproduction was produced for subscribers, this being the first publication of the drawings in print.

There have been a number of studies and discussions of the drawings, which are now easily available in print, the basic text being Albert S. Roe's *Blake's Illustrations to the Divine Comedy* published in 1953. More recently, in 1980, Milton Klonsky published his *Blake's Dante*. The two books are in some ways complementary. Roe offers a long, 43-page introduction in which he presents the history of the designs, summarizes Blake's symbolism, and briefly comments on the themes and style of the series. He then comments individually on each drawing, and here he points out in great detail the Blakean symbolism and iconography, citing passages from Blake's poems and prophecies which help to elucidate the symbolism of the designs. He also points out iconographical similarities with other illustrations, so that the reader comes to realize that Blake's Dante forms with other illustrated works, such as Blake's own *Milton* and, in particular, the illustrations to the *Night Thoughts*, a single system of narratives and icons.

Klonsky provides a much shorter introduction, which is, however, lucid and informative. His comments on the individual drawings are occasionally purely descriptive, but at times offer very revealing and informative interpretations. The quality of reproduction of the drawings is very high; many are in colour, whereas Roe's are all black and white. In addition, alongside each drawing Klonsky places the corresponding passage from Dante, so that the reader sees both source text and Blake's picture. It is particularly unfortunate that Klonsky has chosen the translation by J.A. Carlyle, Thomas Oakey and P.H. Wicksteed (Temple Classics, 1899-1901). This has no historical links with the illustrations, and nor is it a very recent translation, such as would have enabled the modern reader to respond more closely to the text. Moreover, the translation has been manipulated by the editor, who has 'incorporated many changes suggested by other translators' (p. 21), without indicating where he does so. The text is further distanced from the reader by the inclusion in square brackets of explanations of persons and places.

The works of Roe and Klonsky share one basic weakness, in that, although both critics use as method a comparison between the text of the *Commedia* and Blake's illustration, their final analysis of the drawings is based fully on Blake's work and vision, and not on Dante's. This makes their interpretation of the designs at times inaccurate and at times wide of the mark. Moreover, in their views on the *Commedia* they seem to be guided by a preconceived idea which has more to do with the eighteenth century than with the second half of the twentieth. Thus Roe points out that 'the whole theme of Inferno is the terrible nature of God's punishments' (p. 31), and assumes that Blake's belief in forgiveness will naturally make him reject Dante's Hell.

Klonsky is even more disappointing in this respect. For by 1980 Dante scholarship had highlighted the role of the protagonist and the nature of the experience in Hell, and yet Klonsky mentions Dante's 'infernal equations of crime and punishment which would not permit him to exempt or pardon even his closest friends, his benefactors, or his own kinsfolk' (p. 9). The reader can imagine for himself what critics through the centuries would have said of a system in which Dante saved his 'friends, benefactors and kinsfolk' and damned everyone else! Klonsky's words show that he identifies Dante's emotional life with the structure of the narrative, and loses sight of the realism of the vision. One might even think Klonsky was an eighteenth-century or Victorian sentimentalist when he accuses Dante of cruelty in unfeelingly separating a family for all eternity – by placing Corso Donati (who was an enemy, he adds) in Hell, his brother (who was also an enemy, though this is not mentioned) in Purgatory, and their sister in Paradise.

Figure 1

From the "Heads of the Poets": Milton

Figure 2

From the "Heads of the Poets": Dante Alighieri

Figure 3

Plate 1, *Dante Running from the Three Beasts*

Figure 4

Plate 3, *The Mission of Virgil*

Figure 5

Plate 4, *The Inscription over Hell-Gate*

Figure 6

Plate 5, *The Vestibule of Hell, and the Souls Mustering to cross the Acheron*

Figure 7

Plate 8, *Homer and the Ancient Poets*

Figure 8

Plate 9, *Minos*

Figure 9

Plate 69, *Dante Tugging at Bocca's Hair*

Figure 10

Plate 70, *Ugolino Relating His Death*

Figure 11

Plate 80, *Lucia Carrying Dante in His Sleep*

Figure 12

Plate 81, *Dante and Virgil Approaching the Angel Who Guards*
the Entrance to Purgatory

Figure 13

Plate 88, *Dante at the Moment of Entering the Fire*

Figure 14

Plate 91, *Beatrice Addressing Dante from the Car*

Figure 15

Plate 94, *Dante Adoring Christ*

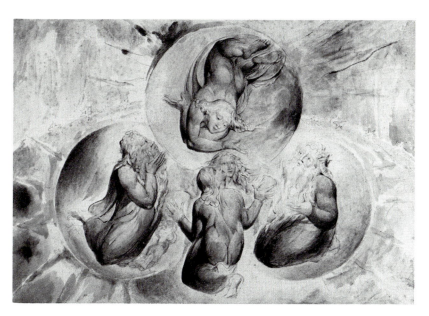

Figure 16

Plate 99, *Saint Peter, Saint James, Dante, Beatrice*

with Saint John the Evangelist Also

Figure 17

Plate 102, *The Queen of Heaven in Glory*

An objective and sensitive reader would simply deduce that in Dante the drama of a family is part of the drama of the individual, and not the reverse, and that here we have the opposite of Racine's *sangue*: each individual has a personal destiny, and his redemption or salvation depends upon himself alone.

It is also a pity that both critics devote very little attention to the series as a whole, so that their comments on the individual drawings do not lead to any cumulative conclusions. Here Klonsky is virtually silent. Roe mentions that the drawings, which are Blake's last work, show the further development of Blake's linearist art, have greater simplicity and purity of line, and that, in the total composition of each drawing, space plays a much greater role than it had ever done: '... imaginative landscape settings are given considerable prominence and take on a new expressive importance that is not accorded them in any of Blake's earlier work' (p. 41).

My comments on Klonsky and particularly Roe should not be construed as an attempt to minimize their achievement. Both (and particularly Roe) provide an excellent *tertium comparationis*, promulgating as they do the widely-accepted view of Blake's illustrations. If there is a criticism to be made of Roe's and Klonsky's work it is of their method. Where the method used is a comparison between two systems, Dante's and Blake's, then both systems must be given equal status, and the critic who is willing to search Blake's canon to see how he arrived at solutions must also be willing to search Dante's total text for the source of the problems. The status of source and target text must be equal, otherwise what is in actual fact a literal solution might appear as a creative one, distorting the analysis completely.

In the following pages I move through the three *cantiche*, analysing a number of the illustrations in terms of literal and of recreative and innovative renderings of the text. Illustrations are, as I proposed in Chapter 1, to be regarded as a kind of translation, and the illustrator is a reader of Dante who reveals, in his work, both how he reads the source text and which outside and inner forces contributed to his reading. I begin, however, by examining Blake's very first drawing for the *Commedia*, in order to establish some basic features of the whole series. I should make it clear that I do not intend to produce a systematic reading of all the illustrations. For a detailed examination of all the illustrations the reader should refer back to Klonsky and Roe. In fact, even some of the drawings that, considered individually and in isolation, are strikingly effective and dramatic will remain outside my discussion here, as will the seven engravings. The basic purpose of the present analysis is to observe Blake's response to Dante, and to retrace the forces which have contributed to this response; the method is an analysis of the iconography as well as the formal means used by Blake for his illustrations.

Blake's illustrations for *Inferno*

Blake's illustration to Canto I of *Inferno* depicts Dante escaping from the forest and from the three beasts, which stand to our right (Fig. 3). Dante faces away from us, his arms outstretched, and with his head turned to the right to look at the beasts. Facing him is Virgil with arms outstretched, floating in mid air. The sun is rising, not from behind the hill, but from out of the sea, a detail not in the text. A basic feature, common to the whole series, is immediately apparent: Dante is represented as a simple human figure, clothed in red, and Virgil is the same human figure clothed in blue, the fact that his feet do not rest on the ground indicating that he is pure spirit. The two figures are aspects of the same man – Dante is Luvah, Virgil Los – so that both the Zoas which dominate the creative artist are present on the scene. Blake adds to the landscape roots and brambles, indicating the error of this world, and the sea of time and space, or the sea of Ulro, threatening Dante with a further fall into chaos.[29] Virgil (poetic genius) will lead Dante (the fallen Albion) through the Fallen World to Beulah and Eden. Though expressing perfectly a moment of the narrative of Blake's own myth, the picture is also a virtually literal visualization of the text. All this has been pointed out by various commentators.

These observations already establish two main points about Blake's illustrations. First, the very fact that Dante has no aquiline nose, no laurel and earflaps means that, when faced with Dante's literal story and the allegorical meaning the story conveys, Blake did not try to suggest both narratives, but specifically chose the latter. Dante is Everyman and Virgil is an aspect of his spiritual make up. Secondly, Blake has created a picture which includes two blueprints superimposed on each other, as it were: Dante's story and Blake's myth are both illustrated by the drawing, some features of which belong to both systems, some to Blake's only. The viewer is, therefore, faced with a picture which communicates both systems at one and the same time. Blake's addition of the sea in fact makes of this first drawing a complete icon of the spirit and its possible destiny in Dante's terms: man falling, at the moment of danger and approaching death, from a high place down into a valley, towards the sea. The landscape, therefore, is spiritual and internalized. Many of Blake's illustrations are of this kind: they create an aesthetic object which can be read in terms of both systems, Dante's and Blake's. This is true also of other illustrations which seem, on the surface, to be purely interpretations of the original text in terms of Blake's own mythology, the most extreme example of which is the drawing which illustrates 'HELL canto 2' (Fig. 4).

Indeed, Rossetti gave this drawing illustrating 'HELL canto 2' the title of *The Mission of Virgil*; and Roe states that it departs considerably from the text, so that 'a reading of this canto will not enlighten us greatly as to what is represented; only a knowledge of Blake's ideas as set forth in his writings will enable us to understand why this subject is portrayed in this particular way' (p. 51). The drawing in divided horizontally into two parts. In the lower part two giants in chains occupy the extreme left and right spaces. Between them there is an opening. Dante faces the opening with his back to us, his head turned left in profile. He is visibly frightened by the appearance of the three beasts half hidden in the bushes which line the left side of the opening. Inside the opening Virgil waits for him. A layer of clouds and figures divides this lower part from the upper part of the illustration, where the figure of Jehovah/Nobodaddy/Urizen, with arms outstretched, towers over the drawing (and Blake has pencilled 'The Angry God of this world & his throne in purgatory' above the figure). Facing him, on his knees and with his back to us, is a figure covered with symbols of earthly power and tyranny (fleur-de-lys, castles, maltese crosses), holding in his hand a smoking censer, with a spiked crown on his head. The layer of clouds, a device which in Blake signifies a separation between spiritual states, is occupied by three flying female figures, and by a fourth woman weaving beneath an alcove enclosed by a vine.

This would be purely Blake's own vision: kings and priests worship a false God in order to oppress man. Dante's Emanation, Beatrice, weaves for him a body so that he can begin his journey through the Fallen World, and she is accompanied by the other Daughters of Beulah. The giants are souls marking the boundary of Ulro, as their stupefied expressions, the flames, and the chains make clear. Roe suggests that the Daughters of Beulah are derived from Dante, who mentions the Virgin, St Lucy, Rachel and Beatrice – this being, presumably, in his view, the only feature, together with the basic figures of Dante and Virgil, suggested by the text.[30]

On the contrary, this picture offers, again, a complete vision of Blake's superimposed on the central point of Dante's second canto of *Inferno*. Blake does not select one moment of the story, such as Beatrice's descent to Limbo to ask Virgil's help for Dante, as Flaxman did, but communicates the narrative of the whole canto – 'HELL canto 2', indeed, being precisely what the drawing is about. The second canto of *Inferno* prepares the mission of Dante in the *Commedia*, and concerns itself with the questions of why and by whom Dante was chosen to go through the worlds of the afterlife when still alive – 'io non Enea, io non Paulo sono' (l. 32; 'I am not Aeneas, neither am I Paul'). Dante's Canto II presents a number of narratives and speaking voices, and a definite picture. First Dante speaks, and remembers the founder of the Roman Empire, Aeneas, and his journey into the underworld – a historical mission, justified by its consequence in the foundation of Rome. He then remembers Paul's later journey in the underworld, his mission being one of confirmation of faith and of the way to salvation. The question which is logically implied is, 'Ma io perché venirvi? o chi 'l concede?' (l. 31, 'But I, why do I go there, and who allows it?'). The answer is Virgil's complicated report of Beatrice's speech to him, in which she reports Lucy's speech to her. When he hears the names of those who interceded on his behalf Dante gathers courage and begins the journey. One more point of interest is that when Virgil first speaks he says that Dante's fear is imaginary and causes him to retreat 'come falso veder bestia quand' ombra' ('as false seeing turns a beast that shies', l. 48).

These major features of Canto II are all in Blake's picture: the Church and the Empire as directing Dante's mission are the picture in the top part of the design, the intercession by the women is in the centre layer, and Dante's fear at imaginary sights – here the three beasts which, indeed, seem to be part of the foliage – occupies the lower part. This lower picture, in fact, is a spiritual, personalized version of the upper scene in which not the individual, but institutions are the actors, and institutionalized religion and government worshipping a False God take the place of the individual soul on his way to Poetic Imagination.

It is true that Dante's text implies that Church and Empire, in their ideal state, are the basic powers which ordain men's destiny, whereas Blake's drawing suggests his own very critical view of these institutions even as ideals. And yet Blake's design can be read as perfectly representing Dante's poetry, in which, as Sinclair puts it, 'for all the great place given to Church and Empire and their institutions in human order and fellowship and intercession, the essential and primary operations of grace are always, for Dante, unofficial, inward, personal, in principle prior and superior to all institutions' (I, p. 43). Again, therefore, Blake's illustration departs from the literal story and directly translates the inner significance of the narrative. Blake's mythology seems very successful in encoding Dante's meaning in an unmediated system to be unravelled by the reader.

Blake is also highly successful in portraying emotion and drama. Dante's facial expression and posture in the illustration just discussed are very dramatic and dynamic. Another illustration (the first to Canto V), representing Minos, is perhaps the best example of Blake's achievement in the creation of complex composition, drama, and movement (Fig. 8). Roe calls this 'one of the finest of the series' (p. 63) because of the sweeping movements in different directions and different layers of the picture, so that the reader feels the composition's dramatic power even if he does not look further into its meaning. To Roe this meaning is the presentation of how man has perverted sexual love. Blake departed from the text by showing a Minos, who in Dante decides the place in Hell for all sinners, only concerned with couples and their love; and thus Blake refers only to the sinners in Canto V, the lustful. The picture presents a powerful Minos sitting on a throne, wearing a crown. He looks at Virgil and Dante with his mouth open and his right arm, with open hand, raised upwards. Flames emerge from the throne and lightning falls from the sky, while the sea (a feature Roe admits could have been suggested by the text) rages behind him. In mid air to the right of Minos (our left) a woman drags a man towards the sea of flames, and to the left of Minos a man drags a woman away, while under the throne one man approaches Minos, a woman is prostrate at his feet, and another woman is being carried away by a demon. To the extreme left Virgil, his lips parted and his arms widely outstretched, moves towards Minos, followed by Dante.

Roe's interpretation of the scene is correct and useful, but at times far too detailed. Of the couple struggling in mid air to Minos' right he says that 'the woman keeps her lover in a state of hopeless frustration by pointing to the authority of moral law' (the woman is pointing to Minos), and of the two figures approaching Minos he says that they 'are doubtless to be thought of as a couple who have led a frustrated married life through ignorant and fearful interpretation of the moral law' (the chain lying nearby).[31] Although this interpretation could all be true, it does nothing to explain the power of the picture. A comparison of the picture with the text offers a more successful means of decoding the dynamism of the picture, which is the source of its power. To begin with, the postures of the souls seen from left to right seem to retrace the process a soul goes through when it faces Minos, as described in the text:

> For when before him comes the ill fated soul,
> It all confesses; and that judge severe
> Of sins, considering what place in hell
> Suits the transgression, with his tail so oft
> Himself encircles, as degrees beneath
> He dooms it to descend. Before him stand
> Always a numerous throng; and in his turn
> Each one to judgement passing, speaks, and hears
> His fate, thence downwards to his dwelling hurled.   (Cary, V 9-17)

The woman prostrate before Minos is, indeed, confessing, the one being dragged away is still turned towards him, listening to her doom, and the one in mid air is being dragged away to her appointed place in Hell; the whole drama of the final doom of a soul in Hell is sketched in terms of the three female figures. In addition, the complex movement of the picture, with souls dragged away, in flight and prostrate, reproduces the throng and the chaos of this place in Hell.

Moreover, the reader of Dante, who knows that the very next episode sees the drama of Paolo and Francesca, cannot but see in the repetition of couples the damnation the two protagonists of that love story have brought upon one another.

The sense of a crowd, the impression of the chaotic movement in all directions that Minos' task in Hell entails are all in Blake's picture. The sense of the drama of the individual soul, and the premonition of the doomed love story to come animate the picture further. Moreover, the attitudes of Minos and of Virgil correspond to another drama which takes place in the text, that of Dante's own journey. In the first lines of the canto Minos speaks to Dante to threaten him, while Virgil replies that it is not for Minos to question the commands of Him for whom will and power are one; and in Blake's picture, too, Minos is addressing Dante and Virgil in a threatening manner, while Virgil is answering him. Blake does not produce a static drawing, which, by definition, selects one moment of time caught in one composition in space, but on the contrary combines different moments in the narrative, so that the address, the answer, and the passing of a judgement on a soul all take place, as it were, in the prolonged time it takes to read the picture. Blake's illustration conveys not only movement (both in space and through time), but also narrative and dialogue.

Taken singly, Blake's illustrations to Dante not only present to the reader an adequate visualization of the significance of the original text, but at the same time give shape to Blake's own vision. Taken as one system, the series has three major characteristics. First, Blake introduces visual links between many illustrations, so that each illustration contributes to one total narrative. Secondly, Blake focuses, at one point of the total narrative, on a particular subject that emerges from the text, which he therefore highlights. Thirdly, Blake does not avoid portraying Lucifer's grotesqueness, does not reduce the role the devils play in the journey, and does not refrain from using, occasionally, gothic touches.

To begin with the first point – the narrative thrust of the series – we have already seen that some drawings depict a sequence of moments in the narrative time of the story or of the canto they refer to. There is, therefore, a narrative progression within a drawing. In addition, drawings contain visual links with each other, underlining the fact that they belong to a sequence. For example, Plate 11 is an overview of the circle of the Gluttonous with Cerberus far away in the left part of the drawing, while Plate 12 is a close-up of Cerberus, with the poets standing next to the monster, and so the two plates together suggest the progress of the journey. Similarly, Plate 45 pictures Virgil and Dante hiding from the devils under a bridge in obvious fright, but just discernible in the left bottom corner of the design are a few heavily cloaked figures walking in a line, and these appear in full as the Hypocrites trudging in a winding line around the crucified Caiaphas in Plate 46. Ugolino, also, appears fully in Plate 70, but his appearance is already prepared for in Plate 68. Here, Dante is shown striking Bocca degli Abbati on the flat frozen plain of Cocytus, which takes up a great part of the drawing, the figures of the poets being placed somewhat to the left of the composition. Dante and Virgil face right, and behind them in the left corner is a rising mound. In the next plate, Plate 69 (Fig. 9), Dante is tugging at Bocca's hair, the figures taking up the centre of the drawing and thereby allowing the mound to be shown fully. It contains, in what seems to be a cave, Ugolino with his teeth set in the neck of Ruggieri. Dante and Virgil face away from them. Then in Plate 70 (Fig. 10) the travellers have turned to face Ugolino, who has left off biting the head and is obviously telling the story of his death. The setting and the landscape around the central figures of a single drawing, therefore, contribute towards unifying the series. In particular, the narrative is highlighted by Blake's use of landscape and space.

Roe has pointed out the scope Blake gives to landscape in this last work of his. In fact, Blake's landscape assumes, here, functions which it did not have in previous works of his. First of all, as in many of Blake's illustrations, landscape is a tool for creating a complex picture and increasing its meaning. But here landscape also has a role of its own in that it creates a contradictory sense of space: it adds sublimity, but also limits it. The view in Plate 17 showing the Stygian lake, which takes up most of the drawing, is characteristically sublime, the huge expanse of the lake being delimited in the bottom part of the drawing by a strong tower, whose powerful structure dwarfs the little figures of the two poets. On the other side of the lake a tiny tower is lit by the light filtering through the clouds. Shown in detail in the following plates, this tower is the city of Dis to which the poets will go. There is a sense of space and the idea of the direction of the poets' journey, but the clouds covering the sky and the mountains on the opposite shore put a limit to the sublimity of the spacious, bright picture.

Similarly, in the illustration for Canto III (Fig. 6) Blake creates a very varied composition, in which the space is divided between the crowd following the flag, the crowd waiting to be ferried over Acheron, and the crowd which has just crossed over. The water between the two last groups extends to the horizon, and its choppy, dark waves attract the viewer's eye and lead it outwards. But the sky above, as dark as the sea and filled with clouds, is occupied by the fallen angels, so that a sense of oppression counteracts the sweep outwards to the sea. The illustration representing Hell's gate (Plate 4, Fig. 5) pictures a high, gothic arch, but the vertical thrust of the arch, which is emphasized by the tall trees lining it on each side, is counteracted by the horizontal lines of the continents visible one above the other beyond the door, so many and high that they fill the scene beyond, blocking the view.

Blake's landscape also gives solidity to Hell as a place. The battlements of the City of Dis, repeated in various illustrations, the rocky landscape further from the city, the bare, rocky bridges criss-crossing the sky-line further on, and the frozen lake of Cocytus create a topography of Hell, a solid world which adds realism to the journey taking place in it. The narrative of the journey is held together by the very fact that it moves through consistent but varying settings.

However – and this is the second of the three points to be discussed – Blake also slows the pace of the narrative in places. Nearly every canto is represented by at least one illustration, many by two, and one by four, but Cantos XXIV and XXV are represented together by no fewer than ten illustrations (and also by two of the seven engravings). Of these illustrations, eight focus on the snakes attacking the men and the transformation of men into snakes and back into men. Blake produces, in this sub-series, some very dramatic drawings, one (Plate 54, *The Six-footed Serpent Attacking Agnolo Brunelleschi*) being peculiarly horrific. In this sub-series the human frame is shown as grotesquely distorted and beautiful, in alternation. Vanni Fucci, for example, is shown making an obscene sign at God, but his frame and stance appear heroic, and the snakes darting upwards alongside his body make of this a very dynamic design.

Both Roe and Klonsky point out that some features of the thieves' punishment in Dante's Hell were also particularly meaningful in Blake's system of symbols. Roe stresses the figure of the serpent as the embodiment of the material world, Satan being the lowest point in the fall. More interestingly, Klonsky sees in the thieves the figure of Orc, who can be identified with the rebellious Satan but also with Prometheus, and is therefore the cause both of the fall and of salvation. It is probably also the very idea of metamorphosis that appeals to Blake, and this concept fits in with the fast moving, dynamic character of these illustrations. In any case, the space devoted to this vision of Hell means, first, that the narrative slows down, and, secondly, that, through repetition, stress is placed on the view that the human form, when at its lowest state of being, is the same as that of a serpent, and that this view of man is the very core of Blake's Hell.

I now turn to the third characteristic of Blake's series, the potentially more gothic aspects of Hell in Blake's rendering – Ugolino, the devils and Lucifer in particular. While the paintings of Ugolino by Reynolds and others represent the pathetic figure of the man in prison, his sons dying around him, Blake's Plate 69 (Fig. 9) shows the scene of his punishment – Hell. Like so many translators of his time, Blake also emphasizes the gore, and his depiction of a man's teeth set in another man's neck causing the blood to flow is quite horrific. Ruggieri's expression is one of agony and horror, and his neck, particularly in Plate 70 (Fig. 10), is mangled. Blake underlines, as many translators also did, the fact that Ruggieri is an 'infernal priest': placed in the bottom pit of Hell, gnawed by another sinner, his tasselled hat and crozier are prominent in the drawing, and appear very striking objects in the frozen waste of Cocytus. Blake does not, on the other hand, include any objects to suggest Ugolino's political role in life, so that if any harsh criticism is suggested, it concerns only Ruggieri as a member of a corrupt church.

A comparison of Plates 69 and 70, moreover, shows that the illustrations succeed in following the text closely precisely through the very creation of a gap between one plate and the next.[32] So Plate 69, illustrating Canto XXXII, presents Ugolino at his beastly occupation, with a savage expression on his face, while Plate 70 illustrates Canto XXXIII, and here Ugolino's expression is one of suffering, his gestures suggesting resignation and powerlessness. In this way the illustrations retrace that break between the two moments of the story, between Ugolino as a beast and Ugolino as a suffering man. But this is more than a simple following of the physical organization of the text, and Blake is deliberately stressing, in the second picture, the pathos and the spiritual state of Ugolino. Roe correctly suggests that here Ugolino looks very similar to Job in Blake's *Illustrations for the Book of Job*, and that probably the likeness is intentional, since both men suffered through the loss of their children. Blake would be stressing, then, also the suffering of Ugolino as a father. This means that Blake, even at this stage, must still see Ugolino as more sinned against than sinning, and so produces a particularly sensitive rendering of the text, using his own iconography to suggest the meaning he sees in it. That Ugolino is finally forgiven in Blake's mind is confirmed by Plate 71 (showing Ugolino in prison), where two angels hovering over the group suggest final salvation.

Blake clearly does not object to picturing horrible punishments so long as they can be used to communicate an important view of man. Similarly he has no qualms about producing illustrations of devils, of which he has many: seven successive plates (Plates 38 - 44) concentrate on the devils themselves and their activities, the last plate being very dramatic. Devils also appear in the next two plates (45, *Dante and Virgil Escaping from the Devils*, and 46, *The Hypocrites with Caiaphas*), but they are pushed more and more into the background, and by the time we get to Plates 47 and 48 they have disappeared. The episode of the serpents follows, so that the two sets of illustrations, of devils and serpents, form two larger groups within the series, and, since they correspond to the text, they re-enact the structure of the original. Blake's varied designs for the devils show that, though he might have believed in forgiveness and rejected the existence of a Hell created by Jesus, he certainly believed in Satan. When he saw him in a vision in his house, he made a drawing which presented him, as Cunningham reports, with large eyes, long teeth and horrific claws: 'It is the gothic fiend of our legends,' Blake is reported to have said.[33] Blake's devils in his illustrations to *Inferno* have bat-like wings, scaly genitals, long fleshy tails like a bull's, large eyes, and claws; and two have tusks. They certainly share many of the features of the traditional picture of a devil.

Similarly, Dis at the bottom of the pit of Hell is a huge figure with bat-like wings. As in the original, he is trapped up to his waist in ice, has three heads, and in each of his three mouths is chewing a man. But the picture is also different from Dante's description in many ways: for example, there is only one set of wings and these are not very large, and through the ice a number of figures appear who are not mentioned in the text, but who could represent the significance of this stage of man's journey within Blake's own system. Nevertheless, the drawing communicates some important aspects of the original: the three heads suggest the monstrous version of the Trinity, and the triple crown the fact that this is 'That Emperor, who sways/ The realm of sorrow' (Cary, XXXIV 27-8). The attitude of the body and arms, and the expression and features of his face, moreover, retrace those of Ugolino, though the face is more monstrous and contorted, so that Lucifer becomes the distortion of God, and also a stage of man's fall, the lowest state that man can reach. In this way Blake renders through his own iconography one aspect of the meaning of the original text. He certainly seems more concerned with meaning than with style, and has no qualms about producing a picture of Dis which might well be called grotesque if set beside the sublime Satan of Milton. This means, further, that while Cary and Coleridge used definite personal preferences as the standard for value judgement, deciding that the Miltonic sublime was 'good' style but the grotesque was 'bad' style, Blake simply takes whichever style is most appropriate for creating the required effect.

Blake's devils and his Lucifer show that, although Blake might have rejected the idea of Hell as a place of punishment devised by the 'justice' of God, he fully accepted it as a metaphor for a state of being. In his illustrations to *Inferno* Blake produces a picture of Hell as the progress of the creative artist through the Fallen World. And so Blake responds to Dante's text fully. His visions provide him with forms to give shape to the devils; and he is moved to produce some of the most effective and complex drawings and engravings of his whole career, such as the Paolo and Francesca illustration. All Blake's powers and craft, and also his feelings as a man find full expression in the illustrations to Dante's *Inferno*: his bitterness at the obscurity in which he spent the last years of his life and which caused his prophecies to go unheard, and also at the poverty which follows the republican artist who is true to his own vision is vented in Plate 15, the picture of the Goddess Fortune, whom Blake apparently places in a cess-pit, coins (or faeces) falling over her. Across the top of the drawing he has scribbled 'the hole of a Shit house' and 'the Goddess Fortune is the devils servant ready to kiss any ones Arse'.[34]

Here Blake's words written on the drawing correspond to the picture. But the question this plate raises is what value is to be placed on the notes Blake wrote on other illustrations. It is in these notes that Blake's rejection of Dante's system are made clear, while the designs themselves are ambivalent, and can be read as endorsing the allegorical value of the journey. Two notes express a judgement on Dante, and they appear in Plates 7 and 22. The latter is still somewhat tentative, and does not directly reject Dante's vision.[35] But the former does directly reject Dante's vision, and deserves to be considered very closely. Representing *Homer, Bearing the Sword, and His Companions*, it precedes Plate 8, *Homer and the Ancient Poets*, and in fact includes an outline description of the total system of the *Commedia*, with Homer in its centre:

> Everything in Dantes Comedia shows That for Tyrannical Purposes he has made This World the Foundation of All & the Goddess Nature Mistress. nature is his Inspirer & not the Holy Ghost as Poor [word unreadable] said, Nature, Thou art my Goddess. Round Purgatory is Paradise & round Paradise is Vacuum or Limbo, so that Homer is the centre of All. I mean the Poetry of the Heathen Stolen and Perverted from the Bible not by Chance but by design by the Kings of Persia and their Generals The Greek Heroes and Lastly by the Romans.
> Swedenborg does the same in saying that in this World is the Ultimate of Heaven. This is the most damnable Falsehood of Satan & his Antichrist.

This condemnation of the *Commedia* is based on a number of notions: first, that Dante was moved by 'Tyrannical Purposes' similar to those which moved kings and warriors from the beginning of history to Roman times; secondly, that the system in the poem is based on the Classics, making Homer 'the centre of all'; and, thirdly, that Dante's muse is nature.

As for the first point, Blake had already rejected Dante as an 'Emperor's man' after reading one of Boyd's introductory essays to the *Inferno*. Reading Cary could not but confirm the view of Dante not as a prophet on a mission of redemption but as a historical figure concerned with the political changes of his city and time. Though Blake's view of Dante might be negative in this respect, it affects his illustrations only in so far as it leads him to improve (in his eyes) on the original by leaving out the historical dimension completely and by concentrating on its spiritual allegory. It does not inhibit Blake from responding to the text, nor does it lead him to express himself continuously in critical terms.

That Blake was not repeatedly criticizing Dante's intentions in his illustrations is confirmed by the second point, the importance of Homer in Dante's poem. A comparison between the words in this plate (Plate 7) and the illustration which follows (Plate 8, which represents Homer and the classical poets in Limbo) shows that Plate 8 does not implement the views expressed in writing in Plate 7. In Plate 8 (Fig. 7) Homer again appears sword in hand, with four more poets. They are placed under the grove of error, but the drawing offers a double view of classical poetry. It is divided horizontally into two parts, separated by a layer of clouds. The upper scene shows Dante and Virgil looking from a rock down into a valley and at a number of figures flying in the space between. Below the clouds is the grove where, in the centre, four poets stand, one of them being Homer with his sword. To the left, a priest worships idols, and on the right Blake introduces (in the place of the castle of the original) a pastoral and Arcadian picture. The layer of clouds is black above the priest, but not above the pastoral scene, in which one of the figures is playing a flute. Clearly the priest corresponds to the heathen religion of the classical poets. But this design is not totally Blake's own creation, devised in order to make clear that these poets lacked inspiration, for it is a visual rendering of a section of the text. Here, Virgil explains that these poets are in Limbo, and not in Purgatory or Paradise, because they are men who 'served not God aright;/ And among such am I. For these defects,/ And for no other evil, we are lost;' (Cary, IV 35-7). The reader is reminded, then, of the very first canto where Virgil introduced himself by saying that he lived 'in the time/ Of fabled deities and false' (1. 67-8).[36] What Blake himself introduces is the composition on the right, showing the Arcadian scene. Pastoral poetry was the only mode of the ancients that Blake accepted as inspired, and so the two extreme parts of the picture would suggest the damning but also the saving aspects of classical poetry.

Roe reads this illustration in terms of the condemnation of the *Commedia* expressed in the previous plate, and he therefore interprets the figures flying above the clouds as 'the graceful, flying forms of the imagination', from which the classical poets are excluded – forms which Blake has introduced 'without any authority for them in the text' (p. 60).[37] Roe's reading is a good example of the danger of using Blake's notes to interpret the drawings, and also of the danger of scanning Blake's works, without referring to Dante's text. Although the figures flying under Dante and Virgil might conceivably suggest imagination, they are without a doubt the souls moving freely in Limbo, which the two poets see as they look into the valley in the original text, the 'men, women and infants' (Cary, IV 28) which had received no baptism.[38] Since, moreover, Plate 7 is barely sketched and Plate 8 is a finished one, the commentator cannot but conclude that Blake's rendering of Dante's presentation of the classical poets is an ambivalent one, in which both their lack of inspiration and their achievement in pastoral poetry are recorded.

The third point in Blake's condemnation of Dante, that he drew inspiration from nature, is very general, but could be clarified by examining Blake's use of sublimity in his drawings. Faced with the sublimity of Boyd's rendering of *Inferno* in terms of the poetry of the *Night Thoughts*, and seeing then Boyd's choice of style confirmed by Cary's use of sublimity, Blake seemingly recognized in Dante a reliance on space and sublimity characteristic of Milton and developed by the eighteenth-century Miltonic poets, particularly Young. Jean Hagstrum finds a source for some features of Blake's illustrations, such as the bridges in Plate 42, in Milton's *Paradise Lost*, and Roe points out similarities in compositions and iconographical traits with the illustrations for Blake's *Milton* and Young's *Night Thoughts*.[39] In fact, Blake's words on Dante's nature in Plate 7 are not justified by any particular section or description in the text, not by any prominence given to nature in Blake's illustration, but they bear a verbal similarity to Young's lines in 'Night the Ninth' quoted on page 260 above, in which Young says that his poem 'echoes what great Nature speaks'. Apparently, therefore, Milton and Young dominate Blake's reading of Dante as far as the landscape and the use of space goes, although the need to picture Hell as an enclosed space forces Blake to limit the sublimity of the scenes. There will not be the same need for him to do so for Purgatory.

Before we move on to Blake's illustrations to the second *cantica*, we can draw certain conclusions concerning the illustrations of the first *cantica*. First, Blake's protagonist is not Dante Alighieri, but an Everyman setting off on a spiritual journey. Secondly, this journey itself becomes the progress of the creative artist (Los and Luvah) through the forms of the Fallen World towards Eden; the reality of the experience of the journey is stressed in the narrative, so that, with the exception of a very spiritualized picture of Ugolino in prison, no reference is made to the earthly lives of the souls (no picture of Ugolino captured by guards, nor a picture of Paolo and Francesca kissing, with a book before them, as in Flaxman). Thirdly, Blake adds sublimity to the landscape, and places the illustrations of many episodes within large expanses of water, cloud, or the ice of Cocytus. These three conclusions combined indicate that Blake seems to be guided in his reading of Dante by his reading of Boyd's *Inferno*, with its Youngian sublimity and the nature of its protagonist. But Blake's rejection of Dante as a political man seems rather to be based on Boyd's introductory essays and, probably, also on Cary's work, which, as we have seen, stressed the 'Life of Dante' and the political destiny of the man. All in all, however, Blake produces a vision of *Inferno* which is partly idiosyncratic, and partly an accurate visualization of the text, the two tendencies being perfectly harmonized within the illustrations.

Blake's illustrations for *Purgatorio*

Blake produced only 20 plates for *Purgatorio* (Plates 73 to 92 in Klonsky's numbering). For many of the cantos there is only one illustration; and there is a large gap between Cantos XXIII and XXVII. Accordingly, the opening and the closing sections of the *cantica* are represented in the *Purgatory* series, but the place given to the progress of the poets through the terraces on which the sins are purged is drastically reduced. This is not, however, the impression one gets when looking at the series, because by far the majority of illustrations show the landscape of the narrow ledges cut in the side of the mountain: three plates are set on the shore of the island (the beginning of *Purgatorio*), three in the garden (the conclusion of the *cantica*), and 12 very clearly on the mountain, while one more scene is also set on the mountain (which does not, however, appear in the illustration). Blake's illustrations to *Purgatorio*, therefore, leave out specific encounters and episodes of the central section, but reflect the basic structure of the original. In fact, if we use landscape as a basis for the analysis, Blake's series divides into three major groups of plates, corresponding to the three stages of the journey in the original text. The narrative of the original is, moreover, remarkably well summarized, especially as far as the journey of Dante as poet is concerned.

The first three plates reproduce the poets' arrival on the islet and picture the small island bound by rushes, which form a fence-like border all around it and suggest its narrowness and enclosed nature. The sea extends to the horizon and meets there the vast expanse of the sky. The sea and sky are moved and animated by wave and cloud respectively – and are of varying colours. They suggest a contrast between the sublime spaciousness and the island. The mountain appears from the start, but in the first three plates it is only a single undulating line thrusting upwards on the left side of the design. In this sense, Blake's illustrations are an adequate rendering of the landscape of the original, since in Dante the mountain seems invisible in the first two cantos, but faces the poets suddenly in Canto III.

The mountain assumes solidity and becomes the basic setting of Plates 76 to 89 (see, for example, Figs. 12 and 13). Encounters, sights, sleep, and dreams all take place on the narrow ledge of the path cut into the steep side of the mountain, while the sea below and the sky behind always appear, adding space, colour and light. The mountain is very barren and rocky so that the contrast with the last three plates (Plates 90-92) could not be more striking.[40] In Plate 90 in particular the ground is carpeted with flowers, and the spaciousness of sea and sky is shifted to the ground of the garden. As in *Hell*, here too Blake creates the impression of vast and towering space to give shape to the experience of the protagonist – his arrival on the islet, his ascent, and his arrival into the garden of Eden.

As for the narrative of the journey throughout the plates, the reader who is familiar with the text can readily see that the series reproduces the story of the poet's progress. In the first of the *Purgatory* plates (Plate 73), Dante is girt with a rush; in Plate 74 he encounters his musician friend Casella, and, in Plate 75, Dante appears between Virgil and Cato, the latter pointing to Hell, the former to Heaven, symbolizing the limits of the poet's journey. In the central section of the plates, Dante encounters the souls of those who repented at the time of death (here they are not mostly men, but are paired in couples to show the reunion with their emanations). We see him at the gate of Purgatory, and with the angel who marks seven 'Ps' (for 'peccato', 'sin') on his forehead. He then meets the proud – and as in the original, bends down with them to purge the sin of pride in himself. Next we see Dante observing the 'visibile parlare' of the bas-relief on the side of the mountain, and talking in Plate 86 to the envious, the sinners among whom Dante meets the miniature-painter and illuminator Oderisi da Gubbio and discusses fame and the fate of the artist in Canto XIII of *Purgatorio*.

It is at this point that the gap in the illustrations occurs. The next three plates (Plates 87, 88, 89) all relate to Canto XXVII, and represent Dante and Virgil approaching the fire of purification, Virgil entering the fire as Dante stands hesitating, and finally Dante asleep and dreaming of Leah and Rachel after having gone through the fire. Blake therefore focuses closely on the final stage of the poet's progress. However, one must also point out that he has, so far, included most of the episodes in the text where art and the artist appeared (music, painting, and sculpture); now, in Plates 87-89, he moves to the fire into which, at the very close of Canto XXVI, Arnaut Daniel disappeared. Indeed, the figure just visible above in the fire in Plate 88 (Fig. 13) could well be the Provençal poet. Blake's *Jerusalem* and the *Four Zoas* also depict a similar purification by fire as one of the final stages in the soul's redemption, so that Canto XXVII not only portrays an important moment of Dante's journey, but also corresponds closely to Blake's own myths, and, further, continues the narrative of the artist in *Purgatorio*. The concluding three plates of the *Purgatory* drawings (90-92) show the conclusion of Dante's journey with his arrival in the garden and the reunion with Beatrice.

The illustrations of *Purgatorio* are similar, in some respects, to those of *Inferno*. Here, too, Blake uses a linking landscape to bind the plates into groups. He also insists upon spatial sublimity, and in fact increases it by extending the limits of sea and sky as Cary had done in his translation (see p. 200 above). Here, also, Blake combines an accurate representation of the text with a personal interpretation of it – again by adding features of his own, in order to make clear the status of that particular stage in the journey within his own narrative. The narrative, too, is only that of the journey – anything outside the actual experience recounted does not become a subject for illustration.[41] And, also as in *Hell*, a single illustration here often combines more than one of the events of a canto, in order to suggest the double view of the experience, as either vision or fall. In this respect, a change comes only in the last plates, where Blake denies Dante his vision.

Some of the designs clearly suggest the possibility of vision as well as of fall, and this accords with Blake's own views, since, as Roe proves, Blake must have seen Purgatory as corresponding to the state of being he called Beulah, where both salvation and fall are at hand. Many of the compositions suggest precisely this double view. So the group of Dante and Casella is placed between two other figures: on the left Cato stands before an enclosure in which idols are placed for worship, while on our right the angel shines in a boat shaped like a crescent moon. Thus both illusion and fall, and also salvation and inspiration surround Dante – the former on the mountain, the latter on the sea.

Other illustrations might suggest either definite salvation or a repetition of the fall. Among the first is Plate 80 (Fig. 11), Dante being carried by Lucia in his sleep – a moment in Dante's story which corresponds with great precision to a moment in Blake's myth of man's progress to salvation. Illustrations which definitely point to a repetition of the fall are very few. Klonsky believes that the approach to the gate of Purgatory is such a design (Fig. 12). According to him, Blake deliberately departs from the text and attempts to suggest that Dante is here entering the cave of Sleep, since he pictures the gate as a large 'open and inviting' door with a gothic arch, whereas the original had a very narrow opening, 'a gap just like a fissure which divides a wall', in the translation which Klonsky quotes (p. 155). Here Klonsky makes the mistake of not checking the translation Blake used, for, in his continuous effort to stress sublimity, Cary had avoided defining the narrowness of the entrance into Purgatory, and had said that when the poets 'Arrived whence, in that part, where first a breach/ As of a wall appeared, I could descry/ A portal...' (IX, 67-69). Thus Blake does not deliberately change the original to communicate a personal judgement of Dante, but is in fact being fairly faithful to the translation he used. Other features of the drawing (the fact that the angel looks like Urizen, for example) could perhaps suggest a criticism of the forms of Dante's vision, but not a definite fall.

This is, however, the case with the final *Purgatory* plates, representing the reunion of Dante with Beatrice. Plate 90 is a panoramic view of the river

Lethe/Eunoe, with Matilda and the pageant (including Beatrice on the car) on one shore, and Dante, Virgil and Statius on the other. The design is highly complex and rich in colour; Beatrice is barely visible on the car. Plate 91 is a close-up of the car with Beatrice on it, and here the interpretation Blake places on the scene in terms of the iconography of the composition is undoubtedly such as to suggest a meaning very different from that of the original (Fig. 14). Both Roe and Klonsky analyse the various figures and icons and show that many details point to Blake's myth of the fall.

Even without a knowledge of these details one realizes immediately that the seemingly blind, statuesque Griffin cannot be taken as an emblem of spiritual renewal and self-knowledge. Also, the four heads, half-human half-animal, sketched on the car obviously represent the Evangelists, who are often iconographically represented as the four animals of Ezekiel (man, lion, ox and eagle); here, however, they have been given dull, beastly faces with a downcast look. The eighteenth-century reader, or the modern reader familiar with eighteenth-century literature, moreover, would have no problem in identifying Beatrice: she is without a doubt presented as the Whore of Babylon. In terms of Blake's myth, she is Vala, the Female Will. Dante, placed below her, is subdued and in obeisance. She is crowned and carried in triumph on the car, her long hair flowing behind; a veil hangs down from the crown to her feet, like a mantle, behind her and at both sides, and a veil-like tunic reveals her body; flowers emblematic of fertility decorate the car. In Blake's system, we should remind ourselves, Vala is the emanation of Luvah in the Fallen World – love distorted. She is also the beauty of the natural world and the goddess of fertility, or Mother Nature. In a fallen state, she becomes a cruel mistress, who enslaves man by seducing him and forcing him to pursue material ends. The scene which in the original text constituted the fulfillment of Dante's love story, the culmination of his artistic career as planned in the *Vita Nuova*, and the regeneration of physical love into spiritual love is turned by Blake into its very opposite.

The reunion of a man with his emanation after the fire and the sleep of Beulah and in the context of Revelation could, theoretically, have been perfectly accommodated to Blake's own myth of salvation. But at this point of Plate 91 it becomes possible to trace some of the ways in which Blake's response to *Purgatorio*, and, in fact, to the whole *Commedia*, could have been directed along particular lines by forces other than his own myths. Below I indicate briefly five other possible influences on Blake's reading of Dante.

To begin with, we have seen that Cary overlaid *Purgatorio*, in particular, with sublimity, thereby attributing to space and nature a role these did not have in the original, where landscape serves as a visible sign of the state of being of a particular soul and of its destiny.

Cary's sublimity was purely external – a huge backdrop dwarfing man with its greatness. Moreover, Cary's footnotes take the reader out of the poem and connect it with real places, and therefore contribute towards reducing the spiritual dimension of the landscape. In the original, the rocky mountain and the flowers of the garden were indications of fallen and of redeemed landscape respectively, but in Cary this differentiation was not made. Blake notices the barrenness of the mountain and the fertility of the garden, and reproduces the difference faithfully.[42] But he misreads Dante's use of mountain and garden imagery. This helps to explain how it comes about that in Blake Beatrice becomes the goddess of fertility, enthroned in flowers, and dwarfing Dante by comparison and enslaving him with the spectacle of nature as a physical reality. Rather than the blossoming of the spirit, the flowers of the garden are seen by Blake as the richness of fertility, emblematic of that physical reality which so charms man that he, like Thomson's botanist, is deluded into turning his eyes to the material world – his vision being a matter of sight and not insight.

Blake's strong interest in Young may well have been a second possible influence, combined with the fact that the Miltonic sublime of Young was used to introduce Dante into England, notably by Boyd, but also by Hayley. All this could well have suggested to Blake a view of nature which makes him distort his reading of Dante. Beatrice on the car among trees, flowers and the river seems the literal visualization of the lines already quoted earlier (p. 260): 'Place at the head of nature/ a Sovereign' describes Blake's drawing exactly.

Thirdly, it must be pointed out that there is no evidence that Blake ever read Boyd's *Purgatorio*. We know that Blake had read Boyd's *Inferno* in the 1785 edition which contained that *cantica* only, and there is evidence that he subsequently read Cary, but no other evidence of translations used by Blake is available. If Blake's acquaintance with Boyd's translation was limited to *Inferno*, that would help explain why he did not see Beatrice as the figure of a beloved and of the Bride in the context of Revelation. Boyd had pictured the reunion of Dante and Beatrice in *Purgatorio* as one between two courtly lovers in a pastoral setting: "Twas my first love!' Dante had exclaimed in Boyd's translation. Also, Beatrice herself was shown as a figure from Revelation, however filtered through Milton's 'Il Penseroso', and appeared in the modest attire described in the original, the attire of a 'nun devout and pure' (see p. 150 above).

Instead of being a beloved and a bride – and now we come to a fourth possible influence – her flimsy and transparent gauze, in Blake, identifies Beatrice enthroned on the car as that very same figure as 'Ch – h' in Hayley's *Triumphs of Temper*, whose 'charms amaz'd the public sight' when she appeared 'in a veil so thin that the clear gauze was but a lighter skin' (VI, 87-88). In fact, Beatrice's veil will be even finer than 'Ch – h''s, since, like the veil of the other version of the same figure in Hayley's poem (the queen of the false Paradise), Beatrice's dress is a thing of heaven, and 'earthly gauze was never half so fine' (V 214). Hayley's poem included the obedient young girl and the harlot as opposites in terms of the kind of love they represent and as possible choice for marriage, thus symbolizing themes and figures of these central concerns of eighteenth-century literature. Blake visualizes Beatrice in terms of Hayley's images.

To come to the final possible influence, however, Blake would probably not have seen Beatrice in these terms had it not been for Cary's greatly distorted version of Beatrice. In Cary's lines, Dante's brief image of her dignified stance becomes the lengthy and detailed metaphor of an admiral enforcing his power over those under him. Indeed, Cary introduces the metaphor of a master and servant and eliminates all expression of feelings, so that Beatrice's initial anger does not appear as that of a caring mother towards her child as clearly as it did in the original. The lack of impact of Boyd's *Commedia* on the one hand, and the remarkable influence of Cary's, on the other, find confirmation here. Blake's illustrations to *Purgatorio* close with a plate showing the Whore of Babylon and the Giant Emperor kissing: love is degraded, spirituality denied, and the marriage of church and state – that is, of history and the future Jerusalem – only appear in their finally corrupt, demonic form.

To summarize, we have seen how Blake's myths influenced his response to Dante's *Inferno* and *Purgatorio*. Furthermore it would seem probable that some or all of the following influences were at work on Blake's response; Cary's sublimity, the role Young's *Night Thoughts* played in the early translations of Dante, Blake's limited reading of Boyd's translation, the figure of the Whore of Babylon – a basic metaphor of eighteenth-century poetry and one which, in Hayley's *Triumphs of Temper*, seems appropriate to Beatrice's appearance – and, finally, Cary's particular version of this episode of *Purgatorio*, in which he stresses the power and haughtiness of Beatrice.

Blake's illustrations for *Paradiso*

There are only ten illustrations for *Paradiso*, one of which is merely a sketch, and Blake makes no attempt to follow the story of *Paradiso*. He begins with Canto XIV, and then chooses a few moments of the journey.[43] According to Roe, the selection is made on the basis of Blake's own myths, each design representing a moment in the experience of Paradise and either corresponding with or diverging from it. Accordingly, the first drawing in Roe's ordering – Plate 94, *Dante Ador-ing Christ*, from Canto XIV (Fig. 15) – reproduces Blake's own vision of Christ and of the spiritual nature of all things in God, a vision he first had in 1800 and which 'influenced the whole further course of his thought and which provided him with a central focus for his belief which he had lacked up to that point' (p. 176). It is with this vision, adds Roe, that Blake's three great prophecies end.

Although, as before, Roe's and Klonsky's detailed interpretations of each drawing are interesting and accurate, the *Paradise* series still deserves some consideration both as one integrated whole, and as part of the total series of Blake's Dante. One must begin by pointing out that Blake's designs for *Paradiso* are unlike anything he had done before. The simplicity of the composition, the radiance of bright colours, the combinations of the human figure with images of spheres and light, the relative lack of detail, and the use of abstract figures are all representations of moments of consciousness and of spiritual states, and have little of the narrative composition of previous illustrations, whether those to Dante or those to Young or Job.

At the same time, although it is true to say that Blake does not picture Piccarda, or St Francis, or Cacciaguida, there remains a narrative element in the *Paradise* drawings. In the *Hell* and *Purgatory* drawings Blake had ignored the historical Dante, and reproduced only an allegorical level of the journey. Here, Blake also discards the fictional line of progress of the journey itself, but does depict the progress of the soul to vision. Accordingly, Plates 97, 98 and 99 retrace step by step the addition of vision upon vision, so that the twofold vision of Plate 97 grows into a perfect representation of the fourfold vision in Plate 99 (Fig. 16). Blake sees Dante's encounter with Saint Peter in Canto XXIV, their being joined by Saint James in the opening of Canto XXV, and their being further by John the Evangelist in the latter part of Canto XXV as the visible form of the achievement of more and more perfect vision. The three spheres which enclose the three saints suggest the Trinity, and echo the three spheres around the hands and feet of Christ in Plate 94.[44]

Moreover, the increase of visionary power represented by the saints in the three drawings is paralleled by the changing attitudes and positions of Dante and Beatrice, suggesting the union of soul and emanation. In the drawing preceding this triptych, Plate 96, Dante and Beatrice are in upright posture, facing each other but at a distance. In Plate 97 they take flight towards Saint Peter, almost joining their hands. In the next plate they are now with arms extended, the lower part of their bodies stretched one to the right and the other to the left, super-imposed, so that the two figures appear partly joined. Finally in Plate 99 (Fig. 16) they are truly the mirror image of one another, both kneeling to face each other, hands lifted, looking at the saints. Blake must have seen Dante as the masculine soul, Beatrice as its female emanation, who, as Klonsky points out, has lost the crown of the Female Will she had been wearing until that point.

Dante as Everyman – or Albion – has achieved the fourfold vision in Plate 99. Plate 101 pictures him drinking at the River of Light. In this plate, images of the fourfold vision are repeated, but in addition there are images of the artist. A poet composing on a scroll, a painter, and an engraver can all be distinguished, and an old woman not present in the text has been identified as the most important of Blake's mythological figures, Eno, the inspirer of visions and the mother of all poetry.[45] Blake's series of illustrations to the *Commedia* has followed the progress of man to salvation and also the parallel progress of the artist to visionary poetry.

It would appear at first sight disappointing, then, to see that the very last design of the complete series should represent the final victory of the Female Will, and, moreover, should be a definite condemnation of Dante's vision as being vitiated. Plate 102, *The Queen of heaven in Glory*, repeats the motifs of Plate 91, related to *Purgatorio*, where Beatrice appears as Vala, and of Plate 7, related to *Inferno*, in which Blake's annotations point both to the poem's foundation in the classics rather than the Bible, and to its misplaced worship of nature. Plate 102 (Fig. 17) represents Mary as the centre of the rose, with Beatrice below her. Many details show that the figure of Mary suggests Vala rather than Christ's mother – for example, she wields a lily as a sceptre. As for Beatrice, she has now shed even the gauze, and she and the three Graces accompanying her form a voluptuous group, suggesting a physical rather than a spiritual state, and natural desires rather than inspiration. Among the various significant details in the plate, two are particularly interesting: on one side of the flower is a book, identified as the Bible, bound in chains, while on the other side, wide open, are books by Homer and Aristotle. Here the features of the drawing in themselves already suggest that in Blake's view this vision in *Paradiso* was based on nature and not the Holy Ghost, and on the classics and philosophy rather than the Bible.

Again one cannot but be reminded of Cary's translation, in this case of *Paradiso*. There, Dante's echoes of Revelation were almost totally avoided, the final vision was presented as something frightening and to be dreaded and was described in terms of the terrible sublime of nature, and the stress in the very final words was not on love, but on will.

Yet it would be inaccurate to state, as Klonsky does, that this last design (Plate 102, representing the rose) is 'the consummation of his own [Blake's] series of illustrations' (p. 162). For the drawing is highly incomplete and therefore its status in Blake's canon is uncertain. The same reasoning suggests that we should not give too much importance to the fact that apparently there are no illustrations to later cantos. After all, the balance in the series is on the achievement of vision rather than a re-enactment of the fall.

Further support for this view may perhaps be found in a re-examination of Plate 94 (Fig. 15). This plate supposedly represents the moment, described in Canto XIV, where Dante sees Christ on the cross, this being the passage in which the name of Christ is repeated three times in rhyming position. The drawing is one of the few on which Blake has not written the canto number, and the attribution to this particular canto of *Purgatorio* is tentative.

The picture does correspond, however, to the passage in Canto XIV in various ways. Christ does not appear as the epitome of suffering humanity, nailed to the cross, but in triumph amidst flames and light: 'quella croce lampeggiave Cristo' ('Christ beamed on that cross', Cary, or 'that cross so flamed forth Christ') suggests the triumph, not the suffering, of Christ. Appropriately, in the drawing there is no cross, but Christ himself is represented in the attitude of the crucifixion.[46] Flames and beams encircle the figure, and Blake has added three flaming discs, similar to those enclosing the three saints in the later plates, placed behind Christ's hands and his feet. This feature re-enacts the threefold repetition of the name of Christ, and in this way Blake could have found a visual equivalent of Dante's repeated rhymes. But a design representing Christ uniting in himself the three circles of the Trinity, with Dante worshipping him, his arms outstretched like Christ's own in a mirror image of him, certainly represents the coming together of Everyman and Christ, and could well represent Dante's final vision of the Trinity.

The very fact that this drawing seems to be a visual rendering of Blake's own vision, in 1800, of the unity of all things in God, a vision which Blake used, as mentioned earlier, to conclude his three major prophecies suggests that Blake may have imagined this to be the culmination of Dante's prophecy. To read Blake's description of his vision is to retrace the text of Dante's final vision in many ways:

> My Eyes more & more
> Like a Sea without shore
> Continue Expanding
> The Heavens commanding
> Till the Jewels of Light
> Heavenly Men beaming bright
> Appeared as One Man
> Who Complacent began
> My limbs to infold
> In his beams of bright gold
> Like dross purgd away
> All my mire & my clay
> Soft consumd in delight

In his bosom Sun bright
I remaind. Soft he smild
And I heard his voice Mild
Saying This is My Fold
O thou Ram hornd with gold
Who awakest from Sleep
On the Sides of the Deep
On the Mountains around
The roarings resound
Of the lion & wolf
The loud Sea & deep gulf.[47]

Whether the illustration refers to Canto XIV or to the final vision of the *Commedia*, the fact that this plate gives shape to Blake's central belief in Apocalypse as the unity of all things in Christ means that at this point Dante, as the soul whose progress we have been following, has reached the highest state of being and has been granted the same vision Blake had been granted at Felpham.

This drawing seems to mark the fulfilment of the mission of Dante also in terms of Blake's series as a whole, for it repeats the composition and the theme of Plate 3 of *Hell*, entitled *The Mission of Virgil* (Fig. 4). There, a double picture also appears. Above, Urizen, his arms outstretched in the crucifixion, rests his hands on shapes like clouds, which spiral downwards; before him kneels man as the subject of Church and Empire, man under tyranny becoming the worshipper of the false god. Below, the individual's journey is represented by Dante, who, frightened at the illusion of the beasts, is hesitating before Virgil. Here in Plate 94 of *Paradise* Nobodaddy has been replaced by the true Christ, his hands resting on the suns of energy; before him, his arms outstretched and turned upwards rather than downwards, kneels Dante.[48] Christ's hands expand into flames and billowing clouds which assume circular shapes. Dante has followed Virgil and, at the end of his journey, has not turned into man under the constriction of morality and law, but man who recognizes the warmth, brightness and energy of Christ as the source of vision.

Blake's illustrations to the *Commedia* are a more faithful rendering of the original than people so far have acknowledged. A close look at the text of a canto and, in particular, at a version of the text contemporary with Blake's work (and particularly Cary's) shows that, in some of the instances where critics have assumed that Blake has deliberately departed from the original, he was in fact following it quite closely. Thus, while his verbal comments on Dante's vision are few, Blake produces a pictorial version of the *Commedia* which is, essentially, both an adequate rendering of the significance of the poem and also a re-shaping of Dante's narrative in terms of Blake's own vision.

Blake's illustrations can be read in both of these ways. The nineteenth-century viewer ignorant of Blake's system and myths would be faced with a number of the most important issues which a modern reader of the text identifies – he would envisage the protagonist as a Universal Man, the journey as a spiritual journey, and the goal of the journey as visionary, and he would see that there was, running alongside this journey, a narrative of the progress of the artist. The viewer familiar with Blake's prophecies would notice Blake's adoption of the *Commedia* as a means of giving voice to his own myths in a new way, and would see that Blake had indeed found in the text images, forms and narratives identical with his own, so that he could readily invest them with his own idiosyncratic iconology and symbolism. But the viewer familiar with Blake's prophecies would note also that Blake was moved by Dante's work to extend the visualization of his own prophecies even further. Blake had searched the Bible, and also Milton and the Miltonic poets for a language and a set of metaphors and had developed his system on that basis; in his last work he combined his Biblical and Miltonic system with the new iconology discovered through Dante.

The nineteenth-century viewer and reader of Blake's Dante (a reader being taken as both a knowledgeable viewer of the drawings and a reader of the comments) would be faced with a particularly perceptive view of Dante. Blake was not blinded by his own views of history to such an extent that he saw Dante as a revolutionary prophet of the Risorgimento and of political liberties, as so many other readers of the time did. Neither was Blake blinded by the horrors of Hell into a purely gothic and horrific reading of *Inferno*, and, consequently, of *Purgatorio* and *Paradiso* too. Dante is not the prophet of revolution, but he is a visionary poet – something Cary had not seen, or at least had not used as the guiding notion in his translation. Blake achieved what so few readers of Dante before him had managed to achieve – both a clear view of his own historical distance from Dante, with Dante's belief in the possibility of an ideal Church and State, and a clear view of the context of eternity of the poem. Blake in fact distinguishes Dante the man, with his historically-determined views, from Dante the visionary artist who received and communicated a vast, all-inclusive vision set in the context of eternity.

Blake's illustrations also indicate the status and role of one of the links in the chain of responses to a text. Blake, though a very perceptive and independent reader of Dante, could go beyond the fashionable current view of the poet, but could not possibly free himself from the restrictions of the then current scholarship (the translations and information then available).

At the same time, Blake himself could have contributed little to the course of Dante's role in English literature had his own major contribution to it not achieved some status or acceptance in the Canon. We have seen that Cary's translation marked the end of creative translations of Dante. Henceforth, translators of Dante would be interested purely in the language and prosody of the text and the scholarship surrounding the text. The creative response to Dante withdrew into the personal response of individual poets. Blake's illustrations might have contributed towards suggesting the possibility of a less literal, less referential, more fundamental version of the poem. Alternatively, they might have fallen on deaf ears – or blind eyes. But the question does not even pose itself, for Blake's drawings remained unexhibited and unpublished until the end of his century and the beginning of ours. The Pre-Raphaelites, being interested in Dante, were also interested in Blake, and their work was a step towards the establishment of Dante as a force in English literature. But the particular nature of Dante's presence in modern literature is due rather to the three great poets mentioned in the first chapter of this work – Yeats, Pound and Eliot. And indeed it was Yeats who first published critical comments on Blake's illustrations of Dante. In his *Ideas of Good and Evil* he first discusses 'William Blake and the Imagination', where he states that 'There have been men who loved the future like a mistress, ... William Blake was one of these men'.[49]

To introduce at this point a comprehensive discussion of Yeats' views on Dante or Blake would be beyond the scope of this work, but a few points can be noted. First, Yeats established a sympathetic view of Blake's vision when he explained (in the essay following the one just quoted, on 'Blake's Illustrations to the Commedia') that the word vision in Blake means a 'symbolic image', 'a reproduction of what exists really and unchangeably' – a necessary basis for accepting Blake's prophecies as more than the ravings of a madman. The view that symbolic, imagistic or visionary poetry – in the varying vocabulary (and its varying meanings) of the age – is the only mode which maintains its significance for all times is voiced here by Yeats in his words on Blake and on Dante. Yeats displays the recreative stance of the modern reader faced with the poetry of the past when he disagrees with J.A. Symonds' statement that Dorè, for example, has 'given us something of the world of Dante, but Blake and Botticelli have builded worlds of their own and called them Dante's',

> as if Dante's world were more than a mass of symbols of colour and form and sound which put on humanity ...; as if it was not one's own sorrows and angers and regrets and terrors and hopes that awaken to condemnation or repentance while Dante treads his eternal pilgrimage; as if any poet or painter or musician could be other than an enchanter calling with a persuasive or compelling ritual.[50]

These words firmly state the need for a personal and intimate response to Dante, which is characteristic of the modern view, and which a poet like Shelley had also felt, but which only Blake had consistently used within a ritual of his own. Yeats' words also indirectly suggest the recreative role of the translator or illustrator, which finds fulfilment in the most recent translations of Dante, such as those by Sisson, Mandelbaum, and Phillips, as well as in original poems of, for example, Heaney and Davie (see p. 5 above).

An examination of Blake's illustrations to the *Commedia* explains why Blake's Dante must indeed be recognized as an antecedent of modern views on Dante as a poet of vision, who presents to reader and translator alike images and narratives to be fully internalized, rather than passively studied and imitated. But looking, as we are in the present context, not back to Blake from the present, but on towards Blake from the beginning of the eighteenth century, Blake's illustrations are not an antecedent, but a climax. We have reached a point where Dante has become fully integrated into the Miltonic tradition of visionary poetry, and into the most challenging work of a great English poet and artist.

12

Final conclusion

The aim of this study was to trace some of the forces at work in English poetry in the late eighteenth century and early nineteenth century, using as a tool translations of Dante into English, a procedure justified by the fact that the changes in taste and aesthetics of that period – called a 'revolution' by many scholars – coincided with the steady increase in translations of Dante, which culminated in the great popularity of Dante and his *Inferno*. This aim is fulfilled in the exploration itself, which, alone, can do full justice to the interplay of ideas, their changing meaning, and the different emphasis placed on them. A critic cannot but be satisfied if his work sheds some light on the genesis of poetry written by a poet like Blake, and on the process through which certain notions develop, join with others, and move from the background to the foreground. This process I hope to have demonstrated in my foregoing analysis. Accordingly, I now focus on three other points: the first is concerned with the figure of Dante, the second with the contributions of Dante translations to the Miltonic line of English poetry, and the third with a possible motivation for Dante translations and an interest in Dante at the end of the eighteenth century.

The figure of Dante

Readers of Dante in the last decades of the eighteenth century were accustomed to reading into a text the 'sentiments' of its author, and so were shocked by Dante's lack of high moral values and of mercy. Dante became established as the poet of Hell, grim and unforgiving. He is tainted by his own creation, Ugolino: a gothic hero/villain, symbolizing the collapse of moral and political values, and one human being's oppression of another. The later Dante, envisaged as Byronic hero, is a specific development of this ambivalent gothic and dark romantic hero (see above, pp. 53-4). Steve Ellis has convincingly shown that the figure of the Byronic hero was, in part, based specifically on Dante. But the first translations of the *Commedia* offered little support for such a view of Dante. Boyd's Dante was a visionary poet whose work was philosophical in nature, and as protagonist he was a morally good man. Cary, through stressing the life of Dante Alighieri, played down the grimness of Hell and avoided excesses of passion.

But Boyd, and other translators such as Hayley, used as a model for Dante's poem Young's *Night Thoughts*, and thus fostered the natural association of the two poems in the eyes of eighteenth-century English readers. Indeed, the figure of Dante as grim, unsmiling and unforgiving was, in part, undoubtedly fleshed out in imagery drawn from Young's own protagonist. We have seen that the understanding of Dante's system of justice in terms of passionate allegiance to vengeance was supported by the corresponding belief firmly and directly stated in Young's poem (p. 260 above). A further characteristic of the English Dante is his rejection of levity, and his grim and disdainful stance. As Macaulay's words well suggest, this was a very important aspect of the English view of Dante, a view which ignores large parts of the poem on which it is based:

> We think that we see him standing amidst those smiling and radiant spirits with that scowl of unutterable misery on his brow, and that curl of bitter disdain on his lips, which all his portraits have preserved, and which might furnish Chantrey with hints for the head of his projected Satan.[1]

This Satanic, Byronic Dante could hardly have been suggested by a sentence on Dante's presumed melancholy in Boccaccio's life of Dante, and certainly did not proceed from Cary's presentation of Dante in his 'Life', since he left out this very detail from his report of Boccaccio's life of Dante. But such is precisely the stance that the speaker of the *Night Thoughts* recommended. The protagonist and speaker of the *Night Thoughts* (a visionary figure, who evidently epitomized fashionable attitudes) had urged Lorenzo, and so his own readers, to 'Retire, and read thy Bible to be Gay' (VIII 771). Indeed he had gone so far as to condemn 'Laughter, [which] though never censured yet as Sin,/ ... Is half immoral' (VIII 748-50).

The figure of Dante acquires not only the ambivalent attitudes embodied by Ugolino, but also some of the characteristics of Young's protagonist. Like Ugolino, Dante is morally ambivalent, tormented and tormenting, but in addition, like the protagonist of the *Night Thoughts*, he has journeyed into space and brought back an apocalyptic message of redemption. All this sheds light on the genesis of the figure of the Byronic hero, around which a myth has arisen. Jerome McGann has explained that the Byronic hero is a figure 'cast into antithetical sets of terms whose significance can only be determined by a reader's self-implicating decision', and one which is designed 'to foster ambivalent perspectives'.[2] The present discussion has highlighted some of the forces which added to the complexity and ambivalence of this figure, and which were brought into it by the figure of Dante.

But the nature of this figure can also help explain the popularity of Dante. Dante as protagonist is an egocentric hero whose morally ambiguous behaviour in Hell contrasts strikingly with Dante Alighieri's fight in defence of his country and his role as a poet. It is in *Inferno* that the tension between opposing sets of values is most striking, whereas in *Purgatorio* and *Paradiso* the tension dissolves, an effect intensified in a translation like Cary's. The result of unsolved tension in all poetry, as in *The Seasons*, is that the reader is not led to give the poetry a determinate meaning; on the contrary, the poetry will fit the meanings or the feelings which the reader brings to it. It is probably this tension that contributed to readers' fascination with Dante, and with Hell. Dante's position as an outcast and a political exile no doubt also contributed to establishing Dante's place in English poetry, for it would seem to confirm the emerging view that the true artist is above and beyond society. One important aspect of the culture of the time which helped create this view was that many young writers were such active critics of the existing structure of society, that some were arrested and even imprisoned under the charge of high treason, particularly in the troubled decades of the 1780's and 90's. Blake himself was the victim of such an accusation, although it was soon dismissed as a mistake. Within this context it becomes all the more significant that both Ugolino and Dante had been condemned by their respective systems of government as traitors.

The Miltonic tradition

The early translators of Dante experimented with various literary forms (opera, drama, the cosmic journey, primitivist poetry) and various systems of versification (couplets, *terza rima*, blank verse). Partly, they were attempting to find the English medium most appropriate for Dante, but partly also they were using Dante as a testing ground, where different possibilities could be tried out and experimented upon. The *Commedia* was not a classic and had not been translated before. Dante was therefore a Modern, who could be made to speak the current language of the day.

Hayley placed two basic models in tension: the balanced logic of Pope, and the expansive, emotional tone of the visionary poetry of Young and the eighteenth--century Miltonic style. In his own poem, *The Triumphs of Temper*, these models alternate, but eventually coalesce: Pope provides the language for the daily life of Serena, whereas Dante, Ariosto and Young provide the images and the language for the excursions at night into space and imagination. In Hayley's translation of Dante the two models corresponded to the activity of the writer and the experience of the protagonist, the latter being conveyed in terms of vision, prophecy and, occasionally, the gothic. Thus, rather than reject one mode and extol the other, Hayley tries to manipulate both, merging them, and suggesting the need for English poetry to find a medium which harmonizes both. This medium became the poetry of Milton.

Milton was the final choice of the first translators of a complete *cantica*, and of the whole *Commedia*. Rogers chooses a kind of Miltonic style, but this is limited to the blank verse paragraph. The relatively plain diction of Rogers moves his blank verse away from verbal sublimity and very near to prose, so that the first English version of *Inferno* can be seen to be a literal translation of the original, Rogers' attitude being probably motivated by his antiquarian interest. But Boyd, in his translation of the *Commedia*, brings together the whole range of the Miltonic tradition as it was understood in the eighteenth century. His *Inferno* is a Spenserian allegory, his *Purgatorio* repeatedly echoes various poems by Milton himself (*Lycidas*, 'Il Penseroso', *Paradise Lost*), and his *Paradiso* has the narrative thrust, the biblical gestures, and the spatial sublimity of Young. Boyd's choice of a stanza form similar to Spenserian stanzas stresses the antiquity and formality of the tradition he is writing in – not classical, but rather 'gothic'. This formal choice corresponds to two notions inherent in the Miltonic tradition. First, like Cowper's blank verse, it is a challenge for the poet because it lends itself to the creation of individual effects of great complexity and variety, although it produces an overall effect of simplicity (whereas in the heroic couplet, for example, the work of the writer is very apparent). James Beattie explains his choice of the Spenserian stanza for his poem *The Minstrel* by saying that the measure has 'harmony, simplicity, and variety' (words of a similar kind to those used by Cowper to explain the characteristic beauties of blank verse, see above, pp. 33-4), and that

> it pleases my ear, and seems, from its Gothic structure and original, to bear some relation to the subject and spirit of the poem. It admits both of simplicity and magnificence of sound and of language, beyond any other stanza that I am acquainted with. It allows the sententiousness of the couplet, as well as the more complex modulation of blank verse.[3]

A stanza form with a complex pattern of rhyme could therefore be seen as a reaction against the classical balance of the couplet and its strict fetters, and as a medium in which imagination could range more freely. The second notion inherent in the Miltonic tradition, that poetry is vision and prophecy, is also exemplified by Beattie's poem. For the stanza form he has chosen is well suited to the subject of the verse, this being the presentation of a Minstrel or 'itinerant Poet', a character who, 'according to the notions of our forefathers, was not only respectable, but sacred' (ix). The concept of the poet as prophet or bard makes its appearance here, as it had done in the first words of Boyd's introduction of Dante as a 'venerable old Bard' who had been long neglected (see p. 127 above).

Boyd's translation of Dante is visionary poetry, and it in fact concludes with the poet's soaring to divinity, and becoming 'a human God'.

That Cary saw the *Commedia* as a visionary poem is obvious from its very title of *The Vision of Dante*. But this view remains at the formal level only, and does not animate words and narrative. Cary's use of the Miltonic tradition for his model is, accordingly, limited to the blank verse paragraph and the use of both verbal and spatial sublimity. His version lacks tension, lacks the suggestion of spiritual significance, and lacks the achievement of vision by either the poet or the protagonist. Cary refined the *Commedia* into a poem with a unified, sustained style, and provided a referential apparatus which is informative and learned. He turned the *Commedia* into a 'classic', and consequently his version became the first accepted translation of Dante. But it is probable that Cary was able to adopt the approach he did only because earlier translators, Boyd in particular, had ambitiously struggled to produce an English version of Dante's poetry, thereby drawing it up into English literature.

Certainly 'the truth' of Boyd's translation (as, in Mack's words, it was of Pope's Homer) is in English poetry: and in their creative response to Dante, Blake, Shelley and Byron all follow Boyd's approach, rather than Cary's. So whereas in Cary the *Commedia* found a scholar who attempted to provide the reader with a text which reproduced the surface structure of the original, in Blake the *Commedia* found the first artist who carried to its completion the movement initiated by Gray and continued by Boyd – a movement which aimed to add weight and significance to English visionary poetry, and to interpret and enrich the Miltonic tradition through the adoption of the vision and mythology of Dante. This, therefore, is the process through which Milton and Dante are united so as to offer an overall system to Romantic poetry, as Shelley saw (see p. 1 above).

Dante and Milton contribute to modern English poetry more than a language and a Christian mythology which can be internalized. For although many eighteenth-century poets interpreted the Miltonic tradition as consisting mainly of sublimity (verbal and spatial), a few poets saw Milton as the champion of the freedom of creative imagination, and also of the freedom of religious feelings and political ideals. Milton was a republican and a reformist, yet his poems did not address political questions, but rather the moral, religious and intellectual issues which underlie all political questions. Milton's poems were ambitious experiments which tried to renew poetry, and also to renew religious feelings. This is the Miltonic tradition which poets like Coleridge and Shelley, in adopting Milton's poetic modes, tried to follow. Personal liberty, a belief in civic virtues, and the religious value of human life are the notions which Milton bequeathed to that often radical movement in poetry called Romanticism. And the political and religious mythology attached to these notions is a mythology to which Dante and the *Commedia* contributed heavily, as the example of Blake well shows. Blake's illustrations to the *Commedia* are his own final statement on the powers and duties of the visionary poet, as represented by Dante, Milton, and Blake himself.

Interest in Dante at the end of the eighteenth century

English readers of the *Commedia* at the end of the eighteenth century drew from the poem two points of interest: the figure of Ugolino as a victim of political oppression, and the figure of Dante as a defender of his city-republic and as the spokesman for civil and religious liberty. In Chapter 1 I suggested that Dante could have been discovered by a movement which was as much political as aesthetic, and which ran parallel to the developments taking place in landscape gardening and the fashion for gothic ruins. The early translators of Dante also belong to this movement in various ways.

Early readers of Dante in the eighteenth century were indeed members of the gentry, often just emerging from merchant and artisan classes (see note 2 in Chapter 3). To them Ugolino became an object of pathos, a statue, but also a victim of political persecution, so that his tower became a place of pilgrimage for the young Englishman on his Grand Tour. Furthermore, once Ugolino had been brought into England through the figurative arts and the translation of Richardson, this episode and the rest of the *Commedia* were soon referred to favourably by writers connected, although loosely, with the radical movement, such as Godwin, Fuseli and Blake. Furthermore, the episode and the *Commedia* were translated by writers and scholars who were primitivists and Antiquaries, such as Gray and Rogers. Gray's poems in the tradition of northern mythology and Celtic poetry seem to include Ugolino, like a gothic ruin, in a native English garden. Charles Rogers, the first translator of the *Inferno*, was an Antiquary and a collector, and his translation of Dante could well have been motivated by notions characteristic of the Antiquaries – the desire to bring to light the gothic past, and to give currency to plain, vernacular English.

Boyd had a decided preference for translating Italian authors – Petrarch, Dante, Ariosto. This preference, however, seems more aesthetic than political, since both his translations of Dante and also his introductory essays to these translations are largely philosophical. They do not provide any real evidence to suggest that Boyd was committed to any established movement. Some limited political and social content is to be found, however, in the dedications in his *Inferno* and *Commedia*. These dedications show that he had some knowledge of current events, that the course of his life, which was mainly spent in Ireland, depended in part on the situation there, and that, in sum, he must not be thought of as a simple parson living in the quiet retirement of the English countryside.

The dedication of *Inferno* to the Bishop of Derry is brief, and here Boyd simply extends the moralistic concerns voiced in the introductory essays to social duties. Of the Bishop of Derry's patronage Boyd says that it 'proves your attention even to the humblest claims of industry and application'. He adds:

> To enlightened eyes, it even marks the extensive views of THE PATRIOT, however minute the present object of your attention may seem to vulgar observation. The minds of the multitude are very inadequate to comprehend the liberality of your Lordship's motives: they cannot see, what to you is so evident, that public spirit depends upon an enlargement of sentiment, which can neither be acquired, nor preserved, unless by a due attention to the interests of Learning, and particularly to the Belles Lettres.[4]

Boyd's own contribution to literature cannot but also be a contribution to 'public spirit'. It is hardly necessary to underline the importance of the 1780's in Ireland. Independency was achieved in 1782, and Ireland became a nation: a mood of confidence prevailed, at least among the Anglo-Irish.

By the end of the century, the war with France and the rising of 1798 had shattered this mood. The uncertainty and danger of the new situation is reflected in Boyd's dedication in the *Commedia* (1802). Written at Rathfryland, County Down, where Boyd was vicar, the dedication is addressed to 'Charles William, Lord Viscount Charleville, one of the lords of the Imperial Parliament for the United Kingdoms', with whom Boyd held a further position as chaplain. This dedication is more lengthy than the one to *Inferno*, and most of it consists of Boyd's self-justification at leaving Charleville at the onset of the 'Rebellion', when the Viscount was required to go 'through a country swarming with Foes (whose object was not conquest but extermination), to a remote angle of the Province'.[5] Boyd even obscurely refers to a threatened 'nocturnal assault' on Charleville's garrison, of which the Viscount had received intelligence. Perhaps Boyd left Charleville out of fear, or out of desire to avoid taking sides, or to distance himself, at least in the most turbulent times, from an important member of the Imperial Parliament on a military mission. Be that as it may, Boyd's life was clearly affected by certain current political and military events. His final justification in the dedication is that 'Your Lordship was at the head of a troop of Warriors; I had the charge of a little band of Pilgrims...' (p. v). This reference to 'Warriors' and 'Pilgrims' acquires particular meaning when one remembers Boyd's stress on both the souls in Cantos III and V of *Purgatorio* and also Cacciaguida in *Paradiso* as warriors.

Cary's life was divided between Oxford and London, in the quiet of academic life and the British Museum, the crises of his life being purely private ones –

family sorrows and humiliations at work. Accordingly, he reflects more than Boyd the academic aspect of the preference for Italian over other non-English poetry. Indeed, in an early letter to Anna Seward, Cary makes it very clear to us that his reason for studying Dante is that Dante is one of 'the Italians', who offer a different set of values than the French, and that he himself preferred the former (while Seward, like Lord Chesterfield, preferred the latter):

> I much wonder that you should listen to the idea, that a fondness for Italian poetry is the corruption of our taste, when you cannot but recollect that our greatest English poets, Chaucer, Spenser, and Milton have been professed admirers of the Italians, and that the sublimer province of poetry, imagination, has been more or less cultivated among us, according to the degree of estimation in which they have been held.
>
> The poetry of the French is diametrically opposed to that of the Italians: the latter are full of sublimity, pathos, and imagination; the former of ethics, and descriptions of common life.

Cary sees the poetry of imagination as the native line of English poetry, and places the poetry of judgement in opposition to this. An admiration for the Italians becomes a measure of the role of sublimity and imagination in English poetry. Still at Oxford, Cary notices that 'we have lately condescended to go back a little to our own masters, and to them and the Greek poets we owe all the best writers of our own times, Gray, Warton, Hayley, Mason'.[6]

The brief list of names concluding this statement is remarkable. In the eyes of a student of the time the 'best writers' are not Akenside or Crabbe, but poets connected with the introduction of Dante's poetry into England; and yet the last two, Hayley and Mason, are practically unknown today. Of the names Cary lists, Thomas Warton accepted the place of Poet Laureate in 1785, and both Gray and Hayley were also offered the position (in 1757 and 1790 respectively), but declined to accept it. Hayley preferred to assume the public role of a patron, which was a figure badly needed at the time by republican artists such as William Blake, since they were unsupported by the existing establishment. What Hayley and Mason have in common is that they were both champions of the Gothic Revival, and admirers of England's Saxon past. Poets such as these carried into their own time the political myths which the gothic past contained. Hayley illustrates the concern with national identity in a changed context when, in his *Essay on Epic Poetry* (which presents his translation of Dante as a note), he adds his voice to the chorus discussing that classical genre. He states that 'A national Epic Poem [is] the greatest desideratum of English literature', and suggests that the one poet who seems most suited to fulfil this national task is William Mason (Argument to Epistle V, p. 96). Mason is still known nowadays as the author of *The English Garden*, a poem in which ruins, history and local colour assume clear roles; and he was, in fact, a Whig Antiquary with strong republican tendencies.

So poets such as Gray, Hayley and Mason carried into their own time the political myths which the gothic past contained. I pointed out in Chapter 1 that ruins were ambiguous signs, since they are emblems of the past, but were often read in the eighteenth century as marks of the continuing relevance of England's pre-Norman history, and as emblems of a return to a freedom which had been lost after Saxon times to an absolutist monarchy. Paradoxically, the ruin of a Catholic church or of a Roman temple seen in Italy could be invested with a significance alien to some of its features, and seen as a symbol of the rejection of tyranny within the landscape of England. The figure of Dante assumes a similar significance. Dante was one of the greatest writers of the past: but his exile, the gothicism of his work, and the very fact that his *Commedia* had been ignored make both the author and his work appropriate vehicles for conveying further the political myth of Saxon liberty, which was one of the characteristic innovations of eighteenth-century literature. The barbarism and gothicism in Dante's work, which had been condemned by so many of the established aristocratic judges of literature (including Lord Chesterfield and Anna Seward), were the very features which radical thinkers like Godwin or Fuseli admired. As first suggested on p. 36 above, therefore, translation becomes salvation not only as the justification of the specific vision of an individual poet, who might feel, like Pope, that the poetic genius of Homer is reincarnated in him, but also as a more general ideological gesture, which can in fact be shared by more poets and writers. Such poets and writers find in their chosen original the authority to warrant their own alternative ideology and their alternative literary tradition. Dante as a dark romantic hero, and the *Commedia* as a varying sublime landscape have become part of the English cultural heritage, attracting to themselves the creative imagination of an age, and sanctioning its aesthetic and political myths.

Notes

Notes to chapter 1

1. In 1821 Shelley published his *Defence of Poetry*, in which Dante figures prominently (see further note 3 below). By 1821, moreover, Cary's translation of the *Commedia* had become well known after Coleridge had praised the translation. Coleridge himself mentioned Dante often in his *Biographia Literaria* (1817). Shelley's *Prometheus Unbound* (1820) also shows clear traces of Dantean influence. Byron, too, often referred to Dante or quoted from *Inferno* in *The Corsair* (1814), *Childe Harold's Pilgrimage* (1819), and *Don Juan* (Cantos I and II, 1819); and in 1821 he wrote the *Prophecy of Dante*.

2. That Dante's *Commedia* should have been neglected for so long in England is particularly surprising if one considers, first, that the *Commedia* had been translated quite early into most other European languages, and, secondly, that other Italian writers had been translated very soon after the publication of their works in Italy. The *Commedia* was translated first into Latin (1381), and secondly into Spanish (in 1428 into Castilian and 1429 into Catalan). In 1500 the *Inferno* was translated into French, with the whole *Commedia* appearing in 1550. The first German translation of the *Commedia* only appeared in 1767 (35 years before the first English translation), but the *Monarchia* had been rendered into German as early as 1559, whereas the *Commedia* was the first of Dante's works to be translated into English (followed in 1846 by the *Vita Nuova*).

   Ludovico Ariosto's *Orlando Furioso*, written in 1532, was translated in 'English heroicall verse' by Sir John Harington. The first edition was published in London in 1591 by Richard Field, and was followed by a second imprint by the same publisher in 1607; a third edition, 'revised and amended, with the addition of the author's [i.e. Sir John Harington's] Epigrams' was printed by G. Miller for J. Parker in London in 1634 (the date on the title page is 1633). Harington's translation has been lately reprinted as *Sir John Harington's Translation of the Orlando Furioso*, ed. Graham Hugh, Centaur Press, London, 1962.

   Torquato Tasso's *Gerusalemme Liberata* (1581) was published in England in 1600 in Edward Fairfax's translation, which was regularly reprinted. Five cantos of Tasso's *Godfrey of Bulloigne* had been translated by R. Carew Esq. in 1594. E. Fairfax's translation was entitled *Godfrey of Bulloigne; or the Recoverie of Ierusalem. Done into English heroicall verse*. It was reprinted in 1624. A second edition appeared in 1687, a third edition in 1726, and a fourth edition in 1749. The fifth edition was published in 1817, and was followed by three more, in 1844, 1853 and 1889. As with Harington's translation of Ariosto, the Centaur Press reissued Fairfax's Tasso in 1962.

   Petrarch and Boccaccio had also been translated into English, at least in part – Petrarch most notably by Wyatt and Surrey, and Boccaccio by Chaucer (and here I refer, of course, not to the *Decamerone*, but to the *Teseida* and the *Filostrato*). Chaucer is heavily indebted to the *Filostrato* for his *Troylus*. The influence of the *Teseida* appears in *The House of Fame, Anelida and Arcite*, and *The Parliament of Fowles*, but particularly in the 'Knight's Tale' from the *Canterbury Tales*. For more information and the many questions surrounding the relationship between the work of Boccaccio and that of Chaucer, see Herbert Wright, *Boccaccio in England, from Chaucer to Tennyson*, London, 1957, pp. 59-115. The following information also seems relevant to the present discussion, and is drawn from the same work. The *Decamerone* was first published in an English translation only in 1620 – still very early, compared to the first Dante translation (see Wright, p. 191). But it had already been published in Spain (translated 1429, printed 1496) and Germany (1473 and 1490), and fifty of the tales had been translated by Dirck Cornhert and published in Holland in 1564. However, the very first country to pay attention to the *Decamerone* was France, with a translation dating from 1414 and printed in 1485. This is the translation by Laurent de Premierfait, which was introduced into England by Humphrey, Duke of Gloucester, in 1578 (see Wright, pp. 113, 114). After the first publication in 1620, the translation of the *Decamerone* was reprinted in 1625, 1634, 1657 and 1684. In the eighteenth century, a new translation appeared in 1702, a translation which was 'accommodated to the Gust of the present Age' – which means that the *Decamerone* was deprived of its Proemio and Conclusion, and all the linking narrative between tales was omitted. A second edition was published in 1712, but already by 1741 it was felt that a more accurate translation was needed. Charles Balguy published his more accurate version in 1741, which was reissued in 1762 and in 1774. This suggests that, already towards the middle of the century, ideas about translation were changing, and that there was a desire for greater closeness to the original (see Wright, pp. 261-265). For a discussion of Chaucer's use of and indebtedness to Dante, see Mario Praz, 'Introduction' to Geoffrey Chaucer, *The Canterbury Tales*, Bari, 1961, pp. 61-109. Also see Paget Toynbee's 'The Earliest References to Dante in English Literature', *Miscellanea di Studi Critici*, edita in onore di Arturo Graf, June 1903; in this article Paget Toynbee points out that Chaucer mentions Dante by name no less that 5 times, each time with reference to the *Divina Commedia*, of which Chaucer obviously knew all three parts. Toynbee identifies 19 passages in Chaucer which are translations of or are suggested by passages of Dante's; of these, 9 are from *Inferno*, 6 from *Purgatorio*, and 4 from *Paradiso*.

3. Percy Bysshe Shelley, *A Defence of Poetry*, in *Shelley's Prose, or The Trumpet of Prophecy*, with a critical introduction and notes by David Lee Clark, Albuquerque, 1954, p. 290.

4. I do not analyse the translations by the Wartons because they are in prose. They render the sense of the episode, but cannot shed light on the models used by the translators. Also, I stop analysing translations of individual episodes once a whole *cantica* or the whole *Commedia* begins to be translated.

5. For general information about the translators of Dante, see Gilbert F. Cunningham, *The* Divine Comedy *in English: a Critical Bibliography*, 2 vols, Vol. 1 1782-1900, Vol. 2 1901-1966, Edinburgh and London, 1965-6, pp. 6-10. In the nineteenth century, lawyers seem to have been particularly keen translators of the *Commedia*, accounting for 11 out of 38 translations; they are followed by clergymen (7), scholars (6) and civil servants (4). In the twentieth century (up to 1966), scholars greatly outnumber the rest, accounting for 17 out of 41 translations. They are followed by clergymen (5), and by women translators, lawyers and authors – represented by 4 translators each. The first woman to translate Dante's *Commedia* was Claudia Hamilton Ramsey, whose work, published in 1862-3, has survived, as has her name. But very little else is known of her, not even the dates of her birth or death (Cunningham, p. 108).

6. More specifically, the publication of the *Commedia* by these scholars occurred in the following order: Laurence Binyon, *Inferno* 1933, *Purgatorio* 1938, *Paradiso* 1943; John D. Sinclair, *Inferno* 1939, *Purgatorio* 1939, *Paradiso* 1939; Geoffrey L. Bickersteth, *Paradiso* 1932, the *Commedia* 1955; Dorothy L. Sayers, *Hell* 1949, *Purgatory* 1955, *Paradise* (with Barbara Reynolds) 1962.

7. Few eighteenth-century scholars mention Dante. There is no evidence that Edmund Burke knew Dante, apart from the fact that, according to James Northcote, author of the *Memoirs of Sir Joshua Reynolds* (1813), it was Burke who suggested to Sir Joshua Reynolds the subject of Count Ugolino for his painting (see Paget Toynbee's introduction to *Dante in English Literature from Chaucer to Cary*, 2 vols, London, 1909, p. xxxvii). Whenever I refer to this work I use the form *DEL* for volume 1 and *DEL* II for volume 2, following William De Sua and Steve Ellis. For the interesting story of

the origins of Reynolds' painting, see *DEL* II, p. 135. Samuel Johnson is reported to have mentioned Dante once in his conversation. Only the Wartons discussed Dante at any length.

8. Thomas Carlyle, 'The Hero as Poet', in Sartor Resartus *and* On Heroes and Hero Worship, Everyman's Library, 1908; rpt. 1959, p. 318.

9. John Ruskin, *The Stones of Venice* 1851-3; 7th edn, London, 1896, Vol. 2, Appendix I, Sec. 67, p. 207.

10. Pound's indebtedness to Dante, and the role Dante played within Pound's own art have been the subject of extensive studies. See Giovanni Giovannini, *Ezra Pound and Dante*, Nijmegen, 1961, and James J. Wilhelm, *Dante and Pound: the Epic of Judgement*, Orono, 1974.

11. Eliot, *Dante*, in *Selected Essays*, London, 1932; rpt. 1953, p. 268. Three essays by Eliot are specifically about Dante: the 'Dante' essay written between 1917 and 1920, the longer *Dante* (1929), and 'What Dante Means To Me' (1950). I distinguish the later, longer essay on Dante by italicising the title, following Steve Ellis. The earlier 'Dante' essay was published in *The Sacred Wood* (1920); the edition used here is the 1957 reprint of the seventh edition (1950). In the opening page of *Dante* Eliot claims that '...there is an immense amount of knowledge which ... is positively undesirable' (p. 237), and the argument continues into page 242, in which, for example, Eliot discourages the reader from worrying about identifying the allegorical meaning of the three beasts, since the purpose of the allegorical method is to communicate with 'simplicity and intelligibility'; 'It is really better not to know or care what they mean. What we should consider is not so much the meaning of the images, but the reverse process, that which led a man having an idea to express it in images.' The quotation stating that 'allegory means clear visual images' also comes from p. 242. Concerning Dante's allegory Eliot also says that it is in his use of images that the core of Dante's art resides, because they make up one total system: 'Proceeding through the *Inferno* on a first reading, we get a succession of phantasmagoric but clear images, of images which are coherent, in that each reinforces the last' (p. 246). This process of coherence continues throughout the poem, according to Eliot, who says, in the shorter 'Dante' essay, that the disgust one might feel at Dante's *Inferno* 'is completed and explained only by the last canto of the Paradiso', because 'The contemplation of the horrid or sordid or disgusting, by an artist, is the necessary and negative aspect of the impulse toward the pursuit of beauty' ('Dante', pp. 168-169).

As far as he himself was concerned, Eliot acknowledged in 1950 that 'I still, after forty years, regard his poetry as the most persistent and deepest influence upon my own verse...', and that his debt to Dante 'is the kind which goes on accumulating' ('What Dante Means To Me', in *To Criticize the Critic*, London, 1965, pp. 125, 126). In the same article, he points out the references to Dante in his own poems such as *The Waste Land* and *Little Gidding*, but in fact one could simply list most if not all of Eliot's poems and plays. For the traceable impact of Dante on Eliot, see for example Sean Lucy, *T.S. Eliot and the Idea of Tradition*, London, 1960, p. 154.

12. 'Repertoire' is the word Wolfgang Iser uses to denote the social norms and literary allusions which shape a literary text and create the 'unique relationship between the literary text and "reality"' (p. 72). To be more specific, the repertoire of a text includes 'social and cultural norms' and it also 'incorporates elements and, indeed, whole traditions of past literature' – hence, literary allusions. The two quotations are from pp. 72 and 79 respectively of *The Act of Reading: A Theory of Aesthetic Response*, Baltimore and London, 1978. In fact the whole of chapter three is devoted to 'The Repertoire' (pp. 53-85).

13. One exception was Thomas Gray. The first line of the 'Elegy Written in a Country Churchyard' – 'The Curfew tolls the knell of parting day' – bears a note by Gray himself, in which he simply quotes the Italian of Dante: '"... Squilla di lontano,/ Che paia 'l giorno pianger, che si muore.", Dante, Purg. I.8.' The reference is in fact to *Purgatorio* VIII, 5-6, as pointed out in *DEL*, p. 234. Gray often refers to Dante in his *Observations on English Metre* and in *Observations on the*

Pseudo-*Rhythms*, both works having been written in 1760-61, and published in the *Works of Gray* in 1814. For a brief survey of references to Dante in the eighteenth century see Chapter 3, note 2.

14. George Gordon, Lord Byron, *The Poetical Works of Lord Byron*, London and New York, 1892, p. 284. For Dante and the Byronic hero, see in particular Steve Ellis' chapter on 'Dante as Byronic Hero', in *Dante and English Poetry: Shelley to T.S. Eliot*, Cambridge, 1983, pp. 36-65.

15. Medwin reports that reading Dante drove Shelley to despair of his own potential as a poet; but instead of despairing Shelley, like Byron, attempted to learn from Dante by translating and imitating his work. He translated two sonnets and a *canzone*, besides some passages from the *Commedia*. The impact of Dante is traceable in the *Triumph of Life* (1822) and in *Prometheus Unbound* (1819). The former is an exercise in *terza rima*, as well as a vision modelled on Dante. As for the latter, the influence of Dante on the last act is, in the words of Ellis, not a question of a few references, but of 'nothing less than the whole act itself' (p. 3). For Medwin's memoirs of Shelley (including a version of the opening of *Inferno* and of the Ugolino episode, both done in collaboration with Shelley) see *The Shelley Papers*, 1833, in *DEL* II, pp. 380-389. Also in *DEL* II reference is made to Shelley's translations from Dante: two sonnets and a fragment, a *canzone* from *Convivio*, three short extracts from *Purgatorio*, and the Ugolino episode with Medwin. George Watson claims that Shelley's *The Triumph of Life* was inspired by Petrarch's *Trionfi*, also written in *terza rima* (*The English Petrarchans*, London, 1967, p. 5). For the vision of Shelley's poem as indebted to Dante see for example T.S. Eliot, 'What Dante Means to Me', in *To Criticize the Critic*, p. 127.

Of the three *cantiche*, Shelley preferred the *Paradiso*. In *A Defense of Poetry* he says that 'Shakespeare, Dante and Milton (to confine ourselves to modern writers) are philosophers of the very loftiest power' (p. 281). 'His [Dante's] apotheosis of Beatrice in *Paradiso* ... is the most glorious imagination in modern poetry. The acutest critics have justly reversed the judgement of the vulgar and the order of the great acts of the *Divina Commedia* in the measure of the admiration which they accord to the *Hell*, *Purgatory*, and *Paradise*. The latter is a perpetual hymn to everlasting love' (p. 289).

16. I am referring in particular to Tennyson's 'Ulysses' (written in 1833, published in 1843). Tennyson himself mentions two sources for 'Ulysses' in the notes to the poem: *Odyssey* XI, 100-137, and *Inferno* XXVI, 90 to end of canto. Critics have pointed out Tennyson's indebtedness to Dante rather than Homer. See for example Christopher Ricks' 'Tennyson Inheriting the Earth', in *Studies in Tennyson*, ed. Hallam Tennyson, London and Basinstoke, 1981: 'Tennyson ... takes more from Dante than from Homer' (p. 122). See also A. Dwight Culler, *The Poetry of Tennyson*, New Haven and London, 1977: 'Tennyson's task it was to take the narrative of Dante and the spirit of the Renaissance and Romantic age and make Ulysses into a symbol of the eternally restless, the insatiable element in the mind of man' (p. 94). One can differ as to the interpretation of Ulysses as symbol, but the basic similarity between Tennyson's and Dante's Ulysses remains valid. Culler also points out the role a knowledge of Dante played within the group of Cambridge students known as the Apostles, at the time when Tennyson was there. They 'deplored the narrowness of the university curriculum and determined to explore for themselves the wealth of contemporary literature, philosophy, politics and theology...'. Further, 'they acknowledged a mission, as Merrivale put it, "to interpret the oracles of transcendental wisdom to the world of Philistines and Stumpfits." Among these oracles were Niebur, the Roman historian, ...; Dante, Shakespeare and Calderon; and all the English Romantic poets, except Byron' (pp. 59 and 60).

For his *Sordello* (1840) Browning lifts a character and episode from *Purgatorio*. By recreating a character first presented by a fourteenth-century poet Browning finds a way of dramatizing his own central belief in the evolution of culture and poetry. As Ellis suggests, 'Browning can show how far poetry has come in the contrast between the two Sordellos' (p. 68).

Dante Gabriel Rossetti translated the *Vita Nuova* (1861) and some of Dante's poems; he also wrote poems such as 'Dante at Verona' (1861) and produced many paintings on Dantean topics.

17. W.B. Yeats, 'Ego Dominuus Tuus', first published in *Per Amica Silentia Luna*, 1918; in *Selected Poetry*, ed. Norman Jeffares, London, 1971, p. 77. Of this poem, Richard Ellman says that it represents 'the first synthesis in didactic verse of his [Yeats's] new philosophy' (*Yeats, the Man and the Mask*, London, 1961, p. 201).

18. Seamus Heaney, *Field Work*, London, 1979, pp. 44, 57.

19. Donald Davie, 'Summer Lightning', *TLS*, 25 July 1981, p. 841.

20. This is confirmed by seventeenth-century references to Dante. See for example Henry Reynolds' *Mythomystes, wherein a short survey is taken in the nature and value of true poesy and depth of the ancients above our modern poets* (1632, quoted in *DEL*, p. 118), in which Tasso, Ariosto and Marino are preferred over Dante. Also see George Wither, *The Great Assises Holden in Parnassus*, 1645, where Tasso is made 'Lieutenant Generall of that proud Brigade/ Of the Italian Poets' to the displeasure of Dante and Petrarch (*DEL*, p. 136-7).

21. The low ebb of Dante's fame in Italy is well illustrated by the number of editions which appeared in the different centuries. After the three first editions in 1472, fifteen editions appeared in the rest of the century, thirty editions in the sixteenth century, but only three in the seventeenth. The eighteenth century saw thirty-one editions, and the nineteenth about 320. I am following the counting of Werner P. Friederich, *Dante's Fame Abroad, 1350-1850*, Chapel Hill, 1950, pp. 77-79 (rather than the different counting of Plumptre, which, however, also shows a drastic drop in the seventeeth century). A few more details taken from Toynbee's *Dante Dictionary* (Oxford, 1968) are of interest. The *editio princeps* of the *Commedia* was at Foligno in 1472. The first Florentine edition was in 1481; it was illustrated by Botticelli and contained the commentary of Landino. A Venice edition of 1555 bore for the first time the title of *"Divina" Commedia*.

22. Oscar Kuhns, *Dante and the English Poets from Chaucer to Tennyson*, New York, 1904, p. 107; Werner P. Friederich, *Dante's Fame Abroad*, pp. 81-2; Oswald Doughty, 'Dante and the English Romantic Poets', *English Miscellany*, Vol. 1, Part 3, 1950, pp. 125, 126; Charles Peter Brand, *Italy and the English Romantics*, Cambridge, 1957, p. 228. Doughty says that to state that Dante was brought into fashion in England by Sir Joshua Reynolds' Ugolino is an exaggeration, 'But the picture certainly widened and intensified the growing interest in Dante by its popularity' (p. 129). The importance of the figurative arts is also underlined by Marco Besso, *La fortuna di Dante fuori d'Italia*, Firenze, 1912.

23. Dorothy L. Sayers, 'The Art of Translating Dante', in *Nottingham Medieval Studies*, ed. Lewis Thorpe, Vol. 9, 1965, p. 16.

24. William J. De Sua, *Dante into English*, Chapel Hill, 1964, pp. iii-iv.

25. Giuseppe Baretti spent many years of his life in England and died there. While in England (between 1751 and 1760, and from 1766 till his death in 1789) he published many works in English, among them *A Dissertation upon the Italian Poetry* (1753), in which he translated passages of the *Commedia*, and discussed Dante, attacking Voltaire for his criticism. Ugo Foscolo was a political exile, first in Switzerland and then, from 1816 until his death in 1827, in England. An English connection is traceable very early, since in 1813 he completed the translation of Laurence Sterne's *A Sentimental Journey Through France and Italy* which he had started in France between 1804 and 1806. When in England he wrote a number of critical works on Italian literature, among them *Essays on Petrarch* (with a comparison between Dante and Petrarch), and a commentary on the *Commedia*, of which only one volume was published in his lifetime. He also translated the 'Letter of Dante' at the time of the projected amnesty of the Florentine exiles.

26. See George Walley, 'Coleridge and Vico' in *Giambattista Vico: An International Symposium*, Baltimore, 1967. The information that Coleridge read Vico in 1825 occurs on p. 255. See also René

Wellek, 'The Supposed Influence of Vico on England and Scotland in the Eighteenth Century', ibid., pp. 215-223. Wellek argues that a direct influence of Vico in the eighteenth century in England is non-existent, that he was 'discovered' in the nineteenth century, but that in fact 'only Croce, in 1901, saw the full import of his ideas on aesthetics and poetics' (p. 223).

27. Watson, *The English Petrarchans*. The 'Introduction', from which most of the information in the next paragraph is taken, takes up pp. 1-5.

28. ibid., p. 5.

29. Doughty, p. 126.

30. This is the view of the eighteenth century convincingly discussed by Margaret Anne Doody, *The Daring Muse: Augustan Poetry Reconsidered*, Cambridge, 1985. Doody draws on many examples to illustrate the views that the Augustans wished 'to flow out and expand' (p. 61), that the poets of the age had a 'typical Augustan desire for complexity and inclusiveness' (p. 64), that the Augustans discovered ways of 'including all the world and grabbing all it had to offer' (p. 74), and that the English intellectual climate had particularly an 'interest in inner individual consciousness' (p. 73).

31. Boileau's *L'Art Poetique* was published in 1674, and was translated immediately by Rhymer. See Samuel Monk, *The Sublime: A Study of Critical Theories in Eighteenth-Century England*, Ann Arbor, 1962, p. 29.

32. John Hoole's *Orlando Furioso* went through two more editions in 1799 and 1807; his *Jerusalem Delivered* saw eight editions between 1763 and 1802. It should also be pointed out that Henry Brook translated Books I-III of Tasso's work and that this was published by Dodsley in 1739.

33. See T.R. Steiner, *English Translation Theory 1650-1800*, Assen and Amsterdam, 1975, particularly pp. 1-2.

34. For radicalism and radical societies in Britain at the time see H.T. Dickinson, *British Radicalism and the French Revolution 1789-1815*, Oxford, 1985. Also see Marilyn Butler's 'Introductory essay' to *Burke, Paine, Godwin, and the Revolution Controversy*, Cambridge, 1984. See further notes 1 and 2 to Chapter 11.

35. See Michel Baridon, 'Ruins as a Mental Construct', *Journal of Garden History*, Vol. 5, No. 1, 1985, pp. 84-96. Baridon says, for example, that 'Gothic ruins in eighteenth-century gardens, like classical ruins, had ideological connections with the political myths of the time. To understand what they stood for one has to remember that the Society of Antiquaries ... was then secularizing the "antiquities" of the kingdom' (p. 87). Baridon also points out how, like all myths, the political myth was reflected in the use of ruins in guises which do not follow strict logic, but appear often as paradoxical.

36. For the implications of the choice of the Italian garden, see John Dixon Hunt, *Garden and Grove*, London, 1986, particularly p. 142 and pp. 176-177.

37. Gilbert F. Cunningham's *The Divine Comedy in English* (1965-6) is a bibliography with basic, short, critical introductions to each translation. Werner P. Friederich's *Dante's Fame Abroad, 1350-1850* (1950) is a historical study of translations of Dante in manuscript and print. Oscar Kuhns' *Dante and the English Poets from Chaucer to Tennyson* (1904) is a very brief survey of the area of study specified. Marco Besso's *La fortuna di Dante fuori d'Italia* (1912) is dedicated to illustrators and painters, but uses a few passages in translation. In addition, there are a number of the following: 1. shorter articles, such as Mario Praz, 'Dante in England', *Forum for Modern Language Studies*, Vol. 1, No. 2, April 1965, pp. 99-116; 2. articles and books of more limited scope, such as Oswald Doughty, 'Dante and the English Romantic Poets', *English Miscellany*, Vol. 1, Part 3, 1950, pp. 125-169, and John Arthos, *Dante, Michelangelo and Milton*, London, 1965; 3. monographs on

Dante in relation to a single English author, such as Mary Reynolds' *Joyce and Dante: The Shaping Imagination*, Princeton, 1981. Many short articles have been written on the problems the translator has faced and solved – for these, see the bibliography.

38. Paget Toynbee's *Dante in English Literature from Chaucer to Cary* is a compilation of primary material.

39. Charles Dédéyan published in 1962 *Dante en Grande-Bretagne* (Paris) – mainly a selection of high points from Toynbee's material, duly acknowledged and translated into French. In the preface Dédéyan expressed his intention to continue the survey up to our own day, in subsequent publications. In fact, in 1983 there appeared *Dante Dans Le Romantisme Anglais* (Paris), which focuses on pre-Romanticism and Romanticism. In this last work, although most of the sections only offer information of bibliographical interest and quotations from current texts, some of the sections also contain considerable critical commentary on the material.

40. De Sua, pp. iii-iv; the quotations in this and the following paragraph are from these two pages.

41. John D. Sinclair, 'Preface' to Dante, *The Divine Comedy of Dante Alighieri, Vol. 1: Inferno*, London, 1975, p. 9.

42. A further example of the reductive nature of the chronological approach is provided by De Sua's brief evaluation of the translation by Dorothy L. Sayers. According to De Sua, Sayers' is a 'critical' translation because she chooses one aspect of Dante, such as his 'humour', and attempts to give voice to it; and also, her style is colloquial – an obvious 'critical', modern feature. De Sua contrasts Sayers' theoretical standpoint (she states she will imitate Dante's rhyme scheme and other stylistic features of the translation), which seems a mixture of 'Romantic and critical theories', with her actual translation, which is, according to De Sua, only 'critical'. This is incorrect. To again use De Sua's own framework, Sayers is a modern translator at times, a Romantic at others, and she is even a 'Victorian translator', since, besides being, in places, colloquial, her diction and style are, in other places, archaic, a characteristic of Victorian translators according to De Sua – see his comments on p. 63 regarding the translation by John A. Carlyle (1849).

43. 'without destroying all its softness and harmony'. Dante Alighieri, *Convivio*, I, vii, 14, Bologna, 1966.

44. Luigi Pirandello, 'Illustratori, attori e traduttori', first publ. in *Nuova Antologia* (16 January 1908); in *Saggi*, ed. Manlio Lo Vecchio Musti, Milano, 1939, pp. 227-246. The difficulty of finding a critical approach is mentioned on p. 242.

45. James S. Holmes, 'Describing Literary Translations: Models and Methods', in *Literature and Translation*, eds James S. Holmes, José Lambert, and Raymond van den Broeck, Leuven, 1978, p. 74.

46. In this respect my analysis approaches the area of reception and response studies, and for it I have relied, as a referential frame, upon the ideas on aesthetic response of Wolfgang Iser, particularly as they are developed in his *The Act of Reading*.
   This choice might seem surprising. Of the two major names which cover the field of reception and response studies, the name of Hans Robert Jauss would perhaps seem more appropriate, since it is Jauss who develops a historicist approach to the subject. Moreover, it is true to say that Jauss's survey of the history of literary investigation on the basis of his theory of the change in paradigms – or interpretative norm on the basis of which the litarary canon is defined – would help explain what happens in the eighteenth century (see in particular Hans Robert Jauss, 'Paradigmawechsel in der Literaturwissenshaft', *Linguistische Berichte*, No. 3, 1969, pp. 44-56, as quoted and discussed in Chapter I of Robert C. Holub, *Reception Theory: a Critical Introduction*, London and New York, 1985). But this is exactly the reason why his ideas are less helpful in the present context than those

of Iser. The latter's close analysis of the relations between text and reader and between text and reality results in a system which traces the ways in which the reader encounters in the text 'spots of indeterminacies' as well as the author's encoded strategies, which the reader himself must then attempt to fill in and recreate respectively. Such a system has proved very helpful in a study which, time and time again, comes across the fact that the translator fills in himself what he sees as gaps (which, often, can simply be explained as things he does not understand, due to lapse of time and difference in referential frame) and rewrites in contemporary ways features he thinks he does understand.

47. Throughout this study I use the word 'model' to refer to a writer and his work which serve as a basis for imitation by other writers. The extent and manner of the imitation will be discussed as and when appropriate in the relevant parts of the study.

48. T.R. Steiner, p. 2. Alongside Steiner, I have chiefly relied on Susan Bassnett-McGuire, *Translation Studies*, London and New York, 1985.

49. Joseph Anthony Wittreich jr., 'Opening the Seals: Blake's Epics and the Milton Tradition', in *Blake's Sublime Allegory*, eds. Stuart Curran and Joseph Anthony Wittreich jr., Madison, Wisconsin, and London, 1973, p. 58.

50. Henry Francis Cary, 'Life of Dante', in *The Vision*, 'Albion' edn, London and New York, 1889, p. xxxvi.

51. John Ruskin, 'Of Medieval Landscape', in *Modern Painters*, Vol. 3, London, 1906, p. 223.

52. T.S. Eliot, *Dante*, in *Selected Essays*, p. 243.

53. C.F. Goffis, 'Canto I', in *Lectura Dantis Scaligera*, ed. Mario Marcazzan, Firenze, Vol. 3, 1968, pp. 3-4. 'The sense of the real, which we have admired in the Inferno, is the very nerve of Dante's art, and enables him even in Paradiso to translate a metaphysical reality into forms which are new and concrete ...'.

54. *Ottimo Commento* (about 1334), quoted in A.C. Charity, *Events and their Afterlife: the Dialectics of Christian Typology in the Bible and Dante*, Cambridge, 1966, pp. 228-229. 'Dante presents himself in the common guise of a man ... leaning to sensuality.'

55. Angelo Jacomuzzi, *'L'Imago al Cerchio': invenzione e visione nella* Divina Commedia, Milano, 1968, p. 198. 'If we translate Contini's underlining (Dante protagonist/poet) into the distinction it implies (Dante *protagonist/poet*) we obtain a view which, besides being a necessary criterion of exegesis and a helpful heuristic probe, can also assume the function of an important methodological criterion ...'.

Notes to chapter 2

1. For a recent discussion of classical scholarship in England at the time see C.O. Brink, *English Classical Scholarship*, Cambridge and New York, 1986.

2. Alexander Pope, 'Preface' to his translation of *The Iliad*, *The Twickenham Edition of the Poetry of Pope*, ed. M. Mack, London and New Haven, 1967, 7, p. 116, n. 600. References in the text by Arabic numbers are to Pope's 'Preface'; Roman numbers are references to Mack's 'Introduction' in the same volume.

3. Homer, *The Iliad*, with a translation by A.T. Murray, Cambridge Mass., and London, 1924; rpt. 1971, pp. 36-9. I quote from the English version in this edition:

So he spake in prayer, and Phoebus Apollo heard him. Then, when they had prayed, and had sprinkled the barley grains, they first drew back the victims' heads, and cut their throats, and flayed them, and cut out the thighs and covered them with a double layer of fat, and laid raw flesh thereon. And the old man burned them on billets of wood, and made libation over them of flaming wine; and beside him the young men held in their hands the five-pronged forks. But when the thigh-pieces were wholly burned, and they had tasted of the inner parts, they cut up the rest and spitted it, and roasted carefully, and drew off the spits. Then, when they had ceased from their labour and had made ready the meal, they feasted, not did their hearts lack aught of the equal feast.

4. Homer, *The Iliad*, trans. Andrew Lang, Walter Leaf and Ernest Myers, 1882; first Globe edn 1914; reset and rpt. London, 1930, p. 14.

5. See note 2 to Chapter 1 for an example of the way in which expectations regarding translations had changed around the middle of the eighteenth century.

6. This is in agreement with Mack's views; see his 'Introduction' to Pope's *Iliad*, pp. cxli-cxlii.

7. Henry Home, Lord Kames, *Elements of Criticism*, 1762, quoted in Samuel Monk, *The Sublime*, p. 116.

8. Reuben Arthur Brower, *Alexander Pope: The Poetry of Allusion*, Oxford, 1959, p. 129.

9. Josephine Miles, *The Primary Language of Poetry in the 1740's and 1840's*, Berkeley and Los Angeles, 1950; Miles particularly lists the major words like *bright* replacing *fair*, and *light* and *sun* (and *night*) replacing words such as *nature* and *power*. Such new words reveal the 'shift to implicative particularity', and are 'more inward and more personal' (p. 355). See also pp. 356, 366.

10. Pope's translation of Homer, *The Iliad*, Book XIII, n. xxxix to v. 721.

11. John Dryden, *Dedication of* the Aeneis, 1697; in *Essays of John Dryden*, ed. W.P. Ker, Oxford, 1926, Vol. 2, p. 228.

12. For examples of similar statements of intention, see T.R. Steiner, pp. 39-42. A translator of Horace, Oldham went very far indeed in transferring his original into England; he saw his task as that of putting 'Horace into a more modern dress than hitherto he has appear'd in, that is, by making him speak, as if here living and writing now. I therefore resolv'd to alter the Scene from Rome to London ...' ('Advertisement' to Oldham's imitation of the *Ars Poetica*, 1681, quoted in Hunt, *Garden and Grove*, p. 201).

13. William Cowper, 'Preface' to *The Iliad of Homer*, Vol. 7 of *The Works of William Cowper*, ed. Robert Southey, illus. with engravings by W. Harvey, 8 vols, London, 1854, p. x.

14. Throughout this study I use the word 'style' to refer to the manner of linguistic expression characteristic of a particular writer. The main traits of linguistic expression I take to be sound patterns, vocabulary, and syntactic structures. As Josephine Miles specifies, 'when used in poetry all these [main traits of language] will be formalized in some degree', sound into rhythm and rhyme, vocabulary into 'a special selectivity', syntax into 'the poem's logical structure. The relation between these formalizations helps define the total style' (Miles, p. 167, n. 1). The extent to which I will discuss the style of a particular author or translator will depend upon my criterion of usefulness to the argument of the study.

'Style' is also used, in this study, to refer to the linguistic expression of an author as it is understood at a particular moment in time. The main example of this is the notion of the Miltonic style in the eighteenth century. Havens' *The Influence of Milton on English Poetry* (New York, 1961) is the basis for the notion of the pseudo-Miltonic style as it is used in the present work.

15. C.H. Sisson, 'On Translating Dante', in *The Divine Comedy*, Manchester, 1980, p. viii.

Notes to chapter 3

1. Dorothy L. Sayers, 'The Art of Translating Dante', in *Nottingham Medieval Studies*, p. 16.

2. Toynbee provides the material for the ensuing exploration in the text, especially pp. 120-683 of the first volume of *DEL*. These pages cover the period from Milton to Cary, roughly 1635-1805, listing the brief and less brief comments of 213 readers – of whom 39 between 1635 and 1700. The argument in the text is based on the results of this reading, and often on a selection of the possible quotations. Where appropriate, further references will be provided in a footnote. 7 readers used the term 'gothic' in relation to Dante's work, 9 'satire', and 23 'sublime'. All three terms were used particularly in the second half of the eighteenth century. The first reference to Dante's work as gothic was in John Spence's translation of conversations held in Italy, and was supposedly made by a Dr. Cocchi in 1732; the next reference is in 1764. The generic term 'satire' was first used by Joseph Warton in 1756, and went on being used into the nineteenth century. In view of the argument in the text it should be pointed out that 2 out of the 7 references to 'gothic' actually deny that Dante's work was 'gothic', whereas 'satire' is used as a partial or total description of the *Commedia*.

The real reader of Dante whose comments have been preserved seems to have been the educated person of independent means – often just emerging from the professional or merchant classes. The major artists do not figure prominently in the list. Sir Thomas Browne used Dante's sayings or images as similes in his own writings; while John Dryden, Oliver Goldsmith and Samuel Johnson have passing references to Dante – insufficient to judge to what degree, if at all, they knew him, and even what they thought of his work. Alexander Pope, however, requires a few brief comments.

There is only indirect evidence as to whether Pope knew Dante or not. Owen Ruffhead, author of a *Life of Pope* written in 1769, includes in this work an outline of a projected work by Pope on the schools of English poetry: the first was the school of Provence, the second of Chaucer, the third of Petrarch, the fourth a school of Dante, under which he had listed the 'Mirror of Magistrates, Lord Buckhurst's Induction, Gorboduck – Original of good Tragedy – Seneca (his Model)' (*DEL*, pp. 330-1, 305). Yet it seems that Pope's Italian was weak, and that he knew Dante very little if at all. He could have read him in a French translation, since the *Commedia* had been translated into French already in the sixteenth century, but there is no evidence for this.

Pope used the name of Dante once in his versification of John Donne's fourth satire. Donne's words were:
> ... and a trance
> like his, who dreamt he saw hell, did advance
> It self o'r me: Such men as he saw there,
> I saw at Court, and worse, and more ...(*DEL*, p. 101)

But Pope actually uses Dante's name:

> 'I've had my Purgatory here betimes,
> And paid for all my satires, all my rhymes.
> The Poet's hell, its tortures, fiends and flames,
> To this were trifles, toys, and empty names.
> ...
> There [in Solitude] sober thought pursu'd th' amusing theme,
> Till Fancy colour'd it, and form'd a Dream.
> A Vision hermits can to Hell transport,
> And forc'd ev'n me to see the damn'd at Court.
> Not *Dante* dreaming all th'infernal state,
> Beheld such scenes of envy, sin and hate.'   (Satire iv, ll. 5-8, 187-193; *DEL*, p. 193)

Perhaps the connection of Dante's name with Hell and not the other *cantiche*, with satire, and with vision' might be noted, but as evidence of Pope's knowledge of Dante these verses are very slight.

John Hoole believes that Pope's 'Say, shall my little bark attendant sail,/ Pursue the triumph and partake the gale?', from the *Essay on Man* (Ep. iv), is an imitation of the very opening of *Purgatorio*: 'Per correr miglior acque alza le vele/ Ormai la navicella del mio ingegno,/ Che lascia dietro a sé mar sí crudele' (1783; *DEL*, p. 391; 'To course over better waters the little boat/ of my wit now hoists its sails,/ leaving behind her such a cruel sea'). But surely this, on its own, could be pure coincidence, and provides no proof. Less easy to dismiss are the similarities between various passages of the satires (particularly *Dunciad* II, with the dunces swimming in mud and excrement, and *Dunciad* IV) and scenes from *Inferno*. To claim any direct influence would be pure speculation; still, the similarities would register in the mind of the eighteenth-century reader, who might then recognize passages in *Inferno* as similar to the satires of Pope.

3. Joseph Warton, *An Essay on the Genius and Writings of Pope*, 2 vols, 1756-82; 4th edn London, 1782; facsimile edn Farnborough, 1969, 1, p. 370. Warton describes 'the graceful angles in frontispieces, the spaces between the columns, or the ornaments of the capitals' of Grecian architecture, whose beauty is based on 'the imitation of natural things', and continues: 'Which is indeed, the grand distinction between Grecian and Gothic architecture, the latter being fantastical ....'

4. *Parentalia, or Memoirs of the Family of the Wrens*, London, 1750; facsimile edn Farnborough, 1965. The 'compiler' of *Parentalia*, Wren's son Christopher, reports that his father 'was astonish'd to find how negligent the first Builders had been' although 'They had not yet fallen into the *Gothick* pointed-arch' in the main building of the church. The quotation in the text is from the extract of Wren's own 'Proposal', reported by Wren's son in *Parentalia*, and written early in the year 1666. Still, Wren's son also reports that there was 'great opposition to' the tower being taken down, and 'applications' were made to have the tower simply 'repair'd without deviating from the old Gothick-STILE' (p. 277). The great fire of 1666 prevented the more conservative repairs.

5. In Shaftesbury's *Characteristics* (Treatise I) Palemon is said to be strongly opposed to 'our favourite Novels', clearly described as romances of a gothic kind: 'In short, this whole Order and Scheme of Wit you condemn'd absolutely as *false* and *monstrous*, and GOTHICK; quite out of the way of Nature' (p. 195). In this work, 'gothicism' is synonymous with 'barbarism', both meaning 'savage' and 'primitive', and anything primitive causes 'Discord and Confusion', as the second part of the same Treatise says (p. 234). In the third Treatise, 'Advise to an Author', Shaftesbury says 'So is Symmetry and Proportion founded still in Nature, let Man's Fancy prove ever so barbarous, or their Fashion ever so Gothick in their Architecture, Sculpure, or whatever other designing Art. 'Tis the same case, where *Life* and MANNERS are concern'd. *Virtue* has the same fix'd standard. The same Numbers, Harmony, and Proportion will have place in MORALS' (p. 353). This is all from the first volume of the *Characteristics of Men, Manners, Opinions, Times*, 3 vols, 1711; 2nd rev. edn 1714; 5th edn Birmingham, 1773. The *Charactericstics* includes various treatises published previously, 1699-1710. Dryden, also, saw 'gothic' as synonymous with 'barbaric' and reinforced the comparison between figurative arts and literature: 'The Gothic manner, and the barbarous ornaments, which are to be avoided in a picture, are just the same with those in an ill-ordered play' ('A Parallel of Poetry and Painting', in *Essays of John Dryden*, ed. Ker, Vol. 2, 146).

6. Hester Piozzi, *British Synonymy*, 1794, in *DEL*, p. 449. Often, Dante's sayings (that is, a few lines or, more usually, a tercet from his poem) were used as comments on social or political truths. Of the 39 readers mentioned in note 2 above who briefly mention Dante between the years 1635 and 1700, 4 refer to Dante in this way – some of them a number of times – in their political works. A later example is E. Farneworth, who, in his *The Works of Nicholas Machiavel*, 1762, twice quotes Dante to illustrate a political truth – in one case, the rarity of hereditary virtue (*DEL*, p. 326).

7. Anna Seward, Letters iii, quoted in Samuel Monk, *The Sublime*, Ann Arbor, 1962, p. 214.

8. In this letter she refers to the plot of *Inferno*: 'Then the plan is most clumsily arranged: Virgil,

and the three talking quadrupeds, the guides; – an odd association' (*DEL*, p. 401). It would indeed be a very odd association, but it is, of course, of Seward's own making; nor is it true that the three animals ever talk.

9. Samuel Monk, *The Sublime*. Marjorie Hope Nicolson, *Mountain Gloom and Mountain Glory*, New York, 1963.

10. See John Baillie, *An Essay on the Sublime*, 1747; rpt. Los Angeles, 1953.

11. *DEL*, p. 317: 'His similes are in the greatest part very beautiful, and purely the product of his genius. His descriptions are extremely vivid and highly original, and his sublime is the result of the excellence and depth of the truth of his thoughts, which he expresses in the simplest words. And this is the sublime praised by Longinus. The current exception that the superficial critics of Italian literature make of Dante's style is that it is harsh and obscure. Obscurity, in varying degrees, will always be found in all ancient authors, if one does not first learn the facts they are writing about.'

12. in *Lettres Chinoises, Indiennes, et Tartares à M. Pauw par un Benedictine*, 1776; *DEL*, p. 212.

13. William Godwin says 'Dark as was the age in which he studied and wrote, unfixed and fluctuating as were the then half-formed languages of modern nations, he trampled upon these disadvantages, and presents us with sallies of imagination and energies of composition, which no past age of literature has excelled, and no future can ever hope to excel. ...He [Dante] is not infected, in his immortal part, with the weakness of his age.' (in *Life of Geoffrey Chaucer*, 1803; *DEL*, p. 641-2). An anonymous writer in the *Annual Register* of 1764 denies that Dante is gothic, because he avoids 'the mere trappings of composition and Gothic minutiae' and chooses instead 'a just simplicity'. His assessment is that, because of this choice, Dante is 'the father of modern poetry' (*DEL*, p. 327). In 1790 Thomas Penrose, in *A Sketch of the Lives and Writings of Dante and Petrarch*, underlines the barbarism of past ages, but points out that 'Yet many years before literature received this very valuable acquisition [printing] ... flourished Dante, the Ennius, and father of Italian poetry. After seven hundred years of ignorance and darkness when learning, immured in the cloister, and circumscribed to narrow limits, was uselessly employed in metaphysical disquisitions, this meteor of genius, as it were, blazed out with redoubled lustre' (*DEL*, p. 460). Here Penrose applies to Dante images perhaps derived from Akenside's *The Pleasures of the Imagination* dating from 1744:

> ... Alas! how faint,
> How slow the dawn of Beauty and of Truth
> Breaks the reluctant shades of gothic night
> Which yet involve the nations! Long they groan'd
> Beneath the furies of rapacious force ...
> ... As long immur'd
> In noontide darkness by the glimmering lamp,
> Each Muse and each fair Science pin'd away
> The sordid hours: while foul, barbarian hands
> Their mysteries prophan'd, unstrung the lyre,
> And chain'd the soaring pinion down to earth.
> At last the Muses rose, and spurned their bonds,
> And, wildly warbling, scatter'd, as they flew,
> Their blooming wreaths from fair Valclusa's bowers
> To Arno's myrtle border and the shore
> Of soft Parthenope.   (bk ii, ll. 4-8, 13-23, *DEL*, p. 241)

The place names in the last lines are specified by Akenside in footnotes as referring to 'Petrarcha', Dante and Boccaccio, Sannazzaro and Tasso (*DEL*, p. 241).

14. Joseph Warton, *An Essay on the Genius and Writings of Pope*, 1, p. 266.

15. Nicolson, p. 358.

16. Thomas Babington Macaulay, 'Criticisms on the Principal Italian Writers. No. I. Dante', *Knight's Quarterly Magazine*, January 1824; in *Miscellaneous Writings*, London, n.d., pp. 40-41.

17. Joseph Warton, *An Essay on the Genius and Writings of Pope*, 1, p. 193.

18. Thomas Warton, *The History of English Poetry*, 1781; new edn, 4 vols, London, 1824, 4, p. 64. The comparison with Shakespeare and the Book of Job occurs on p. 71, the mention of the gothic painters on p. 74, the reference to Francesca on p. 67, and to Ugolino on p. 72.

19. *Inferno*, XVIII, 112-113:
    ... and then, down in the ditch,
    I saw people plunged in excrement
    which seemed as if it had flowed out of a cesspit;
    and while I was searching down there with my eyes,
    I saw one so covered with shit
    You couldn't see whether he was layman or cleric.

20. Alexander Pope, *Collected Poems*, Everyman's Library, 1965, pp. 334-5.

21. This is what Martin Price says concerning the use of excrement in Augustan literature: 'The irony turns on the crucial distinction between poetry (or rhetoric) as a making and poetry as the secretion or evacuation of pent-up feeling; between poetry as articulation of meaning and poetry as expressive noise; between poetry as 'issue' (the creation of new living creatures) and poetry as "excrement"'. Martin Price, *To the Palace of Wisdom*, London, 1964, p. 206.

22. ibid., p. 131.

23. The first references to Dante have to do with anecdotes, figurative arts, general history, manuscripts and editions of his works being brought into England. Of the 39 readers, 15 refer to Dante in the course of surveys of literary history, usually in combination with Petrarch and Boccaccio; 4 quote 'sayings' of Dante; 8 mention visits, generally to Dante's tomb in Ravenna or portrait in the Duomo of Florence; 4 refer to lists of manuscripts and printed editions of most of the works of Dante; 2 make mention of the history of Florence and northern Italy; 3 include translations and/or quotations of lines from Dante, one being Thomas Heywood's quotation and translation of 27 lines from *Inferno* 33 (the description of Lucifer, in *The Hierachie of the Blessed Angels*, 1635, *DEL*, pp. 129-30) – which makes this the longest quotation in Italian and translation of a passage before Jonathan Richardson. The remaining two are Sir Thomas Browne (see note 2) and Jeremy Collier, who wrote a 'Life of Dante', based on works by Villani and Petrarch, which was actually published in 1705. The emphasis in these works is therefore on historical facts, though in addition to battles around Florence we are also informed that Dante was a kleptomaniac, and that he had two mistresses and three wives.

24. Iser, *The Act of Reading*, p. 97.

25. .... And I did not open them,
    and it was a courtesy to treat him ill.

26. So, in a letter to H.F. Cary Anna Seward says 'Were you ever struck by the presumptuous malice of that mind which could delight in suggesting pains and penalties at once so odious and so horrid? The terrible graces of the Inferno lose all their dignity in butcherly, grid-iron, and intestinal exhibitions, which become fatal to our esteem for the contriver' (*DEL*, p. 403). She also reports to Cary a conversation with Sir Walter Scott, in which the latter expressed his dislike for Dante's

'personal malignity and strange mode of revenge, presumptuous and uninteresting' (*DEL*, p. 409).

27. There are many comments on Dante and his work in Godwin's *Life of Geoffrey Chaucer* (1803). The following is from Vol. 1, Ch. xi: 'Dante is one of those geniuses who in the whole series of human existence most baffle all calculation, and excite unbounded astonishment. ... His grand poem embraces the whole compass of human invention'. Particularly interesting in the context of ideas on the gothic are the following comments: 'No poet has shown himself a greater master of the terrible, of all which makes the flesh of man creep on his bones,' which makes one think of the gothic of the 'horrid' novels; but an awareness of the existential issues presented by Dante, and even of a didactic function of Dante's poem become obvious when Godwin continues by saying 'and persuades us for the moment to regard existence, and consciousness, and the condition of human beings, with loathing and abhorrence. Dante exhibits powers, of which we did not before know that the heart of man was susceptible, and which teach us to consider our nature as something greater and more astonishing than we had ever been accustomed to conceive it' (*DEL*, pp. 641-2).

28. G.R. Thompson, 'Introduction', in *The Gothic Imagination: Essays in Dark Romanticism*, Washington State U.P., 1974, p. 6.

29. It is odd that Horace Walpole should not have recognized what is superficially a technique he had also used. The huge size of Lucifer makes of him a mirror image of Ugolino, and in its distorted size in fact reveals the true import of the latter's damnation, while his lack of speech deprives him of the possibility of hiding his degeneration under some pathetic tale. Similarly in Walpole's *The Castle of Otranto* the giant ancestor appearing in the castle is supposed to show in proportion the degeneration of his descendant.

30. I am referring to *The Gates of Paradise*, 1793; see further Chapter 11 below.

31. Besso, p. lxx.

32. quoted in Monk, p. 78.

Notes to chapter 4

1. This is not surprising either, since the idea of the closeness of the sister arts in the eighteenth century is not new. In fact, it was early in this century that Prof. Lovejoy circulated his beliefs that the interest in irregularity – which was to grow into a taste for the irregular and, eventually, for the most irregular of shapes and forms, such as rocks and mountains – began with landscape gardening and interior decoration. When the 'natural' garden became more appreciated than the 'artificial' garden, and when the interest in *chinoiseries* introduced, as Lovejoy claims, the Chinese principle of asymmetry, we probably have two indications that the change in taste, which could not be accommodated yet in literature, was, however, finding expression in other fields. The increased pictorial quality of eighteenth-century poetry, which has been argued in various quarters, would then suggest a channel of communication from one art to another. See Arthur O. Lovejoy, 'The First Gothic Revival and the Return to Nature', *Modern Language Notes*, XLVIII, 1932, pp. 419-446. See also 'The Chinese Origin of a Romanticism', *Journal in English and Germanic Philology*, Vol 32, 1933, pp. 1-20. Both articles have been reprinted in Arthur O. Lovejoy, *Essays in the History of Ideas*, Baltimore and London, 1948; rpt. 1970. This is the text I have used. Actually, Marjory Hope Nicolson points out in a note that according to some there was no such principle of asymmetry in China (Nicolson, note p. 317).

2. Monk, p. 186.

3. quoted in Monk, p. 175.

4. ibid., pp. 177, 178.

5. Jonathan Richardson suggests that the bas-relief was actually by Michelangelo when he says 'Michelangelo Buonarroti ... goes on in a *Bas-relief* I have seen in the hands of Mr *Trench*.'. See Jonathan Richardson the Elder, *Two Discourses* [including I: 'an Essay ...', and II: 'An Argument in behalf of the Science of a Connoisseur wherein is shewn the Dignity, Certainty, Pleasure and Advantage of it'], London, 1719, p. 32. It is in 'II' that the Dante translation and the related discussion occur. Further references in the text are to the reprint of 'II' in *The Works of Jonathan Richardson (the Elder)*, London 1773. This edition differs from the first only typographically.

6. Giovanni Villani, *Cronica*, VII, 121, as quoted and translated by Charles Singleton, *The Divine Comedy*, Vol. 1 *Inferno*, Part 2 Commentary, Princeton, 1980, pp. 608.

7. He raised his mouth from the savage meal,
    that sinner, wiping it on the hair
    of the head he had spoiled behind.
Then he began: "You will have me renew
    a desperate grief, which presses on my heart,
    Even to think of it, before I speak.
But if my words are to be seed
    that will bear fruit of infamy to the traitor I gnaw,
    You shall see me speak and weep at the same time.
I do not know who you are, nor by what means
    you have come down here; but when I hear you
    you seem to me Florentine.
You have to know that I was Count Ugolino,
    and this is the Archbishop Ruggieri:
    now I will tell you why I am such a neighbour to him.
That as a consequence of his ill devices,
    trusting him, I was taken
    and then killed, there is no need to tell you;
But what you cannot have heard,
    that is, how cruel my death was,
    that you shall hear, and you will know if he has done me wrong."

8. Modern standard editions and translations do not generally quote this alternative reading (for example Sapegno, Tommaseo, d'Ovidio, Singleton), but Petrocchi mentions a number of codices and manuscripts with the reading 'lume' or 'leuie', and adds that this reading had its supporters but 'il Moore esaurintemente conferma la genuinità di "luce"', in G. Petrocchi, *La Commedia secondo l'antica volgata*, Vol. I, Milano, 1966, p. 255.

9. "When a small ray of sunlight made its way
    into that doleful prison, and I saw
    on four faces my own look,
I bit both my hands for grief;
    and they, thinking I did it because I wanted
    food, without any hesitation rose
and said: 'Father, it would hurt us far less
    if you ate of us; you clothed us with
    this miserable flesh, and you can strip it off.'
Then I calmed myself, not to make them more unhappy;
    that day and the next we stayed all silent:

alas, hard earth, why did you not open?"

10. Thomas Gray, 'Dante. Canto 33, dell'Inferno', probably written 1737-40, first published in *Works*, ed. Gosse, 1884; rpt. in *The Complete Poems of Thomas Gray*, eds H.W. Starr and J.R. Hendrickson, Oxford, 1966, p. 63. Also in *DEL*, p. 234.

11. Thomas Gray, 'The Descent of Odin', ibid., pp. 32-4.

12. Thomas Gray, 'The Fatal Sisters', ibid., pp. 29-31.

13. Gray's translation of Ugolino cannot have contributed directly to Dante's fame in England, since it was first published only in 1884. Indeed, Gray's published correspondence bears no reference to his showing his translation to any friend. However, many poems tentatively identified were referred to in the letters as having been shown in particular to Thomas Warton and Horace Walpole. Another frequent correspondent was the poet Mason. Gray did refer to Dante in his correspondence, as well as in other works of his (see note 13 to chapter 1). But Gray's own note to his very popular 'Elegy in a Country Churchyard' would, of course, popularize the name of Dante and the specific verse quoted. See *Correspondence of Thomas Gray*, eds. Paget Toynbee and Leonard Whibley, 3 vols, Oxford, 1935; rpt. 1971.

14. Earl of Carlisle, *Poems ... by the Earl of Carlisle*, 1773; as quoted in *DEL*, pp. 337-8.

15. Francesco de Sanctis, *Quattro saggi danteschi*, Napoli, 1903, p. 82. The stance of de Sanctis has been traditionally termed 'romantic', and he is partly followed in it by d'Ovidio, Marcazzan and others. There are other, more modern and interesting voices, such as that of Vittorio Russo. In his article 'Il "dolore" del conte Ugolino' he argues for a more detached reading, and calls the romantic school too sentimental. He sees, with some reason, violence and bestiality as the core of Ugolino, and all other elements of the episode as a function of this core. This would explain, he says, why the children only appear so late, just at the point where they exacerbate the father's grief. To further explain the nature of the 'dolore', he quotes Seneca (*De Ira*), San Tommaso (*Summa Teologica*) and others to prove that 'dolore' is not sorrow but wrath, which, as San Tommaso says, comes of fear and causes vengeance and 'augmentum irae quandoque ... ultra procedit, usque ad impediendum motum linguae et aliorum membrorum exteriorum'. In this way Russo explains Ugolino's immobility and silence. The contrast between the different readings is highlighted by the respective choices of de Sanctis and Russo as the climax of the episode. De Sanctis selects the moment in which Anselmo says 'Tu guardi padre, che hai?' and says 'E se un pittore dovesse scegliere una attitudine sintetica che ti ponesse avanti i tratti sostanziali di questa poesia, sarebbe quest'essa: perché qui sei proprio al momento decisivo del racconto: ed hai già nell'attitudine del padre e de' figli tutti i "motivi" del piú alto patetico' (p. 97). Russo denies that the creation of pathos was Dante's intention, and chooses as climax of the episode the moment when Ugolino bites his hands – 'nella rappresentazione del gesto iracondo'. Two points should be made, as far as the present work is concerned. First, the romantic reading probably lays too much stress on the pathetic, on Ugolino as father, and in general on the tender feelings expressed in the episode, but it cannot be denied that all such notions are indeed present in the episode. Russo lays the emphasis on Ugolino himself, seeing as the main point of the episode Ugolino's punishment, and seeing his life in Hell as characterized by bestiality and vengeance. But this still does not contradict the presence of tenderness in the episode. However (and this is the second point of interest here) one must also realize that in the English translations, until very recently, it is the romantic reading that predominates. The quotations of Russo were from V. Russo, 'Il "dolore" del conte Ugolino', in *Atti del convegno di studi su Dante e la Magna Curia*, Palermo, 1967.

16. Mario Marcazzan, 'Canto XXXIII', in *Lectura Dantis Scaligera*, Firenze, 1967-68, Vol. 1 1967, p. 1168.

17.   And, as bread is devoured for hunger,

so the one on top set his teeth in the other,
at the place where the brain joins the nape of the neck.

18. See de Sanctis, p. 95: 'La poesia comincia, e ve ne avvedete alla stessa solenne ed epica intonazione del verso'.

19. Marcazzan, p. 1174.

20. Natalino Sapegno, *La Divina Commedia*, Vol. 1 *Inferno*, Firenze 1981, p. 362, note 1.

21. Marcazzan, pp. 1175-6: 'There is nothing in the text to contradict those readers who point out the horror of the details in the opening of the canto ...; but the movement from the first to the second tercet (from the remains of the atrocious spread to the silent and firm gestures, to the word which redeems that abyss of misery and annihilates that horror) has a poetic and human breath which has great power.'

22. *Purgatorio*, XI, 1-21:

"O padre nostro, che ne' cieli stai,
  non circunscritto, ma per più amore
  ch'ai primi effetti di là su tu hai,   3
laudato sia 'l tuo nome e 'l tuo valore
  da ogni creatura, com'è degno
  di render grazie al tuo dolce vapore.   6
Vegna ver noi la pace del tuo regno,
  chè noi ad essa non potem da noi,
  s'ella non vien, con tutto nostro ingegno.   9
Come del suo voler li angeli tuoi
  fan sacrificio a te, cantando osanna,
  così facciano li uomini de' suoi.   12
Dà oggi a noi la cotidiana manna,
  sanza la qual per questo aspro diserto
  a retro va chi più di gir s'affanna.   15
E come noi lo mal ch'avem sofferto
  perdoniamo a ciascuno, e tu perdona
  benigno, e non guardar lo nostro merto.   18
Nostra virtù che di leggier s'adona,
  non spermentar con l'antico avversaro,
  ma libera da lui che sì la sprona."   21

"Our Father, which art in heaven,
  not circumscribed, but by the greater love
  you have for your first creation on high,
praised be your name and worthiness
  by every creature, as it is appropriate
  to give thanks to your sweet effluence.
May the peace of thy kingdom come to us,
  for we cannot reach it of ourselves,
  if it does not come, for all our striving.
As your angels of their own will
  make sacrifice to you, singing Hosanna,
  so let men also make of theirs.
Give us this day our daily manna,
  without which, through this harsh desert,
  he who tries hardest to advance, goes backward.

And as we forgive everyone the wrong
  that we have suffered, may you also forgive us
graciously, and have no regard to our merits.
Our strength, which is easily overcome,
  do not put to the test with the old adversary,
but deliver us from him who spurs it so."

23. Dorothy L. Sayers, 'The Art of Translating Dante', in *Nottingham Medieval Studies*, p. 18. The statement concerning *terza rima* occurs in Sayers' 'Introduction' to *Hell* (Vol. 1 of *The Comedy of Dante Alighieri*, Penguin 1977, p. 56.

Notes to chapter 5

1. Byron, George Gordon, Lord Byron, *English Bards and Scotch Reviewers*, 1808, in *The Poetical Works of Lord Byron*, London and New York, 1892, pp. 80-81.

2. Quoted in Donald Reiman's 'Introduction' to *William Hayley*, New York and London, 1979, p. viii. This volume prints in photo-facsimile four poems by Hayley, including *The Triumphs of Temper* with Hayley's own 'Preface', and the *Essay on Epic Poetry* with the notes, in which is to be found the translation from Dante. References to the *Essay* and to *The Triumphs* are to this edition, unless otherwise stated. In his introduction, Reiman collects various pronouncements on Hayley by contemporary and later writers, to which I will refer. References to Reiman will be to the introduction, and references to *William Hayley* to the poems and other primary material in the volume.

3. Reiman, p. xiv.

4. William Hayley, 'Preface' to *Plays of Three Acts*, London, 1784. Here Hayley opens the 'Preface' by saying that 'As the following Plays were intended only for the private theatre, I have been tempted by that circumstance to introduce a kind of novelty into our language, by writing three comedies in rhyme.' He continues: 'The Antiquarian, indeed, may remind me that Gammer Gurton's Needle ... with other comic productions of that rude period, was written in rhyme; and possibly some fastidious enemies of that Gothic jingle, as they affect to call it, may consider the present Publication as nothing more than a relapse into the most barbarous mode of dramatic composition...'. This is all on p. ix. Hayley concludes his 'Preface' by returning to the idea of novelty, since the publication of the three plays arose from his wish 'to introduce a striking, and [he trusts] not blameable, variety into the amusements of English Literature' (p. xv).

5. *Essay on Epic Poetry*. The argument of 'Epistle I' is on p. 2 (2 pages before the marked page 4); the reference to the 'inborn vigour' occurs in 'Epistle I', l. 291; the reference to 'daring/ Dante' occurs in 'Epistle III', ll. 81-82; and the reference to the new province for epic poetry is to be found in 'Epistle V', ll. 57-8.

6. William Hayley, 'Introduction' to *The Triumphs of Temper*, 1781. Unless otherwise stated, references in the text will be to this, the first, edition (reprinted in Reiman). However, occasionally I will refer to additions or changes made in later editions; more specifically, I compare the first edition to the later edition published in Paris in 1804.

7. Martin Price, p. 164.

8. I will have to leave Hayley's indebtedness to Ariosto aside. It is possible that the narrator's stance is partly in imitation of Ariosto's – who seems to mingle irony with naive admiration for characters and issues. Also, the movement from a hell in a cave, then to a garden and further upwards to

heaven seems similar to Astolfo's journey in Canto XXXIV of the *Orlando Furioso*. In addition, the attempt to flow from one topic to the other with speed and grace seems an attempt to imitate Ariosto. In all three cases, however, Hayley falls well short of Ariosto's art. I will not, however, move any further into this additional dimension of Hayley's poem.

9. The first is the entrance to Spleen's 'dome', similar to Hell's gate, in lines 53-64; the second is the protagonist's first experience of Hell, with the wailings of the damned, ll. 67-78; the third is the arrival of Charon, ll. 139 ff.; and the last is the comparison of Serena's fears with Dante's, ll. 180-7. Before all these, however, Toynbee draws attention to the motto Hayley placed on the title page of the poem, which is from Dante's *Inferno* (ll. 61-63):

'O VOI CH'AVETE GL'INTELLETTI SANI
MIRATE LA DOTTRINA, CHE SI ASCONDE
SOTTO' IL VELAME DEGLI VERSI STRANI.
Dante, Inferno, Canto 9.'

10. *Purgatorio*, XXIX, 106-108, 113-14:
Lo spazio dentro a lor quattro contenne
  un carro, in su due rote, triunfale,
  ch'al collo d'un grifon tirato venne.   108

...
  le membra d'oro avea quant'era uccello,
  e bianche l'altre, di vermiglio miste.   114

The space between the four of them contained
  a triumphal car upon two wheels,
  which came drawn on the neck of a griffin.

...
The parts in which he resembled a bird were gold,
  the rest of him was white mingled with red.

11. The quotations in this paragraph are not in the first edition of *The Triumphs*. In the first edition, the first group of the 'fav'rite Females' consists of women who were betrayed by their husbands, but managed to 'Lure the lost wanderer back to faithful bliss' (l. 530). They even 'Rear'd the young offspring of a rival fair' (l. 534) and, in short, 'These gentle wives still gloried to submit' (l. 545). The second group is made up of those women who 'Gave up those joys which youthful hearts engage,/ To watch the weakness of parental age' (ll. 561-562). The third group (to which the lines quoted in the text belong) is missing in the first edition, in spite of the fact that 'the leading Spirit' had expressly mentioned 'yon three groups' (l. 515). I assume that the addition in the later edition restores a missing passage.

12. The reference is to one of the most controversial figures of the eighteenth century, the fourth Earl of Chesterfield. Specifically, it points to one of his most admired speeches, delivered in 1737, which was an attack on the restrictions imposed on theatres by Walpole's Licensing Bill – which in its turn was an attempt to stop attacks on Walpole himself by, among others, Fielding. Chesterfield was a rich, aristocratic Whig, and remains famous partly for his 'Letters' to his natural son, which, collected in a work, became a kind of manual of good manners. Seen by some as 'strict in manners, but often loose in morals' (F.L. Lucas, *The Search for Good Sense: Four Eighteenth Century Characters*, London, 1958, p. 131), Chesterfield seems a model for Serena's father, but adds a further twist to the didactic meaning of the poem. Perhaps it is worth mentioning that Chesterfield advised Philip not to read Dante: '...I could never understand him; for which reason I had done with him, fully convinced that he was not worth the pains necessary to understand him' (see Letter cxxxii to Philip Stanhope, dated February 8 1750, in *DEL*, p. 255).

13. Alternatively, the reference could also be to *The Patriot*, a satirical poem by Anstey which appeared in 1767. Thomas Gray mentions it in his correspondence; it was a Pindaric Epistle, aimed chiefly, in Gray's opinion, at Cambridge University. One passage, one of the few Gray enjoyed, describes a great ball. See letter dated 24 December 1767, in *Correspondence of Thomas Gray*, 3, p. 985.

14. Leigh Hunt, *The Feast of the Poets*, 1815, quoted in Reiman, p. viii.

15. William Hayley, 'Notes to the Third Epistle', *Essay on Epic Poetry*, p. 173. The 'Notes to the Third Epistle' take up pp. 116-173 of the *Essay*. Here, Hayley records a history of Dante, taken mainly from Boccaccio, including the description of Dante that will become famous. He further includes the translation of a sonnet, of which I will only quote the first line: 'Guido, vorrei che tu, e Lappo (sic) ed io...' is rendered as 'Henry! I wish that you, and Charles and I...'. After this introduction, the translation follows.

16. The measure employed by Dante, *terza rima*, lends itself to opposing effects. In *Inferno*, Dante often uses the first effect by making his tercets closed, particularly when describing Hell itself. In this manner, he reproduces in the verse the feeling of imprisonment of Hell itself. On other occasions, and particularly in the other *cantiche*, Dante uses the linking middle line of *terza rima* (aba, bcb, cdc, etc.) to stress the continuous flow, which is the second effect to which *terza rima* lends itself. One should stress that the effect of enclosure is created by the very fact that the thought is made to begin, grow and close within one tercet, and has little to do with punctuation; obviously, the punctuation of the text is not necessarily Dante's own, but the sense of the tercets is clearly either closed or continuous. Also, enjambments are used between tercets when the effect aimed at is one of continuity.

17. In the middle of the journey of our life
    I found myself within a dark wood,
    for the straight way was lost.
    Ah, how hard it is to tell
    of that wood wild and harsh and vigorous
    which even to remember renews the fear.
    It is so bitter, death itself is hardly more so;
    but to treat of the good I found there
    I will speak of the other things I saw there.

18. She placed such heaviness on me
    with the fear, which issued from her looks,

19. before my eyes a man a man offered himself to me,
    one who seemed faint from long silence.

20. G. Ungaretti says that 'fioco é vocabolo necessario' (the word needed is 'faint') because the sound suggests distance and therefore increases the sense of perspective, while the light which illuminates the figure is also faint. 'Canto I', in *Letture Dantesche*, ed. Giovanni Getto, 3 vols, Firenze, 1955-61, 1, p. 18.

21. *Inferno*, I, 79-90:
    "Or se' tu quel Virgilio e quella fonte
    che spandi di parlar sí largo fiume?"
    rispuos'io lui con vergognosa fronte.   81
    "O delli altri poeti onore e lume
    vagliami 'l lungo studio e 'l grande amore
    che m'ha fatto cercar lo tuo volume.   84
    Tu se' lo mio maestro e 'l mio autore;

to se' solo colui da cui' io tolsi
lo bello stilo che m'ha fatto onore.   87
Vedi la bestia per cui' io mi volsi:
aiutami da lei, famoso saggio,
ch'ella mi fa tremar le vene e i polsi".   90

"Are you then that Virgil and that spring
   which spreads abroad so rich a stream of speech?"
I answered him, my brow covered with shame.
"O honour and light of other poets,
   may the long study and great love
   that made me pore over your book give me strength.
You are my master and my author;
   it is from you alone that I have taken
   the high style for which I have been honoured.
See the animal that made me turn back;
   help me against her, famous sage,
   for she makes my veins and pulses shudder."

22. The day was going, and the dark air
   was taking the creatures of the earth
   from their labours; and I was the only one
preparing myself to endure the battle
   both of the journey and of the pity
   which memory that does not err will recount.
O Muses, O high genius, help me now!
   O memory, which recorded what I saw,
   here will be shown your worth.

23. See Sapegno, 1, p. 18, note 7.

24. Through me you go into the woeful city;
   Through me you go into eternal pain;
   Through me you go among the lost people.
Justice moved my high maker;
   I was created by divine power,
   supreme wisdom, and primal love.

25. Here sighs, lamentations and loud wailings
   resounded through an air under no stars,
   so that at first they made me weep.
Deformed languages, horrible accents,
   words of hate, outcries of anger,
   voices shrill and faint, and the beating of hands clapped together.

26. "I come to take you to the other shore,
   into eternal darkness, into fire and ice."

27. When he had finished, the murky countryside
   trembled so violently, that the memory of the terror
   even now bathes me in sweat.
The tear-soaked ground gave forth a wind
   that flashed a carmine light
   which overcame all my senses,

and I fell like one that is seized with sleep.

28. Joseph Anthony Wittreich jr., 'Opening the Seals: Blake's Epics and the Milton Tradition', in *Blake's Sublime Allegory*, p. 27.

Notes to chapter 6

1. 'Notes on Essay on Epic Poetry', in *William Hayley*, p. 172

2. Then I descended from the first circle down
    into the second, which girds a smaller space,
    and so much more of pain, that spurs to wailing.
  There stands Minos, horrible and snarling;
    he examines the offences at the entrance,
    judges, and dispatches each according as he girds himself.
  I mean that when the ill-born soul
    comes before him, it confesses all;
    and that discerner of sins
  sees what place in hell is suited for it;
    and encircles himself with his tail as many times
    as the grades he will have it sent down.

3. *The Inferno of Dante*, tr. Charles Rogers Esq., of the custom House London [added in pen], London, 1782. Further references in the text are by canto and line numbers.

4. Love, which is quickly kindled in a gentle heart,
    seized this man for the fair form
    that was taken from me; and the manner afflicts me still.

5. Gallehault (or Galahalt, or Galleot, not to be confused with Galahad) was a character in the Old French Romance of *Lancelot du Lac*. He made war upon King Arthur, but by the intervention of Lancelot was induced to come to terms, and became a close friend of Lancelot, who confided to him his love for Guinevere. Gallehault persuaded Guinevere to meet the knight privately, and this meeting was the beginning of their secret love. The name of this character came to be used in the Middle Ages as a synonym for a pander. See Toynbee, *Dante Dictionary*, pp. 299-300.

6. "A Gallehault was the book and he who wrote it;
    that day we read in it no farther."

7. Henry Francis Cary, *The Vision*, Albion edn, p. 3. Further references in the text are by canto and line numbers.

8. Compare, for example, in the opening passage (ll. 1-2 and 3-4), Rogers' enjambment in 'I found/ Myself entangl'd' (which almost creates narrative tension) with Cary's 'our mortal life,/ I found me'; and also Rogers' 'but to relate/ The horrid wildness' with Cary's 'and e'en to tell/ It were no easy task'. In the latter example, Cary's verses are very static and the word order attempts to add variety to his lines.

9. Some of the passages quoted in the text are, in fact, purple passages, such as the very opening (in which the inversions are much more numerous than in other passages), and the opening of Canto IV with the inscription over Hell's gate. Notice the difference with Virgil's words which follow, or his gesture to Dante, and the plain English in which they are put: 'suspect not that anything is wrong./ It's proper now that fear should be extinct.' or 'And then he kindly put his hand

on mine,/ Giving me comfort with a look of joy,/ And shew me sights within unknown before.'

10. Readers of Dante in the eighteenth century had often seen Dante's work as an example of the early sublime of elevated thoughts and simple language (see above, pp. 44-5), and had also seen it as moving in its diction from the gross to the sublime, including the steps in between. These were readers (including Martinelli and Thomas Warton) who had read Dante in the original. So to reproduce in English the effect these readers had isolated in the original meant to produce an 'aesthetic' analogue of it.

11. William Cowper, 'Preface' to the second edition of *The Iliad of Homer*, Vol. 7 of *The Works of William Cowper*, ed. Robert Southey, pp. xvii-xxi.

12. Cowper's publisher added his voice to that of the readers Cowper mentions – see 'Preface' to *the second edition of The Iliad of Homer*, ibid., pp. xxii-xxvi. This publisher was none other than Joseph Johnson, who was in fact a relative of Cowper and had also published *The Task*. Johnson would probably be aware of readers' reactions to Cowper's Homer, because he had very actively looked for subscribers before Cowper started on his translation of the *Iliad*, in order to help him in his personal and financial difficulties.

13. At the end of his words the thief
    raised his hands, making obscene gestures,
    and called out: "Take that, o God, for I am squaring them at you!"

Notes to chapter 8

1. Henry Boyd translated parts of Ariosto's *Orlando Furioso*, which were published together with his *Inferno* in 1785. He published *Poems Chiefly Dramatic and Lyric* in 1793. In 1805 two more volumes of verse appeared, and in 1807 a verse translation of the *Triumphs of Petrarch*.

2. Anna Seward, letter to Mrs Helen Williams dated 25 Aug 1785 (*DEL*, p. 390). Byron mentions in a letter written from Ravenna (20 March 1820) that there Francesca was born and had been slain 'by Cary, Boyd and such people' (*DEL* II, 38).

3. *Gentleman's Magazine*, May 1785, art. 71, *DEL*, pp. 419-420.

4. Toynbee, for example, says that Boyd's is 'not so much a translation as a paraphrase' (*DEL*, p. 410).

5. De Sua puts forward these notions, and concludes that 'a great deal of pride was taken precisely in the translator's 'creative' abilities, and in his making the translation sound as much like an 'original' as possible' (p. 123). The translator's self-importance would be proved, further, by the fact that he changes the original, 'in order to conform to his idea of neoclassical stylistic demands' (p. 14). It would, therefore, be the translator's attitude of superiority and creative pride that changed the original, rather than, as is indicated here, an attitude dictated partly by the preferences of the reading public, and partly by the desire to insert the foreign text within English literature.

6. Henry Boyd, 'A Comparative View of the Inferno with some other Poems, relative to the original principles of *Human Nature*, on which they are founded, or to which they appeal', in *A Translation of the INFERNO of Dante Alighieri in English verse, with Historical Notes, and the Life of Dante to which is added A SPECIMEN OF A NEW TRANSLATION OF ARIOSTO*, 2 vols, Dublin, 1785, 1, p. 27. The publisher was P. Byrne.

7. Henry Boyd, *A Translation of the Inferno*, 1785, p. 189. In the text I will occasionally also refer to the *Inferno* as it appeared in *The Divina Commedia of Dante Alighieri, consisting of the Inferno, Purgatorio, Paradiso*, trans. into English verse by the Rev. Henry Boyd, A.M., 3 vols, London, 1802.

This later edition was printed by A. Strahan, New Street Square, FOR T. CADELL JUN. AND W. DAVIES, in the Strand.

8. And lo, almost at the beginning of the steep,
    a leopard, lithe and very swift,
    covered with a spotted hide;
and it did not go from before my face
    but instead impeded my way so much
    that I turned many times to go back.

   ...
    so that the hour of day and the sweet season
    gave me cause for good hope
of that beast with the gay skin.

9. In *The Poetical Works of John Milton*, ed. Sir Egerton Brydges, London, 1852, p. 7.

10. Alas, Pisa, shame of the peoples
    of the fair country where the *si* is heard,
    since your neighbours are slow to punish you,
may then Caprara and Gorgona shift
    and make a barrier for Arno at its mouth,
    so that it drown every soul in you!

11. Ellis Waterhouse, 'Introduction', *Reynolds*, London, 1973, p. 27. Waterhouse describes the genesis of the painting: 'the head was a character study, from a favourite model of the time, and one of Reynolds literary friends – it is uncertain whether Burke or Goldsmith – detected in it an appropriate head for the subject of Ugolino, with which it is likely that Reynolds was quite unfamiliar. Reynolds enlarged his canvas, and read some Dante (probably for the first time). The result was noted by Walpole as most admirable; but the taste of today is more inclined to agree with Mrs Thrale's waspish comment – which was not made on this specific picture – that Reynolds showed "a rage for sublimity ill-understood".'

12. In *The Divina Commedia of Dante Alighieri*, London, 1802, 2, p. 3.

13. Frederick Copleston discusses with great clarity the attitude of post-Kantian thinking 'to demythologize Christian dogmas, turning them in the process into a speculative philosophy'; in Hegel's words, '...though philosophy must not allow herself to be overawed by religion, or accept the position of existence on sufferance, she cannot afford to neglect those popular conceptions' and 'the tales and allegories of religion'. The secularization of the legend of the stories of man's fall and future redemption means that they are applied to the here and now, and to the single individual. See Frederick Copleston, *A History of Philosophy*, Vol. 7, London, 1963, p. 12. The quotation from Hegel (from *The Logic of Hegel*, trans. Wallace, Sec. 24, p. 54) is quoted in Abrams, *Natural Supernaturalism*, New York and London, 1971, p. 175.

14. Abrams, *Natural Supernaturalism*, p. 193.

15. I turned to him and looked at him attentively:
    he was fair-haired and handsome and of noble presence,
    but a blow had cloven one of his eyebrows.
When I had humbly disclaimed
    ever to have seen him, he said "Look now!"
    and showed me a wound high on his breast.
Then smiling he said: "I am Manfred,"

16. There are other ways in which Boyd attempts to justify Manfred's future reward, such as his stress on Manfred's innate nobility and original goodness, but they are less relevant to my argument in the text.

17. Umberto Bosco, 'Canto V', in *Dante nella critica*, ed. T. di Salvo, Firenze, 1965, p. 417. Bosco's words refer to Jacopo's own two views of blood: "I was from there [Fano]: but the deep wounds/ whence flowed the blood in which my life resided/ were dealt me in the bosom of the Antenori,".

18. I never saw kindled vapours cleave
  the clear sky at nightfall
  nor August clouds at sunset,
so swiftly as these returned above
  and, arrived there, wheeled back with the others towards us
  like a troop running without curb.
"The people that press on us are many,
  and come to entreat you", said the poet:
  "But go right on, and listen as you go."
"O soul that go to your bliss
  with those limbs with which you were born,"
  they came crying, "stay your steps for a little.
See whether you have ever seen any of us,
  so that you may take news of him back there.
  Oh, why do you go on? Why do you not stop?
We were all slain by violence."

19. Sisson translates 'meteor', though within the context of his lines the word assumes the more familiar connotation of falling star. Singleton quotes Grandgent who explains that 'vapori accesi comprise both meteors and lightning' (Charles Singleton, *The Divine Comedy*, Vol. 2 *Purgatorio*, Part 2 Commentary, Princeton, 1977, p. 95).

20. This is, furthermore, quite illogical, since the third soul to speak is that of La Pia, a woman who had, it is assumed, been murdered, but did not die in battle.

21. *Purgatorio*, V, 103-118:
  "Io dirò vero e tu 'l ridí tra' vivi:
    l'angel di Dio mi prese, e quel d'inferno
    gridava: 'O tu del ciel, perché mi privi?
  Tu te ne porti di costui l'etterno
    per una lacrimetta che 'l mi toglie;
    ma io farò dell'altro altro governo!'
  Ben sai come nell'aere si raccoglie
    quell'umido vapor che in acqua riede,
    tosto che sale dove'l freddo il coglie.
  Giunse quel mal voler che pur mal chiede
    con lo 'ntelletto, e mosse il fummo e 'l vento
    per la virtú che sua natura diede.
  Indi la valle, come 'l dí fu spento,
    da Pratomagno al gran giogo coperse
    di nebbia; e 'l ciel di sopra fece intento,
  sí che 'l pregno aere in acqua si converse:"

  "I tell the truth, and do you repeat it among the living.
    The angel of God took me, and he from hell
    cried out: 'O you from heaven, why do you rob me?

You carry off with you the eternal part of him,
    for one small tear that takes him from me;
    but with the other I will deal in other fashion.'
You know well how in the air is condensed
    that damp vapour that changes to water again as soon
    as it rises to where the cold seizes it.
That evil will which only seeks evil
    he combined with intellect, and moved the mist and wind
    by the power which his nature gave him.
Then, when the day was spent, he covered the valley,
    from Pratomagno to the great ridge,
    with cloud, and charged the sky overhead
    so that the pregnant air changed into water:"

22. I have seen once, at the beginning of day,
    the eastern part of the sky all rosy
    and the rest of it adorned with fair clear sky,
    and the face of the sun rise shaded,
    so that through the tempering of vapours
    the eye could bear it:
so, inside a cloud of flowers
    which rose from the angelic hands
    and fell again within and without,
    over a white veil crowned with olive,
    a lady appeared, under a green mantle
    clothed, in the colour of living flame.

23. Northrop Frye, *The Great Code: The Bible and Literature*, New York and London, 1982, p. 140.

24. Alexander Pope, 'The Key to the Lock', 1715, in *A Casebook*, ed. J.D. Hunt, London, 1968, pp. 33-48.

25. Mario Marti, 'Canto II', in *Dante nella critica*, p. 398. Walter Binni, 'Canto III', ibid., p. 411 (referring to Manfred's story).

26. Marti points out 'la raffigurazione dei due pellegrini smarriti e incerti, piccoli e soli nell'infinito silenzio, nella spiaggia del Purgatorio' ('the picture of the two pilgrims, small and in doubt, in the infinite silence of the shore of Purgatory', 'Canto II', ibid., p. 399); and Binni refers to the details 'che accrescono il senso oppressivo di un paesaggio solitario e paurosamente grandioso' ('which increase the oppression of a landscape which is deserted and so grand as to cause fear', 'Canto III', ibid., p. 406).

27. G. di Pino, 'Canto VIII', in *Dante nella critica*, p. 437 ('siamo nei simboli della preistoria della colpa', 'what we find are the symbols of the pre-history of the fall').

28. John D. Sinclair, *The Divine Comedy of Dante Alighieri*, Vol. 2 *Purgatorio*, New York, 1978, p. 432.

29. 'Preliminary Essay on the Paradiso of Dante', in *The Divina Commedia*, London, 1802, 3, p. 3.

30. 'Extract from the Symposium of Plato', ibid., p. 21.

31. The glory of him who moves all things
    penetrates the universe and shines
    in one part more and in another less.
I have been in the heaven which receives most of his light,

and have seen things which he that descends from it
has neither the knowledge nor the power to tell again;
for drawing near to our desire,
  our intellect sinks so deep,
  that memory cannot follow it all the way.
Nevertheless, so much of that holy kingdom
  as I was able to treasure in my mind
  will now be the matter of my song.
O good Apollo, for the last labour
  make me such a vessel of your worth
  as you require for the gift of the beloved laurel.

32. See, for example, Canto VII, sts XII-XIII, p. 88:
Deep, deep conceal'd within th'abyss of Light,
The mystic reason shuns created sight;
Except to them whom Love's eternal ray
Irradiates all within, and bids extend
Their eagle faculties, to comprehend
The secrets of the Sky, with broad survey.

But how this Truth that numbers vainly scan,
Exalted far beyond the ken of Man,
Fulfils its glorious end, may thus appear:
Love from its source emits a cloudless ray,
And scatters round that pure meridian day,
In which those glorious Orbs their voyage steer.

33. See Jospehine Miles, *The Primary Language of Poetry in the 1740's and 1840's*, 1950, in particular pp. 183, 187, 258. On this last page we read that in the 1840's the fullness of poetic statement lessened, conclusions were more tentative or not reached, while words such as 'nature' and 'power' gave way to 'light', 'night' and 'spirit'. Furthermore, Miles points out, on p. 172, that the poetry of the 1740's, compared to the poetry of one century earlier, shows the statistical proportion of 12-19-9 (adjective, noun, verb) in the place of the previous 8-15-10, therefore having a 'firm increase' in adjectives and nouns, and a decrease in verbs. Young himself has a high proportion of nouns in the sample from the *Night Thoughts* examined by Miles (10-20-10).

34. By not enduring for his own good
    a rein upon his will, that man who was not born,
    condemning himself, condemned his whole issue;
  So that the human race lay sick down there
    for many centuries in great error,
    until it pleased the Word of God to descend
  where he united to himself, in his person,
    that nature which had distanced itself from its maker,
    by sole act of his eternal love.

35. Beatrice was standing with her eyes firmly fixed
    upon the eternal wheels; and I on her
    fixed mine, withdrawn from above.
  Gazing at her I became within me
    as Glaucus became when he tasted the grass
    which made him, in the sea, one with the other gods.

36. Beatrice was gazing upwards and I on her;

and perhaps in the time it takes an arrow,
 to strike, and fly off, and free itself from the catch,
I saw myself arrived where a marvellous thing
 drew my sight to itself; and therefore she
 from whom my concerns could not be hidden,
turned toward me, as glad as she was lovely,

37. Boyd gives a lengthy explanation of how in the early days of their existence the mendicant orders were worthy of respect and love, and then he goes on to show, on the basis of anecdotes and examples, that they later degenerated, particularly in England, into the greedy, lying order similar to the Jesuits the English knew.

38. Marti, 'Canto III', in *Dante nella critica*, p. 503. Marti points out a number of effects, including the following from Canto III:

Quali per ve*tri tra*sparenti e *ter*si (l. 10)
non sí pro*fon*de che i *fon*di sien persi (l. 12)
debili sí, che perla in *bian*ca fro*nte* (l. 14)

He adds that such effects are created by Dante either within a phrase, as in the examples above, or as an internal rhyme:

... Ne' mirabili aspetti
vostri risplende non so che divino
che vi *trasmuta* da' primi concetti:
però non fui a *rimembrar* festino;
a or *m'aiuta* ciò che tu mi dici,
sí che *raffigurar* m'è piú latino (ll. 58-63)

39. Cacciaguida's loving approach is similar to the encounter between Aeneas and his father in the Elysian Fields in the *Aeneid*, bk. VI, ll. 684-686; 'O sanguis meus..', as Sapegno points out (Vol. 3, *Paradiso*, 1981, p. 194, n. 28), echoes Anchises' words about Caesar in the *Aeneid*, bk. VI, l. 836.

40. *Paradiso*, XXXIII, 115-132:
Nella profonda e chiara sussistenza
 dell'alto lume parvermi tre giri
 di tre colori e d'una contenenza;
e l'un dall'altro come iri da iri
 parea reflesso, e 'l terzo parea foco
 che quinci e quindi igualmente si spiri.
Oh quanto è corto il dire e come fioco
 al mio concetto! e questo, a quel ch'i' vidi,
 è tanto, che non basta a dicer "poco".
O luce etterna che sola in te sidi,
 sola t'intendi, e da te intelletta
 e intendente te ami e arridi!
Quella circulazion che sí concetta
 pareva in te come lume reflesso,
 dalli occhi miei alquanto circunspetta,
dentro da sé, del suo colore stesso,
 mi parve pinta della nostra effige;
 per che 'l mio viso in lei tutto era messo.

In the profundity of the clear substance
 of the deep light, appeared to me three circles

of three colours and one circumference;
and the one seemed to be reflected by the other,
  as rainbow by rainbow, and the third
  seemed a flame breathed forth equally from the one and the other.
O how scant is my speech, and how faint
  for my conception! And this, to what I saw, is such that
  it is not enough to call it little.
O light eternal, existing in yourself alone,
  alone knowing yourself; and who, known to yourself
  and knowing, love and smile upon yourself!

41. *Paradiso*, XXXIII, 142-45
All'alta fantasia qui mancò possa;
  ma già volgeva il mio disio e 'l velle,
  sí come rota ch'igualmente è mossa,
l'amor che move il sole e l'altre stelle.

Here power failed high imagination;
  but already my desire and my will were revolved,
  like a wheel that is turned with even motion,
by the love which moves the sun and the other stars.

Notes to chapter 9

1. The Rev. Henry Francis Cary, A.M., 'Preface' to *The Vision; or, Hell, Purgatory, and Paradise, of Dante Alighieri*, London, 1871, p. vi. All quotations of the text are from this edition, the 'Chandos Classics' edition published by Frederick Warne and Co.. I have also used the 'Albion' edition of the same publisher, London and New York, 1889 (see note 8). Cary's *Inferno* appeared in 1805-6 and contained his 'life of Dante'; when he published *The Vision* in 1814 it did not contain the 'life of Dante', but only 'A Chronological View of the Age of Dante'. When, after 1818, Cary's translation was much sought after, a second edition was quickly published in 1819, and this contains the 'life of Dante'. The third edition of 1831 has few changes from the 1819 edition, whereas the fourth edition of 1844 contains many more footnotes than the previous editions. The 'life of Dante' has remained exactly the same as in 1805-6, and the text has also remained essentially the same (see note 62 below for an example of one of the few passages which was changed). The edition I quote from reproduces the 1814 edition. On a few occasions I have referred in the text to footnotes which were added in the 1844 edition, since they seem to explain Cary's particular reading of the original. This is indicated in my footnotes.

2. James Thomson, 'Summer', ll. 142-159, in The Seasons *and* The Castle of Indolence, ed. James Sambrook, Oxford, 1972, p. 41.

3. *The Poetical Works of William Cowper*, ed. William Michael Rossetti, illus. Thomas Seccombe, London, n.d., p. 201. As this edition has no line numbers, references to the text after quotation will be by book and page number.

4. The inclusion of scientific classification in the formation of eighteenth-century diction is examined by John Arthos, *The Language of Natural Decription in Eighteenth-century Poetry*, Ann Arbor and London, 1949. Periphrases of the kind 'plumy loins' are mentioned by Arthos on p. 33.

5. William Blake, *Jerusalem*, in *William Blake: The Complete Poems*, ed. Alicia Ostriker, Penguin, 1977, p. 734. Quotations from Blake are from this edition.

6. William Blake, letter to John Butts November 22 1802, ibid., p. 487.

7. William Wordsworth, 'Prospectus' to *The Excursion*, written 1798, published 1814, in *Romantic Poetry and Prose*, eds Harold Bloom and Lionel Trilling, New York and London, 1973, p. 144.

8. All quotations from the 'life of Dante' are from the 'Albion' edition of Cary's *The Vision* (see note 1 above).

9. Robert W. King, *The Translator of Dante*, London, 1925, p. 37.

10. The Rev. Henry Francis Cary, Letter to Anna Seward May 7 1792, in *Memoir of the Rev. Henry Francis Cary, A.M., Translator of Dante, with his Literary Journal and Letters*, by his son, the Rev. Henry Cary, 2 vols, London, 1847, 2, p. 44.

11. Coleridge's acquaintance with Dante may have had various sources. It may have started with his acquaintance with German authors and been strengthened when he was in Germany in 1798-9, where, as Henry Crabb Robinson reports in his *Account of Tour with Christian Brentano in Germany*, 1802, there was a 'concurrence of opinion among the German philosophers as to the transcendent genius of Shakespeare, Goethe, and Dante' (*DEL*, p. 632). In fact he had referred to Dante in an article in *The Watchman* of 25 March 1796, in which he mentions 'the gloomy imagination of Dante' (*The Notebooks of S.T. Coleridge*, ed. K. Coburn, 2 vols, New York, 1957, Vol. 1, 170 a 165). In that same year he borrowed a copy of Boyd's *Inferno* from the Bristol Library. In the *Biographia Literaria* (1817; Everyman's Library, 1917) Coleridge refers to Dante first in connection with the idea of liberty ('In Pindar, Chaucer, Dante, Milton, and many more, we have instances of the close connection of poetic genius with the love of liberty and genuine reformation', Everyman's Library, 1906; rpt. 1917, p. 110.), then in connection with the idea of the picturesque (which is realized in the highest degree in *Venus and Adonis*, more than in the work of any other poet, 'even Dante not excepted', p. 169), then when arguing for the poet's duty to guard 'the purity of their native tongue', a duty stressed by 'the sublime Dante, in his tract *De la volgare Eloquenza*' (sic, p. 174), again when he discusses the *lingua communis*, adding 'as Dante has well observed' (p. 190), and finally in connection with Wordsworth's poetry (p. 253).

12. Cary's son remembers that 'a thousand copies of the first edition, that remained in hand, were immediately disposed of; in less than three months a new edition was called for.' *Memoir*, 2, p. 28.

13. See, for example, Robert Southey's praise in his 'Advertisement' to *The Works of William Cowper*, ed. Southey, 1, pp. vii-viii.

14. Coleridge, Letter to Cary, Oct [29] 1817, in *Letters of Samuel Taylor Coleridge*, ed. Ernest Hartley Coleridge, 2 vols, London, 1895, 2, p. 677.

15. 'Advertisement' to Cary's *The Inferno of Dante Alighieri*, 2 vols, London, 1805-6, Vol. 1 1805, p. v.

16. In the opening passage, the fourth line has word inversions which make the sentence very different from present day Italian, but the words themselves are simple and clear. For the rest the sentences flow in a simple, straightforward manner; both the words and the syntax are plain. Only a few small points are at variance with modern Italian: 'esta' is the old form of 'questa', 'era' of 'ero'. 'Compunto' and 'mena' are not in current use, but are not particularly 'poetic'.

17. Havens, p. 355.

18. Cunningham, p. 20.

19. See, for example, De Sua, p. 31 and Cunningham, p. 60.

20. She put such heaviness on me
    with the fear which issued from her looks,

that I lost all hope of reaching the top of the hill.

21. Coleridge, Letter to Cary Nov 6 1817, in *Letters*, 2, p. 678.

22. Coleridge, Lecture X, in *The Portable Coleridge*, ed. I.A. Richards, New York, 1950, p. 406. The lecture was on Donne, Dante and Milton, being the tenth lecture of a series given at the Flower-de-Luce in February 1818.

23. Guido Mazzoni, 'Il Canto III dell'Inferno', in *Letture Dantesche*, 1, p. 45.

24. The profound was a term of eighteenth-century aesthetics; it signifies the opposite direction of the sublime. Aaron Hill uses it in *The Progress of Wit* (written in reply to Pope's *Dunciad*), describing it, for example, as follows:

> But far more frightful this! – whose dark profound,
> A death eternal! life wants line to sound:
> Unbottom'd shade roll'd, loose, o'er swallow'd
> light.
> Fancy grew giddy, nor sustain'd the sight:
> But, starting into fear, transposed remark,
> And sought the source less dreadful, though as dark.

(Aaron Hill, *The Progress of Wit*, 1730, in *The Poems of Hill, Cawthorn, and Bruce*, The British Poets Vol. 60, Chiswick, 1822, p. 72.)
The profound, as Hill describes it, seems to have much in common with the notion of 'horror' as described by Radcliffe. Doody forcefully defines the idea of the Profound when she uses it in her description in 'Peter Grimes' to say that at the lowest moment of his degeneration Grimes 'has come to that downhill stop, that place of rest and inertia which is the Profound, where the only life is the small slimy monsters that reflect the small monsters of his own flickering consiousness' (Doody, p. 181).

25. An interesting instance of Cary's stance is his rendering of Dante's adaptation of Virgil's simile of the autumn leaves, also used by Milton. While Virgil's 'quam multa ...' and Milton's 'Thick as ...' stress the number, Dante's 'come ... similmente si levano' ('As leaves in autumn ... are blown away, ... so') suggests the manner in which the leaves fall from the branch one by one; it is the movement that is emphasized, and the general composition of the picture. Cary quotes Virgil and Milton in his footnotes, without adding a comment, but in his rendering 'As ... in a like manner' he reproduces the movement and rhythm of the original. It could be a matter of translating literally, or it could be accident. This is a question that the reader of Cary will often ask himself. The many instances of similar occurrences (where footnotes from Milton or Spenser are provided, but the text follows the original) could suggest either that Cary was aware of Dante's difference from his imitators, and that his translation derived from the conscious choice of the most appropriate reading as far as Dante was concerned, or that he was unaware of the significance of the difference and, quite simply, pedantically adds material for comparison with English literature.
At this particular point too little evidence is given in the text to decide which of the two possibilities is correct. See, however, pp. 188.

26. In Dante, Charon bursts into vision with speed and violence, which are present also in Cary's version:

> ... And lo! Towards us in a bark
> Comes an old man, hoary white with eld,
> Crying "Woe to you, wicked spirits! hope not
> Ever to see the sky again. I come ..."   (III, 76-79)

And indeed within a few lines he is so near that Dante gives a close-up of his face, describing his eyes twice, and referring to his cheeks. Charon then proceeds to beckon to the souls, and strikes those who are lazy: we never see him still. Again Cary seems to be attempting to reproduce the original. A brief comparison with some later translators indicates this clearly enough. Cary's Charon, like Dante's, 'beckons' to the souls. Bickersteth ('With eyes of burning coal that demon hoar/ Charon, makes signs to and collects them all') seems to picture a more dignified and commanding ferryman who only needs to signal with his eyes to be obeyed – forgetting that Dante's Charon makes use of his oar to herd them into the boat. Ciardi and Binyon both maintain some ambiguity. Ciardi says 'and demon Charon with eyes like burning coals/ Herds them in', where the lack of a comma seems to group him with Bickersteth. Binyon's 'Charon, the demon, beckoning before,/ With eyes of burning coal, assembles all' is closer to Cary's rendering.

References are to the *Inferno* as translated by Geoffrey L. Bickersteth (in *The Divine Comedy*, Oxford, 1981), Laurence Binyon (in *The Portable Dante*, Penguin, 1975), and John Ciardi (in *The Divine Comedy*, New York and London, 1970).

27. *The Comedy of Dante Alighieri*, Vol. 1 *Hell*, trans. Dorothy L. Sayers.

28. Giorgio Petrocchi, *La Commedia secondo l'antica vulgata*, Vol. 2 *Inferno*, p. 42, note 31. According to Petrocchi, though there are two readings, the reading 'error' should definitely be chosen, because 'la variante promossa è quella espressa dai testimoni piú puri e piú autorevoli della primitiva bipartizione' (this variant is the one put forward by the most authoritative sources reporting the original division into two readings). In the 'Introduzione' (Vol. 1, p. 168) he further states that 'error' is also to be preferred because the reference is to the head, rather than to the heart or breast.

29. He raised his mouth from the savage meal
    that sinner, wiping it on the hair
    of the head he had spoiled behind.
Then began: "You will have me renew
    a desperate grief, which presses on my heart,
    even to think of it, before I speak.
But if my words are to be seed
    that will bear fruit of infamy to the traitor I gnaw,
    You shall see me speak and weep at the same time."

30. These are probably examples of 'sylvan' words – according to Dante's classifications of words in his *De Vulgari Eloquentia* (bk 2, Ch. 7). In this classification words are childish, feminine, or manly. Manly words are in turn divided into 'silvestria' (sylvan) and 'urbana' (urban). Urban words (which are further subdivided) include words which are generally more varied and noble. Dante's classification is discussed at some length in William Anderson, *Dante the Maker*, London, 1980, pp. 179-181.

31. An example is the break between the first and second line in *Inferno*, XXXIII, 21-3:
    udirai, e saprai s'e' m'ha offeso.
Breve pertugio dentro dalla muda
    la qual per me ha il titol della fame,

    And you will know whether he offended me.
A narrow opening in the mew
    which, because of me, has the name of Hunger,

32. When a small ray of sunlight made its way
    into that doleful prison, and I saw
    On four faces my own look,
I bit both my hands for grief;

33. *Inferno*, XXXIII, 45-54:
    e per suo sogno ciascun dubitava;   45
    e io senti' chiavar l'uscio di sotto
      all'orribile torre; ond'io guardai
      nel viso a' mie' figliuoi sanza far motto.   48
    Io non piangea, sí dentro impetrai:
      piangevan elli; e Anselmuccio mio
      disse: "Tu guardi sí, padre! che hai?"   51
    Perciò non lacrimai né rispuos'io
      tutto quel giorno né la notte appresso,
      infin che l'altro sol nel mondo uscío.   54

    And on account of his dream, each was anxious;
    and I heard below the door of the horrible tower
    nailed up; and then I looked into the faces
    Of my children, without saying a word.
    I did not weep, I so turned to stone within:
    they wept, and my poor little Anselm said:
    "You look so, father, what is the matter?"
    At that I neither wept nor did I reply
    all that day, nor the night after,
    Until another sun came forth into the world.

34. *Inferno*, XXXIII, 76-80:
    Quand'ebbe detto ciò, con li occhi torti
      riprese 'l teschio misero co' denti,
      che furo all'osso, come d'un can, forti.
    Ahi Pisa, vituperio delle genti

    When he had said this, with his eyes bulging
      he seized again the wretched skull with teeth
      which were strong on the bone, like a dog's.
    Ah Pisa! contemptible to all the people

35. *Inferno*, XXXIV, 22-60:
    Com'io divenni allor gelato e fioco,
      nol dimandar, lettor, ch'i' non lo scrivo,
      però ch'ogni parlar sarebbe poco.   24
    Io non mori', e non rimasi vivo:
      pensa oggimai per te, s'hai fior d'ingegno,
      qual io divenni, d'uno e d'altro privo.   27
    Lo 'mperador del doloroso regno
      da mezzo il petto uscía fuor della ghiaccia;
      e piú con un gigante io mi convegno,   30
    che i giganti non fan con le sue braccia:
      vedi oggimai quant'esser dee quel tutto
      ch'a cosí fatta parte si confaccia.   33
    S'el fu sí bel com'elli è ora brutto,
      e contra 'l suo fattore alzò le ciglia,
      ben dee da lui procedere ogni lutto.   36
    Oh quanto parve a me gran maraviglia
      quand'io vidi tre facce alla sua testa!
      L'una dinanzi, e quella era vermiglia;   39

l'altr'eran due, che s'aggiugníeno a questa
  sovresso 'l mezzo di ciascuna spalla,
  e sé giugníeno al luogo della cresta: 42
e la destra parea tra bianca e gialla;
  la sinistra a vedere era tal, quali
  vegnon di là onde 'l Nilo s'avvalla. 45
Sotto ciascuna uscivan due grand'ali,
  quanto si convenía a tanto uccello:
  vele di mar non vid'io mai cotali. 48
Non avevan penne ma di vispistrello
  era lor modo; e quelle svolazzava,
  sí che tre venti si movean da ello: 51
quindi Cocito tutto s'aggelava.
  Con sei occhi piangea, e per tre menti
  gocciava 'l pianto e sanguinosa bava. 54
Da ogni bocca dirompea co' denti
  un peccatore, a guisa di maciulla,
  sí che tre ne facea cosí dolenti. 57
A quel dinanzi il mordere era nulla
  verso 'l graffiar, che tal volta la schiena
  rimanea della pelle tutta brulla. 60

How frozen and how faint I then became
  do not enquire, reader, for I do not write it,
  since any speech would be inadequate. 24
I did not die, and I did not remain alive:
  think now for yourself, if you have any wit,
  what I became, deprived of death and life. 27
The emperor of the woeful kingdom
  stood forth at mid breast out of the ice;
  and I in size compare better to a giant 30
than giants to his arms:
  see now how great that whole must be
  to correspond to such a part. 33
If he was as beautiful as he now is ugly,
  and yet lifted his brow against his maker,
  well may all sorrow come from him. 36
Oh, what a great wonder it appeared to me,
  when I saw three faces on his head!
  One in front, and that was red; 39
the other two joined to this
  just above the middle of each shoulder,
  and all came together at the crown; 42
the right-hand one seemed between white and yellow;
  and the left one had the look of those
  who come from where the Nile descends. 45
Under each came out two great wings
  of size fitting for such a bird;
  sails at sea I never saw like these. 48
They had no feathers, but their make-up was
  like a bat's; and he was flapping them

```
    so that three winds went out from him,              51
  by which Cocytus was all frozen;
      with six eyes he wept, and down three chins
      dripped tears and bloody foam.                    54
  In each mouth he crushed with his teeth
      a sinner, as if with a brake,
      and so he kept three of them in torment.          57
  For the one who was in front, the biting was nothing
      compared with the clawing, for at times his back
      was left all stripped of skin.                    60
```

36. Edmund Burke, *A Philosophical Enquiry into the Origin of Our Ideas of the Sublime and Beautiful*, 1757; rpt. Merston, England, 1970, Part I, Sec. 7, pp. 58-9. Further references will be by Part and Section number.

37. Ann Radcliffe, 'On the Supernatural in Poetry', *New Monthly Magazine*, Vol. 16, 1826, pp. 145-152. This essay is a dialogue which was to be included in Radcliffe's *Gaston de Blondeville* (1826), but was published after Radcliffe's death by Henry Colburn as an article with the title specified above and with the addition 'by the Late Mrs Radcliffe'.

38. In an early letter to Seward, Cary mentions the fact that he had started translating *Purgatorio* 'because the poem is less known than Inferno' (May 7, 1792, in *Memoir*, 1, p. 43). The reasons for the interruption and the new start are not mentioned.

39. As far as the English is concerned, the following is a good example:
```
  "Of truth, kind teacher!" I exclaimed "so clear
  Aught saw I never, as I now discern,
  Where seem'd my ken to fail, that the mid orb
  Of that supernal motion (which in terms
  of art is call'ed the Equator)..."            (IV, 73-77)
```
Cary adds grandiosity and solemnity according to the sublime style, as at the close of Canto IX ('ciò ch'io udiva, qual prender si sòle/ quando a cantar con organi si stea'), where Cary's 'The strains came o'er mine ear, e'en at the sound/ of choral voices, that in solemn chant/ With organ mingle' (ll. 135-7) adds 'choral voices' and 'solemn chant' to the original 'strains'. Cary relies on the established neoclassical diction, for example by adding adjectives to nouns where it is quite inappropriate, as in the exclamatory lament on the degeneration of Italy, where Dante's brief and shocking 'non donna di provincie, ma bordello' (VI, 78) becomes 'Lady no longer of *fair* provinces,/ but brothel-house *impure*' (my italics).

40. *Purgatorio*, VI, 1-9:
```
  Quando si parte il gioco della zara,
      colui che perde si riman dolente,
      repetendo le volte, e tristo impara;              3
  con l'altro se ne va tutta la gente;
      qual va dinanzi, e qual di dietro il prende,
      e qual da lato li si reca a mente:                6
  el non s'arresta, e questo e quello intende;
      a cui porge la man, piú non fa pressa;
      e cosí dalla calca si difende.                    9

  When the game of dice breaks up,
      the loser is left disconsolate,
      going over the throws, and sadly learns his lesson;
```

with the other all the people go off;
    one goes in front, one seizes him from behind,
    another at his side calls himself to his attention; he does not stop,
and listens to this one and that;
    each to whom he reaches out his hand presses him no longer;
    and so he defends himself from the crowd.

The footnote to this passage in Cary's translation is taken from the fourth edition of 1844 (rpt. 'Albion' edn, 1889) but well explains Cary's divergent rendering.

41. *Purgatorio*, I, 13-31:

Dolce color d'oriental zaffiro,
    che s'accoglieva nel sereno aspetto
    del mezzo, puro insino al primo giro,   15
alli occhi miei ricominciò diletto,
    tosto ch'io usci' fuor dell'aura morta
    che m'avea contristati li occhi e 'l petto.   18
Lo bel pianeta che d'amar conforta
    faceva tutto rider l'oriente,
    velando i Pesci, ch'erano in sua sua scorta.   21
I' mi volsi a man destra, e puosi mente
    all'altro polo, e vidi quattro stelle
    non viste mai fuor ch'alla prima gente.   24
Goder pareva il ciel di lor fiammelle:
    oh settentrional vedovo sito,
    poi che privato se' di mirar quelle!   27
Com'io da loro sguardo fui partito,
    un poco me volgendo all'altro polo,
    là onde il Carro già era sparito,   30
vidi presso di me un veglio solo,

Sweet colour of oriental sapphire,
    which was gathering in the clear face of the sky
    pure right to the first circle,   15
gladdened my eyes again,
    as soon as I issued from the dead air
    which had afflicted my eyes and my breast.   18
The lovely planet which prompts to love
    made all the east laugh,
    veiling the Fish which were in her train.   21
I turned to the right, and fixed my mind
    on the other pole, and I saw four stars,
    never yet seen except by the first people.   24
The sky seemed to rejoice in their flames.
    O widowed region of the north,
    since you are deprived of seeing them!   27
When I had withdrawn my gaze from them
    turning a little towards the other pole,
    to where the Wain had already disappeared,   30
I saw near me an old man, alone,

42. *Commedia di Dante Allighieri*, con ragionamenti e note di Niccolò Tommaséo, Milano, 1865, note 5F, p. 14.

43. All round about its very base, this little island,
    down there where the wave beats it,
    bears rushes on its soft mud;

44. *Purgatorio*, II, 13-26:
    Ed ecco qual, sul presso del mattino,
       per li grossi vapor Marte rosseggia
       giú nel ponente sovra 'l suol marino,   15
    cotal m'apparve, s'io ancor lo veggia,
       un lume per lo mar venir sí ratto,
       che 'l mover suo nessun volar pareggia.   18
    Dal qual com'io un poco ebbi ritratto
       l'occhio per domandar lo duca mio,
       rividil piú lucente e maggior fatto.   21
    Poi d'ogne lato ad esso m'apparío
       un non sapea che bianco, e di sotto
       a poco a poco un altro a lui uscío.   24
    Lo mio maestro ancor non fece motto,
       mentre che i primi bianchi apparser ali:

    And lo, as at the approach of morning,
       through the thick vapours Mars glows deep red,
       low in the west, above the level sea,
    so to me appeared – may I see it again –
       a light coming over the sea so swiftly
       that no flight could equal its motion;
    from which when I had taken my eyes
       a little to question my leader,
       I saw it again grown brighter and bigger.
    Then on each side of it appeared to me
       a something white, I knew not what, and from underneath it,
       bit by bit, another came out.
    My master still did not say a word,
       until the first whiteness appeared as wings:

45. Entries in Cary's 'Literary Journal' show that during the same period of time Cary was translating the first cantos of *Purgatorio* and reading Burke: 'Jan 17, Continued Dante, and finished canto i of Purgatorio. Jan 26, Began Burke on the Sublime and Beautiful and read to Part II, with Jane [his wife]. Jan 28, Proceeded in Dante, Purgatorio, canto iii. Jan 30, Proceeded in Dante, Purgatorio canto iii. Continued Burke to Part V.' In *Memoir*, 1, p. 103.

46. Singleton well summarizes the issues here: 'the notion of pilgrim and thus of pilgrimage here appears in the poem for the first time. Strikingly enough, it never was applied to the journey through Hell. Clearly it implies an exodus, a newness of life ...' *The Divine Comedy*, Vol. 2 *Purgatorio*, Part 2 Commentary, p. 33. But while in Dante the crowd is 'selvaggia del loco' (that is, unfamiliar with the place), Cary translates 'that strange tribe'.

47. The dawn was conquering the matin hour
    which fled before it, so that far away
    I recognized the trembling of the sea.

48. *La Divina Commedia*, nuovamente commentata da Francesco Torraca, Roma e Milano, 1908, p. 312. The spirituality of the landscape in *Purgatorio* has been discussed by many critics. As Momigliano says 'In Purgatorio tutto ci richiama senza posa all'animo che si scruta e si riconosce ... e i particolari di quel cammino lungo strade deserte e su per salite faticose in cospetto sempre del cielo, hanno una poesia spirituale superiore ai paesaggi, piu pittoreschi e meno intimi, dell'*Inferno* e del *Paradiso*. ('Tono e motivi del Purgatorio', in *Dante nella critica*, p. 369). In his study of this aspect of *Purgatorio*, Marti says that Dante's opening of Canto VIII, for example, does not give us a sunset, but the feeling of a sunset ('Simbologie luministiche nel Purgatorio', ibid., p. 379).

49. My mind, which had before been constrained,
  widened its range in its eagerness,
    and I set my face towards the hill
    that rises highest heavenward from the sea.
  The sun, which was flaming red behind us,
    was broken before me in the shape of my shadow,
    which was framed by its rays resting on me.

50. We arrived meanwhile at the foot of the mountain:
    and there we found the cliff so steep
    that in vain would legs be willing there.
  Between Lerici and Turbia, the most deserted,
    the most broken scree, compared to that,
    is an open and easy stairway.

51. Ann Radcliffe, *The Mysteries of Udolpho*, Oxford and New York, 1966; rpt. 1983, p. 672.

52. Umberto Eco, editor's preface to *Il Nome della Rosa*, Milano, 1984, p. 13.

53. One can go to Sanleo and get down to Noli;
    one can climb up to the top of Bismatova,
    with feet alone; but here a man has to fly;
  I mean with the swift wings and plumage
    of strong desire, ...

54. A larger opening many a time the peasant hedges up
    with a little forkful of his thorns,
    when the grapes are darkening,
  than was the gap by which climbed through
    my leader, and I after him, we alone
    as the company parted from us.

55. I am referring to a description of the mountain in Canto IV: 'Lo sommo er'alto che vincea la vista,/ e la costa superba piú assai/ che da mezzo quadrante a centro lista' (ll. 40-42). This tells us that the top of the mountain was higher than man's power of sight, and that the steepness of the mountain was greater than 45 degrees; the word 'superba' seems to have no overtones of pride, and in fact that would be strange, considering that pride is the lowest sin in Purgatory and therefore the first to be expiated, and considering that it is the one expiated also by the protagonist. The proud are purified in Canto X, where the essential Purgatory begins. Here Dante's climb reaches its slowest and hardest point, as Sinclair, for one, points out (Vol. 2 *Purgatorio*, p. 139). Interestingly, this is the canto where the sculpted side of the mountain is so beautiful that it seems to speak – the famous 'visibile parlare' (l. 95).

56. So, Jacopo's 'quel d'Este' becomes 'Este's prince', where the stress is not on the place as identification of the man, but on the role and power of the ruler over the place; and the original's

compressed 'in Fano' is turned into the paraphrase of its meaning, 'those who inhabit Fano', which loses the identification completely.

In the fourth edition of *The Vision* the passage is referenced by a number of footnotes. Many of them call to the reader's attention works and authors such as *Alberici Visio* or Albertus Magnus, in order to explain sources of traditional beliefs. Others – those which appeared also in the earlier editions – identify the character mentioned in the text and provide a brief history, or describe more precisely the place names and their position on the map.

57. The seven ladies [stopped] at the edge of a slight shade
    such as mountains cast on their cold streams
    under green leaves and dark branches.

58. In front of them I seemed to see
    Euphrates and Tigris issuing from a single spring
    and, as friends might, slowly parting.

59. This is clearly a reference to the idea of the 'Refrigerium', or heavenly happiness presented as refreshing coolness. It is mentioned also in Jacques le Goff's useful book *La Naissance du Purgatoire*, 1981, translated into English by A. Goldhammer as *The Birth of Purgatory*, London, 1984. The discussion of the idea of 'Refrigerium' occurs on p. 46.

60. King occasionally shows that he knows little of Dante's poem. On page 309 he mentions how in Dante Ulysses set off on his journey only after having been restored to Penelope, which is not what the text says. Moreover, his use of the words 'dignity' and 'sublimity' on page 323 ('the dignity and stark sublimity of the original') suggests that he is reading Dante through Cary, or at least through late eighteenth-century or early nineteenth-century ideas on Dante.

61. Over a white veil crowned with olive,
    a lady appeared to me, clothed under a green mantle
    in the colour of living flame.
    And my spirit, which for so long a time
    had not been overcome with awe,
    trembling in her presence,
    without having more knowledge by the eyes,
    through hidden virtue that came from her
    felt the great power of old love.

62. In the fourth edition Cary altered this passage slightly:
    And o'er my spirit, that so long a time
    Had from her presence felt no shuddering dread,
    Albeit mine eyes discern'd her not, there moved
    A hidden virtue ...

63. Like an admiral who goes to stern and bow
    to see his people who serve on the other ships
    and to encourage them to do well,
    so upon the left side of the chariot,
    when I turned round at the sound of my name,
    which is noted here of necessity,
    I saw the lady ...

It must, however, be pointed out that a commentator like Buti (ca. 1380) gives a similar reading of Beatrice's approach, and could be conveying the views on this passage current perhaps during the nineteenth century, and similar to those Cary could have been familiar with.

64. *Purgatorio*, XXX, 67-81

    Tutto che 'l vel che le scendea di testa,
      cerchiato delle fronde di Minerva,
      non la lasciasse parer manifesta,   69
    regalmente nell'atto ancor proterva
      continuò come colui che dice
      e 'l piú caldo parlar dietro reserva: 72
    "Guardaci ben! Ben son, ben son Beatrice.
      Come degnasti d'accedere al monte?
      Non sapei tu che qui è l'uom felice?"   75
    Li occhi mi cadder giú nel chiaro fonte;
      ma veggendomi in esso, i trassi all'erba,
      tanta vergogna mi gravò la fronte   78
    Cosí la madre al figlio par superba,
      com'ella parve a me; perché d'amaro
      sent'il sapor della pietade acerba.   81

    Although the veil which fell from her head,
      encircled with Minerva's leaves
      did not allow her to appear openly,
    regally, in her mien still severe,
      she went on, like a speaker who keeps back
      his hottest words till last:
    "Look at me well! Indeed I am, indeed I am Beatrice.
      How did you deign to climb the mountain?
      Did you not know that here man is happy?"
    My eyes fell down to the clear fount
      but, seeing myself in it, I drew them back,
      so great a shame weighed on my brow.
    So does a mother seem harsh to her child,
      as she seemed to me; for bitter
      tasted the savour of stern pity.

65. when I turned round at the sound of my name,
    which is noted here of necessity,

66. Sapegno, Vol. 2 *Purgatorio*, 1967, note to Canto XXX, l. 63, p. 342.

67. Cunningham, p. 20: 'There is a strong resemblance between his style and Cowper's, including something of the uncertainty of Cowper's touch.' It is a pity the critic gives no examples, or further explains what he means.

68. Passing beyond the human cannot be put
    into words; so let the example suffice
    for him for whom grace reserves the experience.

69. This reference to Pope occurs in the fourth edition. References in this canto to Ovid, Chaucer, Spenser and Milton are in the earlier editions.

70. Thus she spoke to me, and then began
    singing *Ave Maria*, and, singing, vanished
    as a heavy object through deep water.

71. This is Sisson's translation (p. 318):
    Thus she spoke to me, and then she began

To sing *Ave Maria*, and, singing, vanished
As a heavy object does in deep water.

72. "And in his will is our peace:
    it is that sea to which all things move,
    what it creates and what nature makes."

73. It is a pity that Cary misses the opportunity of pointing out an interesting similarity with Thomson's *The Seasons* – where the English poet, too, suddenly inverts his picture ('Summer', ll. 1244-49):

    Cheered by the milder beam, the sprightly youth
    Speeds to the well-known pool, whose crystal depth
    A sandy bottom shows. Awhile he stands
    Gazing the inverted landscape, half afraid
    To meditate the blue profound below;
    Then plunges headlong down the circling flood.

74. Then, as people who have been under masks
    appear other than before if they take off
    the semblance not their own they disappeared into,
    so were changed before me into a greater festival
    the flowers and the sparks, so that I saw
    both the courts of heaven made manifest.
    O splendour of God, by which I saw
    the exalted triumph of the true kingdom,
    give me power to tell how I saw it!
    A light is there above which makes visible
    the creator to every creature
    who finds his peace only in seeing him.
    It stretches itself in the form of a circle
    so far, that the circumference of it
    would be too large a belt for the sun.
    All its appearance is formed by a radiance,
    reflected from the summit of the Primum Mobile,
    which takes from it its life and potency.
    And as a hillside mirrors itself in
    water at its base, as if to see itself adorned
    when it is at its best with green and flowers,
    so rising above the light round and round about
    in more than a thousand tiers,
    I saw all of us that have returned up there.

75. Here my memory defeats my wit;
    for in that cross flamed forth Christ
    so that I can find no fit comparison:
    but he that takes up his cross and follows Christ
    will still forgive me for what I leave unsaid
    when he sees that whiteness flash out Christ.

76. That one and two and three which lives for ever
    and for ever reigns in three and in two and in one,
    uncircumscribed and circumscribing all,

three times was sung by each

77. But Beatrice showed herself to me
    so lovely and smiling that this must be left
    with those sights which the memory did not retain.
    From this sight my eyes recovered strength
    to raise themselves; and I saw myself translated
    - with my lady alone to a higher blessedness.
    I perceived clearly that I had risen higher
    by the enkindled smile of the star
    which seemed to me redder than ordinary.

78. "O my own blood, and grace of God
    poured forth above measure, to whom as to thee
    was heaven's gate ever opened twice?"

79. *Paradiso*, XV, 88-9:
    "O fronda mia in che io compiacemmi
    pur aspettando, io fui la tua radice"

    "O my leaf, in whom I was well pleased
    only expecting you, I was your root."

80. "But none the less, all falsehood set aside,
    make manifest to everyone your whole vision;
    and let them then scratch wherever is the itch."

81. See note 30 above concerning Dante's notion of words in *De Vulgari Eloquentia*, which he probably put into practice, for example, in Ugolino's 'traditor ch'i' rodo'.

82. And that of which I now have to tell
    never has voice conveyed, nor ink written,
    nor ever was conceived by imagination:
    for I saw and also heard the bird talk,
    and utter with his voice 'I' and 'mine',
    when in conception it was 'we' and 'ours'.

83. Cary does, in fact, translate 'vidi e anche udí' with words which maintain the original's echo of Revelation (as for example in 8:13: 'And I beheld, and heard, an angel ...'), though the words in themselves are common enough, particularly within the sublime style, and really require a clear context around them to suggest their source. Also, the footnotes carry a reference each to Proverbs, to Revelation, to Matthew, and to Milton. In the fourth edition the stress is on English authors, and reference is made for example to a line of Chaucer's *Troylus and Creseide* which uses a similar hyperbole about writing (Note 5, p. 417: 'This joie ne maie not written be with inke. Chaucer, *Troilus and Creseide*, b. 3.').

84. Here the footnotes, which could have highlighted the apocalyptic mode, provide no help in this respect, but refer the reader to Homer, Virgil and Milton. In the fourth edition, moreover, Cary adds an example from Milton which illustrates the literal similarity in the image and the wording rather than an example illustrating the significance of the images (Note 1, p. 471: '...the middle pair/ .../ Skirted his loins and thighs with downy gold. Milton, *P.L.* b.5. 282.').

85. In the profundity of the clear substance
    of the deep light, appeared to me three circles
    of three colours and one circumference

86. *Paradiso*, XXXIII, 127 and 130-8:
   Quella circulazion che sí concetta
       ...
   dentro da sé, del suo colore stesso,
       mi parve pinta della nostra effige;
       per che 'l mio viso in lei tutto era messo.   132
   Qual'è 'l geomètra che tutto s'affige
       per misurar lo cerchio, e non ritrova,
       pensando, quel principio ond'elli indige,   135
   tal era io a quella vista nova:
       veder volea come si convenne
       l'imago al cerchio e come vi s'indova;   138

   That circle which, thus conceived,
       ...
   within itself, and in its own colour,
       seemed to me painted with our effigy;
       and so my sight was wholly given to it.
   Like the geometer who sets all his mind
       to square the circle, and for all his thinking
       does not find the formula he needs,
   such was I at that new sight:
       I wanted to see how the image was fitted to the circle
       and how it has its place there;

87. T.S. Eliot, *Dante*, in *Selected Essays*, p. 251.

88. *Paradiso*, XXXIII, 142-5:
   All'alta fantasia qui mancò possa;
       ma già volgeva il mio disio e 'l velle,
       sí come rota ch'igualmente è mossa,   144
   L'amor che move il sole e l'altre stelle.

   Here power failed high imagination;
       but already my desire and my will were revolved
       like a wheel that turns in even motion
   by the love which moves the sun and the other stars.

89. Coleridge, Letter to Cary Nov 6 1817, *Letters*, 2, p. 678.

90. Ellis, p. 63.

91. in Ellis, pp. 52-53.

Notes to chapter 10

1. This is a bibliography of editions and reissues of Cary's *Vision*, taken from the catalogues of the British Library:
   The Vision, or Hell, Purgatory, and Paradise, of Dante Alighieri, trans. the Rev. Henry Francis Cary, A.M., 3 vols, printed for the Author by J. Barfield, London, 1814.
   2nd edition corrected, with the 'Life of Dante', additional notes and an index, 3 vols, Taylor & Hessey, London, 1819.

Another edition, 2 vols, Samuel Bradfield, Philadelphia, 1822 (The Work of the British Poets Vols 45 and 46).

3rd edition, 3 vols, John Taylor, London, 1831, 8o.

A new edition corrected, William Smith, London, 1844, 8o (previous edn 1831).

The Vision... , Henry G. Bohn, London, 1850, 8o (previous edn 1844).

The Vision of Hell, illus. Gustave Doré, 2 vols, Cassel & Co, London, 1866, folio (published in parts, previous edn 1850).

The Vision... , Alfred Thomas Crocker, London, 1868, 8o (previous edn 1866).

Another edition, Author's corrected edn, Bell & Daldy, London, 1869, 8o.

The Vision... , Chandos Classics, Frederick Warne & Co, London, 1871, 8o (previous edn 1869).

Another edition, *The Vision of Hell*, Cassel, London, 1872-74 (published in parts, a reissue of the edn of 1866).

The Vision... , George Bell & Sons, London, 1876, 8o (a reissue of the edn of 1850).

The Vision of Hell... (with *The Vision of Purgatory and Paradise*), 2 vols, Cassel & Co., London, 1883-87, 4o (published in parts, a reissue of the edn of 1866, previous issue 1872-74).

The Vision... , The 'Albion' edn, Frederick Warne & Co. Ltd, 1889, 8o (previous edn 1883-87).

The Vision... , The 'Albion' edn as above, 1890, 8o (a reissue of the edn of 1889).

The Vision of Hell, illus. with 75 designs of Doré, popular edn, the ed.'s preface signed A.J.B. = Arthur J. Butler, 2 vols, Cassel & Co., London, 1892-93, 8o (previous edn 1889).

The Vision of Hell, illus. by Gustave Doré, new ed. etc. (incl. *The Vision of Purgatory and Paradise*), Cassel & Co, London, 1894-98, 4o (a reissue of the edn of 1866, previous issue 1883-87).

The Vision of Dante Alighieri, trans. the Rev. Henry Francis Cary, revised, with an introduction by Paget Toynbee etc., 3 vols, Little Library series, Methuen & Co, London, 1900-1902, 8o (previous edn 1894-98).

The Divine Comedy of Dante Alighieri, trans. the Rev. Henry Francis Cary, edn with a Life of Dante and Introductory notes by Paget Toynbee, part of Methuen's Sixpenny Library, Methuen & Co, London, 1903, 8o (previous edn 1900-1902).

Another edition, *The Vision...* , George Newnes, London, Charles Scribner & Sons, New York, 1903, 8o.

Another edition, *The Vision...* , London & New York, 1903, 8o (a reissue of the edn of 1889).

Another edition, *The Vision ...* , trans. H.F. Cary, illus. with the designs of Doré, 2 vols, London, 1903, folio (a reissue of the edn of 1866, previous issue 1894-98).

The Vision of Dante, trans. the Rev. H.F. Cary, with an Introduction and notes by Edmund Gardner, Everyman's Library, London, 1908, 8o (previous edn 1903).

The Divine Comedy ... , trans. the Rev. H.F. Cary, revised, with an Introduction by Marie-Louise Egerton Castle, Bohn's Standard Library, George Bell & Sons, London, 1910, 8o (previous edn 1906).

Another edition, *The Vision, ...* , trans. the Rev. H.F. Cary, with 108 illus. by John Flaxman, O.U.P., London, 1910, 8o.

The Vision... , trans. H.F. Cary, ed. G. Fattorusso, illus. with 450 original drawings ... and 429 reproductions of works of art, Florentine edn, Florence, 1930, 4o.

The Divine Comedy, trans. H.F. Cary, with an Introduction and appreciation by James Scott, illus. by John Flaxman, Books that Have Changed Man's Thinking series, Esto-Service, Geneva, 1970.

Notes to chapter 11

1. In particular, one thinks of William Sharp, Fuseli and perhaps Paine. For radical societies and Blake's relations with them see David V. Erdman, *Blake, Prophet Against Empire*, Princeton, 1969, pp. 159-162. Erdman points out that 'The name of Blake's friends and friends' friends are frequent in the public notices' (p. 159). Erdman discusses the impact and role of the American and French

revolutions in relation to Blake's life and work. Bronowski also adduces a further revolution: the industrial revolution in England (J. Bronowski, *William Blake and the Age of Revolution*, London, 1972). This critic also reports on the records and the proceedings following the charges brought against Blake of Treasonable Practices (p. 112). See also note 34 to Ch. 1.

2. In 1772 Blake began his apprenticeship to James Basire, engraver to the London Society of Antiquaries and to the new Royal Academy. In 1774 he was assigned by his master to copy the monuments of ancient British dynasts for the Antiquaries (Erdman, p. 31).

Blake also seems to have belonged to the circle meeting at the regular Tuesday dinners given by the radical publisher Joseph Johnson in the early 1790's. Johnson had published many radical poems and works, including Blake's *The French Revolution* (1791). See Erdman, pp. 154-159, and Geoffrey Keynes, *Blake Studies*, Oxford, 1971, pp. 68-69.

3. See page 257.

4. The full annotation occurs on page 273 and is quoted in Milton Klonsky, *Blake's Dante*, London, 1980, p. 138.

5. *The Marriage of Heaven and Hell* was probably started in 1790, and completed in 1793, a year which also saw the completion of *For Children: The Gates of Paradise*.

6. Public Address (MS), 1809, as quoted in *The Portable Blake*, ed. A. Kazin, New York, 1946, p. 534.

7. Klonsky, p. 18.

8. The basic numbering and ordering of Blake's Dante plates is that of William Michael Rossetti, who was shown the plates when they were still in the possession of the Linnell family in 1862, when he was asked to compile a catalogue of Blake's drawings, paintings and engravings for the second volume of Gilchrist's *Life of Blake*. He grouped the plates into 69 *Hell* plates (1-69), 20 *Purgatory* plates (70-89), 10 *Paradise* plates (90-99) and three 'Additional Drawings' (100-102). In addition, he provided each plate with a title. Roe follows the Rossetti ordering, but Klonsky claims to have discovered the places within the series where the additional drawings belong, and so his order is different from Rossetti's and Roe's, though he retains Rossetti's titles. I partly disagree with Klonsky (see note 10 below), but follow his numbering, since his book is more readily available than Roe's. Hence, the numbers in my text relate to Klonsky. As for John Flaxman, I have used *Compositions By John Flaxman*, London, 1807.

9. Of this plate Roe says: 'For striking and effective creative originality, this is probably the finest design of the series and one of the masterpieces of Blake's life. This is the result, of course, of the highly unusual and yet perfectly appropriate composition which is in keeping, as no attempt at literal illustration could have been, with the lyrical and imaginative essence of the poem itself' (Albert S. Roe, *Blake's Illustrations to the* Divine Comedy, Princeton, 1953, p. 65).

10. Fuseli's drawings of subjects drawn from Dante are mainly wash-drawings in pen and china ink, finished in watercolour. Fuseli sketched some landscape around the figures in his few watercolours; he represents the literal Dante with the characteristic physiognomy. There are two groups of figures which are somewhat similar in Fuseli's and Blake's drawings. I am thinking in particular first of the man carrying away a woman in Blake's *Minos* plate and in Fuseli's sketch for 'Le anime di Paolo e Francesca' (1777). Secondly, Fuseli's 'Studio di figure per illustrazioni dantesche' (1770-78) has, to the right, a group consisting of a male figure reclining over a rock with a female figure sitting on the ground; this is somewhat similar to one of Blake's 'additional drawings', which Klonsky inserts within the series as Plate 27, as being an illustration of the blasphemers in Canto XIV. This latter group in particular could support the idea of the artists having made some sketches together, in which case these would be early sketches which would be better not placed amongst the plates. In this respect, therefore, I disagree with Klonsky. Fuseli's Dante designs are included in *Füssli e Dante*,

a cura di Corrado Gizzi, Milano, 1985.

11. Flaxman's views are not recorded, and there is no other evidence that Blake followed his views.

12. David V. Erdman, *The Illuminated Blake*, London, 1975. Erdman discusses the Ugolino plate (Plate 12) in *The Gates* on p. 274, and that in *The Marriage* on p. 113.

13. *The Marriage of Heaven and Hell*, in *William Blake: the Complete Poems*, ed. Alicia Ostriker, Penguin, 1977, p. 180. References are to this edition, unless otherwise specified.

14. Erich Auerbach has developed this view in various books and essays. In particular, I have used *Dante als Dichter der irdischen Welt*, 1929, trans. R. Manheim, *Dante, Poet of the Secular World*, 1961; 3rd impression Chicago and London, 1974. See also 'San Francesco' in *Antologia della critica dantesca*, ed. Carlo Salinari, Bari, 1966, pp. 217-229.

15. Charity discusses Dante's letter at length in his *Events and Their Afterlife*, particularly pp. 204-207. The quotation is from p. 221.

16. This is the anecdote in Cary's words: 'At the table of Can Grande, when the company was amused by the conversation and tricks of a buffoon, he was asked by his patron, why Can Grande himself, and the guests who were present, failed of receiving as much pleasure from the exertion of his talents, as this man had been able to give them. "Because all creatures delight in their own resemblance," was the reply of Dante'. Cary reports this anecdote to show that Dante 'appears to have indulged too much a disposition to sarcasm' ('Life of Dante', p. XXVI). Ellis discusses the painting by Lord Leighton in *Dante and English Poetry*, pp. 55-56.

17. The information concerning the Heads of the Poets is taken mainly from two booklets published on the occasion of the exhibition of the series in the City Art Gallery in Manchester, April 29 to May 18, 1969. The first booklet, *William Blake's "Heads of the Poets"*, contains a foreword by the Director of the Gallery, G.L. Conran, in which he specifies that the introduction which follows is the work of William Wells, and the postscript (coming at the end of the introduction), with information about the layout of the library, is by Miss Elizabeth Johnson, Keeper of Paintings, and is based on the recent discovery of a plan of Hayley's library. The introduction and postscript are followed by the catalogue of the series, which includes details such as measurements. The catalogue is in black and white. The second booklet (entitled *'For Friendship's Sake': William Blake and William Hayley*) is a shorter catalogue, with an introductory 'Argument towards a conjectural arrangement of Blake's "Heads of the Poets"', written by Elizabeth Johnston. There is a foreword by the Director of the Gallery, who adds the information that the cleaning of the paintings has revealed that they were originally in tempera, and were successively heavily overpainted in oil. The text of the introductory essay is 'based on Mr Wells' booklet', who presumably is then its author. Most of the information contained in these booklets is also to be found in G.E. Bentley, *Blake Records*, Oxford, 1969, pp. 69-71.

18. The larger catalogue includes under the description of each portrait information about the models Blake used. Only for Homer does there seem to have been no specific source. For Milton, Blake used the portrait engraved *ad vivum* by William Faithorne, which appeared in Milton's *History of Britain* (1670) and was often used in other books (*William Blake's "Heads of the Poets"*, p. 23).

19. Figures 1 and 2 are taken from the booklet *William Blake's "Heads of the Poets"*, and the Dante plates are reproduced from Milton Klonsky, *Blake's Dante*, London, 1980.

20. *William Blake's "Heads of the Poets"*, pp. 17-18.

21. For background information on Raphael's painting of Dante, the iconography of a Dante portrait, the scientific discoveries concerning Dante's death mask, and traditions at different times concerning the 'reality' of a portrait, see R.T. Holbrook, *Portraits of Dante from Giotto to Raphael*,

London, Boston and New York, 1911.

22. See Elizabeth Johnson, 'Argument towards a Conjectural Arrangement of Blake's "Heads of the Poets"', in *'For Friendship's Sake': William Blake and William Hayley*, City of Manchester Gallery, Manchester, 1969. How or even whether the portraits ever were used is uncertain, as this publication and its companion by Wells show. With regard to the fact that Blake turned the heads of Dante around in respect to the print he used as model, it is of course possible that he intended to return to the original position as in Raphael's painting. As for Milton, Wells suggests (p. 23) that Blake may have used a version of William Faithorne's engraved portrait (which faces right) as it was reproduced in one of the versions of that portrait by Vertue, some of which faced right, and some left – such as the frontispiece to the 1720 edition of Milton's *Works*.

23. Joseph Anthony Wittreich jr., *Angel of Apocalypse: Blake's Idea of Milton*, London, 1975, pp. 11-12.

24. Flaxman's are well known, and pick moments of the story different from Blake's. Reynold's painting is lost, but can be deduced from engravings, such as the one reproduced in Ellis Waterhouse's *Reynolds*, London, 1973.

25. Blake's annotations to Boyd are included in *The Complete Writings of William Blake*, ed. G. Keynes, London, 1966, pp. 411 ff.

26. Henry Crabb Robinson, diary entries, in Bentley, pp. 541-543.

27. The whole question of Blake's knowledge of Italian, use of English translations of Dante, and reliance on translation should be briefly discussed.
   In the fifties Keynes discovered Blake's annotations to Boyd, the first volume of Boyd's *Inferno* (1785) being one of the volumes in Blake's possession (and one which had been kept back from public knowledge). No other volume by Boyd is known to have been owned or used by Blake (Keynes, *Blake Studies*, p. 149).
   The obituary notice in *The Literary Gazette* of Saturday August 18 1827, describing the room where Blake died, mentions 'books (among them his Bible, a Sessi Valatello's Dante, and Mr Carey's translation, were at the top), ...', the 'Velatello' being presumably the *Commedia* with the commentary of Alessandro Vellutello (1551; rpt. 1554, 64, 71, 78, 96, etc.), which was available and not expensive in London in the 1820's. The obituary notice and associated comments are in Bentley, p. 349.
   Blake is reported to have started learning Italian when he was commissioned to do the Dante plates by John Linnell, in 1824, and to have made so much progress in two weeks that he could read the text. See John Thomas Smith's biography *Nollekens and His Times*, 1828, Vol. II; rpt. in Bentley, pp. 455-476. The reference to Blake learning Italian occurs on p. 476. The first reference in correspondence to Blake's 1824 commission for the Dante plates occurs in 1825.
   There are indications that Blake read Dante in the Italian. He writes the inscription above Hell's gate in Italian, followed by a translation. The Italian is, however, incorrect, and this may suggest that Blake is not copying it from an original, but recalling it from memory. The translation of the Italian phrase is very literal, obviously done by himself, and is, therefore, also incorrect ('Lasciate ogni Speranza voi che en Entrate', 'Leave every Hope you who in Enter', instead of 'Lasciate ogni speranza, voi ch'entrate', which Cary translated as 'All hope abandon, ye who enter here'). Since this phrase had by then become quite current in English (see, for example, Ch. 3, p. 39), Blake could indeed have remembered it from sources other than the original text. More definitely from the text of the *Inferno* comes a single reference included in Blake's 'Diagram of Hell-circles' (Plate 22). Here, after '9 Circles in Canto XI v 18 3' he adds 'Dante calls them Cerchietti'. This is quite accurate. Still it must be remembered that Cary's translation of *Inferno* (1805-6) included the Italian original on the opposite page from the translation. Furthermore, that Blake actually followed Cary's translation quite closely is confirmed by other words in the same plate. For his definition of some of the circles

of Hell in Plate 22 Blake definitely uses Cary's phrasings (such as 'Lesser circle point of the universe' and 'queen of endless woe' for circle 5). In fact the very reference to 'Cerchietti' is preceded by the reference to Canto XI, 18, which corresponds to Cary's 'Are three close circles in gradation placed'.

28. Prints from the engravings were issued to collectors at 2 guineas a set in 1825 – see Geoffrey Keynes, *A Bibliography of William Blake*, New York, 1921, pp. 182-185. There were 7 plates, printed in black on separate leaves, issued either as loose leaves together with a label (which included short extracts from 'Cary's Dante'), or 'bound up as an oblong folio volume with the label pasted on the outer cover' (p. 183). It is possible that Linnell printed more copies of the plates when they were in his possession.

29. Roe explains many features of the picture in terms of Blake's ideas. So the trees, with the roots and brambles Blake adds, signify the dangers of the material world which prevent him from attaining spiritual freedom; the three beasts could symbolize 'the ravening selfhood' (the leopard), 'uncontrolled rationalism' (the lion) and 'the Female Will' (the she-wolf). Virgil would be a figure of Christ, and Roe interestingly points out that he looks like the 'great design of plate 76 of *Jerusalem*, in which the Fallen Albion at the moment of his realization of his error of selfhood and his understanding of the means of his redemption through Christ's love, stands with his back turned and his arms spread in the forms of the cross, facing the figure of Christ crucified upon the Tree of Error' (p. 49). This explanation seems particularly interesting in the light of the similar position of some figures in Plates 3 and 94 (see my discussion, pp. 284-5).

30. See, in the original, l. 94, 'Donna è gentil ...', ll. 97 ff., and l. 102 for Mary, St Lucy and Rachel respectively. Beatrice is present, through Virgil's report of her visit to him, in much of the canto.

31. Roe, pp. 61-63.

32. For my discussion of the gap between the two cantos see Chapter 4, pp. 70 ff..

33. Alan Cunningham, a close friend of Blake's, relates the following: 'For many years ... I longed to see Satan – I never could believe that he was the vulgar fiend which our legends represent him – I imagined him a classic spirit ..., with some of his original splendour. ...' said Blake, introducing Satan's apparition to him at a turn of the stairs in his house, and then 'It is the gothic fiend of our legends, said Blake – the true devil – all else are apocryphal' (Alan Cunningham, *The Lives of the Most Eminent British Painters, Sculptors, and Architects*; rpt. in Bentley, p. 498).

34. Above the Goddess, and her place of abode, is a picture of the spendthrifts and the misers, who face each other and have to push a large stone with their chests until they meet and can go no further, at which point they start again. Blake merely sketched them, and the indefiniteness of the drawing, in combination with the scene down below, makes these figures look like dung beetles.

35. The annotations pencilled on this plate read as follows: 'It seems as if Dantes supreme Good was something Superior to the Father or Jesus. For if he gives his rain to the Evil & the Good & his Sun to the Just & the Unjust He could never have Built Dantes Hell nor the Hell of the Bible neither in the way our Parsons explain it. It must have been originally formed by the Devil Him self & so I understand it to have been.' The sense of this is not absolutely clear. More clear is the following note: 'Whatever Book is for Vengeance and for Sin & Whatever Book is Against the Forgiveness of Sins is not of the Father but of Satan the Accuser & Father of Hell.' Roe (p. 31) points out the verbal similarity with *Jerusalem*, Plate 52, and concludes that 'Obviously, therefore, Blake considered the *Inferno* to be such a book.' Yet Blake is not directly censuring Dante here; rather, he is thinking about possibilities, and clarifying his own thoughts. This is particularly clear in two other comments, which Blake wrote along the right side of the same page but, in relation to one another, the other way up and, as a consequence, running in a different direction: 'This is Upside Down When viewed from Hells Gate *which ought to be at the top*' and then, reversing the

page, 'But right when viewed from Purgatory after they have passed the centre. In Equivocal Worlds Up & Down are Equivocal.' This refers to the poets' journey from Lucifer to Purgatory, at which point they must turn upside down, because they are crossing the centre of the earth.

36. In fact Blake adds a fifth figure half hidden by a tree, which could be an attempt to represent the scene as it is in eternity, Virgil having joined the other poets.

37. Roe has to admit, however, that Blake's views concerning classical poets as expressed in his different works vary, and this probably explains why the division created by the clouds 'is not a very great one'.

38. Notice, also, that Blake faithfully reproduces figures of men, of women and of babies.

39. Jean Hagstrum, *William Blake – Poet and Painter: An Introduction to the Illuminated Verse*, Chicago and London, 1964, pp. 125-126.

40. The contrast is somewhat smoothed over when one notices the flowering vegetation occurring on the mountain in Plate 69, that is, the plate preceding the final three plates. Dante is resting on this mountain after going through the fire, and dreams of Lea and Rachel (pictured within an enormous moon, gathering flowers). In the preceding drawing, too, a few flowering twigs can be seen right under the path on which the fire burns.

41. Blake's drawings all refer to the narrative of the journey. Flaxman, on the contrary, also shows Buonconte da Montefeltro rescued by the angel, with the devil retreating below (Fuseli also has a plate of this episode), the fall of Lucifer, Forese's elevation, and the salutation – this being one of the examples of humility engraved on the mountain.

42. We have seen that the last plates begin to include flowers, and in Plate 90 the ground is covered with flowers; in Plate 79, representing 'the Lawn with the Kings and Angels' in Canto VIII, on the other hand, Blake pictures very thick and luxuriant bushes, but no flowers.

43. This is in fact in Roe's order; the second plate in this order is a 'Design of Circular Stairs', a bare sketch. Klonsky makes of this the first *Paradise* plate (although he also attributes it to Canto XXI), with 'Dante Adoring Christ' from Canto XIV then becoming the second plate.

44. Bernard Blackstone, says that 'Throughout Blake's work the sun is present in his triple aspect of light, heat and motion, the trinity of energy' (*English Blake*, Cambridge, England, 1949, p. 149).

45. Eno is 'the ability of seeing the eternity in all things ... . She is thus the mother of all poetry.' See S. Foster Damon, *A Blake Dictionary*, Providence, Rhode Island, 1965, p. 125.

46. Christ appears a number of times in *Paradiso*, where he is mentioned 34 times. In at least four passages the name of Christ is repeated three times in rhyming position; besides the occurrence mentioned in Canto XIV, others are in Canto XII (ll. 71, 73, 75), XIX (ll. 104, 6, 8), and XXXII (ll. 83, 85, 87). In addition, he is referred to many times through periphrases or attributes.

47. From a letter to Butts 20 October 1800, ll. 45-60, as quoted in *William Blake: The Complete Poems*, pp. 483-4 (in the section 'Poems from Letters').

48. Klonsky and Roe both quote passages from *Jerusalem* and other poems by Blake (some are in fact the same passages), only to come to very different conclusions. Klonsky sees this Christ as 'a God afar off', while to Roe 'this is the final instant in which is made real that unity with Divine Vision of which the poet is aware in all of his inspired moments during his life in the Fallen World'. The one passage from *Jerusalem* (also quoted by Roe) that seems to me to approach this design most closely is the following:

Of the Sleep of Ulro! and of the passage through
Eternal Death! and of the Awakening to Eternal Life.

This theme calls me in sleep night after night, & ev'ry morn
Awakes me at sun-rise, then I see the Saviour over me
Spreading his beams of love & dictating the words of this mild song.   (*Jerusalem* 1:1-5)

49. W.B. Yeats, 'William Blake and the Imagination', in *Ideas of Good and Evil*, London, 1903, p. 168.

50. W.B. Yeats, 'William Blake and his Illustrations to *The Divine Comedy*', ibid., pp. 219-220.

Notes to chapter 12

1. Lord Macaulay, 'Criticisms on the Principal Italian Writers. No. 1. Dante', *Knight's Quarterly Magazine*, January 1824; in *Miscellaneous Writings*, London, n.d., p. 38.

2. Jerome McGann, 'The Aim of Blake's Prophecies', in *Blake's Sublime Allegory*, eds Curran and Wittreich jr., p. 13. McGann points out that the Byronic hero is, in this respect, a figure similar to Shelley's Alastor, Keats' La Belle Dame, or Coleridge's Kubla Kahn, and says that 'To decide that Keats' fairy child is a Circe or a visionary ideal is to pass judgement upon oneself' (pp. 12-13). He connects the function of these figures with visionary poetry (Blake's in particular) – a poetry that is 'a call to judgement, the declaration of a state of affairs in which men have to choose either the light or darkness' (p. 11).

3. James Beattie, 'Preface' to *The Minstrel*, in The Minstrel or The Progress of Genius *with some other Poems*, Edinburgh, 1807, pp. x-xi.

4. Boyd, 'Dedication to the Earl of Bristol, Bishop of Derry', in *Inferno*, Dublin, 1785, 1, pp. v-vi.

5. Boyd, 'Dedication to Charles Williams, Lord Viscount Charleville, One of the Lords of the Imperial Parliament for the United Kingdoms', in *The Divina Commedia*, London, 1802, 1, p. iii.

6. Letter dated 'Christ Church, Oxford, May 7 1792', in *Memoir*, 1, pp. 42-3.

Bibliography

This bibliography is divided into 9 sections according to the area of study covered by the books used:

a) Dante's works
b) Works on Dante
c) Translations of the *Commedia* or parts of the *Commedia* into English (in chronological order)
d) Works on translations of Dante and translation studies
e) Dante and English literature
f) Works on and by William Blake
g) Works on and by other authors
h) England in the eighteenth and nineteenth centuries.
i) General works

a) Dante's works

Commedia di Dante Allighieri, con ragionamenti e note di Niccolò Tommaséo, Milano, 1865.
Convivio, Bologna, 1966.
La Commedia secondo l'antica vulgata, ed. G. Petrocchi, 4 vols, Milano, 1966-67.
La Divina Commedia, a cura di Natalino Sapegno, 3 vols, Firenze, 1955-6; Vol. 1 14a ristampa 1981, Vol. 2 19a ristampa 1967, Vol. 3 13a ristampa 1981.
La Divina Commedia, nuovamente commentata da Francesco Torraca, Roma e Milano, 1908.
Tutte le Opere, a cura di Fredi Chiapparelli, edizione del centenario, Milano, 1965; rpt. 1969.

b) Works on Dante

Anderson, William, *Dante the Maker*, London, 1980.
Atti del convegno di studi su Dante e la Magna Curia, Palermo, 1967.
Auerbach, Erich, *Dante als Dichter der irdischen Welt*, 1929, trans. R. Manheim, *Dante, Poet of the Secular World*, 1961; 3rd impression Chicago and London, 1974.
Avalle, D'Arco S., *Modelli semiologici nella* Commedia di Dante, Milano, 1975.
Bickersteth, Geoffrey L., *Dante's Virgil*, Aberdeen, 1951.
Binni, Walter, *Incontri con Dante*, Ravenna, 1983.
Borges, Jorge Luis, *Nueve Ensayos Dantescos*, introd. Marcos R. Barnatán, pres. por J. Arce, Madrid, 1982.

Bosco, Umberto, *Dante vicino*, Caltanisetta-Roma, 1966.
Branca, V., and Caccia, E., eds, *Dante nel mondo*, Firenze, 1965.
Brentari, Ottone, *Dante alpinista*, Padova e Verona, 1888.
Charity, A.C., *Events and Their Afterlife: the Dialectics of Christian Typology in the Bible and Dante*, Cambridge, 1966.
Fallani, Giovanna, *Dante e la cultura figurativa medievale*, Bergamo, 1971.
Fowlie, W., *Dante's* Inferno, Chicago and London, 1981.
Frattarolo, Renzo, 'Per una teoria della critica dantesca', *A.B.I.*, Vol. 34, 1966, pp. 302-321.
Frattarolo, Renzo, *Studi su Dante dal 300 all'eta romantica*, Ravenna, 1970.
Freccero, J., *Dante: a Collection of Critical Essays*, Englewood Cliffs, N.J., 1965.
Gardner, E.G., *Dante and the Mystics*, New York, 1968.
Getto, Giovanni, *Aspetti della poesia di Dante*, Firenze, 1966.
Getto, Giovanni, ed., *Letture dantesche*, 3 vols, Firenze, 1955-61.
Green, R.G., 'Dante's "Allegory of Poets" and the Medieval Theory of Poetic Fiction', *Comparative Literature*, Vol. 9, 1957, pp. 118-128.
Hawkins, Rev. John C., *The Use of Dante as an Illustrator of Scripture*, London, 1909.
Holbrook, R.T., *Portraits of Dante from Giotto to Raphael*, London, Boston and New York, 1911.
Holmes, George, *Dante*, Oxford, 1980.
Jacomuzzi, Angelo, *'L' Imago al Cerchio': invenzione e visione nella* Divina Commedia, Milano, 1968.
Letture classensi, Vol. 5, Ravenna, 1976.
Mandelstam, Osip, 'Conversation about Dante', trans. C. Brown and T. Hughes, in *Osip Mandelstam: Selected Essays*, ed. S. Monas, Austin and London, 1977, pp. 3-44.
Marcazzan, Mario, ed., *Lectura Dantis Scaligera*, 3 vols, Firenze, 1967-1968.
Marzotta, Giuseppe, *Dante, Poet of the Desert*, Princeton, 1979.
Mineo, Nicoló, *Profetismo e apocalittica in Dante: strutture e temi profetico-apocalittici dalla* Vita Nuova *alla* Commedia, Catania, 1968.
Moore, Edward, *Studies in Dante*, 4th Series, Oxford, 1917; rpt. 1968.
Riestra, Myriam de la, *Dante y los romanticos*, Buenos Aires, 1971.
Salinari, Carlo, ed., *Antologia della critica dantesca*, Bari, 1966.
Salinari, Carlo, ed., *Dante e la critica*, Bari, 1973.
di Salvo, T., ed., *Dante nella critica*, Firenze, 1965.
de Sanctis, Francesco, *Quattro saggi danteschi*, Napoli, 1903.
Sandron, Remo, ed., *Mostra di codici ed edizioni dantesche*, Firenze, 1965.
Scaglione, A.D., 'Periodic Syntax and Flexible Metre in the Divina Commedia', *Romance Philology*, Vol. 21, 1967-8, pp. 1-12.
Singleton, Charles, *An Essay on the* Vita Nuova, 1949; rpt. Baltimore and London, 1977.
Singleton, Charles, *Dante's* Commedia - *Elements of Structure*, 1954; rpt. Baltimore and London, 1977; 2nd printing 1980.
Singleton, Charles, *Journey to Beatrice*, Baltimore and London, 1958; rpt. 1977.
Toffanin, G., *Perché l'umanesimo comincia con Dante*, Bologna, 1967.
Toynbee, Paget, *A Dictionary of Proper Names and Notable Matters in the Works of Dante*, 1898; rev. Charles Singleton, Oxford, 1968.
Volkman, L., *Iconografia dantesca*, Firenze and Venezia, 1898.

c) Translations of the Commedia or parts of the Commedia into English (in chronological order)

Richardson the Elder, Jonathan, 'An Argument in behalf of the Science of a Connoisseur, wherein is shewn the Dignity, Certainty, Pleasure and Advantage of it' [containing a translation of the Ugolino episode into blank verse], in *Two Discourses*, London, 1719.

Richardson the Elder, Jonathan, 'An Argument in behalf of the Science of a Connoisseur, wherein is shewn the Dignity, Certainty, Pleasure and Advantage of it' [containing a translation of the Ugolino episode into blank verse], 1719; rpt. in *The Works of Jonathan Richardson (the Elder)*, London, 1773.

Gray, Thomas, 'Dante. Canto 33, dell'Inferno' [the Ugolino episode], probably written 1737-40, first published in *Works*, ed. Gosse, 1884; rpt. in *The Complete Poems of Thomas Gray*, eds H.W. Starr and J.R. Hendrickson, Oxford, 1966.

Frederick Howard, Earl of Carlisle, 'Translation from Dante, Canto XXXIII' [the Ugolino episode], probably written 1772, in *Poems . . . by the Earl of Carlisle*, 1773; as quoted in Toynbee, *Dante in English Literature from Chaucer to Cary*.

Hayley, William, *William Hayley* [containing facsimile copies of the first editions of *Ode Inscribed to John Howard*, *An Essay on Painting*, *The Triumphs of Temper*, *Essay on Epic Poetry*], introd. Donald H. Reiman, New York and London, 1979.

The Inferno of Dante tr. by Charles Rogers, Esq., of the Custom House London [added in pen], London, 1782.

Boyd, Henry, *A Translation of the INFERNO of Dante Alighieri in English Verse, with Historical Notes, and the Life of Dante to which is added A SPECIMEN OF A NEW TRANSLATION OF ARIOSTO*, 2 vols, Dublin, 1785.

Boyd, Henry, *The Divina Commedia of Dante Alighieri, consisting of the Inferno, Purgatorio, Paradiso*, 3 vols, London, 1802.

Cary, Henry Francis, *The Inferno of Dante Alighieri*, 2 vols, London, 1805-6.

Cary, Henry Francis, *The Vision; or, Hell, Purgatory, and Paradise, of Dante Alighieri*, 1814; rpt. Chandos Classics edn, London, 1871.

Cary, Henry Francis, *The Vision; or, Hell, Purgatory and Paradise, of Dante Alighieri*, 4th edn 1844; rpt. Albion edn, London and New York, 1889.

Longfellow, Henry W, *The Divine Comedy*, Boston, 1867.

Howard, E.P., *Dante in English: a Terza Rima Translation and Critique of Terza Rima Translations of Inferno*, Chicago, 1919.

Hooper, H.J., *The Inferno, a New Rhythmical Translation*, London, 1922.

Bickersteth, Geoffrey L., *The Divine Comedy*, 1931; rpt. Oxford, 1981.

Binyon, Laurence, *The Divine Comedy*, in *The Portable Dante*, ed. Paolo Milano, Penguin, 1975.

Sinclair, John D., *The Divine Comedy of Dante Alighieri*, 3 vols, 1939; rpt. Vol. 1 *Inferno*, London, 1971; rpt. 1975.

Sinclair, John D., *The Divine Comedy of Dante Alighieri*, 3 vols, 1939; rpt. Vol. 2 *Purgatorio*, and Vol. 3 *Paradiso*, New York, 1961; rpt. 1978-79.

Sayers, Dorothy L., *The Comedy of Dante Alighieri*, Vol. 1 *Hell*, Penguin, 1949; rpt. Penguin, 1977.

Sayers, Dorothy L., *The Comedy of Dante Alighieri*, Vol. 2 *Purgatory*, Penguin, 1955; rpt. 1979.

Sayers, Dorothy L., *The Comedy of Dante Alighieri*, Vol. 3 *Paradise*, Penguin, 1962; rpt. 1978.

Ciardi, John, *The Divine Comedy*, 1954; rpt. New York and London, 1970.

Singleton, Charles, *The Divine Comedy*, Vol. 1 *Inferno*, Part 1 Italian Text and Translation, Part 2 Commentary, Princeton, 1970; rpt.1980.

Singleton, Charles, *The Divine Comedy*, Vol. 2 *Purgatorio*, Part 1 Italian Text and Translation, Part 2 Commentary, Princeton, 1973; rpt. 1977.

Singleton, Charles, *The Divine Comedy*, Vol. 3 *Paradiso*, Part 1 Italian Text and translation, Part 2 Commentary, Princeton, 1973; rpt. 1977.

Sisson, C.H., *The Divine Comedy*, Manchester, 1980.

Sisson, C.H., *The Divine Comedy*, rev. edn with introduction, notes and commentary, Pan Classics, 1981.

Mandelbaum, Allen, *The Divine Comedy of Dante Alighieri*, 3 vols, illus. Barry Moser, Berkeley, 1980-82.

Musa, Mark, *Dante Alighieri: The Divine Comedy*, 3 vols, 1971-84; rpt. 3 vols, Penguin, 1986.
Phillips, Tom, *Dante's Inferno*, trans. and illus. Tom Phillips, London, 1985.

d) Works on translations of Dante and translation studies

Bassnett-McGuire, Susan, *Translation Studies*, London and New York, 1985.
Bergin, Thomas G., 'Dante Translations', *The Yale Review*, Vol. 60, 1970-71, pp. 614-617.
Hermans, Theo, ed., *The Manipulation of Literature: Studies in Literary Translation*, London & Sidney, 1985.
Holmes, James S., José Lambert, and Raymond van den Broeck, eds, *Literature and Translation: New Perspectives in Literary Studies*, Leuven, 1978.
Musa, Mark, 'On Translating Dante', *Yearbook of Comparative and General Literature*, No. 19, 1970.
Pound, Ezra, 'Hell', *The Criterion*, 1934.
Reynolds, Barbara, 'English Fashions in Translating Dante', *Forum for Modern Language Studies*, Vol. 1, No. 2, April 1965, pp. 117-125.
Shewring, W., 'Epilogue on translation', in Homer, *Odyssey*, Oxford, 1980.
Steiner, George, 'The Tale of 3 Cities', *Encounter*, May 1984.
De Sua, William J., *Dante into English*, Chapel Hill, 1964.
Webb, Timothy, *The Violet in the Crucible: Shelley and Translation*, Oxford, 1976.

e) Dante and English Literature

Arthos, John, *Dante, Michelangelo and Milton*, London, 1965.
Besso, Marco, *La Fortuna di Dante fuori d'Italia*, Firenze, 1912.
Bidney, Martin, '"The Central Fiery Heart": Ruskin's Remaking of Dante', *The Victorian Newsletter*, No. 48, Fall 1975, pp. 11-15.
Brand, Charles Peter, *Italy and the English Romantics: the Italianate Fashion in Early Nineteenth-century England*, Cambridge, 1957.
Coleridge, Samuel Taylor, 'Dante', in *The Portable Coleridge*, ed. I.A. Richards, New York, 1950.
Cunningham, Gilbert F., *The Divine Comedy in English: a Critical Bibliography*, 2 vols, Vol. 1 1782-1900, Vol. 2 1901-1966, Edinburgh and London, 1965-6.
Dédéyan, Charles, *Dante dans le Romantisme Anglais*, Paris, 1983.
Dédéyan, Charles, *Dante en Grande-Bretagne, Moyen Age - Renaissance*, Paris, 1962.
Doughty, Oswald, 'Dante and the English Romantic Poets', *English Miscellany*, Vol. 1, Part 3, 1950, pp. 125-169.
Eliot, T.S., *Dante*, in *Selected Essays*, London, 1932; rpt. 1953.
Eliot, T.S., 'Dante', in *The Sacred Wood*, 1920; 7th edn London, 1950; rpt. 1957.
Eliot, T.S., 'What Dante means to Me', in *To Criticize the Critic*, London, 1965.
Ellis, Steve, *Dante and English Poetry: Shelley to T.S. Eliot*, Cambridge, 1983.
Farinelli, A., *Dante in Spagna, Francia, Inghilterra e Germania*, Torino, 1922.
Flick, Adrian John, *Dante in English Romanticism*, Diss. Cambridge, 1978.
Friederich, Werner P., *Dante's Fame Abroad, 1350-1850*, Chapel Hill, 1950.
Gizzi, Corrado, ed., *Füssli e Dante*, Milano, 1985.
King, Robert W., *The Translator of Dante: the Life, Work and Friendships of Henry Francis Cary 1772-1844*, London, 1925.
Kuhns, Oscar, *Dante and the English Poets from Chaucer to Tennyson*, New York, 1904.
Ostermann, Theodor, *Dante in Deutschland*, Heidelberg, 1929.
Praz, Mario, 'Dante and T.S.Eliot', in *The Flaming Heart*, New York, 1958.

Praz, Mario, 'Dante in England', *Forum for Modern Language Studies*, Vol. 1, No. 2, April 1965, pp. 99-116.

Steiner, T.R., *English Translation Theory 1650-1800*, Assen and Amsterdam, 1975.

Thorpe, Lewis, ed., *Nottingham Medieval Studies*, Vol. 9, 1965 [containing 'English Awareness of Dante', by B. Reynolds; 'The Art of Translating Dante', by Dorothy L. Sayers; 'Dante's Similes' by C.S. Lewis; 'The "terrible" Ode', by Dorothy L. Sayers; 'Religion and Love in Dante', by C. Williams].

Toynbee, Paget, *Dante in English Art*, Boston, 1921.

Toynbee, Paget, *Dante in English Literature from Chaucer to Cary*, 2 vols, London, 1909.

Toynbee, Paget, *Dante Studies and Researches*, London, 1902.

Toynbee, Paget, 'The Earliest References to Dante in English Literature', *Miscellanea di Studi Critici*, June 1903.

f) Works on and by William Blake

Bentley, G.E., *Blake Records*, Oxford, 1969.

Blackstone, Bernard, *English Blake*, Cambridge, 1949.

Blake, William, *William Blake: The Complete Poems*, ed. Alicia Ostriker, Penguin, 1977.

Blake, William, *The Complete Writings of William Blake*, ed. Geoffrey Keynes, London, 1966.

Bronowsky, J., *William Blake and the Age of Revolution*, London, 1972.

Curran, Stuart, and Joseph Anthony Wittreich jr., eds, *Blake's Sublime Allegory*, Madison, Wisconsin, and London, 1973.

Damon, S. Foster, *A Blake Dictionary*, Providence, Rhode Island, 1965.

Erdman, David V., *Blake, Prophet Against Empire: a Poet's Interpretation of the History of His Own Times*, Princeton, New Jersey, 1969.

Erdman, David V., *The Illuminated Blake*, London, 1975.

Frye, Northrop, *Fearful Symmetry: a Study of William Blake*, Princeton, 1947; rpt. 1974.

Hagstrum, Jean, *William Blake – Poet and Painter: An Introduction to the Illuminated Verse*, Chicago and London, 1964.

Johnston, Elizabeth, *'For Friendship's Sake': William Blake and William Hayley* [booklet accompanying the exhibition of the Heads of the Poets in the City Art Gallery Manchester, 29 April to 18 May 1969].

Kazin, A., ed., *The Portable Blake*, New York, 1946.

Keynes, Geoffrey, *A Bibliography of William Blake*, New York, 1921.

Keynes, Geoffrey, *Blake Studies*, Oxford, 1971.

Klonsky, Milton, *Blake's Dante: the Complete Illustrations to the Divine Comedy*, London, 1980.

Roe, Albert S., *Blake's Illustrations to the Divine Comedy*, Princeton, 1953.

Wells, William, *William Blake's Heads of the Poets*, for Turret House, the residence of William Hayley, Felpham [booklet accompanying the exhibition of the Heads of the Poets in the City Art Gallery Manchester, 29 April to 18 May 1969].

Wittreich, Joseph Anthony jr., *Angel of Apocalypse: Blake's idea of Milton*, London, 1975.

g) Works on and by other authors

Baillie, John, *An Essay on the Sublime*, 1747; rpt. Los Angeles, 1953.

Beattie, James, The Minstrel or The Progress of Genius *with some other Poems*, Edinburgh, 1807.

Bloom, Harold, and Lionel Trilling, eds, *Romantic Poetry and Prose*, OAEL Vol. 4, New York and London, 1973.

Brower, Reuben Arthur, *Alexander Pope: The Poetry of Allusion*, Oxford, 1959.

Burke, Edmund, *A Philosophical Enquiry into the Origin of Our Ideas of the Sublime and Beautiful*, 1757; rpt. Merston, England, 1970.

Butler, Marilyn, ed., *Burke, Paine, Godwin, and the Revolution Controversy*, Cambridge, 1984.

Byron, George Gordon, Lord Byron, *The Poetical Works of Lord Byron*, London and New York, 1892.

Carlyle, Thomas, Sartor Resartus *and* On Heroes and Hero Worship, Everyman's Library, 1908; rpt. 1959.

Cary, Henry, *Memoir of the Rev. Henry Francis Cary, A.M., translator of Dante, with his Literary Journal and Letters*, 2 vols, London, 1847.

Coleridge, Samuel Taylor, *Biographia Literaria*, London, 1906; rpt. 1917.

Coleridge, Samuel Taylor, *Letters of Samuel Taylor Coleridge*, ed. Ernest Hartley Coleridge, 2 vols, London, 1895.

Coleridge, Samuel Taylor, *The Notebooks of Samuel Taylor Coleridge*, ed. K. Coburn, 2 vols, New York, 1957.

Cowper, William, *The Poetical Works of William Cowper*, ed. William Michael Rossetti, illus. Thomas Seccombe, London, n.d..

Cowper, William, *The Works of William Cowper*, ed. Robert Southey, illus. with engravings by W. Harvey, 8 vols, London, 1854.

Culler, A. Dwight, *The Poetry of Tennyson*, New Haven and London, 1977.

Davie, Donald, 'Summer Lightning', *TLS*, 25 July 1981.

Dryden, John, *Essays of John Dryden*, ed. W.P. Ker, 2 vols, Oxford, 1926.

Eco, Umberto, *Il Nome della Rosa*, Milano, 1984.

Ellman, Richard, *Yeats, the Man and the Mask*, London, 1961.

Flaxman, John, *Compositions by John Flaxman, Sculptor, R.A., from the Divine Poem of Dante Alighieri*, quotations from the Italian and translations from the version of the Reverend H. Boyd to each plate, London, 1807.

Giambattista Vico: An International Symposium, Baltimore, 1967.

Gray, Thomas, *Correspondence of Thomas Gray*, eds Paget Toynbee and Leonard Whitby, 3 vols, Oxford, 1935; rpt. 1971.

Gray, Thomas, *The Complete Works of Thomas Gray*, eds H.W. Starr and J.R. Hendrickson, Oxford, 1966.

Hayley, William, *The Triumphs of Temper*, Paris, 1804.

Hayley, William, *Plays of Three Acts*, London, 1784.

Heaney, Seamus, *Field Work*, London, 1979.

Hill, Aaron, *The Poems of Hill, Cawthorn, and Bruce*, The British Poets Vol. 60, Chiswick, 1822.

Homer, *The Iliad*, trans. Andrew Lang, Walter Leaf and Ernest Myers, 1882; 1st Globe edn 1914; reset and rpt. London, 1930.

Homer, *The Iliad*, trans. A.T. Murray, Cambridge, Mass., and London, 1924; rpt. 1971.

Homer, *The Iliad*, trans. Alexander Pope, Vols 7 and 8 of *The Twickenham Edition of the Poetry of Pope*, ed. M. Mack, London and New Haven, 1967.

Lucy, Sean, *T.S.Eliot and the Idea of Tradition*, London, 1960.

Macaulay, Thomas Babington, *Miscellaneous Writings*, London, n.d..

Milton, John, *The Poetical Works of John Milton*, ed. Sir Egerton Brydges, illus. with engravings from drawings by J.M.W. Turner, London, 1852.

Pirandello, Luigi, *Saggi*, ed. Manlio Lo Vecchio Musti, Milano, 1939.

Pope, Alexander, *Collected Poems*, ed. Bonamy Dobrée, Everyman's Library, 1924; rpt. 1965.

Pope, Alexander, 'The Key to the Lock', 1715, in *Pope: The Rape of the Lock, A Casebook*, ed. John Dixon Hunt, London, 1968.

Radcliffe, Ann, 'On the Supernatural in Poetry', *New Monthly Magazine*, 1826, Vol. 16, pp. 145-152.

Radcliffe, Ann, *The Mysteries of Udolpho*, Oxford and New York, 1966; rpt. 1983.

Ruskin, John, *Modern Painters*, Vol. 3, London, 1906.

Ruskin, John, *The Stones of Venice*, 3 vols 1851-53; 7th edn in 2 vols, Orpington and London, 1896.
Shelley, Percy Bysshe, *Shelley's Prose, or The Trumpet of Prophecy*, introd. and notes by David Lee Clark, Albuquerque, 1954.
Tennyson, Hallam, ed., *Studies in Tennyson*, London and Basinstoke, 1981.
Thomson, James, The Seasons *and* The Castle of Indolence, ed. J. Sambrook, Oxford, 1972.
Walpole, Horace, *The Castle of Otranto*, Oxford, 1982.
Waterhouse, Ellis, *Reynolds*, London, 1973.
Watson, George, *The English Petrarchans*, London, 1967.
Wright, Herbert, *Boccaccio in England from Chaucer to Tennyson*, London, 1957.
Yeats, W.B., *Autobiographies*, London, 1926.
Yeats, W.B., *Ideas of Good and Evil*, London, 1903.
Yeats, W.B., *Selected Poetry*, ed. Norman Jaffares, London, 1971.
Young, Edward, *Young's Night Thoughts*, with Life, Critical Dissertation, and Explanatory Notes by the Rev. G. Gilfillan, Edinburgh, 1853.

h) England in the 18th and 19th centuries

Arthos, John, *The Language of Natural Description in Eighteenth-century Poetry*, Ann Arbor and London, 1949.
Baridon, Michel, 'Ruins as a Mental Construct', *Journal of Garden History*, Vol. 5, No. 1, 1985, pp. 84-96.
Dickinson, H.T., *British Radicalism and the French Revolution 1789-1815*, Oxford, 1985
Dickinson, H.T., ed., *Politics and Literature in the Eighteenth Century*, introd. H.T. Dickinson, London, 1974.
Doody, Margaret Ann, *The Daring Muse: Augustan Poetry Reconsidered*, Cambridge, 1985.
Havens, Raymond Dexter, *The Influence of Milton on English Poetry*, New York, 1961.
Hunt, John Dixon, *Garden and Grove*, London, 1986.
Hunt, John Dixon, *The Figure in the Landscape: Poetry, Painting and Gardening during the Eighteenth Century*, Baltimore and London, 1976.
Hunt, John Dixon, 'Ut Pictura Poesis, Ut Pictura Hortus, and the Picturesque', *Word and Image*, Vol. 1, No. 1, March 1985.
Lucas, F.L., *The Search for Good Sense: Four Eighteenth Century Characters*, London, 1958.
McGann, Jerome J, *The Romantic Ideology: a Critical Investigation*, Chicago and London, 1983
Miles, Josephine, *The Primary Language of Poetry in the 1740's and 1840's*, Berkeley and Los Angeles, 1950.
Monk, Samuel H., *The Sublime: A Study of Critical Theories in Eighteenth-Century England*, Ann Arbor, 1962.
Nicolson, Marjorie Hope, *Mountain Gloom and Mountain Glory*, New York, 1963.
Pocock, J.G., *The Machiavellian Moment*, Princeton, 1975.
Price, Martin, *To The Palace of Wisdom*, London, 1964.
Shaftesbury, Anthony Ashley Cooper, 3rd Earl of Shaftesbury, *Characteristics of Men, Manners, Opinions, Times*, 3 vols, 1711; 2nd rev. edn 1714; 5th edn Birmingham, 1773.
Spacks, P.S., *The Poetry of Vision*, Cambridge, Mass., 1967.
Sutherland, James, *Preface to Eighteenth-century Poetry*, Oxford, 1948.
The Victorian Vision of Italy 1825-1875, A Handbook to the Exhibition at the Leicester Museum and Art Gallery, 11 October - 10 November 1968.
Thompson, G.R., ed., *The Gothic Imagination: Essays in Dark Romanticism*, Washington State U.P., 1974.
Tillotson, Geoffrey, *Augustan Studies*, London and New York, 1961.
Ware, Malcolm, *Sublimity in the Novels of Ann Radcliffe*, Lund, 1963.

Warton, Joseph, *An Essay on the Genius and Writings of Pope*, 2 vols, 1756-1782; 4th edn London, 1782; facsimile edn Farnborough, 1969.
Warton, Thomas, *The History of English Poetry*, 1781; new edn, 4 vols, London, 1824.
Watson, George, *The English Petrarchans*, London, 1967.
Wren, Christopher, *Parentalia or Memoirs of the Family of the Wrens; ...but chiefly of Sir Wren, Christopher, compiled by his Son Christopher*, published by his Grandson Stephen Wren, London, 1750; facsimile edn, Farnborough, 1965.

i) General works

Abrams, Meyer Howard, *Natural Supernaturalism: Tradition and Revolution in Romantic Literature*, New York and London, 1973.
Brink, C.O., *English Classical Scholarship*, Cambridge and New York, 1986.
Copleston, Frederick, *A History of Philosophy*, Vol. 7, London, 1963.
Frye, Northrop, *The Great Code: The Bible and Literature*, New York and London, 1982.
Holub, Robert C., *Reception Theory: A Critical Introduction*, London and New York, 1985.
Iser, Wolfgang, *The Act of Reading: A Theory of Aesthetic Response*, Baltimore and London, 1978.
Le Goff, Jacques, *La Naissance du Purgatoire*, 1981, trans. A. Goldhammer, *The Birth of Purgatory*, London, 1984.
Lovejoy, Arthur O., *Essays in the History of Ideas*, Baltimore and London, 1948; rpt. 1970.
Thorslev, Peter L. jr., *The Byronic Hero: Types and Prototypes*, Minneapolis, 1962; 2nd printing 1965.

Index